CONTENTS

Dedicated to the memory of
Carl J. Couch
born 9 June 1925
died 15 September 1994
'He will always be here'

THE CINEMATIC SOCIETY

Theory, Culture & Society

Theory, Culture & Society caters for the resurgence of interest in culture within contemporary social science and the humanities. Building on the heritage of classical social theory, the book series examines ways in which this tradition has been reshaped by a new generation of theorists. It will also publish theoretically informed analyses of everyday life, popular culture, and new intellectual movements.

EDITOR: Mike Featherstone, *University of Teesside*

Recent volumes include:

The Body and Social Theory
Chris Shilling

Symbolic Exchange and Death
Jean Baudrillard

Sociology in Question
Pierre Bourdieu

Economies of Signs and Space
Scott Lash and John Urry

Religion and Globalization
Peter Beyer

Baroque Reason
The Aesthetics of Modernity
Christine Buci-Glucksmann

The Consuming Body
Pasi Falk

Cultural Identity and Global Process
Jonathan Friedman

The Established and the Outsiders
Norbert Elias and John L. Scotson

THE CINEMATIC SOCIETY

THE VOYEUR'S GAZE

Norman K. Denzin

SAGE Publications
London • Thousand Oaks • New Delhi

First published 1995

Published in association with *Theory, Culture & Society*,
School of Human Studies, University of Teesside.

SAGE Publications Ltd
6 Bonhill Street
London EC2A 4PU

SAGE Publications Inc
2455 Teller Road
Thousand Oaks, California 91320

SAGE Publications India Pvt Ltd
32, M-Block Market
Greater Kailash – I
New Delhi 110 048

British Library Cataloguing in Publication Data

A catalogue record for this book is available
from the British Library

ISBN 0 8039 8657 2
ISBN 0 8039 8658 0 (pbk)

Library of Congress catalog card number 94-074913

Typeset by Mayhew Typesetting, Rhayader, Powys
Printed in Great Britain by Redwood Books, Trowbridge,
Wiltshire

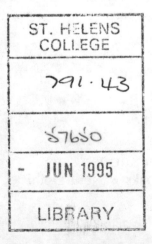

ACKNOWLEDGMENTS

I would like to thank Mike Featherstone and Stephen Barr for their support of this project. Interactions in the Unit for Criticism and Interpretive Theory at the University of Illinois, and conversations with Mitch Allen, Robert Carringer, William R. Schroeder, Bryan Cooke, Ben Agger, Carl Couch, David Altheide, Patricia Clough, Laurel Richardson, James Carey, Avaid Raz, Katherine Ryan, Nate Stevens, Johanna Bradley, Richard Bradley, Rachel Denzin, Dilip P. Goaonkar, Larry Grossberg, Stanford M. Lyman, and Norbert Wiley helped to clarify my arguments. I wish to thank Rosemary Campbell for her careful copy editing and her patience and assistance throughout the production process and Paul Benson for his meticulous reading of the page proofs and the production of the index.

Portions of the materials in Chapter 1 appeared in Norman K. Denzin, 'The Birth of the Cinematic Society', *Current Perspectives in Social Theory*, 14, 1994; portions of the materials in Chapter 4 appeared in Norman K. Denzin 'Chan is Missing: The Asian Eye Examines Cultural Studies', *Symbolic Interaction*, 17 (1): 63–89, 1994; portions of the materials in Chapter 5, Chapter 6 and Chapter 8 appeared in Norman K. Denzin, 'The Voyeur's Desire', *Current Perspectives in Social Theory*, 13: 139–58, 1993; and in Norman K. Denzin, 'The Conversation', *Symbolic Interaction*, 15 (2): 135–49, 1992.

Norman K. Denzin

For now we see through a glass darkly;
but then face to face: now I know in part;
but then shall I know even as also I am known.

I Corinthians, 13: 12

I was brought up to be a spectator . . . I was
raised to be a voyeur.

John Irving, *The World According to Garp*, p. 1

INTRODUCTION

Voyeur: One who derives gratification from surreptitiously watching sex acts or objects; a Peeping Tom; one who takes a morbid interest in sordid sights; one who sees; may also be called a spy, reporter, peeper, detective, psychoanalyst, sociologist, or anthropologist.

The Voyeur's Gaze: 'Just a gaze. An inspecting gaze, a gaze which each individual under its weight will end by interiorizing to the point that he [she] is his own overseer, each individual thus exercising this surveillance over, and against him[her]self. A superb formula: power exercised continuously and for what turns out to be a minimal cost'.

Foucault, *Power/Knowledge*, p. 155

Cinematic Society: That twentieth century social formation that knows itself through the cinematic apparatus.

I'll bet you that nine out of ten people, if they see a woman across the courtyard undressing for bed, or even a man puttering around in his room, will stay and look; no one turns away and says, 'It's none of my business.' They could pull down the blinds, but they never do; they stand there and look.

Alfred Hitchcock quoted in Truffaut, *Hitchcock: The Definitive Study of Alfred Hitchcock*, p. 216

The postmodern is a visual, cinematic age; it knows itself in part through the reflections that flow from the camera's eye. The voyeur is the iconic, postmodern self. Adrift in a sea of symbols, we find ourselves, voyeurs all, products of the cinematic gaze.

Between 1900 and 1995 Hollywood made at least 1,200 films[1] in which the warranted and unwarranted voyeuristic activities of one or more of the main characters has been presented as a problem which the character, the film, and by implication the other members of society self-consciously struggle to resolve. Hollywood's voyeur comes in multiple forms: reporter, detective, sleuth, spy, psychoanalyst, sexual pervert, psychopath, murderer, rapist, photo-journalist, cameraman, accidental tourist.

In this book I study the voyeur's film and its place in the cinematic society. Four generic questions organize my analysis. First, how has this gaze been regulated by gender, race and social class, such that only particular types of individuals are given the right to look at others? Second, what motivates this gaze? The voyeur's perverse desire to look and see what others are unable, or unwilling, to see is always directed to a valued, cultural end and structured by personal and social motives. What are these motives and goals? Third, what functions, or purposes does this gaze (in each historical moment) serve for the larger society? Fourth, what are the costs and consequences of this gaze for the individual and society?

The contemporary cinematic society was born in the 1900s, with the first moving picture shows (see Mayne, 1988: 3). This society capitalized on the camera's gaze as a method of creating and documenting reality. The voyeur implemented this gaze which became central to the workings of the new surveillance societies of the twentieth century (see Foucault, 1980). From the early silent Peeping Tom films of the 1900s (*Uncle Josh at the Moving Picture Show* (1902); *The Story the Biograph Told* (1904)), to such contemporary productions as *sex, lies and videotape* (1989), *Silence of the Lambs* (1990), *Pacific Heights* (1990), *Sleeping with the Enemy* (1990) and *What About Bob* (1991), the voyeur and his or her difficulties have been a central preoccupation of the Hollywood filmmaker.[2]

Hollywood's reflexive treatment of the voyeur has vacillated over the years, criss-crossing genres, film categories, and dramatic forms, moving between newspaper, reporter and private eye films (*Front Page, Harper, Salvador*), to spy and espionage movies (*The Spy Who Came in From the Cold*, the James Bond series), women's films (*Rebecca, Suspicion, The Cat People, Stella Dallas, Betrayed, Black Widow, I've Heard the Mermaids Singing*), avant-garde cinema (*Meshes of the Afternoon*), Gothic melo-dramas (*Psycho, Secret Beyond the Door*), unclassifiable classics (*Citizen Kane*), family melodramas (*Ordinary People, Terms of Endearment*), murder mysteries with happy endings (*Rear Window*), to comedies (*High Anxiety, Cheap Detective, Dead Men Don't Wear Plaid, Stakeout*), sport dramas (*The Natural*), biographies (*If You Could See What I Hear*), horror (*Dracula*), science fiction (*Fahrenheit 451, The Prisoner*, (the TV series)), documentaries (*Man with a Movie Camera, The Thin Blue Line*) and westerns (*Pale Rider*). In these texts the voyeur's obsessive desire to look defines the gaze of normal human beings. Films such as those analysed in this work serve as distorted reflections of the filmmaker's preoccupations with the truth and accuracy of the cinematic gaze and the necessity of the voyeur's look for an understanding of society.[3]

I study a category of cinematic productions, called reflexive-voyeuristic cinema (see below and Chapters 1 and 2).[4] The voyeur, a key to such texts, becomes a metaphor for the knowing eye who sees through the fabricated structures of truth that a society presents to itself. This is the cinematic version of Foucault's gaze. That gaze which each of us has interiorized. That gaze which has been institutionalized in contemporary, postmodern everyday life; the gaze which I may pay you to perform for me; that gaze which you may ask me to perform for you. This is the gaze of surveillance, the gaze of power, the gaze which unveils the private and makes it public. It is the ethnographer's and the fieldworker's gaze; the gaze which seeks to expose the social and reveal the hidden truths that lie therein. It is the camera's gaze instantiated in cinema and TV.

This investigation differs from earlier studies (Everson, 1972; Todorov, 1977; Tuska, 1978, 1984; Penzler, 1977; Rubenstein, 1979; Gamman, 1989;

Gamman and Marshment, 1989), which have been guided by purely historical, structural, or popular concerns. These earlier works have not sought to anchor the voyeur's presence within an interpretive framework that transcends the particularities of a specific genre, for example the spy, detective, reporter, murderer or sexual pervert film (but see Mulvey, 1989; Burch, 1990; and Mayne, 1990). With few exceptions, these investigations have not analysed Hollywood as a meaning-making institution and examined the systems of discourse that have shaped the creation and production of the voyeuristic subject. Nor have they followed the evolution and development of the voyeur in the cinematic society and in American film.[5]

The Voyeur's Discourse

While the voyeur's film presumably speaks to the untoward, obsessive gaze in contemporary life, it does so by creating a very specific type of discourse. The voyeur is presented as a 'diseased', often paranoid, violent individual who violates the norms of everyday life. Films validate these depictions of the voyeur by having persons in power (family members, editors, supervisors, the police) articulate how and why the voyeur is a sick or deviant person and why his or her gaze is inappropriate. These tellings shape the public understanding that surrounds the abnormal gaze and the voyeur's presence in society.

These films make voyeuristic looking a problematic activity, but they do so in a very specific way. A taken-for-granted double and triple reflexivity organizes these texts. The cinematic apparatus of course turns the spectator into a voyeur who gazes at the screen. This gaze is focused in the voyeuristic gazing of the voyeur, so a voyeur watches a voyeur gaze. Often, however, the voyeur's gaze is returned by an on-screen voyeur (for example the early reciprocated gaze between the protagonist and the villain in *Bedroom Window*), in which case a third level of voyeurism occurs as the spectator is drawn into the gaze that connects the two voyeurs gazing at one another. In such moments the viewer-in-the-theatre may experience the emotions of shame, embarrassment and fear that are felt by the illicit looker who has been caught looking (see Goffman, 1963: 67).

Each version of the voyeur and the gaze makes a spectacle out of this individual and simplistically equates visual knowledge with interactional interpretive understanding (see Chapters 2 and 8). Each version deploys a particular version of the voyeur's desires to look and to know. These desires are multiple: erotic, political, scientific, medical, investigative, criminal, personal. Their analysis and their place within the voyeur's agenda, as practised in the current historical moment, should make those of us who act as voyeurs more sensitive to the looking eye that casts its gaze on us and our reflective practices.

This Work

This work begins where *Images of Postmodernism: Social Theory and Contemporary Cinema* (Denzin, 1991a) ended; with the voyeur and the eye of the postmodern. As I did in this earlier work, I analyse the most popular of the popular,[6] examining award-winning films for the time period of my study[7] (basically 1940 to the present).[8]

Selecting the Films

I am analysing what I regard as the best exemplars of the reflexive-voyeuristic film. All of the films analysed share one or more of the following characteristics. They (a) are regarded as classics (for example, the Hitchcock texts), (b) are included on the lists of other researchers, reviewers and critics (for example, Gamman, 1989; Everson, 1972; Penzler, 1977; Tuska, 1978; Springer, 1991; Ryan and Kellner, 1988), (c) have been nominated for awards, or (d) were (and are) top video rentals, or big moneymakers when they were released. (I use these criteria as measures of the film's popularity and importance.)[9]

In the eight chapters which follow I take up the institutionalization of the cinematic apparatuses in American society (Chapter 1), the voyeur's aesthetic, the history of the voyeur's film and the emergence of the voyeur as a valued, yet feared social type (Chapter 2). Chapter 3 examines a select number of reflexive-voyeuristic comedies (*Broadcast News* (1987), *Dead Men Don't Wear Plaid* (1982), *Blue Velvet* (1986), *sex, lies and videotape* (1989)) from the classic and contemporary periods, I argue that in the comedy form the dangers of voyeurism are neutralized, making voyeurism, in its multiple forms (detective, reporting, political, spies, erotic) acceptable to the members of the surveillance, cinematic society. These films also present the female gaze as an inevitable supplement to the masculine eye and the male project.

Chapters 4 and 5 examine the positioning of the voyeur during Hollywood's classic, and postwar periods (1930–66). Chapter 4 investigates the minority group member who is given this privileged gaze (*Charlie Chan at the Opera* (1936), *Mr Moto's Last Warning* (1939), *Chan is Missing* (1982)). These films show how the pre and post-World War II cinematic American society made a place for the 'foreign' voyeur, turning his 'evil' eye to good use.

Chapter 5 studies the voyeurism of the classic, mid-century male photographer-detective. I examine Hitchcock's *Rear Window* (1954) and Antonioni's *Blow-Up* (1966). These two modernist directors make their voyeur a part of the spectacle that is filmed. They explore the malevolent uses of the camera in the surveillance society. They mourn the loss of community that the cinematic society experiences as it comes increasingly to rely on images for its understandings of how everyday life operates.

Chapters 6 and 7 move to the contemporary period. These chapters interrogate the obsessive, postmodern gazes of female (*Fatal Attraction* (1987), *Black Widow* (1986)) and male voyeurs (*The Conversation* (1974)), who are on both sides of the keyhole, watching one another, women watching women, men watching men. Following Irigaray (1985), I suggest that the female voyeur often experiences a form of self-knowledge that is not available to the male. The conspiratorial film, as a type of masculine, voyeuristic text, is examined in Chapter 7. Chapter 8 offers reflections on the future of the voyeur and the cinematic society. Here I review various ethical codes that have been brought to the voyeur's project, while developing arguments for a post-pragmatist epistemology that does not solely rely on the voyeur's look.

Throughout, I attempt to deal with the multiple forms of the voyeur's gaze. In so doing my purpose is to expose the cultural logics which have led the postmodern self to interiorize this investigative gaze. This investigative gaze is more than a gaze, it is the exercise of power in its rawest, yet most sophisticated forms. This gaze unmasks all of us, and makes each of us a willing participant in the regimes of surveillance, deterrence, power and control that threaten to destroy the very fabric of postmodern life.

A loosely knit framework organizes the eight chapters that follow. I seek a reflexive framework which will objectify and make problematic the ideological presuppositions that underwrite the cinematic society, and the traditional, realist cinematic, scientific, literary and ethnographic voyeuristic texts this society appears to require. A brief overview of this framework is necessary.

Interpretive Framework

As indicated, the voyeur is a recognizable social type. He or she takes morbid pleasure in looking at the sordid, private activities of others.[10] The voyeur and his or her gaze come in the following forms: the clinical gaze of medicine, psychoanalysis and science (including archaeologists, anthropologists, sociologists, psychologists, physicists, etc.); the investigative gazes of the police state, including crime detection, and the work of the private investigator and the spy; the informational gaze of news reportage, including the reports and work of news and criminal reporter and photojournalists; the erotic, violent gaze of Peeping Toms, usually men looking at the bodies of women;[11] and the accidental, unexpected gaze of innocent by-standers, including children who happen to see what others don't want seen; the inquisitive, assertive, peering gaze of the tourist (Urry, 1990).[12]

Five complex, and interrelated propositions organize my analysis of this figure and his or her place in the cinematic society. The first asserts that the figure of the voyeur, in whatever form, defines personal, sacred, private spaces in social life. By invading these spaces, the voyeur keeps alive the concept of a private world that is distinct from the public spheres of everyday life.[13] The cultural logics of capitalism and democracy require that these two spheres be clearly separated and protected (see Baran and Sweezy, 1973: 122; Zaretsky, 1976: 65; Mayne, 1988: 69). Together the ideologies of capitalism and democracy reproduce and inscribe the concept of the free, interacting, autonomous individual. This individual, and his or her private spaces, are central to the mythologies of the capitalist-democratic society. The voyeur simultaneously challenges and protects the spaces this individual inhabits.

My second proposition is epistemological and concerns claims about truth and knowledge. I propose that throughout the twentieth century, cinema, and society's voyeurs, in their gazing, investigative actions have progressively elaborated the epistemologies of scientific realism (see Chapters 1 and 2). This epistemology argues that truthful statements about the world can be made. These statements will be based on direct observation and the methods of induction and deduction. However, the methods of proof of the voyeur have always gone beyond strict deductive, hypodeductive reasoning. They have traditionally been pragmatic, moving always from consequences (dead bodies, committed crimes), back to the causes of those effects (on pragmatism and its history see Denzin, 1991a; on the scientific methods of detection of the detective see Truzzi, 1976).

The cinematic apparatus introduced into American society new methods of proof and verification, most importantly the picture, or the image, of a person, event or thing. The camera provided solid evidence of the events that the investigative voyeur attempted to explain. He or she then worked back from the scene of the crime (its consequences) to its causes. The voyeur implemented the pragmatic method and made pragmatism, and its ways of knowing and verifying truth, a central part of the American way of life (on the history of pragmatism in American philosophy see West, 1989). The voyeur taught Americans how to be both scientific and furtive in their daily investigative activities.

The pragmatic method of knowing is now under assault. This method, which the cinematic apparatus has elaborated, through its development of the voyeur's film, always depended on the ability of the voyeur to faithfully reproduce reality, either through the direct gaze, or through the camera's lens. Since the modern period reflexive-voyeuristic cinema has systematically attacked this assertion. Starting in the modern period, with films like *Blow-Up*, and *The Conversation*, and continuing to the present, with conspiratorial texts like *Rising Sun* and *JFK*, Hollywood has systematically attacked the assertion that reality can be unquestionably captured with the camera. This attack undermines the voyeur's pragmatic epistemology, for consequences can no longer be firmly established. Dead bodies disappear, pictures are destroyed, and reality, as it was previously known is erased.

Accordingly, the postmodern period confronts an epistemological crisis. Firm claims about truth, knowledge, consequences, causes and effects can no longer be made. The postmodern voyeur searches, then, for a new epistemological framework. Holding still to the pragmatic method, the voyeur searches (without success) for a pragmatism fitted to the cinematic age. This is the topic of Chapter 8.

My third proposition argues that Hollywood progressively incorporated the voyeur into its own cinematic apparatus. The history of Hollywood's treatment of the voyeur reveals the progressive formation, development and elaboration of a film genre, here called the *reflexive-voyeur* film.[14] This type of film builds upon and draws from several film genres, or categories, including the detective, news reporter, thriller and Gothic romance traditions (for recent discussions of film genre theory see Altman, 1984/1986, 1987; Neale, 1990; Schatz, 1981; Brunette and Wills, 1989; and the discussion below). However, the *film noir* tradition is perhaps most central to the history of this type of film (see Krutnik, 1991; Kaplan, 1978; Schrader, 1972/1986; Place and Peterson, 1974/1976; Telotte, 1989, for discussion of this genre).

Following Altman's (1984/1986: 32–4; 1987: 95) structural approach to genre study, I propose that the voyeur's film is defined by the following semantic (common traits, attitudes, characters, shots, locations) and syntactic (structural-relational) elements. Many of these features derive from the film noir tradition:

- a preoccupation with the illicit gaze;
- the use of cameras, sophisticated recording equipment, wire-taps, and so on;
- an epistemology which assumes that the truth can be discovered through a logical process of cause and effect deduction (see Gledhill, 1978: 14); and knowledge gained through visual means, including spying;
- characters (reporters, psychiatrists, policemen, everyday voyeurs) called Peeping Toms by their peers;
- titles which suggest danger, looking and gazing (*Rear Window, Bedroom Window, Stakeout, sex, lies and videotape*);
- A visual code borrowed in part from *film noir*, is deployed and includes the use of: long, telephoto lenses, wide, high-angle, subjective, shot-reverse and close-up camera shots, the reflexive use of off-screen space (i.e. windows); scenes lit for night and an emphasis on oblique and vertical lines and vertical slits; actors hidden by shadows; tension emphasizing visual paranoia and claustrophobia which is created by compositional, cinematic manipulations and not physical action (that is, claustrophobic framing devices such as doors, windows, shadows, framed portraits and mirror reflections. See Schrader, 1972/1986: 175–8 on these *noir* stylistics; also Place and Peterson, 1974/1976: 335; and Telotte, 1989, Chapter 1).

This visual code violates the compositional principles of traditional narrative cinema, creating fear and 'a *mise-en-scene* designed to unsettle, jar, and disorient the viewer' (Place and Peterson, 1974/1976: 333).

The voyeur's film deploys an investigative narrative structure, often presupposing a male hero 'in search of the truth about an event that has already happened, or is about to come to completion' (Gledhill, 1978: 14). This code stresses the importance of:

- 'action defined in male terms with violence connoting the male sphere' (Gledhill, 1978: 14);
- women as the object of the male's investigative activity;
- a romantic triangle with women treated either as *femmes fatales* or wives and long-suffering girl friends.

Within this framework the voyeur's film, again borrowing from film noir, 'probes the secrets of female sexuality and male desire within patterns of submission and dominance' (Gledhill, 1978: 15).[15]

My fourth proposition suggests that as an emerging genre type, Hollywood's treatment of the voyeur has passed through four interconnected aesthetic, historical and structural phases, termed, following Jameson[16] (1990: 155–66) realism, modernism, late modernism, and postmodernism.[17] This history of the genre suggests that it, like all genres, is always in a process of formation and change (Altman, 1987: 98). Furthermore, this change has occurred at the intersection of the syntactic and semantic dimensions which define the form; namely the coalescence and solidification of a narrative and visual style focused solely, or primarily on the voyeur's situation. This emerging coherence in the genre reflects and constitutes 'the very site of negotiation between Hollywood and its audience, and thus between ritual and ideological uses of [the] genre' (Altman, 1987: 98).

The voyeur under realism is represented by the naïve, innocent blatant voyeurism of early primitive cinema (1900–1920; see Burch, 1990: 202–43). This voyeurism is transformed into the repressed, never openly acknowledged voyeurism of modernist and classic Hollywood narrative cinema, the 1930–1960 period (see Bordwell et al., 1985, Parts Five and Six; that is Hitchcock's *Rear Window* and *Vertigo*).

The modernist voyeur, in turn, is to be contrasted to the voyeur of the late modernist period (1960–1970), given, for example, in Antonioni's *Blow-Up* (1966), a direct parody of Hitchcock's style. The postmodern voyeur appears in the late 1970s and continues to the present, given in De Palma's Hitchcock parodies (*Obsession* (1976), *Blow Out* (1981) and *Body Double* (1984)), Lynch's *Blue Velvet* (1986), Soderbergh's *sex, lies and videotape* (1989), and Stone's *JFK* (1991).

The postmodern treatment of the voyeur returns to the blatant voyeurism of the primitive and realist period, only now the audience is openly drawn into the voyeur's activities. At the same time, pastiche, not parody, comes to define the filmic treatments of this figure. Pastiche, a defining feature of the postmodern aesthetic (Jameson, 1990: 156), reflects a nostalgia for earlier treatments of voyeurism, while locating the voyeur's practices squarely in everyday life (for example, *Bedroom Window* (1987), *Sleeping with the Enemy* (1990)).[18]

These four film phases (primitive cinema/realism, modernism, late modernist, postmodernism) roughly correspond to the three major structural phases of capitalism in the twentieth century: local, monopoly, and multinational-consumerism (Jameson, 1990: 156). Each film phase carried out specific ideological tasks for capitalism and its surveillance needs. Primitive-realist cinema introduced the cinematic gaze and the screen voyeur into American culture. Modernist cinema kept the camera's gaze alive, but distanced it from everyday life. Under late modernism this gaze was parodied. With postmodernism the gaze is openly acknowledged, and its presence everywhere, including in the living room, is treated as commonplace.

Accordingly the genre called the voyeur's film may be seen as emerging within each of the above moments. Transformed in each phase, the voyeur's film emerged most clearly in the early Hitchcock era, was parodied in the late modernist period (De Palma), and is now treated with pastiche in the contemporary, postmodern moment. In each phase the voyeur's gaze was kept in front of American film-going audiences, serving always to remind them that even as they gazed on another, they too were being gazed at.[19]

My fifth proposition extends the above argument. I want to use the voyeur's cinematic text as a backdrop for reading current (and historical) interpretive practices in the social sciences, especially the practices of ethnography and cultural studies (see Clough, 1992).[20] The cinematic apparatuses of contemporary culture stand in a two-fold relationship to ethnography and cultural studies. First, the cultural logics of the post-video, cinematic culture define the lived experiences that a critical culture studies project takes as its subject matter. Television, cinema, ethnography, and the panoptic gaze of the cultural voyeur are the keys to the production of these authentic, realistic accounts of lived experience. Secondly, in these texts, there is a subtle and sudden switching of surveillance codes, from Foucault's panopticon to a system of deterrence (Baudrillard, 1983b: 53), where the person gazed upon is the person doing the gazing; the voyeur as newsmaker, tourist, travelling ethnographer.

The voyeur moves back and forth between both forms of textuality, the cinematic, visual representation of reality, and the ethnographic text. The unstable relationship between the ethnographer, the cultural subject, the ethnographic text and cinematic-video representations cannot be avoided. However, current cultural critics of ethnography and cultural studies have yet to seriously interrogate and question their own licence to gaze. They appear, that is, to justify the gazing eye of the voyeuristic, cultural critic by appealing to the politics of resistance that they attempt to write. They remain, accordingly, under the protective umbrella the surveillance society has traditionally made available to the voyeur disguised as ethnographer or fieldworker. My goal is to unmask this voyeur.

Notes

1 This figure is tentative, and meant to be indicative, not definitive. It is taken from The American Film Institute and *Magill's Cinema Annual Cumulative Indexes: 1982–1986*, and catalogue codes for films listed under the categories of columnists, newspaper reporters, journalists, photographers, police, psychoanalysts, detective, espionage, film noir, filmmaker, horror, law, lawyers, trials, murder, mystery, and obsessions (see Munden, 1971; Krafsur, 1976: Magill, 1986).

2 It can be easily argued that Alfred Hitchcock established this preoccupation for Hollywood (see discussion in Chapters 5 and 8). The contemporary director most directly influenced by Hitchcock appears to be Brian De Palma whose films consistently elaborate Hitchcock's violent, voyeuristic themes (e.g. *Sisters, Carrie, Blow Out, Body Double, Obsession, Dressed to Kill*). Hitchcock's films have also been central to feminist theory and criticism, especially theories about 'male voyeuristic and sadistic impulses' (Modleski, 1988: 1–2; and see discussion in Chapters 2 and 5).

3 Throughout this investigation I assume that films define, mediate, contradict and create new understandings of reality. These understandings mirror and distort the realities of everyday life, which are themselves often contradictory. In opening up previously unexamined corners of reality, and by exaggerating particular sets of experiences over others, films perpetuate stereotypes, fears and anxieties that exist in the culture at large. Subversive readings of films, like the one offered here, are intended to expose these tensions and contradictions (see Denzin 1991b: 10–11, 255–62 on the structure of such readings). All interpretations are subject to multiple readings, and necessarily the site of political and ideological controversy. Subversive readings are neither right nor wrong, but they do attempt to exhaust, or illuminate the multiple (consensual, conflictual, negotiated, oppositional) meanings that can be brought to and extracted from a text.

4 Briefly, reflexive-voyeuristic films include any mainstream, popular film which critiques from within its own political ideology, refuses the demands of narrative closure, and positions the voyeur (and the spectator) in the unstable position of doubting what has been seen.

5 Burch's (1990) comparative analysis of the modes of representation, and the treatment of the voyeur and the spectator during the primitive (1895–1909) and institutional (1909–1950) moments in cinema's history is a major exception to this statement.

6 With the exception of the films examined in Chapter 3 (including the Charlie Chan movies, and *The Conversation*), every movie is listed on *Variety*'s 1990 list of 'All-Time Film Rental Champs, by Decade' (*Variety*, 1990). In many cases the films won awards, or were nominated as the outstanding films of their decade.

7 Following Ray (1985) I divide my study into three basic time periods: classic Hollywood (1930–45); the postwar period (1946–66) and the contemporary period (1967–present). In Chapter 1 I complicate this breakdown, drawing on Burch (1990: 186–201), adding the phases of primitive and silent cinema (1895–1932), early classic (1932–45), classic (1945–62), early postmodern (1962–72), the middle postmodern period (1972–80), and the contemporary period (1980–present).

8 Two of the films taken up in Chapter 3 fall in what I call the pre-classic phase of Hollywood production (1930–46). In making these temporal designations I am mindful of the problems involved in specifying both historical moments and genre types (see also footnote 1 above, Chapter 1, and Brunette and Wills (1989: 36–8)).

9 Each decade since the 1940s has seen the production of at least one major annual top moneymaking Hollywood reflexive-voyeurism film: (1940s, *Spellbound*; 1950s, *Rear Window, Vertigo*; 1960s, *Blow-Up*; 1970s, *High Anxiety, Taxi Driver, Clockwork Orange, Dirty Harry, China Town*; 1980s, *Broadcast News, Stakeout, Field of Dreams, The Big Chill, The Killing Fields, Blade Runner, Dead Men Don't Wear Plaid, sex, lies and videotape*; 1990s, *JFK, In The Line of Fire, Final Analysis, Basic Instinct* (see *Variety*, 1990)).

10 Frequently this figure is presented as suffering from, or exhibiting psychopathological and psychoanalytic deficiencies (e.g. a fear of women based on faulty mother–son relations,

and so on). *Silence of the Lambs*, the story of a man who sexually molests, murders and then skins women is a recent (1991) example of this theory.

11 In Chapter 2 I take up the post-Mulvey discourse on the voyeur's gaze (see Mulvey, 1975/89, 1989 and Modleski, 1988).

12 The sociologist-as-voyeur has used each of these forms of the gaze.

13 As Mayne (1988: 128, 147) observes, the detective's itinerary typically involves a movement from private to public, the 'disentangling of the private sphere from the public' (1988: 128) via the efforts of the protagonist (usually male). The Gothic mystery (i.e. *Psycho*) exaggerates this preoccupation with the private by assigning special significance to the Gothic mansion and the female's place in that setting and its (and her) connections to the world outside (see Mayne, 1988: 128).

14 I do not wish to enter into a complex argument over what constitutes a film genre. I am simply attempting to identify a category, or type of film which privileges the voyeur's gaze in ways that transcend the ordinary treatment of the gaze in mainstream, narrative cinema (i.e. Mulvey's gaze; on the gaze in classical, mainstream Hollywood cinema see Bordwell et al., 1985, Part Five; but see also Mayne, 1988: 7–8).

15 Additional characteristics of the voyeur's film will be given in Chapter 1, and in the discussion below. Despite its reliance on the noir tradition, the voyeur's film is not to be confused with this genre. Missing (or down-played) in the voyeur's text are such standard noir features as the influences and themes of German expressionism, postwar existential disillusionment, documentary realism and the hard-boiled detective tradition. (Often, for example, the voyeur's story is told within a comedic, or black comedy frame, i.e. *Rear Window, Stakeout, Blue Velvet*.) Preoccupations with problems of crime, political corruption, police routine, psychotic action, suicidal impulses and street crime, while often present, are also de-emphasized. Finally, the use of voice-over/flashbacks, excessive subjective cameras and the documentary-realist visual style are seldom seen in the voyeur's film (on these features see Schrader, 1972/1986; Telotte, 1989: 11–39).

16 Robert Carringer suggested the use of Jameson in this context.

17 Definitions of terms – *realism*: the attempt to accurately reproduce a real, objective world of objects (see Jameson, 1990: 158); *modernism*: high art, including abstract expressionism, the modernist poetry of Pound and Eliot, the international style of Joyce, Proust and Mann, the films of Hitchcock, Fellini, Bergman, and Kurosawa (see Jameson, 1990: 159; 1983: 111–12); also a historical moment, from the 1920s through the 1960s; *postmodernism*: a nostalgic, eclectic, elaboration of modernist and realist tendencies, often through the use of parody and pastiche (Jameson, 1991: 16–17); that historical moment that extends from the 1960s to the present; a movement in the arts and architecture (see Denzin, 1991a, Chapter 1).

18 Following Jameson (1991: 16–17) I define *parody* as burlesque and imitation with a satiric thrust (i.e. the shower and casket scenes in De Palma's *Body Double*). *Pastiche* is blank parody, a potpourri composition made-up of bits and pieces of other works, or the imitation of another's style, but without the biting edge of satire. Parody presumes an original (e.g. the high modernist style) which can be mocked, while pastiche operates within a system (the postmodern) characterized by great stylistic diversity, the absence of clear-cut originals, unique, private, aesthetic styles, the predominance of reproductions and simulations of the real, and an eclectic, nostalgic longing for the past (see Jameson, 1983: 114–16). For the sake of explication, consider Hitchcock as a high modern original, De Palma, as late-modern parody and Lynch (*Blue Velvet*) as postmodern pastiche.

19 It can be seen that the voyeur is a historical, cultural, medical and ideological construction. Films produced during the silent era (1900–25) reflected the puritanical values of the temperance movement. These early films stressed Peeping Tom, *risqué* situations where women undressed in front of windows, unfaithful husbands cheated on their wives, and were peered upon through keyholes, and detectives discovered sick criminals who were menaces to women, children, family and the state (e.g. *Peeping Tom* 1901; *Getting Evidence*, 1906; *Sherlock Holmes in Deadly Danger*, 1908; see Mayne, 1990: Chapter 5; Everson 1972: Chapter 2). Films made during prohibition and the jazz era (1919–34) elaborated (and overlapped

with) the sexual themes of the silent era, bringing to the screen private investigators and news reporters who balanced Peeping Tomism with an official sanction to look in the name of the public (e.g.; Bull Dog Drummond, Charlie Chan, Hildy Johnson, *Dr Mabuse*, 1922; *Star Reporter*, 1921; *Headlines*, 1925; *Telling the World*, 1928; the *Thin Man* series, *Paths to Paradise*, 1925; *While the City Sleeps*, 1928; *Curtain at Eight*, 1934; see Everson 1972: Chapters 3 and 5; Pitts, 1979, 1990). The two World Wars brought to the screen the FBI agent (the J. Edgar Hoover series), film noir and other detectives (Philip Marlow, Philo Vance) and the state spy (e.g. *Spies*, 1928; *The Thirty Nine Steps*, 1935; *Confessions of a Nazi Spy*, 1939; *Foreign Correspondent*, 1940; *Casablanca*, 1942; *Watch on the Rhine*, 1943; *Cloak and Danger*, 1946; *Iron Curtain*, 1948). This figure would be transformed during the cold war era (*North by Northwest*, 1959; *Dr No*, 1963; *Ipcress File*, 1965; see Rubenstein, 1979: 221–3; Pitts, 1979; Parish and Pitts, 1974, 1986, 1991) and feminized in the 1960s (e.g. *Modesty Blaise*, see Penzler, 1977: 9–10). The aftermath of the Civil Rights movement and the race riots of the 1960s brought black (African-American) private eyes and super spades to film (*In the Heat of the Night*, 1967; *Shaft*, 1971; *Shaft's Big Score*, 1972; *Shaft in Africa*, 1973; *Cotton Comes to Harlem*, 1970; *Lethal Weapon*, 1989, 1990). The American and British conservative backlash to the liberal protests of the late 1960s produced throughout the 1970s and into the 1990s (e.g., *Q & A*, 1990; *Hard to Kill*, 1990), law and order, loner cops, and militaristic films, including those starring Bruce Lee, Chuck Norris, Charles Bronson, Clint Eastwood and Steve Seagal (see Ryan and Kellner, 1988: Chapters 7 and 8). Finally, the emergence, by the end of the 1980s, of third-world investigative films which position the 'spectator in the role of the cultural outsider by virtue of techniques that encourage identification with the reporter protagonist' (Springer, 1991: 168). Films in this grouping include *The Year of Living Dangerously* (1982), *Last Plane Out* (1983), *Under Fire* (1983), *The Killing Fields* (1984), *Salvador* (1985), *Cry Freedom* (1987) and *Deadline* (1987).

20 Borrowing from and modifying Stacey (1994: 22–3) I make a distinction between the textual (cinematic) and the empirical (ethnographic) voyeur. This is arbitrary because the two versions of the voyeur are hybrids, folded into and derivative of one another.

1

THE BIRTH OF THE
CINEMATIC SOCIETY

Almost all sciences owe something to dilettantes, often very valuable view-points. But dilettantism as a leading principle would be the end of science. He who yearns for seeing something should go to the cinema, though it will be offered to him copiously today in literary form . . . Nothing is farther from the intent of these thoroughly serious studies than such an attitude.

Weber, *The Protestant Ethic and the Spirit of Capitalism,*[1] p. 29

All great and unusual men and women sooner or later march through the lens of the sound-recording camera to appear and talk to all the peoples of the earth. Everybody everywhere by grace of the motion picture enterprise eventually can meet face to face every living person of interest or importance.

Hayes, quoted in Davis, *Response to Innovation:
A Study of Popular Argument about New Mass Media,* p. 67

Thus the mechanical eye reproduced the naked eye, becoming, in the process, a 'hearing gaze and a speaking gaze . . . a moment of balance between speech, [vision] and spectacle'.

Foucault, *The Birth of the Clinic,* p. 115

In the space of 30 years (1900–30) cinema became an integral part of American society. Going to the movies became a weekly pastime for a majority of Americans. American films were regularly exported to Europe. Motion pictures became a national institution. Hollywood stars became personal idols, fan clubs were formed and a movie theatre with its marquee was a permanent part of virtually every American community. A new visual literacy was being produced. Americans were learning to look and see things they hadn't seen before.[2]

The sociological impact of cinema on the newly industrializing societies and its import for social theory was virtually ignored, or slighted by the great classical social theorists, as illustrated by Weber's remarks, quoted above. Only the American pragmatists paid attention to this new industry and its effects on society. They (Cooley (1902/1922, 1909); Mead (1925/1926/1964); Park (1926/1967); Blumer (1933)), like their German counterparts in the 1930s (the Frankfurt School) and C. Wright Mills in the 1950s, viewed the movies with distaste and disdain (see below pp. 19–20 and Denzin, 1991a, Chapter 8).

Hollywood's cinematic apparatus ushered into American civil society a new scopic regime which initially privileged the visual over the aural (see Jay, 1988: 3). This visual culture muted the voice of the other, producing a loss of aurality (silent film), a privileging of imagery over sound. But quickly this loss of voice was overturned, merging the panoptic with the panauditory. The cinematic, surveillance society soon became a disciplinary structure filled with subjects (voyeurs) who obsessively looked and gazed at one another, as they became, at the same time, obsessive listeners, eavesdroppers, persons whose voices and telephone lines could be tapped, voices that could be dubbed, new versions of the spoken and seen self.[3] A certain madness of vision and sound (Jay, 1988: 19) was created, a complex, new scopic and ocular culture based on an overarching gaze that turned each individual into a surveillance agent for the state, the self and the other.

American cinema created a space for a certain kind of public, communal urban life. Inside the new movie palaces Americans entered the public realm. But this was a self-contained realm, the public made private by the darkness of the theatre, and here in these dark places a version of Bakhtin's carnival was enacted (Bakhtin, 1968; Stam, 1989, 1991). In these darkened spaces utopian stories, political fantasies and mythic narratives were told. These stories effectively erased the corrosive consequences and features of an oppressive racial and gender stratification system in the United States. The kernels of utopian fantasy contained in these stories 'constituted the fulfillment of what was desired [yet] absent within the status quo' (Stam, 1989: 224); that is, an emotionally harmonious gender and racial system that had successfully integrated racial and ethnic differences into the core emotional elements of the American self.

It can be argued, modifying Stam (1989: 224) who elaborates Bakhtin, that these stories were heard and seen within the framework of the 'carnival'. In the carnival glitter of the theatre, the 'dystopian realities of contemporary urban life under ... capitalism [were] ... through an artistic "change of signs" turn[ed] into the simulacrum of a playful and equalitarian communitas, a world characterized by communicative transparency and "free and familiar contact"' (Stam, 1989: 224). As Nasaw (1994: 10) suggests 'All felt equally welcome inside the picture palaces because all were equally out of place.' The embourgeoisement of the movies made them safe places for family entertainment. Thus did cinema create its particular version and vision of public, civil society.

Cinema made voyeurs out of spectators (Metz, 1982: 94). In the shadows of the theatre is reproduced the concept of a private, sacred space which the spectator enters. In that darkened space the spectator voyeuristically enters the public and private worlds that the on-screen voyeur trespasses.[4] A double reflexivity of vision and experience was produced. The spectator could simultaneously (and vicariously) experience the thrill, desire, dangers and invasions of being both a voyeur and the subject gazed upon. At the same time, the cinematic apparatus operated as a technology of gender (and race) which reproduced the structure of patriarchy (and racism) by implementing a concept of looking and spectatorship which often made women (and non-whites) the objects of the male (white) gaze (de Lauretis, 1987: 15). Thus did the movies create the gender and race-biased cinematic eye and an attendant cinematic imagination fitted to the values of the larger American culture.

Cinema elaborated the epistemology of scientific realism already deeply rooted in American culture. This epistemology held that faithful, direct and truthful knowledge of the actual world could be produced. This system was firmly established in nineteenth century American religion, philosophy, science and technology, and it had quickly taken hold in journalism and photo-journalism (Persons, 1958: 332). It elaborated the pragmatic, instrumental set of beliefs that organized American popular culture (West, 1989: 5), a 'hotel civilization'[5] impatient with abstract theories and obsessed with mobility and new inventions (West, 1989: 5). It found its expression in literary works, especially the novels of Stephen Crane, Frank Norris, Jack London and Theodore Drieser, that were both naturalistic and realistic (see Persons, 1958: 332–7). Cinema reproduced a realistic and naturalistic discourse about the universe of experience and appearance.

The movies became a technology and apparatus of power that would organize and bring meaning to everyday lives. They would function as adjuncts to the twentieth century surveillance societies, deploying the cinematic gaze and its narratives in the service of the state.[6] Cinema would create a new social type,[7] the voyeur,[8] or Peeping Tom, who would, in various guises (detective, psychoanalyst, crime reporter, investigative journalist, innocent by-stander, sexual pervert) elevate the concept of looking to new levels (see Chapter 2).[9] This voyeur, as argued in the Introduction, would gaze into the sacred, hidden places of society. By invading private spaces the voyeur defined the sanctity of such spaces, even as their presence was being erased by the surveillance structures of the democratic societies.

The archaeological and genealogical history of how this happened is my topic in this chapter. This history is complex, and can be told many different ways.[10] Following Comolli (1971–72/1985) I examine the links in the ideological and historical chain that begins with Thomas Edison's kinetograph, and moves through the birth of the picture palace, the Hollywood scandals of the 1920s, the birth of sound and colour film, production codes, and early narrative cinema. I then cycle back into the archaeology of the camera's gaze, the new visual codes that followed from this gaze, and the insertion of this gaze into everyday American life.

I ask how this figure of the voyeur and his or her gaze became a central part of the contemporary cinematic society. The cinematic gaze, visual and auditory to the core, instantiates and defines the medical, psychiatric, military, criminological, ethnographic, journalistic and scientific gazes that Foucault (1980: 148) locates at the centre of today's disciplinary societies.

In the Beginning

The active promotion of motion pictures in the United States was begun on June 13, 1891 (Davis, 1976: 12). On that date George Parsons Lathrop, the son-in-law of Nathaniel Hawthorne and a prominent magazine writer of the day, announced in *Harper's Weekly* that Thomas Edison had invented the kinetograph, a combination of 'the moving picture machine and the phonograph' (Davis, 1976: 12–13).[11] This machine, Lathrop argued, was a device to 'set down and permanently record exact images of men walking, trees waving in the wind, birds flying, machinery in active operation . . . just as though we were looking at reality' (Davis, 1976: 13). This new machine would project the figures from its lens 'greatly enlarged, upon a screen, where they may be shown, if need be, as of life size' (Davis, 1976: 13).

This machine was immediately linked with science. It was a perfect tool for recording reality with precision (Branigan, 1979/1985).

The 1902 Sears catalogue described the Kinetoscope as follows:

THE UNRIVALLED EDISON KINETOSCOPE, moving picture machine, giving pictorial presentation, not lifelike merely, but apparently life itself, with every movement, every action and every detail brought so vividly before the audience that it becomes difficult for them to believe that what they see before them can be other than nature's very self. (1979/1985: 135)

Nature's very self, the soul of life, this new machine made the real more real than the real itself.

The Uses of this New Machine

The moving picture machine would have many uses, including being a great fund of entertainment. It would repeat 'in life-like shadow-play all sorts of dances, the rhythmic whirl of ball-rooms, scenes from the theater . . . horse races, prize fights, athletic games, famous baseball players batting or catching, college crews swinging with a racing stroke in their boat, and the contortions of acrobats' (Lathrop, 1891: 447). Its uses would extend beyond entertainment. This machine could be used politically, it could record 'exciting debates in Congress. Military processions, camp scenes, street scenes (with their accompanying noise and stir)' (1891: 447). The kinetograph could also be used for educational purposes. Actors could study their own art, the public could see for themselves the 'majestic tumult of Niagara . . . a locomotive with rods and wheels in full swing of motion . . . and the animated presence of far-off peoples' (1891: 447).

In 1893 the Columbian Exposition featured nickel-in-the-slot movie machines.[12] The Atlanta Exposition of 1895 'had projected pictures until the tent burned down' (Davis, 1976: 14). In 1896 Vaudeville houses started running short films as part of their programmes. The first motion picture was commercially exhibited in New York City in 1896 (Allen and Gomery, 1985: 143). By 1899 store front movie houses were in operation in New

York City and Chicago. The Nickelodeon, 'the movie house whose name became a generic term for the new amusements, opened its doors in Pittsburgh in 1905 and played to standing room only for weeks on end' (Davis, 1976: 14). In 1907 as many as 10,000 people a day came to the nickelodeons in Chicago. The pictures that were shown in these entertainment sites offered, their promoters explained, 'harmless diversion for the poor, and were a "nightly amusement ground of the masses . . . a recreative school for the whole family, the academy of the working man, his pulpit, his newspaper, his club"' (*Harper's World*, 1907, p. 1246, quoted in Davis, 1976: 14–15).

The Picture Palace: A Theatre For Everyone

By 1909 the 'movies were well established in America' (Davis, 1976: 15). They had become the pre-eminent national amusement and had to be taken seriously. Walter Prichard Eaton the theatre critic observed:

> when you first reflect that in New York City alone, on a Sunday, 500,000 people go to the moving picture shows, a majority of them perhaps children, and that in the poorer quarters town every teacher testifies that the children now save their pennies for picture shows instead of candy, you cannot dismiss canned drama with a shrug of contempt. It is a big factor in the lives of the masses, to be reckoned with. Eighty percent of present day theatrical audiences in this country are canned drama audiences. Ten million people attended professional baseball in 1908. Four million attend motion picture theaters, it is said, every day . . . Chicago has over 300 theaters, New York, 300, St. Louis, 205, Philadelphia 186, even conservative Boston boasts more than 30. Almost 190 miles of film are unrolled on the screens of America's canned drama theaters every day of the year. Here is an industry to be controlled. (Eaton, 1909: 498, quoted in Davis, 1976: 15)

The period of 1910–15 saw the rise of the theatre chain. These theatres, soon to be called picture palaces, were located near middle-class neighbourhoods, in densely populated areas, along retail shopping thoroughfares, and along public transportation routes (Allen and Gomery, 1985: 203). They brought this new visual culture to the middle classes. Many were modelled after a vaudeville operation. They had live music and live performers. From 1926 to 1946 in the city of Chicago one local chain, Babalan and Katz, completely controlled first-, second-, and third-run releases (Allen and Gomery, 1985). These picture palaces manipulated the status symbols of the new middle classes. They created visual environments which simulated the life styles of the rich and the famous. On the screen, in these palaces, the middle class audiences would see lives of wealth and prestige played out by famous Hollywood stars; themselves simulations of the life styles they were portraying. (African-Americans were allowed to enter these palaces, but they were forced to sit apart from white patrons, usually in the balcony (Allen and Gomery, 1985: 206)).

The B and K theatres 'resembled baronial halls . . . [they were like] the most conservative and respectable of community institutions – churches and banks. . . . Chandeliers, paintings and rich draperies decorated their anterooms where pianists entertained' (Allen and Gomery, 1985: 199–200). By 1930 the five major studios and the three minors controlled most of the market for commercial entertainment films (1985: 197). The B and K theatres offered child care, had a nurse in residence and employed college students as ushers, who referred to patrons as gentlemen, ladies and children. A large orchestra accompanied all films and live stage shows preceded the showing of the films (1985: 201).

In 1909 there were over 1,300 theatres in America's major cities, with an attendance of 'two and a quarter million admissions per day' (Austin, 1989: 30). By 1935 this figure had reached 80 million a week; Americans were going to an average of three movies a week. By 1919 virtually every American small town had at least one movie theatre (Austin, 1989: 31–2). In 1941 the annual movie attendance was 2.1 billion. During the period of 1910–30 the Hollywood majors bought up local chains. (This monopoly was challenged in 1947 by the Supreme Court.)[13]

This new cinematic apparatus and the stories it told had to be regulated. The apparatus itself was fine. The stories were the problem. The gaze was looking at and telling stories about the wrong things.

Regulating the Gaze

The first motion picture magazines appeared in 1912 (Mast, 1976: 117). Fan clubs soon followed. The fan magazines (for example, *Photoplay*) 'featured pictures, stories and interviews that made the figure on the screen an even more intimate and personal being for each member of the audience . . . the exotic and erotic activities of the stars . . . became objects of household gossip' (Mast, 1976: 117; see also Levin, 1977: 7–8; Izod, 1988: 45, 47). With stars, fans, and fan magazines came scandals. The content of the new movies reflected a moral relativism that aroused public passion. As early as 1909 Chicago police assumed the role of censors, eliminating from films scenes of 'murder, robbery and abduction' (Sklar, 1975: 126). A rating system was soon put in place. By 1914 Chicago's censorship ordinance created a category of films 'approved for showing to persons over twenty-one' (Sklar, 1975: 128).

This censorship system reproduced the categories that had been established in 1909 by the National Board of Censorship of Motion Pictures. Working in conjunction with the YMCA, YWCA, the Children's Aid Society, the Woman's Municipal League, the Purity League and the Women's Christian Temperance Union, this Board attempted to counter early criticisms that the movies were teaching children how to commit crimes and engage in debauchery (Davis, 1976: 16). The Board published a list of subjects to be avoided by filmmakers, including all obscene subjects, attacks on religion, all crime pictures 'showing gruesome details or tending to teach the techniques of crime . . . [all] suggestive crime . . . like arson or suicide . . . unmitigated sensationalism and malicious mischief . . . marital infelicity . . . and kidnapping' (Davis, 1976: 17). Prize fights were allowed if they were not extremely brutal.

Deflecting the Critics: High Art for the Masses

Praised for its voluntary self-censoring, the fledgling movie industry continued to promote its new product to the American public. Edison would demonstrate his new sound pictures in four New York vaudeville theatres in February of 1913, predicting that 'great drama and opera would be taken to the masses, that the "political orator can appeal to thousands while remaining at his own fireside; the world's greatest statesmen, actors and singers can be heard and seen in even the smallest hamlet, not only today, but a hundred years hence"' (Davis, 1976: 19). This new technology, then, would be put to the services of this great democratic society. It would be taken into classrooms and become an educational tool, even if its flickering, scratched films were hard on the eyes.

But the critics would not be stilled. Controversy erupted in 1914 with the release of the film *Traffic in Souls*. A rather explicit treatment of sexuality, the film created a new moral controversy and the National Board of Review was labelled ineffective. Individual states began to establish their own censorship boards. A Federal Motion Picture Commission was proposed in 1914. It failed when presented to Congress, but the agitation continued. In 1917 the motion picture industry formed The Motion Picture League with D.W. Griffith as its first chairman. Its purpose was to oppose censorship.

World War I quieted the critics, destroyed the European film industry and placed the American filmmakers in control of this new entertainment form. They aggressively marketed their commodity, arguing that the movies were of value to the church and the schools, and that the industry had helped in the war effort (Davis, 1976: 21).[14] The critics again responded that the movies only presented crime, sex and nudity.

Scandals and the New Codes

In 1921 a series of scandals involving Fatty Arbuckle, William Desmond Taylor, Mabel Normand and Mary Miles Minter made national news (Sklar, 1975: 78–9).[15] A blacklist of 117 stars was compiled. Thirty-two state legislatures debated censorship bills. In 1922 Hollywood created the Hayes Commission to confront the censors and to promote self-censorship. Hayes argued that his purpose was 'the attaining and maintaining, for the motion picture industry, a high educational, moral and business plane' (Davis, 1976: 21). He stressed that the movies had a duty to America's youth,

We must have toward that sacred thing, the mind of a child, toward that clean and virgin thing, that unmarked slate – we must have toward that the same responsibility, the same care about the impression made upon it, that the teacher, or the best clergyman, the most inspired teacher of youth, would have. (Hayes, quoted in Davis, 1976: 22)

The filmmakers were just as pure as the clergy. The movies were important to national life. They were a national institution, a national amusement, one of the largest industries in the country. Most importantly, they were 'an instrument and means of immeasurable education and moral influence' (Hayes quoted in Davis, 1976: 22). Under Hayes the industry formed what was facetiously called the 'Purity Code' (Cook, 1981: 214); its chief purpose was to ward off government control of the industry.

The critics would have none of this.[16] In 1928 William H. Short, Executive Director of the Motion Picture Research Council, a pro-movie censorship group, sought and received funds from the Payne Study and Experimental Fund, a private foundation for the scholarly investigation of motion pictures and youth (Sklar, 1975: 135). Nineteen psychologists, sociologists and educational researchers from seven universities joined the project. University of Chicago participants included L.L. Thurstone, R.E. Park, Herbert Blumer, P.M. Hauser, Frederick Thrasher and P.G. Cressey. W.W. Charters, director of the Bureau of Educational Research at Ohio State University was chairman of the research group (Sklar, 1975: 135). Ernest Burgess, for example, argued, 'the facts are grave . . . it [the movies] is a social problem which touches everyone of us' (quoted in Forman, 1933: 5–6).

Hollywood responded by creating a Production Code Administration headed by Joseph Breen. The Breen Commission's task was to supervise all motion pictures from scenarios through to final release and to issue certificates of approval for each film. From this commission emerged the 1934 version of the Production Code (which would hold until the mid-1950s). It prohibited the cinematic presentation of adultery, illicit sex, seduction, rape, profanity, racial and religious epithets, any implication of prostitution, miscegenation, sexual aberration, drug addiction, excessive drinking, cruelty to animals, childbirth, crime, and criminal violence (Cook, 1981: 267). Thus was this new apparatus regulated.

Paradoxically, these criticisms from the vocal moral minority and the academic community emerged and took shape during the very period (1907–32) when film was becoming established as a new, international art form. Not only was D.W. Griffith inventing editing and camera strategies for modern narrative cinema during this period, but German (Lang), Soviet (Eisenstein), French (Feuillade, le Bargy, the Societé Film d'art) and Italian (Caserini, Guazzioni) filmmakers were bringing forth expressionism, the theory of montage, and early forms of realism and social consciousness films. At the same time, film stars of the stature of Chaplin, Keaton, Lloyd, Pickford, Garbo and Fairbanks, and directors like Griffith, Chaplin, Roach, and De Mille were making their presence felt in this new medium, as were a host of European filmmakers, including Von Stroheim, Lubitsch, Murnea, Hitchcock, and Leni. As Cook (1981: 46) notes 'in some sectors the American film was gaining respectability as an art form: serious books were written about it (for example the poet Vachel Lindsey's *The Art of the Moving Picture* (1915) and the philosopher Hugo Munsterberg's *The Photoplay: A Psychological Study* (1916)) and newspapers established regular columns for "photoplay" reviews'.

The New Regime of Realism

Colour entered 'cinema at approximately the same time as sound' (Cook, 1981: 245), the mid-1920s. The drive toward cinematic realism, the impulse to recreate a realistic order of discourse that mapped everyday life, required that sound 'complement and vivify the experience' (Cook, 1981: 235) of watching a movie. However only a small number of exhibitors could afford full-scale orchestras, or even Wurlitzer organs. At the same time there was a desire to add colour to the black and white films Hollywood was producing. (As early as 1925 filmmakers were experimenting with Technicolor.) By 1925 Western Electric and Bell Telephone Laboratories had developed a sophisticated sound-on-disk system called Vitaphone (Cook, 1981: 237). The major Hollywood studios refused this new sound system because of its cost. In 1926 Warner Brothers established the Vitaphone Corporation and immediately released the film *Don Juan*, the first film to be accompanied by sound. The first major talking film, of course, was the *Jazz Singer* (1927). During this time Fox was perfecting sound newsreels, and, on May 20, 1927, presented footage with sound of Charles Lindbergh's takeoff for Paris (Allen and Gomery, 1985: 123).[17] By 1932 the three-colour Technicolor system was in place, fully complementing the talking pictures (Cook, 1981: 247).

Thus technology was able to 'reinvest "realism" into cinematography' (Allen and Gomery, 1985: 127). More importantly, colour was responding to 'a deeper structure – a realistic order of discourse' (Branigan, 1979/ 1985: 137). Colour was not only 'more scientifically accurate . . . it was also able to "repeat" the dominant forms of the culture. . . . The coming of color begins [not with Technicolor] but with the Renaissance's interest in color and linear perspective' (Allen and Gomery, 1985: 127). This order of discourse, tinted with the colour and filled with sound, would then interact with the previously established systems of black and white realism. With sound and colour Hollywood had perfected a system of representation which modelled their version of everyday life and its appearances.

Sound and colour radically transformed American cinema (Cook, 1981: 259). They ushered in a new regime of cinematic realism which complemented the rise of naturalistic realism in the American novel (Cowley, 1950), the emergence of hardnosed, journalistic reporting by the major

American newspapers (and radio stations), an ethnographic, psycho-analytic, life history approach in the social sciences (Carey, 1975, Chapter 6) and a civic liberalism which turned attention to America's major social problems (Carey, 1975, Chapter 1).[18]

This was the system of ideas and representation the movies implemented as they moved into the sound and colour phase. These discursive systems, and their reproduction in Hollywood films, aligned the industry with dominant American values. Conservative to the core, they fostered an 'ideology of improvisation, individualism and ad hoc solutions for problems depicted as crises' (Ray, 1985: 63). By 'helping to create desires, by reinforcing ideological proclivities, by encouraging certain forms of political action (or inaction), the movies worked to create the very reality they then "reflected"' (Ray, 1985: 68). This was a reality that would be successively transformed as capitalism moved from market to monopoly to its contemporary, multinational forms. This reality would be fitted, that is, to three successive stages of representation, realism, modernism and post-modernism, which correspond to capitalism's three stages of development (Jameson, 1990: 155). Over-arching this representational structure would be patriarchy and the traditional gender and racial stratification system.

Stories to Tell and the Origins of the Reflexive Text

Hollywood's newly found realism required stories to be told and new genres to be created. The stories were already there, present in American (and British) literature, classic theatre, Broadway, the newspaper, the highly successful novel, the historical biography and the slapstick, screwball comedy. These texts were just waiting to be translated into the new technology. And they were. Narrative cinema reproduced the systems of reality and morality already present in the older systems of storytelling in Western culture. With sound and colour came the Broadway musical turned into a film musical. Walt Disney created the animated cartoon. Organized crime was quickly adapted to 'a cycle of tersely directed urban gangster films which exploited armed violence and tough vernacular speech in a context of social alienation' (Cook, 1981: 261). A cycle of prison films soon followed, as did films about the wayward delinquent from the broken homes of inner cities. The historical biography emerged as another genre form, reflecting the desire to tell the 'real' story of important historical figures (*The Private Life of Henry VIII*, 1933). The screwball comedy, the detective story, movies about the movies, family melodramas and melodramatic stories about New York City, photographers, school teachers, and scientists soon followed.

Realism was taken to another level in the newspaper picture, which included *The Front Page* (1931), *Scandal Sheet* (1931), *Five Star Final* (1931), *Platinum Blonde* (1931), *Front Page Woman* (1935), *Libeled Lady* (1936), *Mr Deeds Goes to Town* (1936), *Nothing Sacred* (1937), *Stanley and Livingston* (1939), *His Girl Friday* (1940), *Meet John Doe* (1941), *Woman of the Year* (1942) and *Citizen Kane* (1941), forerunners to *The Parallax View* (1974), *All The President's Men* (1975), *Broadcast News* (1987) and 'TV shows (*Lou Grant*) using reporting as a central element of plot' (Cook, 1981: 262). The investigative journalist told the cold, hard facts about American life. The newspaper picture cycle 'was immensely popular during the thirties and important for helping to refine the technique of dialogue in film' (1981: 262).

Such texts recapitulated two key cultural myths of American democracy, namely the beliefs that the truth will always prevail (wrongs will be made right) and that the powerful in this society can be brought down by the little people who are represented by the truth-seeking reporter (see Roberts, 1989: 80). Of equal importance, these texts contributed to the mythical standing of the press as the Fourth Estate (alongside the Presidency and Congress, the Church and the citizens) in the United States. By positioning the journalist within the cinematic apparatus, and by telling stories about his or her investigative activities, Hollywood attempted to bring to itself the same power that had previously been given the press; that is the filmmakers were also seekers of truth.

But in this move, perhaps unintended, the film producers introduced a reflexive impulse into narrative film. By telling stories about people who tell stories and make news, they began to break down the fourth wall that had, since the days of naturalistic theatre, always separated the audience from the story being told. By letting the audience into the newsroom they cracked the barrier that had traditionally separated storytelling from everyday life. They shattered, if only momentarily, the willing suspension of disbelief (that is, things that go on here do not go on in everyday life) that audiences brought to the cinematic experience.

Mysteries, Detectives and Private Eyes   The reflective realism of the newspaper movie naturally complemented another film cycle focused on crime, the criminal and the private investigator. From such silent melodramas as *The Perils of Pauline* to *The Cabinet of Dr Caligari*, *Dr Mabuse* and *Warning Shadows*, emerged in the 1930s, the 'thunderstorm mystery' with its spooky house and mysterious servants (for example, *The Bat*, *The Terror*, *Murder by Clock*). This genre would soon give way to the detective series with films built around such protagonists as Charlie Chan, Sherlock Holmes, Philo Vance, Nick Carter, The Crime Doctor, The Saint, The Falcon, Bulldog Drummond, the 'Thin Man', Sam Spade and Philip Marlowe (see Gramsci, 1934–5/1975; Halliwell, 1990: 809; Everson, 1972; Tuska, 1978; Pitts, 1979, 1990, and for a spoof of these early 1930s films, Groucho Marx as Wolf J. Flywheel in *The Big Store* (1941)).

This genre worked alongside the gangster and prison films of the 1930s and would soon form itself into the *film noir*, urban crime film cycle of the 1940s and 1950s, especially the film versions of the novels by Hammett, Chandler, Cain and McCoy (for example, *City Streets*, *Glass Key*, *The Maltese Falcon*, *The Big Sleep*, *Double Indemnity*, *Farewell, My Lovely*,

Murder, My Sweet, Kiss Tomorrow Goodbye; see Silver and Ward, 1979: 1–5, and Chapter 2; also Tuska, 1984; Hirsch, 1981 and Kaplan, 1978, on women in film noir).[19]

The newspaper, crime, detective and film noir served two key functions at the same time. They addressed Hollywood's need to be anti-crime and to show that crime could be stopped by well-meaning citizens. They made Hollywood pro law enforcement (Davis, 1976: 125) and contributed to arguments that the movies promoted justice, punished criminals and taught law abiding ways. Hence the films made the streets of America safe for America's women and children.[20]

Hollywood was now in control of its own destiny. It had sound and colour, its own Production Code, picture palaces with ready-made audiences in every community, stories to tell America's enthusiastic movie-goers, star and production systems that worked, and an insatiable new national entertainment habit.

The Birth of the Cinematic Society

Thus was born, in three swift decades, American cinema and its counterpart, the cinematic society. Fittingly defined in its early modern form by Griffith's racist film, *The Birth of a Nation*, the movies entered American culture, as argued above, under an immediate cloud of suspicion. Introduced as a new form of entertainment for the masses, an art form for some, a source of profit for a few, a challenge to Christian morality for others, a threat to the human eye for some, an educational vehicle for others, this new apparatus fundamentally transformed American society.

With this birth American society became a cinematic culture, a culture which came to know itself, collectively and individually, through the images and stories that Hollywood produced. By 1900, then, with Edison's invention, the cinematic eye had become firmly ingrained in American society (see Comolli, 1971–2/1985: 55).[21] This cinematic impulse arose out of an attempt to accurately capture reality, 'to compensate for the imperfections of the human eye by substituting the objective, scientifically accurate eye of the camera lens' (Branigan, 1979/1985: 133–4).

Producing the Camera's Gaze

This desire to replace the imperfect eye with the scientific lens reflected the operation of several interrelated ideological processes, most centrally the belief that the human eye was no longer perfect (Comolli, 1971–2/1985: 52). (It was Leonardo da Vinci who first challenged the supremacy of the eye with the simple lens of the camera obscura.) With this challenge to the eye and its inability to render the visible world with full accuracy, came the understanding that the photographic image produced by this new scientific apparatus (the camera and its lens) was perfect; it could not be argued with. It did not distort reality; in fact it could show the real in all its truth. The human eye was displaced as the final authority on reality and its recording.

When, in 1839, Daguerre made public his new method of fixing an image on a metal plate, the field of photography was created (Becker, 1986: 223) and a new class of experts would now enter and explore society visually. There were immediate social, scientific and practical uses of this new technology. Families began to photograph one another, or went to professional photographers, and thus was born the family photo album and every family would soon own, or desire to own its personal camera.[22] Medical science required better images of the human body (Foucault, 1975: 113) and medical art now became more photographically real. The new forensic science of crime, called criminalistics (Mannheim, 1960: 249), required photographic experts who could provide objective data on criminal conduct. In 1893 the Bertillion system of criminalistics was introduced in France. This system included photographs of criminals, the *portrait parle*, or spoken picture, and a picture file (rogue's gallery, see Caldwell, 1965: 321).

Benjamin (1973: 48) and Gunning (1988: 44) summarize this relationship between capitalism, the camera and crime. As Gunning notes, in 'industrializing capitalism, photography posed a technological solution to the problem of establishing and maintaining the personal identity of malefactors and subversives' (1988: 40). Benjamin elaborates: 'photography made it possible for the first time to preserve permanent and unmistakable traces of the human being. The detective story came into being when this most decisive of all conquests of a person's incognito had been accomplished. Since then the end of efforts to catch a man in his speech and action has not been in sight' (1973: 48). Thus did civil society deploy this new visual technology as a way of keeping track of its citizens.

Scientific journals and monographs immediately began to replace human drawings with photographs (see Ekman, 1973: 263–4 on Charles Darwin's early use of photographs).[23] Mathew Brady and his staff photographed the Civil War (Becker, 1986: 225), and soon photographs were being used by the major national newspapers to report the news and record important social events (Becker, 1986: 225). Photographic commercial advertisements for products soon appeared in major national weeklies and newspapers.

The Visual Code and Visual Truth

This process of displacing the human eye with the scientific image retained a commitment, as Pleynet argues (quoted by Comolli, 1971–72/1985: 43), to the visual code that had been 'laid down by Renaissance humanism'. The film camera became (and is) an 'ideological instrument in its own right, it expresses bourgeois ideology. . . . It produces a directly inherited code of perspective built on the scientific apparatus of the Quattrocento'[24]

(Pleynet, quoted in Comolli, 1971–72/1985: 43). This code, which domi-
nated Western painting for five centuries (1971–2/1985: 44) perpetuated
the 'hegemony of the eye, "visualization", and the ideology of the visible
linked to the Western tradition centered on a single point' (Comolli,
1971–72/1985: 46; also Berger, 1972: 18–19; and Verdon and Henderson,
1990).

The image produced by the camera 'could not fail to confirm and
reinforce "the visual code defined by renaissant humanism" which placed
the human eye at the center of the system of representation' (Comolli,
1971–2/1985: 46). This had the effect of displacing other systems (smell,
touch) of knowledge and representation. It assured 'the domination of the
eye over all the other organs of senses; the eye (Subject) enthroned in the
place of the divine (humanisms's critique of Christianity)' (Comolli, 1971–
2/1985: 46). This visual code was intensely realistic, and preoccupied with
the human body, the face and the eyes. It created a fixed presence for the
human subject, making his or her experiences the centre of what was being
represented. It reproduced the ideology of humanism's subject, a subject
who embodied the Renaissance's cult of the individual.[25] This subject's
body would be realistically depicted in paintings, and his (or her) experiences recorded in biographies (the early printed books) and Renaissance
drama (see Gardner 1959: 288).

In displacing the naked eye with its own scientific lens, the camera (and
the cinematic apparatus) created a spectorial gaze that made the spectator
(as argued above) an invisible presence in what was seen. Unlike a
Renaissance painting, where the painter or his subject gazes at the
observer, the camera's gaze created an invisible place for the spectator (see
Foucault, 1970: 5–6). It made voyeurs out of viewers. Still, the sovereign
gaze of the camera reproduced the gaze of the eye and the spectator
entered the photo through the invisible eye of the camera's lens (see
Nichols, 1981: 166–7). This elaborated the double reflexivity of vision,
already present in the classic painting, where 'we observed ourselves being
observed by the painter, and made visible to his eyes by the same light that
enables us to see him' (Foucault, 1970: 6). Now, with the camera's image,
the observer observes another's observations and codes those observations
within the new criteria of scientific realism; that is the camera's lens is
more real than the eye.

This new reflexive gaze, however, still worked within a frame (canvas).
It centred its subject in that frame. It presented the subject in minute detail
(close-ups). It reproduced the ideology of the subject and the sacredness of
his, or her, presence. It brought the viewer into the picture, but with an
immediacy and nearness that had not been previously possible. The
photograph could be held. However, the motionless gaze of the picture
was replaced by the moving picture of cinema. This allowed the viewer to
engage the subject of the gaze in real life detail; in the detail which
accompanies movement through time and space. Thus the mechanical eye
reproduced the naked eye, becoming in the process (to repeat Foucault), a

'hearing gaze and a speaking gaze . . . a moment of balance between speech [vision] and spectacle' (Foucault, 1975: 115).

The Empty Gaze

Paradoxically, human understanding was excluded from the epistemological equation which converted human knowledge into visual perception. Lonergan exposes this inconsistency:

> Now if human knowing is conceived exclusively, by an epistemological necessity, as similar ocular vision, it follows as a first consequence that human understanding must be excluded from human knowledge. For understanding is not like seeing. Understanding grows with time: you understand one point, then another, and a third, a fourth . . . and your understanding changes several times until you have things right. Seeing is not like that, so that to say that knowing is like seeing is to disregard understanding as a constitutive element in human knowledge. (1963/1977: 121–2)

Several implications follow from this formula. They involve the exclusion of the conscious subject from the knowing process. Lonergan elaborates:

> [a] further consequence of conceiving knowledge on the analogy of the popular notion of vision, is the exclusion of the conscious subject. Objects are paraded before spectators, and if the spectator wants to know him [her] self, he [she] must get out in the parade and be looked at. There are no subjects anywhere; for being a subject is not being something that is being looked at, it is being the one who is looking. (1963/1977: 121–2)

The knowing, conscious subject now becomes someone who is looked at, but being looked at, or looking itself, do not constitute understanding, for understanding involves a progressive involvement in the world of the subject who has been turned into a visual object. Hence the knower who wishes to understand another has to build up an understanding based on multiple visions; that is, on seeing more and more. Correct interpretations are presumably dependent on multiple sightings of the visible subject.

But the interpreter-observer is not a neutral spectator. As Springer observes, what is suppressed in the seeing-knowing equation is the fact 'that interpretations are produced in cultural, historical, and personal contexts and are always shaped by the interpreter's values' (1991: 178). Hence, as the records of visual perception were invested with the power of truth, truth itself became an unstable phenomenon, dependent on the viewer's interpretive framework for its empirical grounding. The very processes that joined truth and perception undermined from within the observer's ability to point with certainty to what was seen, and hence known about the visual world and the subjects who inhabited that world. Thus was born a special type of viewer, the voyeur who looked repeatedly in order to know.

The Reflective, Narrative Gaze

Like a mirror, the camera's cinematic gaze answered a double reflective desire to see and be seen (see Metz, 1982: 45). This reflection was visual and narrative. At the visual level it articulated the twentieth century's version of the reflected self, 'each to each a looking-glass reflects the other that doth pass' (Cooley, 1909/1956: 184). This reflected self saw itself reflected back in the face, gaze, figure, and dress of the cinematic self; that larger-than-life self that gazed back from the theatre's screen. From this reflection arose self-ideals and self-appraisals, self-feelings and feelings towards others. The reflected, everyday self and its gendered presentations attached itself to the cinematic self. Blumer provides an example:

> *Female, 19, white, college freshman* – When I discovered I should have this coquettish and coy look which all girls may have, I tried to do it in my room. And surprises! I could imitate Pola Negri's cool or fierce look, Vilma Banky's sweet and coquettish attitude. I learned the very way of taking my gentlemen friends to and from the door with that wistful smile, until it has become a part of me. (1933: 34)

And a male, 20, white, college sophomore:

> The appearance of such handsome men as John Gilbert, Ben Lyon, Gilbert Roland, and the host of others, dressed in sport clothes, evening attire, formals, etc., has encouraged me to dress as best as possible in order to make a similar appearance. One acquires positions such as standing, sitting, tipping one's hat, holding one's hat, offering one's arm to a lady, etc., from watching these men who do so upon the screen, and especially if they do it in a manner pleasing to your tastes. (1933: 33–4)

These selves, reflected back from the screen, were interiorized in the imaginations and fantasies of the movie-goer. They became part of the individual's imagined self-feelings and were incorporated into their interactions with others.

This reflective gaze elevated the look to new levels. The movie-goer became an invisible voyeur and this look complemented the scopic, sexual desire to 'look at another person as object' (Mulvey, 1975/1989: 17). At the extreme, this form of the look became 'fixated into a perversion, producing obsessive voyeurs and Peeping Toms whose only sexual satisfaction can come from watching in an active controlling sense, an objectified other' (1975/1989: 17).[26] Cinema's reflective gaze would answer a wish for pleasurable looking, and it would structure its gaze so that women were the looked at sexual object and men the voyeurs who took pleasure in seeing women so displayed: woman would be the image and man would be the bearer of the look (Mulvey, 1975/1989: 19).

The Everyday Gaze and Narrative Reflexivity

The spectorial gaze of cinema would elaborate and build upon the structure of the gaze as it already operated in everyday life (Simmel, 1924;

Goffman, 1963). It would, that is, bring more precision and more voyeurism to visual interaction. It would increase the sensual pleasures derived from gazing at the other and introduce an increased emotionality to the forms of 'civil inattention' persons would accord one another. Goffman suggests, in this regard, 'what seems to be involved is that one gives to another enough visual notice to demonstrate that one appreciates that the other is present (and that one admits openly to having seen him), while at the next moment withdrawing one's attention from him so as to express that he does not constitute a target of special curiosity or design' (1963: 84). Cinema placed the everyday gaze in the darkened spaces of the picture palace. It taught people how to violate the norms of civil inattention.

The boundaries between the everyday and the cinematic experience were repeatedly transgressed in 'the primitive era' of early cinema (1895–1911) (see Mayne, 1990: 157). *Uncle Josh at the Moving Picture Show* (1902) is exemplary. In this film a naïve spectator goes to the movies for the first time. He becomes involved in the screening of the three films-within-the-film. As the last film begins 'Josh tears down the screen, imagining that he can enter the fictional world on screen; instead he confronts the rear-projectionist and the film concludes with a tussle between them' (Mayne, 1990: 31). If *Uncle Josh at the Moving Picture Show* exposed the threshold that separates the cinematic from the everyday, other films like *The Story the Biograph Told* (1903) took the cinematic eye directly into society. *The Story the Biograph Told* has a boy secretly film a man and his secretary kissing in the biograph office. The film is then screened 'at a motion-picture show attended by the man and his wife' (Mayne, 1990: 169).

In these movies cinema immediately and directly implicated itself in voyeurism and everyday life. It made the camera the new way of establishing social and moral transgressions in private life. At the same time it established a reflexive interaction between cinematic representations and the real life experiences that occur off-screen.

This visual structuring of the spectator's gaze (see Chapter 2) had to be embedded, as argued above, in a narrative, a story, a system of discourse. As Metz observes, 'the cinema was born . . . in a period when social life was deeply marked by the notion of the *individual*' (1982: 95, italics in original). Cinema was made for private individuals and their fellows. Like the classical novel it told realistic, Gothic and melodramatic stories about the lives of men, women and children in contemporary society (see below pp. 32–3). In narrativizing cinema's gaze, the filmmakers introduced a new form of visual and oral storytelling into the new industrial societies. Hollywood's stories were myths, public dreams, secular folktales (see Silverstone, 1988: 23). Ritualized and emotional, these stories allowed people to make sense of their everyday lives. They used the logic of the hero and the heroine to tell stories about individuals and their families. They unified audiences by reinforcing key cultural values (for example, the horrors of violent crime, etc.).

They produced a reflective illusion that the world-out-there was controllable and under control. That is the modern individual, like a screen character, could take control of his or her life. Blumer again:

Male, 20, white, Jewish, college junior – When I was sixteen years old I saw the picture . . . The Ten Commandments . . . and from that time on I have never doubted the value of religion. The many hardships which my people went through for the sake of preserving our race was portrayed so vividly and realistically that the feeling of reverence and respect for my religion was instilled in me. (1933: 177)

And, a female, 16, white, high school junior:

I can remember very distinctly that when I was thirteen years old, I saw a moving picture in which the heroine was a very young, pretty girl. In school she had taken a business course and after working hard she had been promoted to the position of private secretary. To this very day I would like to be a private secretary. I used to sit and dream about what my life would be like after I had that position. (1933: 169)

In these dreams and fantasies the movies created emotional representations of self, sexuality, desire, intimacy, friendship, marriage, work and family. These reflective representations drew upon the ideological structures of everyday life. They created an everyday politics of emotionality and feeling that shaped real, lived emotional experiences (see Grossberg, 1988a: 17).

The cinematic gaze was visually hegemonic; it left no corner of society untouched. Its storied gazes entered the worlds of home, work, leisure, sexuality, sport, medicine, science, prisons, schools, church, the courts, and war. The movies and the cinematic eye, introduced into the social world forms of feeling and thinking that mediated the harsh realities of the everyday with the fantasy world of Hollywood dreamland. These stories were gender and racially specific and were moulded by the ideological structures of domination that existed in the larger social structure. This visual hegemony opened up the cinematic society to itself and destroyed forever the boundaries that would separate the private life of the individual from the public life of the larger society. All personal, political, sociological, cultural and economic dilemmas were converted into personal melodramas (Ray, 1985: 57). By making public stories out of personal troubles the movies would 'trivialize issues into personal squabbles, rather than humanize them by asserting their meanings for you and for me' (Mills, 1956: 335).

Controlling and Structuring the Cinematic Gaze

Classic cinema subordinated the technical problems of production, including camera placement, lighting, focus, casting, framing, editing (and later the soundtrack) to 'the interests of a movie's narrative' (Ray, 1985: 32). Lighting remained unobtrusive, camera angles were shot at eye-level, framing placed the subject in the centre of a scene, 'cuts occurred at logical points in the action and dialogue' (1985: 32). The shot-reverse shot made it possible as Burch notes 'to implicate the spectator in the eye contacts of the actor (and ultimately in their "word contacts"), to include him or her in the mental and "physical" space of the diegesis. Clearly such a procedure was basic to the illusionist fantasy/identification situation' (1979: 158). This style of editing naturalized 'the cinematic narrative by concealing the role of the filmmaker' (Ray, 1985: 39). The suturing of one shot into another, 'whereby one shot completed a predecessor [that is, a single shot of a house followed by a man looking out of the window of the house], prevented the viewer from becoming conscious of a film's status as an object made by individuals with particular biases' (Ray, 1985: 39). In such strategies Hollywood made the operation of the technical cinematic apparatus invisible. A film's narrative, or storyline took precedence over the operation of the unseen camera and its visual fields. This invisible style made the spectator part of the text. The effect, as Ray notes, was to increase the ideological power of the cinematic text. Even the most manufactured stories 'came to seem spontaneous and "real"' (1985: 55).

This new gaze was owned by the state, perfected by its agents, the scientists, and the Hollywood filmmakers. The next link in the ideological chain that defines cinema's history connects the camera and its images to the moving, motion picture, and finally to fully realized cinema with colour and sound. The ideological (and scientific) heritage of the camera and photography would not reap economic benefit until the rise to power of the surveillance society where there was an ideological demand to see the social world in its entirety, to capture, through the totalizing scientific apparatus, all of the features of modern life (see Foucault, 1980: 155, 162).[27] Those in control must now have multiple uses for this new mechanical vision. And uses they had; uses which would be immediately framed by the ideological needs of democracy.

There was, that is, the belief that a form of democratic surveillance was needed if an informed public opinion in the industrialist and capitalist societies was to be produced (Foucault, 1980: 162). In particular, there was a need for an impartial, objective source of information about society and its workings. The early filmmakers built on this point. They argued that 'there would be no longer need for interpretation of information by reporters. The audience member would be permitted to see for himself . . . if the individual had the chance to see first hand, the assessment would be more accurate' (Davis, 1976: 77). Such surveillance was first conducted by the journalist and the photo-journalist, and then by the masters of the new cinematic visionary eye, the filmmakers and the newsmakers who would create accurate newsreels of the events of the day (see Foucault, 1980: 162).[28]

The impartial renderings of reality that the camera, photography and cinema could produce were beneficial for democracy. They made the American citizen an informed participant in history (Davis, 1976: 72).

These pictures and stories awakened public interest in democracy. They aided the war effort (1976: 95), promoted national solidarity and patriotism, and, by being available to all people, made all citizens equal, thereby reinforcing basic democratic principles (1976: 61).

There was an immediate economic demand to make this new form of seeing profitable; to make movies out of what the camera could see. Within months of Edison's invention, it was clear that millions of people would pay to see these images. The early films were cheaply made ($200–$500, Cook, 1981: 32). By 1914 movie-making had become a multi-million dollar a year enterprise with a small group of men presiding over this multi-million dollar empire (Cook, 1981: 43).[29] By the 1930s a handful of banks and corporations (Rockefeller, Chase National Bank, RCA, General Electric, Morgan, AT & T, Western Electric) exerted direct and indirect control over what was to become called the nation's fourth industry (Cook, 1981: 232, but see Gomery, 1979).

What could be seen, could then be used for purposes of profit and social control. It is to these several impulses that the cinema and the cinematic society owe their being (Comolli, 1971–2/1985: 55).[30]

Cinematic Reality and the Cinematic Imagination

Several implications followed from the cinematization of American society. Reality, as it was visually experienced, became a staged, social production. Real, everyday experiences, soon came to be judged against their staged, cinematic, video-counterpart.[31] The fans of movie stars dressed like the stars, made love like the stars, and dreamed the dreams of the stars. Blumer provides an example.

> *Female, 24, white, college senior* – During my high-school period I particularly liked pictures in which the setting was a millionaire's estate or some such elaborate place. After seeing a picture of this type, I would imagine myself living such a life of ease as the society girl I had seen. My daydreams would be concerned with lavish wardrobes, beautiful homes, servants, imported automobiles, yachts, and countless suitors. (Blumer, 1933: 64)

Another person comments: 'I used to look in the mirror somewhat admiringly and try to imagine Wallace Reid or John Barrymore kissing that face' (1933: 66).

The metaphor of the dramaturgical society (Lyman, 1990a: 221), or 'life as Theater' (Brissett and Edgley, 1990: 2; Goffman, 1959: 254–5) ceased to be just a metaphor. It became interactional reality. Life and art became mirror images of one another. Another Blumer student:

> I have fallen in love with movie heroes . . . I imagined myself caressing the heroes with great passion and kissing them so they would stay osculated forever . . . *I practiced love scenes either with myself or the girl friends. We sometimes think we could beat Greta Garbo, but I doubt it.* (Blumer, 1933: 71, emphasis added)

The main carriers of the popular in the cinematic society soon became the very medium that was defining the content and meaning of the popular; that is popular culture quickly became a matter of cinema and the related media, including television, the press and popular literature.

Cinema entered a metropolitan American culture that would soon be filled with segregated public spaces, including baseball fields, amusement parks, boardwalks, libraries, museums, picture palaces, theme and national parks, world fairs. These carnivalesque sites erased while they maintained racial, gender and ethnic differences. These forms of urban entertainment nurtured a sense of public community, a 'republic of [voyeuristic] pleasure seekers' (Nasaw, 1994: 2).

The cinematic apparatus systematized the new urban gaze. A new visual and auditory subject was inserted into an increasingly complex scopic (ocular) and auditory regime. Multiple visual cultures or regimes, what Jay (1988: 18) terms Cartesian, Baconian and Baroque, interacted with one another in these public places. The visual and representational codes connected to Cartesian perspectivalism (Rorty's mirror of nature), Baconian empiricism (positivism), and a self-conscious, reflexive Baroque aesthetic found different spaces within the representations produced by the cinematic apparatus.[32]

Hollywood manipulated its mass audiences, creating texts which located spectators within these multiple visual and auditory cultures. By the early 1930s marketing specialists had learned how to carve up this mass audience into innumerable segments based on gender, age, income and race. This segmentation of the audience destroyed the republic of pleasure seekers.[33] 'Common habits of consumption were no longer able to create a coherent culture and a population with a sense of itself as a unified public' (Lears, 1994: 29). The public spheres of civil society collapsed. The integration of public spaces destroyed the 'race-based privilege that had [previously] held the white audience together' (Lears, 1994: 29). The spread of television and the increased privatization of suburban entertainment further contributed to the destruction of this common visual culture.

The Cinematic Imagination

This instantiation of the gaze, in its multiple forms, led to the production of a cinematic imagination, an imagination which circulated through the private and popular cultures of American life. This imagination was visual, narrative and aesthetic. It defined central personal experiences, especially those anchored in the cultural identities of race, class and gender, within a master narrative derived from classic theatre and Victorian melodramatic literature (Mast, 1976: 123). This imagination suggested that lives had beginnings, middles and ends. It argued that the preferred cultural self found its fullest expression in the love and marriage relationship (Clough, 1992: 13).

This imagination argued for stories with happy endings and it valorized the central American values of individualism, freedom, the frontier, love, hard work, family, wealth and companionship (Ray, 1985: 56–9). Such stories became engrained in the cinematic imagination; they became master tales, myths, which structured how lives were evaluated and judged. Aesthetically, this imagination mediated the individual's relationship to the popular and the everyday world. It judged stories and images in terms of their human element. It valued a realist aesthetic grounded in a realist epistemology (see below, p. 36).

The cinematic imagination mediates these complex, intersecting visual cultures, constantly attempting to make sense of two versions of reality: the cinematic and the everyday. But a paradox is created, for the everyday is now defined by the cinematic. The two can no longer be separated. A single epistemological regime governs both visual fields. Cinema not only created the spectator in its own eye; it created what the eye of the spectator would see. It then subjected that eye and its vision to the unrelenting criteria of realism and the realistic image of reality given in the camera's image.

But still, throughout this history, the voyeur's gaze has held steady. There was (and is) a need for this figure. He or she points to the dangers that lurk outside (and inside) the home. And in its own hegemonic way Hollywood has kept this figure under control. The reflexive text is the key to this control.

Reflexive Cinema

Reflexive cinema, as argued above (pp. 28–9), is that cinematic-narrative formation that tells stories about how stories are told, and challenges the camera's truth-telling gaze. It breaks through the fourth wall of naturalism and brings the viewer into the spaces where reality is socially constructed. In the reflexive text actors may step off stage and speak to audiences. Shots will show cameras photographing actors, or directors directing a scene. Scenes with television shows playing where actors in the scene are also on the TV show, also speak to this reflexive strategy, as do blow-ups of photographs of real events whose traces later disappear. The 1932 Marx Brothers' film *Horsefeathers* provides a comedic example. Groucho turns to address the camera as his brother Chico begins a piano solo: 'I've got to stay here, but there's no reason why you folks shouldn't go out into the lobby until this thing blows over' (Ray, 1985: 37).

Reflexive cinema interrogates the regimes of realism our modern and postmodern culture have come to value. It questions the illusion that everything is captured by the camera's eye. It violates the tenets of classic, realist film. It suggests that the world-out-there may not be under the control of a panoptic gaze which is objective because nothing escapes its neutral, truth-seeking eye. It suggests that this gaze, which is subjective and ideological, is flawed, and that it only tells a certain version of the truth. It suggests that those who own the cameras may only tell their version of the truth. Thus power and knowledge are ideological, cinematic, textual productions. Reflexive cinema challenges those texts which purport to truthfully represent reality.

Knowing the Real

In this challenge, the reflexive text goes against cinematic, ethnographic realism, the code of traditional cinema, which is organized around a specific set of epistemological assumptions concerning truth and accuracy (see Nichols, 1981, Chapters 6 and 7).[34] Such texts implement a version of positivist realism which is connected to the camera theory of reality. The camera theory of reality asserts that accuracy and truth are directly related to the nearness to the event being recorded. It assumes that the scientific eye of the camera (or the trained observer) is better than the naked eye of the untrained observer. It presumes that an event not directly and immediately recorded cannot later be accurately recorded and interpreted. Reconstructions are always subject to error. Cinematic (and television) historiography (all journalistic forms share this commitment) then classifies news sources (and stories) in terms of their reliability and validity, including sources which are first- and secondhand in nature. Secret, confidential (backstage) sources are often granted more validity than public sources. Trained observers are given more credibility than untrained, casual reporters, although an untrained reporter who lived through an event is given high credibility.

This epistemological theory, severely criticized in *Citizen Kane* (1941) and raised to new levels in *All the President's Men* (1976), distinguishes hoaxes (inauthentic reports), from truthful (authentic) reports.[35] This leads to a preoccupation with the dating of reports; that is when they actually occurred in relation to the event recorded. Anachronisms in dating and authorship are given special attention. Three criteria for evidence are typically employed. (1) Was the source of the story able to tell the truth? (2) Was the primary witness willing to tell the truth? (3) Is there any external corroboration of the details under examination? Witnesses may be able to tell the truth, but be unwilling to. Corroborating evidence may, or may not be available. When it isn't, a lie, rather than a fact, may be corroborated, and hence reported.

This theory of realism rests on the presumed fallibility of human memory. It assumes that an event's *meanings* must always be measured against its original representation. The original event, that is, becomes an original which can then be endlessly copied, described and interpreted. But without the original, all subsequent interpretation is in doubt. Hence the preoccupation with the real and its representation.

This theory is not without its problems. As suggested above (pp. 27–8), it equates knowing with visual representation. It excludes the acting subject from the interpretive text. This text is not a neutral production, it is based on the interpretive biases of the observer. This theory also assumes that there is no original, that there are only multiple instances, recordings, recollections and records of an event. Assume that an event is not a thing that stands still to be recorded, but rather is a process dramaturgically constructed through the process of interpretation. Assume that cinematic and televised events are staged productions, made to look real. Assume that they are compared, in their stagings, to copies of prior events, which were copies of prior events, any one, or none of which is an original, and so on. The 'realism' of an event, then, is a function of the degree to which the event as a staged event is made to look like a real event.

Cinema's Epistemology and Historiography

Cinema's historiography presumes a fixed, stable social world that can be accurately recorded. This was the goal of total cinema (Bazin, 1971: 17–22); a goal then joined with an aesthetic argument that cinema was the seventh art form that finally allowed man to recreate 'the world in its own image' (1971: 21) and to reproduce himself at the same time (Comolli, 1971–2/1985: 48). Cinematic realism presumes that the facts can be dug out of the social world; that is, its essential structures of meaning can be revealed through careful naturalistic, journalistic historiography. But the technologies for producing the real distort the real that is produced. And, in these moves, cinema (and television) create the realities they analyse.

The cinematic imagination is now asked to work between two versions of reality; the cinematic and the everyday. Yet the everyday is now defined by the cinematic. The two can no longer be separated. A single epistemological regime governs both visual fields. The hegemony of the camera's eye, with its fine-grained realism, elevates to new heights the visual gaze and the narrative text that contains and explains what is seen. Cinema not only created the spectator in its own eye; it created what the eye of the spectator would see. It then subjected that eye and its vision to the unrelenting criteria of realism and the realistic image of reality given in the camera's image.

The voyeur, the subject of the next chapter (and the key to the reflexive text) challenges the camera's hegemonic control over reality. Transformed by cinema, the voyeur undermines from within cinema's control over reality and what is seen. In his (or her) most grotesque forms, this individual cuts close to the contemporary moment where taped images from monitoring cameras define our very presence in the world and become the measure and record of how we talk, make love, exchange money and claim to know what we know. With this figure the naked human eye is placed up against the camera's vision, and the cinematic look is found to be fatally flawed. The voyeur exposes the underlying power structures which ideologically code truth with the camera's vision. More importantly, the voyeur's gaze is nearly always coded with violence and vicarious danger (see James, 1991: 1). This suggests, of course, that there are dangers involved when the cinematic code is transgressed.

Conclusion

But reflexive cinema is duplicitous. The very agency that purports to be undermining its own agency is in control of this cinematic apparatus which is doing these tellings. So the apparatus attempts its own epistemological privileging as it critiques from within its selfsame representations of reality. The machine that mocks the copy controls the copies that are made.

By insinuating itself within the central structures that it helped create, the cinematic apparatus, from the early silent Peeping Tom films of the 1900s (*Uncle Josh at the Moving Picture Show* (1902); *The Story the Biograph Told* (1904)), to such contemporary productions as *sex, lies and videotape* (1989), *Silence of the Lambs* (1990), *Pacific Heights* (1990), *Sleeping with the Enemy* (1990), *What About Bob* (1991), *JFK* (1991), *Sliver* (1993), has made the voyeur and his or her difficulties a central topic of concern. Films such as these serve as distorted reflections of the filmmaker's preoccupations with the truth and accuracy of the cinematic gaze and the requisite necessity of the voyeur's look for civil society and its understandings.

But these films are not without problems. They valorize the transgressions and violence that accompany the voyeur's project. Even as they reflexively deconstruct the voyeur's search for truth, they hold out the belief that absolute truth can be found, as in Oliver Stone's use of Abraham Zapruder's film of the Kennedy assassination in his own film (*JFK*) of the assassination (see Chapter 7, and see Zelizer, 1992: 38). In holding to the camera theory of reality (and truth) these reflexive texts perpetuate the power of the visual image as the ultimate arbitrator of truth. And here at the end, locked into their own cinematic apparatus the filmmakers seem unable to grasp the truth of the simulacrum which knows that there is no truth beyond the image. The simulacrum is true (Baudrillard, 1983b: 1).

So we are trapped, like birds in a cage. This cinematic apparatus will not set us free. It only changes the cage that traps us. We seek, here at the end of the postmodern, a new epistemology of truth. One that will build a new simulacrum (see Zizek, 1992). This is the topic of Chapter 8. In the next chapter I turn to the voyeur's aesthetic and the theories which attempt to interpret this dangerous gaze.

Notes

1 I am indebted to Patricia T. Clough for this quote from Weber.

2 In McLuhan's terms Americans were learning how to relate to a hot medium, one with high visual saliency, one which would define the meaning of a message in terms of the changes

it produces in an image, or sequence of images. Concern would shift from meaning to effect, from truth to impression management.

3 I thank Aviad E. Raz for this formulation.

4 This darkened space of the theatre was viewed negatively by some early students of the movies. Blumer observed,

> it is important to note that the movies do not come merely as a film that is thrown on a screen; their witnessing is an experience undergone in a very complex setting. There is the darkened theater – itself of no slight significance, especially in the case of love or sex pictures; there is the music which is capable not merely of being suggestive and in some degree interpretive of the film but is also designed to raise the pitch of excitement, to facilitate shock and to heighten the emotional effect of the picture; there are the furnishings – sometimes gaudy and gorgeous, which help to tone the experience. (1933: 195)

5 This is Henry James's phrase, quoted by West (1989: 5).

6 The surveillance society is not, of course, a twentieth century invention. The earliest civilizations (Egyptians, Harappan, Minoan, Mesoamerica, etc.) had systems of centralized administration, control and surveillance, including quasi-scientists, state police and palace guards (see Couch, 1984: 245; and Foucault, 1970, Chapter 10 and 1977, Part Three, on the transformations of this state from the Renaissance onward; see also note 26 below).

7 According to *The Oxford English Dictionary* (1989, 2nd edn, Vol. 4, pp. 544–5, Vol. 11, pp. 433–5; Vol. 13, pp. 652–3; Vol. 14, pp. 573–4; Vol. 16, pp. 382–4; Vol. 19, p. 779) this social type appeared in the English language first as a spy (1250), then as a reporter (1386), then as a person who detected things (1447), then a peeper (1652), who looked through peep holes (1681), and a Peeping Tom (1796), then as a detective (1843) on a private force (1872), and finally, with Freud and psychoanalysis, as a voyeur (1900, 1913, 1924, 1927) with scopophilic desires (1924, 1928, 1930). The reporter was soon transformed into a legal reporter (1617), a dishonest reporter (1726), and then a newspaper reporter (1797). The Peeping Tom became a spy (1926), a reporter (1933) and then a detective in (1940) with Raymond Chandler's *Farewell My Lovely.*

8 More correctly, then, the voyeur, the person whose sexual desires are stimulated or satisfied by covert observation of the sex organs or sexual activities of others, was an already existing social type (Peeping Tom, spy, detective, reporter) transformed by cinema and psychoanalysis. Generically, this figure was changed into the person who sees what shouldn't be seen, and is punished for it (often by having their eyes put out and then death). He or she has been present in virtually all ancient mythology, from Oedipus, to Medusa, to the medieval accounts of the saints, to the folktales of Europe, Asia and Africa, culminating in twentieth century cinema's various treatments of this figure (see de Lauretis, 1984: 114). In fairness to de Lauretis (see also Edmunds, 1985), it must be noted that I generalize from her treatment of the Oedipus myth, to the story of the voyeur, the Peeping Tom, the detective, reporter and the spy; to the story of the person 'who cannot rest until [he or she] has solved all the riddles' (Edmunds, 1985: 2).

9 It is significant that the voyeur, cinema and psychoanalysis are born (1900–13), almost in the same instant (see Metz, 1982: 97–8). The 'Peeping Tom' films produced in the 1900–13 period exploited the concept of the voyeur peering through keyholes, using cameras and telescopes (see Gunning, 1988). In the same period Freud (1915/1959) would recount, in 'A Case of Paranoia Running Counter to the Psychoanalytic Theory of the Disease,' the story of a woman who told him about a man who 'had abused her confidence by getting an unseen witness to photograph them while they were making love, and that by exhibiting these pictures it was now in his power to bring disgrace on her' (Freud, 1915/1959: 263, also cited by Gunning, 1988: 43). Thus did cinema and psychoanalysis come to apply the term voyeurism and the related problems of scopophilia to the looker's gaze.

10 This is not a continuous history, but is rather discontinuous, made up of breaks and ruptures in various discursive systems which interacted to create particular practices (i.e. the struggles to introduce sound and colour) and micro-power structures (i.e. the relations

between the early producers, technology, Congress, the Church, the military, and the American banking community).

11 See Mast (1976: 11–12) for a discussion of the history of the technology of cinema prior to Edison's invention. Edison's kinetograph was designed for individual customers who would look at his pictures through a little peephole (the first Peeping Tom?). Edison quickly formed his own movie studio. However in 1885 the Lumière brothers of France opened the first movie theatre to the paying public, showing films like *Workers Leaving the Lumière Factory* (Mast, 1976: 19). While this early film world was initially ruled by Edison and the Lumière brothers, it was quickly challenged by other French, British and American filmmakers (Méliès, Pathé, Urban, Dickson) who would launch the film careers of Sennett, Pickford, Chaplin and others. It was not until D.W. Griffith that cinema would get first its essentially modern editing techniques and narrative structure. This all came together in Griffith's 1915 film *The Birth of a Nation*. Taken from the novel *The Clansman*, the film was immediately attacked by liberals for its bigoted, racist portrayal of the Negro (Mast, 1976: 78). Griffith, Sennett, Chaplin, emerged as the three major figures in cinema's second decade (1905–15) (Mast, 1976: 115). World War I destroyed the European film industry, placing such early American producers as Selznick, Zukor, Loew, and Mayer on top of a virtual monopoly which controlled the production, and distribution of all American film (Mast, 1976: 116). These producers created a system of production which emphasized the single feature film and the star system with its social types (i.e. Latin leading men, swarthy swashbucklers, the pure women, the fallen woman, the virile male, the little comic) and stars (Valentino, Novarro, Fairbanks, Menjou, Gish, Swanson, Fatty Arbuckle, Harold Lloyd, etc. (Mast, 1976: 118)). By 1915 the major film companies had permanently located in Hollywood. The early majors were all in place (Paramount, Metro-Goldwyn-Mayer, United Artists) to be joined in the 1920s by Warner Brothers, Twentieth-Century Fox, RKO and the minors (Universal, Columbia, Republic, Monogram, Grand National).

12 The kinetoscope, as Mayne observed, was based on 'a simple principle of voyeurism: one person peers at an image' (1988: 77). These machines were set up in viewing parlours specifically designed for this purpose, but also in department stores, saloons, drugstores and hotels (Mayne, 1988: 77).

13 In 1949 Hollywood was challenged by the advent of television and suffered a severe drop in attendance by the American public (from 90 to 70 million from 1948 to 1949). By 1959 90 per cent of American homes had television sets. In 1990 virtually every American home had at least one TV (the average is 1.9); every other home had a VCR and was connected to Cable TV. Television turned the cinematic society inward, making the home a new version of the movie theatre. By 1955 the studios had entered into arrangements with television to produce movies for the home screen (Izod, 1988: 165). By the late 1980s Pay or Cable Television had become major factors in studio production, especially Home Box Office, which is owned by Time-Life and Warners. Although the studios still count on 1 billion admissions a year, rentals in VCR form now account for a major part of the revenue for any new release. Movies made directly for TV by the studios, and then released in VCR rental form also constitute a major source of revenue. The VCR format has also altered the way in which movies are now made (Canby, 1990). All of this means that Hollywood no longer has to get the filmgoer out of the house, and into the theatre in order to see a movie. They do have to go to a video store to pick up the film, and increasingly the studios are creating chains of video stores, much like they used to control movie theatres (see Izod, 1988: 122–3). The oligopoly which anti-trust action split apart in the 1940s 'is now being put together again through openings . . . in cable and satellite' (Izod, 1988: 179). This oligopoly increases the likelihood of an even greater overdetermination in the generic, melodramatic representations films bring to all subjects.

14 During World War I Hollywood created the war newsreel, training films for the military and military surveillance films depicting, among other things, German troops marching into Brussels in 1914, the invisible German super-submarine, the gun-works of the Krups shell factories, army camps and small-arms factories (see Davis, 1976: 97–8). Propaganda films were also produced, both by the Americans and the Germans.

15 Arbuckle was implicated in the death of a woman with whom he had been partying for several days. Taylor was found murdered in his home. The prime suspect was Mabel Normand, who was eventually cleared (Sklar, 1975: 78–9).

16 For a more detailed discussion of this period of film history and the part that American sociologists played in the creation of this Production Code see Denzin (1991a: Chapter 8; also Sklar, 1975: 135 and Leff and Simmons, 1990).

17 Fox followed the success of this broadcast by wiring all of its theatres for sound, and by making the 10 minute newsreel a regular feature in all its theatres. They soon added a permanent staff of camera operators and world-wide stringers who would provide film for these weekly features (Allen and Gomery, 1985: 123).

18 The rapid conversion to colour would not occur until television's attack on the movies in the 1952 and 1955 time period (Cook, 1981: 413).

19 Alfred Hitchcock would modify this genre with the mystery involving the hero on the run (*Thirty-Nine Steps, The Lady Vanishes, Saboteur, Spellbound, Strangers on a Train, North by Northwest* and *Torn Curtain*).

20 When television entered the national scene it was soon predicted that it 'would diminish crime by instantly showing pictures of criminals on air' (Davis, 1976: 125). Needless to say, the crime and newspaper films of the 1930s and 1940s immediately incorporated the latest communication technologies into their story lines, including sending pictures of criminals over the wire to aid in their capture.

21 Actually Comolli (1971–72/1985: 55) refuses to give a precise date, but locates (with Deslandes) the pivotal moment in cinema's history with Edison's kinetoscope and the fact that with a nickel, or 25 centimes, the American (and European) viewer could glue his [her?] eye to Edison's machine and see a picture.

22 The major producers of the personal camera (especially Kodak) would soon begin to compete within this newly created market. The instant camera (Polaroid Land camera) would be introduced in 1948 and by the mid-1960s half of the households in the US had acquired Polaroid cameras (Pace, 1991: 1). This new technology would be quickly fitted to the nation's first attempts at launching spy satellites. By 1960 these space crafts 'were routinely sending pictures back to earth, opening a new era in military surveillance' (Pace, 1991: 13) and introducing yet another order of the reflexive gaze into, first American, and then world, society.

23 The *American Journal of Sociology* 'routinely ran photographs in connection with muckraking reformist articles for at least the first fifteen years of its existence' (Becker, 1986: 225).

24 The fifteenth century in Italian art and literature.

25 The Renaissance reactivated the representational codes of Antiquity. This coincided with 'a new spirit of man: a new subjective, psychological self-awareness as well as an objective interest in the world . . . . One of the outstanding characteristics of the Renaissance was the interest in and the importance placed on the individual. There was a pride of personal achievement and a desire for lasting fame rarely known in the Middle Ages. Everywhere the individual stood out from the crowd' (Gardner, 1959: 287).

26 Thus would be born overtly sexual, or pornographic cinema. According to Mulvey (1975/1989: 19, 26) nearly all traditional cinema exhibits this feature.

27 For Foucault this urge is embodied in the 'Panopticon' (a prison in which all prisoners could be watched from a single point). The panoptic vision is all embracing. The principle of the panopticon (taken from Bentham) was then taken up by physicians, penologists, industrialists and educators. This technology of power was designed to 'solve the problems of surveillance' (Foucault, 1980: 148) of the new industrial societies.

28 Foucault notes that the nineteenth and early twentieth century theorizers of the democratic state neglected to consider 'the economy and power . . . of the press, publishing, and later the cinema and television . . . and . . . that these media would necessarily be under the command of economico-political interests' (1980: 161–2).

29 It was estimated by some that in 1908 the profits from this new industry exceeded $75,000,000, including the sale of $4,000,000 worth of films to rental agents, who derived a

rental profit of $8,000,000 from the nickelodeons, who took in over $65,000,000 in paid admissions. The size of the industry, at this time, included 90,000 persons working in the theatres and rental agencies, and four times that number employed in the manufacturing and production of the films (Davis, 1976: 115).

30 Standard film histories (Sklar, 1975; Cook, 1981; Mast, 1976; Allen and Gomery, 1985) reveal that the technical and scientific conditions for cinema were present perhaps a full century before its emergence in the 1890s as a commercial and entertainment force in American and European cultures. Jean-Louis Comolli (1971–2/1985) and Branigan (1979/ 1985) document the presence of the camera obscura in the Egypt of the Pharaohs 347 years before Christ and to Arab science in the ninth century.

31 Here a dialectic was operating. The ideological demand for realism in cinema produced technological changes which invested cinema with greater realism, including sound film, and colour cinematography (Allen and Gomery, 1985: 127). Now cinema became more realistic than everyday life.

32 Jay (1988: 3–4, 18–20) distinguishes four visual subcultures, or scopic regimes, what he calls the Cartesian, Baconian, Baroque and hysterical. The Cartesian regime embodies the transcendental eye of the solitary, objective voyeur. Baconian vision is fragmentary, descriptive and less explanatory. The Baroque eye stresses textuality complexity, a surplus of images, the bizarre and the disorienting, while the hysterical eye (the madness of vision) underscores the unseeable, that which cannot be captured objectively, from the standpoint of an all-knowing eye. These scopic cultures were progressively incorporated into the realist, modernist and postmodern aesthetic formations that Jameson (1990: 155–6; 1991) connects to capitalism's three major structural phases in the twentieth century (local, monopoly, multinational).

33 Separate cinemas for women, minorities and youth soon appeared.

34 These assumptions have a great deal in common with standard historiographical methods (Gottschalk et al., 1945).

35 In *Citizen Kane* there is the unsuccessful quest to discover, through the interrogation of multiple witnesses and social texts (newsreels, memoirs), the real Charles Foster Kane. *All The President's Men* introduces a journalistic version of triangulation, wherein neither Woodward nor Bernstein would act on a piece of information unless it had been confirmed by at least two sources.

2
THE VOYEUR'S DESIRE

I have just glued my ear to the door and looked through a keyhole. I am alone . . . all of a sudden I hear footsteps in the hall. Someone is looking at me! What does this mean?

Sartre, *Being and Nothingness*, pp. 259–60

The cinematic voyeur's gaze is violent, political, sexual and personal. Several theories of the voyeur's gaze have been offered. Feminist film theorists, elaborating Mulvey's now classic arguments (1975/1989), have built complex psychoanalytic interpretations of the masculine gaze as it is articulated in classic narrative cinema (see Metz, 1982; Mulvey, 1975/1989; Bellour, 1974; Doane, 1987; de Lauretis, 1987; Modleski, 1988; Gamman and Marshment, 1989; Penley, 1989; Mayne, 1990; Tseëlon and Kaiser, 1992; Clough, 1992; Stacey, 1994). Recent feminist theorists of women's films (including those made by women) have further developed these arguments (see Mayne, 1990; Johnston, 1975/1988; Bergstrom, 1979/1988; Penley, 1988; Erens, 1990a, especially the chapters in Part IV, and Erens, 1990b).

Alongside the psychoanalytic, feminist readings of the gaze (and its pleasures) exist Sartre's phenomenology of the look (Sartre, 1943/1956: 252–302; Schroeder, 1984: 186–202); Lacan's (1988) reworking of Sartre's gaze (see Silverman, 1992; Bozovic, 1992); Merleau-Ponty's phenomenology of perception (1962, 1964a, 1964b; see also Andrews, 1978/1985, 1984: 172–90; and Robbe-Grillet, 1958), and Foucault's political gaze (1980, 146–65).[1] These theories will be examined as they bear on my central questions concerning the cinematic representation and regulation of the gaze, its functions, and its costs and consequences for the voyeur and society. Theories first, then the voyeur's place in the cinematic society.

Mulvey's Voyeur and his Pleasures

In a now classic article, 'Visual Pleasure and Narrative Cinema' (1975/1989, 1989) Laura Mulvey applied Freudian psychoanalysis to interpret how 'the unconscious of patriarchal society has structured film form' (1975/1989: 14) in particular classical narrative cinema which has coded 'the erotic into the language of the dominant patriarchal order' (1975/1989: 16). This is a theory of the voyeur and the pleasures that are derived from his gaze. It rests on the following assertions. Women in classic Hollywood cinema are treated as objects of male voyeuristic and sadistic impulses. Women exist to fulfil the desires of the male spectator. Women spectators can only have a masochistic relationship to classic cinema which offers the basic pleasure of scopophilia (pleasure in looking); a pleasure which takes other people as objects of a controlling and curious gaze. Women are cast in the classic role of exhibitionist; they are looked at and displayed as sexual objects. They have a *looked-at-ness* which turns them into the site of the screen's spectacle, from strip-tease 'to Ziegfeld to Busby Berkeley she holds the look, and plays to and signifies male desire' (1975/ 1989: 19).

Cinema produces three types of looks: the gaze of the camera as it records events, the look of the audience as it watches, and the looks of the characters as they watch one another. Narrative cinema denies the first two gazes, subordinating them to the third (1975/1989: 25). In this world visual pleasure is organized in terms of the active and passive voyeuristic mechanisms that turn the woman's body into a spectacle of desire. Visual pleasures, then, are masculine, for the spectator is always masculine.

Mulvey's theory has been attacked on the following grounds: its uncritical use of the psychoanalytic model (de Lauretis, 1984: 45; Tseëlon and Kaiser, 1992); its simplistic conception of the female spectatorship position (Hansen, 1986); its failure to adequately deal with masochism and voyeurism (see Deleuze, 1971; Studlar, 1985); its use of the male sexual pervert as its model of the gaze (Tseëlon and Kaiser, 1992); its conflation of spectacle and narrative, and its unquestioning acceptance of the 'screen' as a fixed ground where narrative and spectacle are played out (Mayne, 1990: 38–40); its biased reading of the Hitchcock's films as support for the theory (Modleski, 1988: 2; Lurie, 1981–2; Wood, 1989; Rose, 1976–7/ 1988); its over-emphasis on binary opposition (Hansen, 1986; de Lauretis, 1984: 145; Kaplan, 1988: 5; Mayne, 1990: 45; Gledhill, 1978; Penley, 1989: 11; Cowie, 1979/1988; Bergstrom 1979/1988); its inability to interpret those films where the categories of the gaze collapse and male and female figures interchangeably identify with and gaze upon one another (Tseëlon and Kaiser, 1992); and its conflation and potential confusion of the textual and empirical spectator (see Stacey, 1994: 24–31 for a review of the most recent criticisms of Mulvey's theory and its revisions).[2]

Clearly Mulvey's theory of the voyeur and his pleasure is too narrow for present purposes. It is based on a limited conception of looking and voyeurism. It ignores alternative models of spectatorship and gazing. It fails to articulate the interaction and interplay between desire and identification, which often involves multiple identities for the male and female figure. It does not conceptualize any positive version of the female gaze, or the female character (beyond transvestism and the masquerade). (Nor does it present the male gaze in a favourable light.) It represses female desire, while clinging to a single meta-narrative about male and female sexuality. It does not permit, that is, an active, interactional relationship between the spectator, the gaze, narrative, spectacle and the screen.[3]

Sartre, Merleau-Ponty and Foucault

It is necessary to embrace a phenomenological and interpretive view of the gazing subject which is fully responsive to the complexities of the cinematic experience, and the experiences of looking and being looked at in everyday life. The foundations of such a perspective, as indicated above, can be found in the works of Sartre (1943/1956), Merleau-Ponty (1964a, 1968), Lacan (1988) and Foucault (1980) who offer phenomenological treatments of the gaze, and the voyeur (on Sartre see also Schroeder, 1984).[4] Their voyeurs come in several forms: Sartre's man at the keyhole; Merleau-Ponty's individual who sits as a spectator in the theatre watching the screen, or his painter, like Cezanne, who gazes at a landscape; Lacan's person caught in the glare of the camera's gaze; Foucault's medical or psychoanalytic gaze, or the gaze of the person of power who looks through the spaces of the panopticon. Each theorizes a generic gaze which is gendered and then filtered through the apparatuses of power that operate in society. Each treats psychoanalysis as a framework which structures the gazes of those in power.[5]

Each begins with a phenomenological conception of vision, the eye, the look, the gaze, the voyeur, spectacle and specularity.[6] Vision refers to my perception of the visual field that confronts me. My eye, my act of looking, renders that field visible, brings it into play, and makes it real for me. However, what I see is projected against a screen, a set of culturally generated images through which subjects and objects are 'differentiated in relation to class, race, sexuality, age and nationality' (Silverman, 1992: 150). I perceive, that is, gendered, embodied subjects. My vision is ideologically screened.

The gaze emerges from within this field of vision, for as I look at the world and give it my attention, others look at me, and fix me in their attention. This fixed look is the gaze of the other. In this visual field we are each spectator and spectacle, the viewer and the viewed. The other's gaze hides behind their eyes, for as Sartre observes the eye 'is not at first apprehended as a sensible organ of vision but as the support for the gaze . . . if I apprehend the gaze, I cease to perceive the eyes' (1943/1956: 258). As I engage the eyes of the other I disarm their gaze, and render it impotent. But I cannot perceive the 'world and at the same time apprehend a look fastened upon me' (Sartre, 1943/1956: 258). To perceive a look is to look at it, to engage it. To apprehend a look I become conscious of being looked at, of being vulnerable. I have been seen. The other's look connects me to myself. It is an intermediary (1943/1956: 259).

Imagine Sartre's person who has just glued their ear to the door and looked through the keyhole. All of a sudden they hear footsteps in the hall. Someone is looking at them. This gaze, as Lacan (1973/1978: 84–5) observes, surprises the person in the function of voyeur (desire). It reduces he or she to a feeling of shame. This gaze reveals a subject caught in an act of desire to see a scene (spectacle) on the other side of the keyhole. The gaze destroys this look, annihilates it. It casts the subject who was looking into the position of being the person looked, or gazed at.

Both Sartre and Lacan agree that I can feel myself 'under the gaze of someone whose eyes I do not see. . . . All that is necessary is for something to "signify to me that there may be others there"' (Lacan, 1988: 215). (In *Rear Window*, Thorvald's lighted cigarette, glowing in the darkness of his apartment signals to Jeff that he may be under the gaze of this threatening other.) Sartre elaborates:

> the gaze will be given as well . . . when there is a rustling of branches, or the sound of a footstep followed by silence, or the slight opening of a shutter, or a light movement of a curtain. During an attack men who are crawling through the brush apprehend as a gaze to be avoided, not two eyes, but a white farmhouse which is outlined against the sky at the top of a little hill. . . . Now the bush, the farmhouse are not the gaze, they only represent the eye . . . [which is] the support for the gaze.[7] (1943/1956: 257-8, also quoted by Bozovic, 1992: 166-7)

A window, curtain or a bush do not gaze at me, eyes behind them see me. Yet I anchor the eyes of the other in the curtain and its movements. I thus see the window and it is gazing at me. The window 'is split into itself, it both signifies and is the site of the other's gaze' (Bozovic, 1992: 168). The gaze, then, is always connected to the look of the other, and it is through their gaze (which is always outside), that I am constituted as a subject. Lacan (1973/1978: 106) argues '[w]hat determines me at the most profound level, in the visible, is the gaze that is outside. It is through the gaze that I enter light and it is from the gaze that I receive its effects. Hence it comes about that the gaze is the instrument through which light is embodied, and through which . . . I am *photo-graphed*' (italics in original).

Silverman (1992: 150-2), extends this argument, 'the subject can only be "photographed" through the frame of culturally intelligible images'. She continues, 'the gaze always emerges . . . within the field of vision . . . we ourselves are always being photographed by it even as we look'. From this observation she concludes, 'all binarizations of spectator and spectacle mystify the scopic relations in which we are held . . . [and this exposes] the impossibility of anyone ever owning the visual agency, or of him or herself escaping specularity.'

My gaze, as Merleau-Ponty argues, renders the invisible world visible.[8] It brings into being the existence of my own body, the flesh of my being, as I am caught up in what I see (1968: 139). I create my visible world through my acts of perception, through my contact with that which I make visible through my actions (1968: 134, 136). My 'body simultaneously sees and is seen . . . it sees itself seeing; it touches itself touching; it is visible and sensitive for itself' (1964a: 162). Through such actions I constitute myself as a self. 'This is a self . . . that is caught up in things, that has a front and a back, a past and a future' (1964a: 163). The perceptual acts of this self, so constituted, bring into existence a vivid world of experience, a world filled with depth, colour, form, line, movement, contour and physiognomy (1964a: 188). Like Cezanne who always doubted what he saw (1964b: 9), and hence painted, the gazing self in everyday life finds its perceptual world constantly changing.

The pleasures of the look are not just erotic and sexual, violent and political. The voyeur's look has its own aesthetic. This aesthetic turns always on the fact that the look produces a double subjectivity; an awareness of self both for the person who looks and for the person who is looked upon. This fact produces the pleasure (and pain) of self-recognition and speaks always to the person's presence in the situation at hand. This look, which creates the other, passes across more than their face. It touches their carnal body, and produces an embodied impression which defines their fleeting subjectivity in the situation. This gaze is structurally empowering: with my eyes I create you (Sartre, 1943/1956: 259–60). The look's pleasures flow from this basic facticity.

In creating you, I give you a history, an erotic reading, and a standing in the situation. I may treat you with indifference, and let my gaze brush across your face, as it would across a distant cloud in the sky (Sartre, 1943/1956: 379). Or I may seize you in my gaze, and draw you near to me. Now my pleasure comes in being able to control your presence for me. As I bring you near I arouse myself, using you for my fantasy purposes. On the other hand, my gaze may be purely clinical and investigative. I find in your presence clues and evidence about your doings (and the doings of others) that are pertinent to my ongoing investigative assignment. Here my pleasure is purely textual and factual. You are an instrumental means to a goal. Or, I may use my gaze to help you. Thinking I am altruistic, I use my control over you to manipulate your body and your mind.

My visual pleasure may be more malefic (Athens, 1980). I define you as evil and I hate you. I must destroy you. I may define you as harmful, as a threat to my safety. My gaze tells me to stay out of your way. I take pleasure, then, in ensuring my personal safety. Finally, my gaze may be one of control. I am your guard and you are under my supervision. When you stray from my sight I react with alarm. You have disobeyed my visual orders. I take pleasure in bringing you back into my visual field, for with my sight I control you.

Foucault (1980) politicizes the gaze and the look of Sartre and Merleau-Ponty. His gaze is given by the omnipresent eye of power that is embedded in all the micro-power structures of the surveillance society. We are always under the control of the eye of the other. This gaze is relentless and we can never successfully fight back against it. (Foucault is unlike Sartre in this regard.) Foucault's gaze (like Sartre's) becomes a metaphor for what the other can do to me. They can intrude into my body, they can punish me, mug me in the dark, stab me in the back, define me as mentally ill, punish me for my sexuality, or brand me a criminal.

I have interiorized this gaze of the other, and have allowed that gaze to control my own subjectivity and social experiences. I have become the eye of power (Foucault, 1980: 155). This eye is everywhere, from the press, to television, cinema and the police. Its gaze defines me within the dominant subjectivities of the surveillance society; namely my race, my class and my gender. This gaze comes at me through the official ideologies of truth which verify the realities of everyday life. These ideologies are present in systems of discourse and centred in those institutional formations which produce truth, including the universities (1980: 131). Taken to new heights by the advanced technological societies, these ideologies of truth are implemented through ever more sophisticated systems of surveillance, encompassing not only aerial viewing and listening devices, but also radar and contact microphones, hidden transmitters, satellite monitoring systems, body microphones, data surveillance systems, computer monitors, hidden cameras, polygraphs, population surveys, international detective agencies, wiretaps, electronic intelligence kits, intercom systems, personality and projective tests, lip-reading, miniature surveillance devices, two-way mirrors, credit card monitoring systems, undercover agents, parabolic and shotgun microphones, photochromic micro-images, television-eye monitoring, public opinion polls, managed news releases, subliminal suggestion methods, radio-detection and frequency probes, radioactive tagging, faked documents, scrambling and signalling devices, sniperscopes, sonic-wave devices, spectograms, super-spy devices, video-tapes, high powered telescopes, voice-prints, DNA prints, X-rays, and Ultra-violet surveillance techniques (see Westin, 1967).

Redoing the Voyeur's Gaze and its Pleasures

Multiple views of the voyeur's gaze and its pleasures: for Mulvey and others, the voyeur's gaze is punishing, repressive, exhibitionistic, narcissistic, fetishistic and almost entirely sexual. It is a structurally overdetermined gendered gaze, a gaze grounded in the politics and ideologies of patriarchy. Mulvey's voyeur looks, not to investigate, or to constitute the world, but to take sexual pleasures in the visual oppression of the other – the figure of woman. Mulvey posits an active-passive gendered system of gazes which reproduce patriarchal domination in the cinematic experience.

Sartre and Lacan's gaze constitute my subjectivity for me, it turns me into an object for the other and a subject for myself. This gaze can embarrass, humiliate, humble and shame. It can produce fear, slavery, desire, love, hate, indifference, masochism and sadism. The other's gaze is everywhere (and nowhere), as is mine, and in the fitting together of our gazes we can destroy or recreate one another. Merleau-Ponty's look is one of wonderment, creation, action and doubt. I create my world by looking at it: my look is always embodied, an extension of my carnal being. Foucault's look is negatively empowered, politically inscribed in the structures of surveillance that reach from medicine to cinema to the prison.

Types of Looks

A typology of gazes may now be offered, building on the above formulations. A gaze is not simply voyeuristic. It is regulated, has a trajectory, and evokes emotions and conduct which are differentially reciprocated, and erotic. A gaze may be active, or passive, direct, or indirect and indifferent. It will always be engendered, reflecting a masculine or feminine perspective. A gaze may be a gaze of power and domination (for example Frank's looks at Dorothy in *Blue Velvet* (1986)). It may be investigative, medical, or psychiatric. It may be erotic or non-erotic, or both. The erotic gaze will move across Sartre's three poles of desire and love, masochism and sadism which define our concrete relations with others (1943/1956: 252–302; Schroeder, 1984: 186–202). It can move from male to male, male to female, female to male, or female to female.

A gaze may be conducted under full interactional awareness, where two parties exchange mutual glances (Lisa and Jeff in *Rear Window* (1954)). On the other hand, the gaze may be covert and secret, where one party has no idea that they are being spied upon by another (Jake's surveillance of Hollis Mulwray in *Chinatown* (1974)). A gaze may be suspected, and a person takes measures to secure privacy (Debra Winger's fears of being seen by Tom Berenger in *Betrayed* (1988)). And, a person may pretend to gaze, or to look, when they in fact are not giving their attention to another (Richard Dreyfuss's early investigative gazes in *Stakeout* (1987)).[9] A person may also be positioned to be deliberately gazed upon (the opening shots of *Atlantic City* (1980), with Susan Sarandon in front of a window). The emotionality produced by the gaze, for the bearer of the look, will move from indifference, to shame, pride, fear, hysteria, paranoia, humility and sexual desire. The conduct produced by the gaze will range from flight and an attempt to escape the other's gaze (Thorvald in *Rear Window*), to a startled reaction (Thorvald again), to a mutual acknowledgment accompanied by no change in action (for example, Jeff and Lisa at the end of *Rear Window*).

Finally, every gaze is regulated, structured by underlying systems of power and gender (see Doane, 1987: 177). This leads to the production of official and unofficial looks (and spectators), furtive, secret looks, looks which commodify, and make the subject beautiful, or erotic, or masculine and powerful. The looked-at-ness of any gazed upon subject, is regulated, then, by a system of meanings that leads the looked-at-subject to act in a particular way. These meanings will reflect the deference and demeanour structures of everyday racial and sexual etiquette (Goffman, 1959). The trajectory of a gaze, male or female, will vary by the context in which it is framed.

In medical discourse, as Doane has shown for the woman's films of the 1940s, woman becomes the object of a pure, clinical gaze. She is deprived of subjectivity. In the maternal melodrama the distance between the mother and her child may be defined by pure voyeurism, as when, in the film *Stella Dallas* (1937), 'Stella Dallas watches her daughter from afar' (Doane, 1987: 178). In the love story, the gaze may become erotic, narcissistic, and framed by gazes in a mirror (Doane, 1987: 178). Paranoid Gothic films, in contrast, offer instances of an aggressive, violent look directed against women (Doane, 1987: 179).

The interactional structures which surround the gaze in everyday life (open, closed, suspected, pretended) must be transferred to the screen, where the same structures will apply. The classic theory of the screen (and everyday life) voyeur has presumed (or emphasized) only one of the above contexts (closed). That is the person who looks takes a secret pleasure in looking at the unsuspecting other. (Although Mulvey's theory, in its most elaborate form, assumes a full masculine gaze directed towards the woman's body which is displayed for his visual pleasure.)

Classic narrative, voyeuristic cinema is filled with each of the above structures and types of gaze (and some postmodern cinema as well, for example *Blue Velvet*). *Rear Window* moves from Jeffries's hidden voyeuristic gazes on the apartments across the way (especially Miss Lonely Heart), to his open exchange of glances with Lisa, to the final discovery by Thorvald that he has been spied upon by Jeffries, and Jeffries's discovery that Thorvald is returning his gaze. In each instance the gaze produces changes in emotions and conduct.

In everyday life the gaze is seldom, if ever, fully regulated, or fully structured. It is an uncertain, unstable production; a fleeting process, leaving its invisible traces, now here, next there, constantly on the move, an absence defined by its moving presence. Thus a person or a thing is seldom, if ever, a full presence to be captured in entirety. Only the frozen, still frames of the camera produce a certain presence; but this look of the camera, as Barthes (1981) has noted, reflects a presence that 'has been,' not one that 'is now'.[10] Cinema's voyeurs, of course, work to overcome the inherent uncertainty of the everyday gaze. This they do through the frozen, close-up looks they direct to their subjects, thereby reproducing the belief that full presence can be given through the look.[11]

Many gazes and many pleasures: supervising, controlling, malefic, investigative, destructive, self-protective, clinical, erotic, indifferent, self-constructive. Each visual pleasure reasserts the power of my look, for with my eyes I have been empowered to make you over into my image. Thus emerges the voyeur's pleasures and its doubts, for I can never be sure that I have created you correctly. Moreover, you always escape the grasp of my gaze, for your subjectivity is always yours, not mine to give. Now cinema's voyeur . . .

The Investigative Voyeur[12]

With the cinematic imagination and the apparatuses of seeing that the cinematic society produced, came, as argued in Chapter 1, a new way of seeing the visible world. The cinematic culture made vision an analogue for knowing (see Ong, 1977: 122–3). The visible world was recorded in terms of the images it left on a strip of film projected as a still or moving photograph. However, the visible was suddenly transformed into a 'continual flux . . . [it] became fugitive' (Berger, 1972: 18), unstable, no longer a thing that could be grasped with certainty. This instability in the visual field could only be overcome through the certainty of the images produced by the camera.

Consider the early film *Getting Evidence* (1906). Here a detective 'armed with a camera pursues a couple and is frustrated in his repeated attempts to capture them on celluloid' (Mayne, 1990: 168–9). Reality escapes the camera's eye. In *A Search for Evidence* (1903), another investigative, voyeuristic film, an angry wife and a private detective search for her adulterous husband. The woman 'peers into one room after another, and the camera imitates her look. When she finds her husband, the detective is shown peering through the keyhole' (Mayne, 1990: 170). The detective's investigative look is thus reinforced by the camera's gaze, and this gaze is superior to the woman's peeping look through the keyhole. In *A Subject for the Rogue's Gallery* (1904) a woman prisoner mugs for the police photographer. The look of the camera, the photographer and the police are joined in a frozen frame which shows the woman crying (Mayne, 1990: 161, 171). The surveillance society has captured its subject.

Thus was produced, with the invention of cinema, a transformation in a previously valued social self, called the voyeur, spectator, or the looking self.[13] This self became an extension of the camera's looking eye.[14] It would know itself and others through the investigative, inquisitive, often erotic gaze, the gaze which would render the other interactionally naked.[15]

Trapeze Disrobing Act (1901) provides an early classic example. Two men, 'seated in a theater box, watch a woman, seated on a trapeze, strip' (Mayne, 1990: 161). In *As Seen through a Telescope* (1900) a man with a telescope peers 'eagerly at a woman passerby and a shot of the woman's angle in close-up' (Mayne, 1990: 158) is shown. In the recent past, *Body Double* (1984), Jake, the gullible, unemployed, house-sitting actor, becomes obsessed with the telescopic viewing of the nightly striptease act performed several blocks away by a beautiful woman in front of her open window. In films like these, the spectator assumes the voyeuristic gaze of the voyeur in the film, thereby transforming the figure of woman into a pleasurable sexual object for the male viewer in the theatre.

The appearance of the voyeur, as the iconic self, ushered in the desire to create, from within the class of all persons who gazed, a special looking self; a voyeur who takes the business of looking seriously, indeed a person who would make looking a livelihood. This person would bring a special interpretive vision to the act of looking. He or she would be able to understand when others could not. This person would emerge as a new version of the conscious subject who joined vision with knowing, and truth with seeing. Thus emerged, within popular culture, the journalist and the detective, professional lookers whose investigative gaze was special, gifted, out of the ordinary, even almost scientific in its objectivity. Indeed, the origins of scientific, investigative sociology can be found in these impulses, wherein the sociologist, like the journalist, would enter society and return with news about the affairs of everyday people.[16] The prototypical gaze was organized, as argued in the last chapter, under the interests of the state and its protection. In its most powerful form this was the gaze of the police state, the gaze of the agent of the police, the detective.[17] This inspecting agent then utilized the scientific gaze of other surveillance experts in his or her work.

Alongside the official, state-sanctioned agents of surveillance, soon appeared a class of private inspectors. PIs (eyes), called shamuses, private detectives and crime reporters. These individuals were often jaded, having had unsuccessful careers as official gazers and inspectors for the state and its various agencies.[18] At times they were burned-out journalists or journalists who fought with their editors. Their presence in society spoke to the general belief that the state and its control agencies were corrupt, inept, brutal and ideologically biased in the direction of the ruling class. The private detective and the reporter spoke for the underclass, those persons who were mistreated by the police, and the other official agencies of society.

This character, as an image-maker and truth finder, would often use a camera to record his or her images. In *Getting Evidence* (1906), the detective finally manages to catch the couple on film, only to discover that it is the wrong couple (Mayne, 1990: 168–9). Or consider the reversal of this pattern in the 1960 version of *Peeping Tom*. Here the filmmaker, as a murderer, photographs his victims, a theme played out in the opposite direction not only in *Blow-Up* (1966) but also in *Blow Out* (1981) where the voyeur's images become evidence of violence, but the incident recorded on film (or tape) is suddenly erased; so what was real no longer is. And then there is *Chinatown* (1974), where Jake's original photographs of marital infidelity become symbols of the deeper transgressive infidelities examined in the film concerning power, violence, truth, reality, patriarchy and incest. Consider too the real live, violent voyeur who takes the film's narrative and its images, as reasons for his violence in the world. As John Hinckley,[19] a star in the recent film *Assassins*, sings to his unnamed love, 'a picture of Jodie Foster in *Taxi Driver* is clearly visible on a table next to him' (James, 1991: 21).

Raymond Chandler described this man, this new investigator, as he would appear in his benevolent form, over and over again, in Hollywood cinema, and in the detective story:

Down these mean streets a man must go who is himself not mean, who is neither tarnished nor afraid. The detective of this kind of story must be such a man. He is the hero ... a man of honor ... a relatively poor man ... a common man ... a lonely man .. a proud man .... He talks as the man of his age talks – that is, with rude wit, a lively sense of the grotesque, a disgust for sham, and a contempt for pettiness. The story is this man's adventure in search of a hidden truth . . . *He has a range of awareness that startles you, but it belongs to him by right, because it belongs to the world he lives in.* If there were enough like him, the world would be a very safe place to live in. (1950: 22, emphasis added)

This man of the world has a visionary power, a range of awareness that makes him extraordinary; yet this power belongs to the world, which is itself visible to all who will look. His gaze is always gendered and shaped by the presence of women, who are themselves contained within the violent structures of patriarchy.

Take *The Big Sleep* (1946), where Philip Marlowe, Chandler's man who walks these mean streets, is hired by General Sternwood to deal with Geiger who is blackmailing him for reasons connected to his daughter Carmen. Marlowe's task is to get rid of the Geiger problem, a problem which involves a hidden camera and missing photographs of the wayward Carmen. In order to do this he is led into a labyrinthine world of clues, double crosses, lies, deceptions and misrepresentations. Everywhere he turns the figure of Carmen or Vivian appears. As objects of sexual spectacle (Mayne, 1990: 27), the sisters function as unreliable eyes to the film's basically incomprehensible plot, which turns on the investigative gaze that is always filtered through erotic desire.

As if he learned his lesson from Marlowe, Jake Gittes in *Chinatown*, will also become erotically involved with the subject of his investigative gaze, Mrs Mulwray. Unlike Marlowe, Gittes will use cameras, and broken watches to record the wrongful doings of others. But like Marlowe, Jake's voyeuristic activities will be in the service of a higher truth, unmasking, that is, the hidden truths about this evil world.

Here is the PI's journalistic counterpart, Hildy Johnson, the protagonist of *The Front Page* (1931):[20]

He is brash, fast talking, and streetwise. He knows who to bribe, where to get a drink, and assumes on principle that any government official or person in a position of authority is corrupt and should be treated like a two dollar whore. On the other hand, two dollar whores, cleaning women, and any other persons working for a living deserve a measure of respect. For all his brashness, Johnson is a rank sentimentalist, easily touched for loans and in love. (Martin, 1985: 47–8, also quoted by Ehrlich, 1991: 23)

Like the shamus, the jaded, sexist journalist knows the streets and the underside of life. A common man, who has contempt for those in power, he is on the side of the little person. As discussed in Chapter 1 (pp. 22–3), the newspaper picture, with the investigative journalist as the hero, kept alive the key cultural myth of democracy concerning the belief that the truth will always be told.

The journalist-crime reporter employed the investigative techniques of the private eye, including the use of surveillance devices, cameras, and the deployment of an official gaze that would ultimately reveal the hidden truths about the social order. Numerous newspaper films of the 1930s, including *The Front Page, Hi, Nellie, The Strange Love of Molly Louvain, Blessed Event, Advice to the Lovelorn* and *Behind the Headlines*, focused on the journalist as crime buster. James Cagney's role in *Picture Snatcher* was typical of this series. Cagney's presence is defined by his ever-present camera which he uses to photograph a murderer in action (Barris, 1976: 26). The reporter-as-photographer was further developed by network television in the 1952 weekly series, 'Crime Photographer', starring Darren McGavin. Two years later Charles Bronson would star in a series entitled, 'Man with a Camera' (Barris, 1976: 195). In both series the hero used his camera to record criminal actions which usually escaped the attention of the police.

A separate category of the journalist film involved the female reporter. Often teamed with a lover or husband who was also a reporter, women reporters were used to cover the human angle of a story. Barris (1976: 139) observes, 'if someone accused of a crime happened to be a woman, a female reporter might be assigned to play up the emotional aspects of the story. Or, if the accused was a man, he might have a wife, girlfriend or mother, and the woman reporter would be sent to interview such interested parties, again playing up the heart-tugging angles.' Such stories came to be called sob stories, and the 'sister reporter doing such work came to be known as a sob sister' (Barris, 1976: 139). Countless films in the 1930s developed these gendered-based themes (*Big News* (1929), *Young Man of Manhattan* (1930), *The Finger Points* (1931), *Hold that Girl* (1934)). *The Philadelphia Story* (1940) turned the female reporter (Ruth Hussey) into a photographer, while *Deadline for Murder* (1946) and *Perilous Holiday* (1946) presented the gutsy female reporter as an aggressive crime fighter. A *Face in the Crowd* (1957) and *All The King's Men* (1949) transformed this character into a soul-searching reporter-aide who charted the moral decline of a strong male figure. These shifts from sob sister reporter to crime fighter and moralist were prefigured in the silent period in the *Exploits of Elaine*, and the *Perils of Pauline* series where 'detectives' Elaine, or Pauline (played by Pearl White), accompanied by scientific criminologist Craig Kennedy, pitted their efforts against the master criminal known as the Clutching Hand (Everson, 1972: 24–5).

The contemporary, cinematic culture created, then, a gendered class of surveillance experts, persons whose ability to look and see was extraordinary and legitimated in terms of the key cultural values. These experts put into place the epistemology of realism and its attendant theories of truth which were examined in the last chapter. In particular, they applied, with varying degrees of emphasis, the methods of modern science to the solving of problems, not always criminal, which flowed from everyday life (see Truzzi, 1976: 52).

Sherlock Holmes, the screen's first detective (1903) (Everson, 1972: 4), was cinema's early model of the application of these principles to the solving of crimes. His methods employed the techniques of deduction, induction, abduction and negative case analysis. He believed in a determinate universe, the empirical verification of conjectures, methods that were intersubjective, the clear presentation of evidence, the power of observation, the factual basis of hypotheses, the use of multiple theories, unobtrusive methods, free association and the other devices of psychoanalysis (Truzzi, 1976: 54–77). As Truzzi (1976: 67–8) observes, Holmes's investigative procedures often combined the methods of deduction and induction with the pragmatism of C.S. Peirce. Peirce's pragmatic method emphasized the importance of abductive reasoning, that is the formulation of 'conjectures about reality which need[s] to be validated through testing' (Truzzi, 1976: 68). This procedure, for Holmes, worked from consequences (dead bodies, committed crimes) back to reasonable interpretations about the causes of these effects. These interpretations were then tested against the realities, facts and details of the actual crime. Consequences (effects) informed causal hypotheses (causes). In this inversion of the usual scientific method Holmes, and the detectives who would follow him, elaborated a pragmatic theory of truth, reality and causality

The task of the surveillance expert was to discover things about society that others could not see. Gittes, for example, simultaneously discovers repressed incest and a corrupt political system that extends from Chinatown to the canals that bring water to Los Angeles, and Charlie Chan, like Sherlock Holmes, always uncovered the hidden murderer. These were the professional 'gazers', or voyeurs of the new capitalist state. Their gaze came in several forms, including medical, penal, educational, scientific, sexual and legal. Indeed, in order to implement their gaze, they often had to rely upon technical experts who were proficient in other forms of gazing and looking. Thus Marlowe would turn to the police for help, or they to him, while other filmic versions of this figure would have him consulting ballistics experts, medical anthropologists, forensic scientists, psychiatrists, fortune tellers, psychics and witch doctors (see Lyons and Truzzi, 1990; Wilson, 1985).

The Costs and Consequences of Gazing

The professional voyeur challenges the ordinary make-up of everyday life. He or she questions the way things are. The voyeur's gaze unravels the untruths that others tell, including their lies, violence, illicit affairs, cover-ups, murders, political assassinations, illegal acts, briberies, personal indiscretions and deeply held secrets.[21]

These professionals who do the gazing, investigative, surveillance work of the cinematic society pay a high prize for their gazing, often alcoholism, personal violence, or insanity. The complex relationships between these costs, their consequences, and the voyeur's activities occurs too frequently to be coincidental. In exposing the truths that others cannot, or will not, see the voyeur functions as a social critic and a menace to the existing social order. These activities place the voyeur under threat of harm; his or her life may be endangered. At the same time these activities produce instabilities in the personal life of the voyeur: a life which is already unstable because of the voyeuristic position he or she has assumed in society (see Penzler, 1977).

The previously unsettled situation of the voyeur is shown in tendencies toward alienation, isolation, alcoholism, drug addiction, personal violence, fractured personal relationships and a proneness to insanity or paranoia. Consider Harry Caul (the wiretap expert in *The Conversation*, 1974; see also Chapter 7), and Scotty, the obsessive voyeur in *Vertigo* (1958). Both men go insane when they discover events (including murder) that others attempt to deny. Sherlock Holmes, in several of his versions, suffered from drug addiction. His addiction supposedly sharpened his powers of perception, but it was also attributable to an attempt to deal with the horrible crimes he uncovered in society. Marlowe, Chandler's PI, drank too much and experienced black-outs, often during those moments when his investigations turned most ugly. Richard Boyle, the photo-journalist of *Salvador* (1986), like his counterpart Russell Price, in *Under Fire* (1983) also drank to excess, as did Don Stevens, the isolated reporter in *Deadline* (1987). In each case the reporter was uncovering political facts that went against the official version of reality. Al Pacino as the detective-voyeur of *Sea of Love* (1990) is an alcoholic, in part because he cannot handle the fact of his divorce and the ugly murders he has to deal with on his job. Graham (see Chapter 3), the video-voyeur of *sex, lies and videotape* (1989) experiences sexual impotency as punishment for his past deeds, but also as a price for his voyeurism. Dorothy, the female voyeur in *Blue Velvet* (1986), who knows and sees too much, is brutalized by Frank. Alex, the detective-voyeur of *Black Widow* (1986) suffers from an obsession with Catharine, an obsession due, perhaps, to the absence of a man in her own life; that void being caused, in part by her job (Mayne, 1990: 48). Ingrid Bergman, the female psychoanalyst of *Spellbound* (1945) is slandered by her co-workers because of her failure to have an active love life, and she requires the assistance of male psychoanalysts in order to unravel Gregory Peck's amnesia.

The voyeur-investigator is obsessed with looking. Detached from others, a perpetual outsider, this figure can, however, never be aloof; he or she always gets involved. As Penzler (1977: 3–4) says of Lew Archer (*Harper*, 1966, *The Drowning Pool*, 1975), Ross Macdonald's version of Philip Marlowe, 'he simply cares too much, and his sensitivity makes him vulnerable to pain. He has experienced it often enough to be exhausted from it, and he lives his lonely years as an outsider, peering into the hopeless pains of others, trying somehow to relieve them.'[22]

The compulsion to look is coupled, then, with the altruistic motive to help others in the name of justice. But this compulsion extends beyond the normal range of involvement in the lives of others. It becomes a mania, a fixation which borders on insanity. For example, Harry Caul's obsession with listening to others and to prying into their lives leads him to have no private life of his own (see the discussion in Chapter 8, pp. 167–73). He refuses to tell his girlfriend where he lives. His telephone number is unlisted. When his landlady delivers his mail to him he asks how she got into his apartment, orders her out and tells her that he will now change his address to a post office mail box. When the company calls him at home and tells him that they will now be watching him, he tears his apartment apart looking for the bug they have planted.

Driven by a private morality which often goes against the public conscience and public morality (Penzler, 1977: 7), investigative voyeurs set their own standards of right and wrong. These standards, or codes of conduct, lead the voyeur not to report certain crimes, thereby practising a vigilante version of law and order. Harper (Lew Archer) for example, lets family members kill one another, if such acts are required. Nick Nolte (*Under Fire*) alters a photograph to make a dead political leader appear to be alive. Philip Marlowe destroys a photograph that could incriminate an innocent victim. Mike Hammer (*I the Jury*, 1953, *Kiss Me Deadly*, 1955, *My Gun is Quick*, 1957, *The Girl Hunters*, 1963) was given to lines like the following, 'there's no shame or sin in killing a killer. David did it when he knocked off Goliath. Saul did it when he slew tens of thousands. There's no shame to killing an evil thing' (Penzler, 1977: 78). In such gestures the voyeur-vigilante invokes a higher moral authority, often locating him- or herself on the same plane as God.

The manic obsession to look, joined with the commitment to a private morality, which often justifies violence and the distortion of the official order of truth, places the voyeur-reporter-detective inside and outside society at the same time. They are outside the official order of society, while adhering to a moral code that their version of society appears to require. As a consequence, they embody an alternative version of the social, a version that the larger order requires if it is to appear to be humane, just and orderly.

This figure upholds the social by going against it; he or she thus represents the ideal version of the just and good society. As such they are mythical figures who re-enact the mythic principles of heroism, justice, kindness, compassion and honour that have been eroded, if not destroyed, by the functionaries who control and manipulate the contemporary, cold-hearted bureaucratic societies. Of equal importance, this figure maintains the illusion that evil will always be destroyed and truth and justice will always prevail.

Thus their personal obsessions, which border on the pathological, are justified by an appeal to these higher goals. Paradoxically, when his or her activities begin to challenge the official social order, a double instability and insanity of place is experienced. They have nowhere to turn, except inward to the destructive personal habits which increase the instability and isolation that is felt. They may have to be sacrificed for the higher good.

As a consequence, the voyeur is simultaneously a hero/heroine and an anti-hero/heroine. In heroic form, voyeurs prevail over adversity. In anti-hero (heroine) form their personal maladies (alcoholism, insanity, paranoia, etc.) reflect and embody, as Spender (1984: ix) has said of the alcoholic 'an extreme external situation through his [her] own extremity'. That is the voyeur's story, like the alcoholic's, however briefly told, 'becomes the dial of an instrument that records the effects of a particular stage of civilization upon a civilized individual' (Spender, 1984: ix; Denzin, 1987: 201). The telling of this story, then, becomes a moral concern, for the voyeur's tale is an account of a person driven to find a truth that others will not accept.

A message with moralistic overtones is conveyed in these stories. In order for the social order to be made right, someone has to pay a great price. That price is worth paying because in the end the benefits for society outweigh the personal costs to the voyeur. More deeply, the voyeur, as an already unstable person, embodies the fact that only the unstable person will be drawn to the underlife of society and its crimes, misdemeanours and other assorted evils. They experience their own version of anhedonia, unable to experience pleasure or happiness, they resort to looking and voyeurism as methods of producing pleasure (see Lyman, 1990b on anhedonia). His or her story, then, is seldom comic. It is nearly always melodramatic, and sometimes tragic.[23]

The Erotic, Pornographic Gaze

Recall the opening shots of *Chinatown* (1974): Jake and a client are examining photographs (taken by Jake) of the client's semi-nude wife having intercourse with a male in a nature setting. Jake attempts to comfort his client, as the two Peeping Toms experience, not just sexual arousal, but outrage at this show of marital infidelity. This scene blurs the dividing line between the detective as voyeur of the truth and voyeur of the sexual; for clearly Jake takes some morbid pleasure in having uncovered this sexual infidelity for his client. His pleasure is two-fold; he has fulfilled his detective obligation to discover the truth about the client's wife, and he has been sexually aroused in the process.

Consider another scene: Harry, our detective in *Dirty Harry* (1971), finds himself in a dark alley on a stakeout of Scorpio. Standing on a garbage can he peers into a window where a woman, undressed to the waist, is engaged in sexual activity with a male. Four bums disrupt his activity, knock him to the ground and call him a dirty Peeping Tom who is interfering with Mary's work.[24] Harry, like Jake, crosses the dividing line between detective or investigator and sexual voyeur. Indeed each film suggests that the two activities cannot be separated, for sex, violence and illegal conduct all go together. Hence Harry's name, 'Dirty Harry' for with this name he takes his place with those sexual voyeurs, and Peeping Toms who have preceded him in the history of cinema.

In the blurring of the investigative with the sexual gaze, the voyeur's story seldom crosses over to pure popular pornography (hard, soft, sadomasochistic, lesbian, gay, etc.).[25] Instead the sexual content of the investigative look is subordinated to the truths revealed by the gaze of the detective. (For example the sexual gazes in *Body Double* ultimately give way to a gaze which tells the truth about the murderer in the situation.) However, popular pornography (see Ross, 1989, Chapter 6; Lewallen, 1989) does deploy the investigative gaze for sexual, erotic and pornographic purposes. In films like *Pink Champagne* (1980), *Mouthwatering* (1986), *Infatuation* (1990), *Dream Lover* (1990), *Trinity Brown* (1984), *Secrets of Love* (1986) the gaze of the 'sexiologist', the virgin, the sexually frustrated, frigid, or impotent male or female, the rapist and the seducer are used to tell a sexual story of self-discovery and domination. A doubling of the spectator's voyeuristic gaze operates in such films. He or she watches the watchers watch the sexual activities of another. Voyeurism is thus justified in terms of a higher goal, or the pleasures it brings another.

The Gendered Ethnic Gaze

The Gendered Gaze Always a gendered production, usually male, but not necessarily, the voyeur exposes the erotic, political sides of everyday life. In doing so this figure shows how the gaze is inevitably gendered and structured by the laws of patriarchy. The female's passive gaze, for example, is typically countered by the active, aggressive gaze of the male: her investigative look is made subordinate to the power of the masochistic and sadistic patriarchal gaze. Her gaze simply lacks power and is often used as a supplement to the investigative look of the male. As such it also functions to affirm his project and underline her admiration and love for him. The highly popular David Lynch film *Blue Velvet* (1986) is representative in this regard (see the discussion in Chapter 3). While Lynch allows Dorothy to control Jeffrey's gaze in the pivotal closet scene ('Don't look at me!'), Sandy's gaze is pure supplement to Jeffrey's investigative project. She sits in the car and watches while Jeffrey searches. In refusing to give her a powerful, reflective gaze, Lynch keeps her trapped within the traditional feminine investigative position. She is the object of, or the adjunct to, the male's gaze.

The Ethnic Gaze The gaze of the voyeur is also racially structured, for typically racial minorities are not allowed to gaze on majority group members (see the discussion in Chapter 4). The concept of the colour line (Blumer, 1965/1988: 208) structures the gaze of race. This line assigns whites and African-Americans different positions in the social order, giving to each different rights and privileges, including how visual, face-to-face interaction is to be organized. When a member of a racial or ethnic minority does appropriate the voyeur's investigative gaze, he or she is often relegated to a secondary position, for example, the helper of a white man; the minority gaze is prohibited from crossing the colour line that separates the races (see Vidich and Lyman, 1988: 69). Texts which invert this structure (*In The Heat of the Night*, 1967) challenge a racial order predicated on a privileged structure of gazing and being seen: African-Americans, even if they are detectives from the big city of Philadelphia, cannot gaze on white Americans. Likewise, Captain Davenport, the African-American lawyer (Harold Robbins) of *A Soldier's Story* (1984), confronts racial bias and continual attempts to thwart his investigation, when he is called upon to solve the murder of Sergeant Waters, also an African-American.

The issue of racial bias and the investigator's gaze was partially circumvented in the 1930s and 1940s in the Charlie Chan and Mr Moto film series (for example, *Charlie Chan in Egypt*, 1935 and *Think Fast Mr Moto*, 1937) (see also Goode, 1982a,b, 1983 a,b,c).[26] In these films Charlie Chan and Mr Moto cultivated Western images of the inscrutable Asian who could, because of his cultural ancestry and educational training, see things that were not apparent, due to their biases, to Westerners. Chan was given to uttering such aphorisms as 'Theories like fingerprints, everybody has them', or 'Man without enemies, like dog without fleas' (Penzler, 1977: 47). Yet these films reproduced biases within Asian culture. Chan, for example, was anti-Japanese ('cooking business begins to get tiresome, like the company of Japanese'), and Mr Moto was an apologist for Japanese imperialism (Penzler, 1977: 142). Chan's methods were often referred to as 'that chop suey stuff' (see the discussion of *Charlie Chan at the Opera* (1936) in Chapter 4).

Often these films used the figure of the Asian detective to mock the attitudes of whites. In *Charlie Chan in Egypt* a racial analogue operates (Tuska, 1978: 115). The true heroes of the film are Charlie, the plodding Chinese, accompanied by seemingly inept Stepin Fetchit (Tuska, 1978: 115). The Europeans are arrogant and self-assured, and their 'conceits toward the nonwhite races [are] parodied by Chan and Fetchit' (Tuska, 1978: 115). At one point Fetchit tells Chan that 'according to a fortune teller in Mississippi his ancestors came from Egypt' (Tuska, 1978: 116), implying that they were perhaps Nubian kings.

These films continued to be made even after the attack on Pearl Harbor (see Chapter 4). They created the concept of the Oriental as hero, or a benevolent entity, but in so doing reproduced a series of racial stereotypes concerning the sinister Oriental, the beautiful Oriental woman, 'as slender as the bamboo is slender, beautiful as the blossom of the plum' (Penzler, 1977: 44), the obedient, dumb Oriental son, and the ageing, wise Oriental grandparent. Such images would be shattered in *Chan is Missing* (1982; see the discussion in Chapter 4; but the concept of the evil Oriental other returns with the 1994 film *The Shadow*). Cinema's investigative voyeur thus reproduces the racial and gender structures of seeing that interact and operate in everyday life.

Conclusion

As a cultural creation, Hollywood's treatment of the voyeur and voyeurism has been shaped by the following:

- the temperance movement and its sexual, puritanical, Victorian legacies (Gusfield, 1963)
- the production (1900 onwards) in popular culture of the idea of a criminal underclass, often connected to membership in a racial or ethnic minority group (see Manning, 1977)
- the nineteenth century creation and legitimation of the science of criminalistics (1860s), the centralized police department (1850s) and the concept of the private detective (1900) (see Haycroft, 1972; Mayne, 1988)
- World War I and the need for special agents and spies who could monitor the activities of the international German enemy
- the jazz era (1926–34), including its attendant liberalizing of sexual relations between males and females (Room, 1985), coupled with the concept of females being able to move freely in public spaces, leading to the female investigator (*Perils of Pauline*) as well as the female who gets in trouble
- the rise in popularity of the newspaper and private eye film in the 1930s (Halliwell, 1990)
- Hollywood's (and the popular culture's) turn to psychoanalysis as a psychology capable of explaining the disturbed, criminal mind (see Gabbard and Gabbard, 1987)
- World War II and the German and Asian scare (see Rubenstein, 1979, Chapters 7 and 8)
- progressive elaborations in Hollywood's Motion Picture Production Code (1922, 1930, 1934, 1938, 1940, 1955, 1960) permitting the showing of increased violence and sexuality on screen (see Cook, 1981; Leff and Simmons, 1990)
- the Cold War era (1950–62) and the perceived communist threats to the American way of life (see Bell, 1960)
- the Civil Rights movement (1950–70), leading to new leading roles for minority actors and women in mainstream cinema (see Lyman, 1990c)
- the conservative decades of the 1970s and 1980s, emphasizing criminal assaults on women, and the family, and a corresponding greater need for official voyeurs who could monitor the doings of the violent voyeur (see Ryan and Kellner, 1988, Chapters 5 and 8)
- transformations in the cultural logics of late, multinational capitalism, which brought Third World peoples into the centres of postmodern discourse (Hall, 1988), while making international tourists out of the white middle class (see Featherstone, 1990; Urry, 1990)
- the sustained production of literary and novelistic works focusing on the voyeur and his or her doings (for example Gothic thrillers, spy novels, detective stories, etc.)

- the desire by filmmakers to turn such works into mainstream films
- the creation of an audience of filmgoers who would attend such productions and the ability of Hollywood to make money from them.

Cinema's serious voyeur is a moral, compassionate being who saves people in danger. A logical, rational, objective observer of social life, he or she exposes the brutality and stupidity of the state and its official agents. Not above using surveillance devices, this individual attempts to capture the truth about reality, exposing, in the process, corruption and evil in the social world. Speaking always in the language of the ordinary person, this voyeur shows contempt for pettiness and official protocol. Operating with a private morality, these persons justify violence in the name of justice. Not above erotic temptation, they will sometimes become Peeping Toms and fall in love with good and bad beautiful women (and men). They pay a price for their voyeurism, including insanity, alcoholism and death.

On occasion the voyeur's gaze can be a laughing matter. I turn now to those film voyeurs who make their looking a topic of comedy. Such persons mock the above conventions.

Notes

1 There exist, as well, recent poststructural, Derridian (and postmodern) readings of the camera, the gaze and the cinematic text (see Kaplan, 1988: 5; Tseëlon and Kaiser, 1992; Derrida, 1972/1981; Brunette and Wills, 1989; Mayne, 1990: 45–6).

2 Stacey fits female spectatorship to the actual cinematic experience, showing that British female movie fans in the 1940s and 1950s actively used filmic images of women for purposes of utopian fantasy and personal identification. There is thus a gap between textual studies of the spectator and empirical studies of real people watching movies.

3 As Kaplan (1988: 5) argues, it is time to abandon the binarisms, and sexual determinisms of psychoanalysis and its theoretical interpretations of the voyeur's gaze.

4 Throughout this section I am indebted to William Schroeder for our discussions of these four theorists.

5 Of the four, Merleau-Ponty most directly addresses the cinematic experience of watching the screen.

6 Silverman (1992: 129) argues for a sharp distinction between the look and the gaze, the former referring to Lacan's eye, that which sees only from one point of view, while the gaze is grounded in otherness, that which is outside the person. Silverman (1992: 130), after Lacan, situates the look in desire, and the gaze in otherness, noting that the 'French language does not . . . sustain my distinction, offering only one word – le regard – in place of two primary English signifiers of vision: look and gaze' (1992: 129). Silverman's look, following Lacan (1973/1978: 84–5) is always within desire, while her gaze remains outside desire. I will use look and gaze somewhat interchangeably, anchoring desire in both activities, viewing the gaze as the look of the other. My look becomes a gaze for you, and your look a gaze for me. Looking and gazing are thus always interconnected processes anchored in the subject's field of vision. In this field you and I are, respectively, spectator and spectacle to one another. Neither one of us owns the look and the gazes that come from it, nor can either of us ever escape specularity.

7 Bozovic (1992: 167) argues that Sartre and Lacan disagree on whether or not a window constitutes a gaze.

8 Andrews (1984: 21–2, 34, 93–4, 176) describes other theorists who have continued Merleau-Ponty's phenomenological approach to vision and cinema, including Bazin, Cavell, Morin, Perkins, Mitry, Poulet and Ricoeur.

9 These contexts of gazing parallel Glaser and Strauss's (1964) four contexts of awareness (open, closed, suspicion, pretence) which refer to the total combination of what each interactant in a situation knows about the identity of the other and his own identity in the eyes of the other.

10 Hence the attraction of cinema, for those 'moving pictures' supposedly fill in the spaces that have occurred since the last frame was shot.

11 On the problem of full presence ever being given see Brunette and Wills (1989: 58) who develop Derrida's position on this point.

12 This voyeur's gaze (clinical, investigative, informational, erotic, accidental) would be fitted to the 'whodunit', thriller, and/or suspense formats outlined earlier.

13 Cinema, of course, as argued in the last chapter, did not invent voyeurism by itself; it also took psychoanalysis and the rise to power of the investigative sciences, including sociology, anthropology, psychology and medicine (for earlier accounts of the voyeur and the gaze in history see Foucault, 1975). In this century phenomenology made the voyeur's gaze and the act of perception central to one's being in the world (see Robbe-Grillet, 1958, 1991). Cinema, though, took the voyeur to new heights. In the 1901 film *Peeping Tom* a hotel porter looks 'through the keyholes of a series of rooms, with keyhole masks imitating his vision' (Mayne, 1990: 169). Primitive cinema repeatedly returned to the voyeur looking through the keyhole, or the male spectator looking through a window at a woman undressing.

14 Recall the meanings of vision, and visible: the act of seeing, being visible; the Visible Church, a look, a glance, a person of great beauty, an apparition; visionary – capable of seeing visions; voyeur – a Peeping Tom, and; eye – the organ of sight; voir – to see.

15 In some cultures the eye is akin to a sexual organ, where looking too intently at a woman is akin to 'ocular rape' (Flam, 1991: 3).

16 See Sanders (1976: 2) on the similarities between the detective and the sociologist.

17 Haycroft (1972: 312–18) suggests that the detective story emerges as a literary form with the rise of democracy and the modern police organization, and in that moment when the citizen's sympathies shifted to the side of law and order and not to the criminal who attempted to escape from justice. He dates the beginnings of this genre from Voltaire's *Zadig* (1748), marking Poe as the father of the detective story, with help from Dickens, Collins, Hugo, Dostoevsky, Stevenson, and most importantly Conan Doyle (see also Frisby, 1992; Benjamin, 1973, 1989; Ginzberg, 1986; Thompson, 1993 and Kracauer, 1971). As noted in the last chapter the word detective enters the modern English language in 1843. As the detective genre developed it assumed several forms, including the Doyle derivatives, the police procedural, the hard-boiled detective, the romantic and Gothic melodrama, the psycho-analytic detective, the priest as detective, the attorney as detective, and more recently the gay detective, the recovering alcoholic detective and the hard-boiled female private eye. In each decade of the twentieth century this genre has fitted itself to the major social problems of the day; from Hammett's concerns with labour conflicts and political corruption in the 1920s and 1930s, to the more contemporary concerns for organized crime, drug wars, serial murders and violence against women and children. But nearly always an Oedipal framework has organized the narrative, coupled with a psychopathological view of criminal human nature. The espionage novels of Ambler, Greene, Le Carre, etc. mapped the underside of the world political system during the world wars. These texts, and the others just cited, then were turned into major films.

18 A variant on this theme is the spy, secret agent and double agent, who, in the over 450 spy films produced by Hollywood since the silent era, have been presented as part hunted man (*The Thirty-nine Steps*), deadly agent of the state (*North by Northwest, Three Days of the Condor, The Parallax View, Quiller Memorandum, Manchurian Candidate, Killer Elite*) a secret agent, a super spy (James Bond), and a cynic (*The Spy Who Came in From the Cold*). Rubenstein (1979) presents a reading of this figure, who, in his trapped, hunted version, was a favourite topic in the Hitchcock films (see also Parish and Pitts, 1974, 1986).

19 He attempted to assassinate President Ronald Reagan in 1981, claiming he was doing it for his lover, Jodie Foster, who he had repeatedly watched in *Taxi Driver*.

20 *Front Page* would inscribe in American culture a recurring image of the journalist as a romantic hero, a man always involved and at odds with, a beautiful, independent woman. *The Front Page* format would be repeated, with variations, in nearly every decade, through films like *It Happened One Night* (1934), *Mr Deeds Goes to Down* (1936), *His Girl Friday* (1940), *Woman of the Year* (1941), *Teacher's Pet* (1958), *Lonelyhearts* (1959), *Front Page* (1974) and *Switching Channels* (1988). Ehrlich (1991) offers an analysis of these variations on the Hildy Johnson character, and Barris (1976) treats the depictions of the journalist in a variety of subgenres (reporter as crime buster, reporter as crusader, the overseas reporter, the reporter as human being, the sob sisters, editors and publishers and the newsman as villain).

21 On the lies that the police tell see Hunt and Manning (1991: 52, 67). Schopen describes lies and the work of the private investigator, 'I spend most of my time trying to get information people don't want to give me. This means most people lie to me. I lie to them' (1989: 141).

22 However, as Ross Macdonald observes of Lew Archer, he 'is a hero who sometimes verges on being an anti-hero. While he is a man of action, his actions are largely directed to putting together the stories of other people's lives and discovering their significance. He is less a doer than a questioner, a consciousness in which the meaning of other lives emerge' (1973: 23–4). This means, as Donnelly notes, that 'most of Archer's descendants ... act as characters who precipitate the actions that resolve the puzzle and yet remain separate from the consequences of the action once it is set in motion. They may express grief at the tragic nature of the outcome, but it is difficult to sustain a significant change of character within the series format' (1990: 13).

23 A major exception would be the Woody Allen comedies (e.g., *Crimes and Misdemeanors*).

24 This scene is preceded by another scene where Harry spies on a naked woman in her apartment.

25 Koch (1973) explores the complex relationship between filmic voyeurism and pornography, especially in the films of Andy Warhol.

26 There was a third series, with Boris Karloff as Mr Wong (see Chapter 4).

3

THE COMIC VOYEUR'S GAZE

In the comedy form, as argued in the Introduction, the dangers of voyeurism are neutralized, mocked, and parodied, thereby making the voyeur's activities acceptable to the members of the surveillance society (see Schatz, 1981, Chapter 6, and Horton, 1991a, b on the major forms of film comedy). Cinema's voyeur is a favourite Hollywood comic figure. This character is the frequent focus of mixed-genre comedies, including comedies about detectives for example, screwball comedy (*The Last of the Secret Agents* (1966), *The Big Store* (1941)), reporters (*Broadcast News* (1987)), families (*I Love You to Death* (1990)), cowboys (for example, the western, *Destry Rides Again* (1939)), gangsters (*Crimewave* (1954)), musicians (for example, the musical *A Hard Day's Night* (1964)), scientists and the military (for example, the black comedy, *Dr Strangelove or How I Learned to Stop Worrying and Love the Bomb* (1969)), ordinary lovers (for example, the romance comedy, *Roxanne* (1987)), and people defined as craze, or insane (for example, the comedy of manners, *Harvey* (1950), also *High Society* (1977)).

In such films the screen's comic voyeur emerges as a figure with whom the audience identifies, as they laugh at the complications his, or her voyeuristic activities produce. From the bumbling Inspector Clouseau of the *Pink Panther* (1964), and *Shot in the Dark* (1964) series, to the mad scientist in *Dr Strangelove*, to Steve Martin's private eye in *Dead Men Don't Wear Plaid*, to Woody Allen's mournful Cliff Stern, the documentary filmmaker of *Crimes and Misdemeanors* (1989), laughing matters are produced out of the comic voyeur's ability to see and not see what is obvious to others.

How comedy works its effects on the voyeur's project is the topic of this chapter. I offer detailed readings of four highly popular, recent films: *Dead Men Don't Wear Plaid* (1982), *Blue Velvet* (1986), *sex, lies and videotape* (1989) and *Broadcast News* (1987).[1] Each of these films, in its own way, mocks and ridicules the voyeur's situation. Each struggles with the meanings of voyeurism, while attempting to locate the voyeur's activities in the contemporary moment. Each deals with the voyeur as a recognizable, and gendered social type. In each film the voyeur is a detective, a news reporter, or an innocent bystander who then becomes erotically involved with the object of his attention.[2]

While 'affectionately dedicated to all the brilliant technical and creative people who worked on the films in the 1940s and 1950s', *Dead Men Don't*

Wear Plaid is essentially a pastiche-like parody of the 'lone wolf' and 'psychotic actor' private eye, film noir movies of the 1945–6, and 1949–53 periods of Hollywood production (on these films see Schrader, 1972/1986: 177–9; also Krutnik, 1991: 16, 182, 226). *Blue Velvet*, a black comedy, coming of age Gothic thriller that borders on the soft pornographic, represents male and female sexual and investigative gazes in ways which are comic and serious (on its comedy elements see Jaehne, 1987; Biga, 1987; Denby, 1986; and Hoberman, 1986).[3] *Sex, lies and videotape*, also a dark comedy, undermines, as argued in Chapter 1, the current cultural impulse which turns ordinary people, with their video cameras, into filmmakers (see Benson, 1989 on the film as a psycho-sexual comedy). *Broadcast News*, a romantic comedy, and a recent extension of *Front Page*, the classic journalistic-reporter film (see Ehrlich, 1991), humorously distorts the investigative, editing and reporting gaze of the female news producer. Taken together these four texts reflect, and reflexively deconstruct the postmodern, post-television gaze and the desire to find a firm, and valued, if only laughable place for the voyeur in this society. Each, in its connection back to modernist formulations, moves back and forth between parody and pastiche.

The Comedy Project

General matters first: the following themes organize the relationship between voyeurism and comedy. Gender norms, as argued in Chapter 2, traditionally structure the female's gaze in passive forms, as in Sandy's supplemental-investigative gazes in *Blue Velvet*. Similarly, the female's comic and shocked reactions to events that males find non-troublesome further illuminates this passive dimension of the gendered gaze. For example, Veta Louis Dowd, the matronly sister of Elwood, faints when she sees Harvey, the over six-foot-tall rabbit, and Sandy nearly faints when she confronts the hysterical Dorothy in her mother's front yard. Life is messy, or untoward things are not to be seen by women.[4] Males can gaze where females cannot.

Comedy unravels the voyeuristic eye, showing that such persons miss what is obvious to others, while they spend their time looking at things that either don't matter, or do matter, but in ways that the voyeur does not understand. In this sense the comic voyeur's gaze is guided by a misdirected social realism based on an inability to see and hence understand the obvious. Clouseau, for example, fails to see the clues which point to Elke Sommer as a murderess (every time she leaves a room a dead body appears).

At the same time, the comic voyeur's gaze often produces embarrassing situations (Inspector Clouseau in the nudist colony). Their untoward eye moves them and their body into the wrong spaces. This exposes them to the reverse voyeur's gaze; they become the figure gazed upon. In violating the norms of civil attention that operate in everyday life (Goffman, 1963: 83–98), they expose the taken-for-granted meanings that organize the underlying visual structures of daily interaction. This becomes a laughing matter. The audience identifies with the looks that fall upon the person who is caught looking when they shouldn't be.

Comedy reflexively attacks, mocks and satirizes the sombre conventions, as outlined in Chapter 2, that organize serious voyeuristic texts; in particular those norms stressing truth, rationality, objectivity, compassion, violence and erotic attachment.[5] (In this sense comedy, in its most critical forms, is always parody.) Often a double visual reflexivity organizes the texts. The audience sees what the protagonist does not see. Two versions of reality exist on the screen at the same time. Humour arises from this situational incongruity. A double laughter ensues. The audience laughs at what the protagonist does not see, while laughing at what is seen, which may be quite painful, or frightening. Thus, for example in *High Anxiety* (1977)[6] two psychoanalysts, Mel Brooks (Thorndyke) and Harvey Korman (Montague), are talking with a patient (Mr Cartwright) who has dreams about werewolves and suffers from a severe pain in his neck. As Brooks talks with the patient, Korman takes on the face and actions of a werewolf and shoots rubber bands at the patient's neck, causing sudden pain. The audience, but not Brooks, observes Korman's actions. The patient who had previously reported doing fine, suddenly takes on the symptoms of his illness. Brooks decides he needs more treatment. Here the audience laughs both at what Brooks cannot see, and at his diagnosis of the patient.

By simultaneously presenting at least two versions of a situation, the comic text, following Todorov (1977: 83), establishes its own verisimilitude, or relationship to reality and what is real. What is perceived as a presence by the audience is an absence, or non-presence of the voyeur. What is a presence for the voyeur is negated, or overruled, by the audience, for it sees what the voyeur cannot see. An incongruous, often ironic situation is produced, permitting the appearance of ludicrous, amusing sequences of action that build upon themselves. Of course one of humour's impulses arises out of incongruity; that is incongruity complements comedy's unique version of verisimilitude. Together these processes introduce a new level of reflexivity into the text, allowing the audience to achieve a measure of superiority over the voyeur, thereby mocking, laughing at and diminishing the seriousness of his or her project.

Comedy undermines the image of the voyeur as a gifted, rational, objective, compassionate, larger-than-life hero or heroine. For example, Inspector Clouseau (*Shot in the Dark*) is a bumbling, irrational detective taken in by the beautiful murderess, while his supervisor is the insane, rational, logical, objective observer. Charlie Chan's dimwitted Number One Son saves the wrong woman from murder, or always solves a crime after the real criminal has been killed. Groucho Marx in *The Big Store* (1941) ridicules Holmesian deductive logic when he convinces a man who has lost six of his 12 children in the department store that a man with his salary could not possibly have so many children.

Comedy presents the voyeur's gaze as painless solace for the lonely, anhedonic, sorrowful (usually male) individual (on anhedonia see Lyman, 1990b). Thus Richard Dreyfuss's early investigative-erotic gazes at Madeleine Stowe (*Stakeout*, 1987) are justified because his girlfriend has just left him. (He flips the pages of *Playboy* as he looks through his telescope.) Similarly, the tragic, but comic, voyeuristic moments in *Monsieur Hire* (1989) come when the lonely, sad, bald Peeping Tom suddenly realizes that the object of his gaze has returned his look. In like fashion, James Spader's pathetically aggressive voyeuristic camera gazes (*sex, lies and videotape*) are mocked by Cynthia. 'Are you kidding! He gets it off by photographing women talking about masturbation!' Pathos and a loss of innocence surrounds this gaze and the reactions to it. (Charlie Chaplin's little tramp was a master of this gaze.)

This gaze, and its desires are structured by a paradox and a fear. The sexual voyeur seeks more than the anonymity of pornography (parodied in *Stakeout*). He desires intimacy. He wants to know the person he gazes upon. But he cherishes the image, the fantasy of the other, and fears that the image will not match up with reality. Moore (1989: 4) elaborates this point in her discussion of *sex, lies and videotape*. The 'voyeur's darkest fear is peculiarly double-sided: that the object of desire is not what it seems, in which case he loses control over the fantasy, and that the object is *exactly* what it seems, in which case total separation is hard to maintain'. Comedy is produced when these two images clash. Thus Jane Craig (*Broadcast News*) experiences enormous conflict when she realizes that the object of her sexual desire, Tom Grunick, while dashing and handsome, is dull, boring, unethical, unfaithful and unintelligent.

The negative reactions to the voyeur's gaze produce and reveal a loss of innocence about the world. This innocence is commonly connected to voyeuristic gazes of the female body. The voyeur gazes on a woman who is above (seldom below) his (or her) position in the class structure. The voyeur is inevitably punished for this seemingly innocent act. In *Stakeout*, Dreyfuss, finally caught in his voyeurism,[7] is rejected (later to be taken back) by Stowe as a dirty Peeping Tom. Underneath the voyeur's gaze, of course, exists the reality that the sexual privacy of the spied upon person has been violated. Hence, while the comic voyeur's gaze reveals truths that others do not want to confront (Hire discovers the real murderer), it can only do this by transgressing, or violating sexual and class (and racial) boundaries and proprieties. A double or triple slander, or slight is produced. The voyeur's gaze has attacked two sacred structures (sexuality and class) which should not be questioned. The punishment such gazes receive underscores the deeper belief that the gaze held too long is never appropriate. But then comedy's voyeur is always misinterpreted, and these misinterpretations reveal the serious meanings voyeuristic gazing is given in everyday life. The lesson is clear. There can be no purely innocent gaze.

Broadcast News (1987)[8]

Holly Hunter (Jane Craig) is an unlikely voyeuristic heroine. Scratchy voiced, skinny, frizzy hair, unconcerned with fashion, she is an obsessed, highly intelligent, quick-witted television newswriter-producer. She holds to the beliefs that the news should be truthful, and that a story should be covered by the best-qualified person (see Ebert, 1989e: 98). As a protagonist, Jane Craig seizes and controls the camera's eye. Her feminine gaze organizes the narrative.

Ostensibly *Broadcast News* is about how TV news has become entertainment and how the news industry, like other capitalist enterprises, has a paranoid fixation on market shares, which leads to glossy marketing practices and sudden terminations of loyal and faithful employees. Underneath, *Broadcast News* is a multi-layered text. It is partially a love story, or romance. Jane is torn between two men. Tom Grunick (William Hurt) is highly successful, unintelligent, attractive and a bad reporter. Aaron Altman (Albert Brooks), is smart, a good reporter, but not especially sexually attractive, and destined to do good journalism in a small market (Portland). Both men love her, and she marries neither.

Broadcast News is also about a specific story about date rape, and whether or not the tear that Tom sheds when he listens to the victim is real or faked. If the tear is faked then Tom is a fraud and Jane must rethink her love for a man who fakes his emotions. By replaying the tapes of the interview she discovers that the tear is a fake. Thus ends her romance with Tom.

However the film is about more than reality and its reproduction and misrepresentations in televised news. It is about the omnipresence of the television (and cinematic) eye in everyday life. It is about the effects of that gaze on the lives of professional voyeurs who purport to tell the truth about reality to the members of American society. But it is a feminine gaze that is represented. As the protagonist of the film, Jane appropriates the camera's lens. It is through her eyes (and voice) that the viewer comes to see the effects of the televised gaze on everyday life. From its opening, voyeuristic comic gazes at Tom, Aaron and Jane as young children, especially its close-up of adolescent Hunter obsessively working at her typewriter, to its closing shot of Jane fading into the distance, *Broadcast News* turns the feminine voyeur into a visual aggressor. It is she who manipulates and controls the masculine eye of the camera. By feminizing the gaze, *Broadcast News* deconstructs and attacks the masculine, visual logic that organizes cinema's traditional representations of television and its news productions. Hence this film simultaneously attacks the genre (*Front Page*) it belongs to, while showing how a feminist critique of this genre also undoes and challenges the surveillance codes that currently operate in this society at the level of the evening TV news.

Two extended scenes embody this clash in visual and narrative codes. The first involves Jane, as executive producer, directing Tom in an emergency special weekend news broadcast, the second focuses on the date rape story reported by Tom and unravelled by Jane.[9]

Jane Doing the News through Tom's Ear

Pulled aside at a party for network employees, Jane is informed by Ernie, the bureau chief, that she will executive produce a special report. A Libyan plane has just shot-up one of the US airbases in Sicily. Tom, not Aaron, will be the anchor.

In a rapid-paced sequence of shot-reverse shots and close-ups Jane is shown in the newsroom, Tom in his office and Aaron at home. In the newsroom Jane demands that Blair, the assistant director, makes sure that Tom's 'earpiece works – have back-ups ready . . . he must be able to hear me at every second, and clearly'. As Jane prepares for the broadcast Tom kills time in his office, brushing his hair, primping in front of a mirror, picking out a clean shirt and the right tie to wear. Aaron, meanwhile, is drunk at home, playing loud rock music on his stereo, angry that he isn't doing the story.

The scene set, anxiety high, wished good luck by Paul and Ernie, Jane gets down to work. She checks each camera, her fingers move across the control board. She speaks into Tom's ear, with no effect: 'Tom, can you hear me? Tom, Tom, Tom!' The camera cuts to Tom who is sorting papers on his desk, and then back to Jane who screams at Blair, 'Damn it! I told you, if there is one thing. He can't hear me!' The camera cuts back to Tom who raises his head, gazes at Jane, and, laughing, says 'I was just teasing.' Tom then moves directly into the broadcast, 'Good afternoon, a Libyan fighter plane . . .' as Jane stares at him on camera on the set.

The camera cuts first to Aaron, obviously drunk: 'I can't sing while I read,' as he turns on his TV and watches Tom reading the news. Jane is next shown, centre screen, shouting out commands in the control booth, 'All remotes stand-by'. Aaron, mumbling out loud, 'Anxious anchors placed in powerful posts.' calls Jane. The screen then splits showing Aaron on the phone to Jane, as he watches Tom on the TV, and she monitors Tom's delivery on the set. Aaron informs Jane that 'the pilot who shot down the Libyan plane in 1981 is stationed right here. Also, Tom should say that the 14 is one of the hardest planes to fly.' Jane feeds these lines directly to Tom, who repeats them over the air. The camera cuts to Aaron, 'You say it here and it comes out there.' The screen is now split three ways: Tom, Aaron and Jane. Aaron, 'How does it feel to be executive. Gotta go. Very busy here.'

The camera cuts back to Jane, hand on control panel, hesitating on Tom's button. The screen fills with a full shot of Jane, feeding lines to Tom. The camera slowly rotates on Tom, moving round the back of his body, showing the monitors in front of him, coming up close on the side of his head, where the earpiece carries Jane's lines to him. The camera then moves back to Jane's mouth as she feeds lines to Tom. The shot continues showing the wire to his earphone running up his suit jacket into his ear. Jane whispers, 'You're doing great!' Her fingers caress Tom's control button as she speaks. A smile crosses her face. A split screen moves from Aaron to Tom to Jane, who is still feeding instructions to Tom, 'You're going to Mark for a message from Libya, and then you're gonna have the carrier pilot . . . fill for a minute'. The screen fills with a split shot of Jane's mouth on the phone to Tom and Tom's ear receiving the message. Tom ends, 'This is Tom Grunick reporting from Washington'.

Broadcast over, the set erupts with applause and nervous laughter. Jane and Tom are congratulated. Tom thanks everyone as he takes off his earpiece. Minutes later in the newsroom Tom rushes up to Jane who is seated, watching the replay of the broadcast. Knees on the floor, hands on the chair arms, 'You're an amazing woman! What a feeling – having you inside my head'. Jane, 'It was an unusual place to be'. The camera pulls back into a medium close-up of the two of them. Tom grabs the chair. 'Indescribable. You knew the second before I needed it.' He lunges forward, and then back, 'It was like a rhythm [full shot of his head], we got into it. It was like, I'll tell you what it was like [pulling her forward], it was like great sex!' Jane laughs as Tom stands up. 'You have to celebrate with me. Everybody's going to the bar down the street.'

Tom undercuts Jane's brilliant production by calling what they did together great sex – not exactly oral sex. By placing Jane inside his head Tom assumes the traditional position of the male being sexually stimulated and then satisfied by the female. This reverses the viewers' definition of the interaction. At all times the camera revealed Jane's, not Tom's relationship to the broadcast, including the shots of her fingers caressing the monitor panel and her voice speaking into his ear.

By immediately undermining Jane's relationship to the news perform-ance, the film sides with Tom's definition of the situation. This interpret-ation is elaborated through the recurring insertions of Aaron into the broadcast. The implication is clear. Aaron fed Jane the lines that she fed Tom. Those lines made the performance work. Hence two men did the work. Jane was their helper.

It is this reading, which the film implies, that I want to challenge. Return to the text of the broadcast. At all moments Jane is in control of the situation. Her commands, her lines, her advance preparations (the earpiece), her snap decisions, risk-taking (rushing to get the pilot on the air), her technical knowledge, expertise and her interpretations of Aaron's comments all dictate the specifics of Tom's performance. Furthermore, the viewer's subjective position is, with few exceptions, given through Jane's eyes (and voice), or from over her shoulder. We see the scene as she sees it. Her panoptic gaze structures the scene.

Jane's gaze appropriates the technological wizardry of the television apparatus. Like a female Leonard Bernstein, she plays with, or rather conducts, that apparatus and all its high-powered, electronic equipment and capabilities (last second, spliced tape inserts, multiple live cameras, on-site camera crews, large film libraries to draw from, etc.) as if it were an orchestra. As the conductor of this orchestra she has a single purpose: to produce the best possible news broadcast.

Best for Jane means three things. The broadcast must be honest and truthful, hence her insistence, in the Central America story, that the shot of the Contra soldier putting on his boots shouldn't be staged. Second, the best story must draw upon all relevant materials (for example, the pilot in Washington DC). Third, it must have a personal, emotional touch, and that touch must be sincere and authentic.[10] These three principles are realized in the Libyan story.[11]

However, Jane's production of a news story extends beyond the above three points. The construction of the story, like the performance of an experimental orchestral suite, must be spontaneous, emergent, and continuously problematic, until its on-air conclusion. This means the performance is constantly emotional and filled, for all participants, with tension and anxiety. Like a conductor, whose gaze organizes each musician's part in a performance, Jane's gaze and her voice command and direct the activities of her assistant producer, the on-site correspondents, the audio and tape engineers, the camera crew and the on-set news reporter.

By defining her (and their) experience in sexual terms, Tom elevates his own position in the news event and reduces Jane's to the level of a sexual object. He thereby takes away from her full range of conducting/producing activities, and sees the performance only through his own eyes. Of course this goes beyond sexism in the newsroom.

What is at issue is the control of the news event and the television apparatus itself. Jane controls both. Her power, as given in her commanding gaze and authoritative, if at times emotional, voice feminizes the production of this news event. The masculine narrative and visual logic which traditionally structure what is called broadcast news have been subverted by her performance. Yet because her effects flow through the voice and body of Tom he, not Jane, defines the fruits of her labours. Hence his sexualization of their experience and his diminution of her work, even as he praises it. Jane succumbs to this definition. When she later meets with Aaron, she thanks him for calling in the information. 'You are the classiest guy I know.'

Jane's subversive power lies, not only in her panoptic, visual control of the newsroom, but also in her voice. After all it is her words that Tom speaks, thus she supplies the text that creates his presence in the situation. In this she performs the traditional maternal function associated with the female voice. As Silverman observes 'the maternal voice introduces the child to its mirror reflection . . . the child also learns to speak by imitating the sounds made by the mother, fashioning its voice after hers' (1988: 80). Like a child Tom imitates Jane's voice, repeating her words in his broadcast. Thus, as he peers into the TV monitor, he sees himself as a mirror reflection of Jane. More deeply, he is an acoustic reflection of Jane for her sounds run into his ear and come out of his mouth. This 'acoustic mirror' (Silverman, 1988: 80) refracts the sounds of Jane's voice, which the viewer also hears, sounds which construct Tom's subjective presence before the camera. Two mirrors (looking-glass and acoustic – the monitor and the voice-over soundtrack) carry Jane's voice (and presence) into Tom's body.

Herein lies part of the film's comedy for in this scene there is a violation of the 'general dictum that female voices should proceed from female bodies, and male voices from male bodies' (Silverman, 1988: 47). While the violation is only temporary, its effects are humorous, as they are played (by Tom) in a deadpan fashion. But this deadpanning is deliberate, for Tom's rational, calm voice contrasts to the 'typically' hysterical, feminine voice that Jane embodies.

In this move the film subverts, while it conforms to cinema's traditional, normative control over the female voice. Traditionally (Silverman, 1988: viii) the female's voice is controlled by the male, who uses her words for his own pleasure, or manipulates what she says for her own benefit. This is not how Jane works. She takes pleasure in controlling the text that others speak. Thus while Tom thinks he is in control of Jane's words, in fact it is her text that he speaks.

However, by appropriating the content of Jane's voice for his own purposes, Tom hears her 'maternal voice through himself' (Silverman, 1988: 81), finding his own voice by interjecting and refining hers. He thus projects onto (and into) her voice his own subjectivity, thereby erasing her feminine, maternal (and hysterical) claim to power and sexual difference (see Silverman, 1988: 81). In this gesture she becomes him. No wonder he reads the interaction in sexual terms, and no wonder she is sexually attracted to him.

Thus, while she will soon be promoted to bureau chief, Jane's intense, personal, obsessive approach to producing the news will always be defined under, and within, the narrative and visual logics of the masculine gaze, even as her gaze subverts the authority of that look. Still, her commitments to her principles will not waver, even as she remains, half-trapped, inside the hegemonic control of the masculine, television eye. (This commitment is observed in her refusal to accept the emotional and visual logic of Tom's date rape story and the faked tears that were shed for that story.)

The Feminine Eye

There is something plaintive in all of this. Jane is trapped within the structures of the simulacrum which says the hyperreal is more real than the real. Her fate is both comic and tragic. Like a classic heroine she attempts to establish personal integrity in the face of insurmountable odds. The age of television rewards appearances. Jane's investigative voyeurism which uncovers fakes and holds to the highest ethical standards leaves her, at film's end, dating a boyfriend who is teaching her how to water ski (surfaces again), and now working as Tom's managing news editor in the New York office of the network. There is no escaping the masculine eye (and voice).

But this film's version of the comic female voyeur promises more than it can deliver. Jane is trapped inside the acoustic and reflective mirrors that define the inner structures of *Broadcast News*. She is a doubly comic figure: comic in her always frantic attempts to produce authentic news and laughable in her attempts to have a serious love life. That she fails on both scores only serves to reaffirm her final status as a comic figure who cannot see what is painfully obvious to some (Aaron) and not even an issue for others (Tom). A comedically serious voyeur, Jane Craig is, in the end, satirized by those classic voyeuristic norms which stress rationality, truth, objectivity and compassion. Her compassion for the truth undoes her, suggesting that these terms cannot be easily combined for the female voyeur. Troubled always by her feminine sexual appearance, she resists those traditional male gazes which give her that looked-at-ness Mulvey assigns the female in mainstream narrative cinema. Thus her sexual and professional identities remain forever anchored in her attempts to control the masculine gaze which simultaneously produces news and erotic sexuality.

Still, *Broadcast News*'s treatment of Jane's gaze goes beyond earlier representations of this gaze as given in the figure of the assertive female TV news reporter (for example, Sigourney Weaver in *Eye Witness*). Indeed she has more in common with the loveless but fanatically-obsessed-with-her-job Faye Dunaway of *Network*. But unlike Dunaway she is not cut off from her emotional and sexual roots. Jane knows who she is. Who she is is someone who can produce the news with feminine authority and the highest ethical integrity.

Hers, then, is not the supplemental, investigative gaze of Sandy in *Blue Velvet*. It is not the sexually violent gaze of such female aggressors as Dorothy in *Blue Velvet* or Glenn Close in *Fatal Attraction*. Nor is it the stumbling, fumbling, comically inept gaze of Madeline Kahn in *High Anxiety* (this is Tom's gaze), or the aggressive, pathological investigative gaze of Debra Winger in *Black Widow*. Jane's is the gaze of the television network news camera turned to feminine ends. But the power of the patriarchal eye is difficult to escape, for even when it is challenged by the feminine gaze, its traces, as Jane now understands, remain in place. *Sex, lies and videotape* offers a unique feminist challenge to this masculine way of seeing.

sex, lies and videotape (1989)[12]

I focus on a single extended sequence, the film's penultimate moment when Ann takes the video camera out of Graham's hands, and begins taping his story.[13] The sequence begins with Graham, the video-voyeur, complying with Ann's request to tape her talking about sex. The sequence divides into three separate scenes or frames. The first scene presents Ann's request to be taped. The second scene involves John, Ann's husband, watching the tape of Ann at Graham's house, while Graham listens outside the door. We as audience are viewers over John's shoulders. The third scene moves into the first frame and shows Ann turning the camera on Graham. The viewer watches this scene along with John, as Graham listens. A triple-reflexivity thus organizes this voyeuristic sequence: Graham taping Ann, Ann taping Graham, John watching the two of them. The sequence ends with Graham destroying all of his tapes. The tables have finally turned on him. He is no longer able to justify his video sexual voyeurism. This transformation occurs because of Ann's refusal to be a passive, sexual object for his video camera. The significance of the scene thus lies in the fact that a female *sexual voyeur* successfully challenges and undermines the authority of the male gaze.

Here is how it works. Discovering that John has been having an affair with her sister Cynthia, Ann comes to Graham and asks him to make a tape. He cautions against this. 'Do you think that's such a good idea?', but she insists. He opens a new box of videotapes and turns on the camera. Her on-camera story begins, 'My name is Ann Bishop Millaney'. The screen turns black, then to an exterior shot of Graham's house. It is nightime. Next, Graham is shown stopping the video recorder at the number 46.02. Ann sits on the couch next to him, stroking his hair and looking into his eyes. The actual taped story has not been told.

Two scenes later John storms into Graham's house. He has just learned from Ann that she wants a divorce and that Graham has made a tape of her. He violently attacks Graham, forcing him outside his house on to the porch. Finding Ann's tape, he turns on the monitor and Ann's story is now told. Graham listens through the keyhole. Ann discusses, in answer to Graham's questions, her sexual experiences with John, who watches the screen in mute anger. Graham continues to listen. Ann's face fills the monitor. As the questions become more intimate ('Did you have sex before you were married?', 'Did the person you made love with satisfy you more than your husband?') Ann becomes agitated, 'I don't mind answering the questions so much but if somebody were to *see* this?' Their conversation continues. She reveals that she has fantasized about having sex with Graham.

The camera now cuts back to the previous afternoon, to the actual taping. The audience no longer watches Ann on the monitor. We see her watching Graham as they made the tape. The action is now given from Ann's point of view. She suddenly shifts from the interview subject, to the interviewer, and begins to ask Graham questions. 'You said you weren't always impotent', 'So you have had sex', 'Who was the last person you had sex with?' Visibly upset, Graham sets the camera down. Ann picks it up, points at him and demands that he tell the story of his relationship with Elizabeth, to whom he lied and was violent. As he begins to reveal the history of the relationship Ann moves to him and caresses his hair. She touches his face and puts his hand against her face. She lowers herself into a sitting position on his waist. They begin to kiss and become intimate. They each become almost dazed as they enter a shared state of accepting ecstasy, which is both gentle and erotic. Smiles are shared as Graham gets up and slowly moves to turn off the camera.

Video snow appears on the monitor. The camera pulls back from the monitor to John, who gets up, turns off the tape and goes outside. He stops for a moment and speaks to Graham who is huddled in the corner of the porch. 'I never told you this . . . I fucked Elizabeth before you broke up. Before you were having trouble even. So you can stop making her into a saint. She was good in bed and she could keep a secret. And that's about all I can say about her.'

John, the man who was unfaithful to his wife, and who has just been made into a cuckold by Graham, now returns the favour. Graham's moral high ground has been further stripped away by John. Together he and Ann have penetrated and destroyed Graham's tightly wound moral universe.

Back in 'real' time, Graham enters the house and destroys his tapes and video camera. For all practical purposes the film ends at this point, it remains only for the two lovers (Ann and Graham) to be reunited at the film's end – which they are.

This extended scene serves three purposes for our project. The video camera has become the eye of power and truth. Its gaze sees through lies and exposes the hidden secrets about our sexual selves. However this gaze and its power are gendered. It reveals different truths depending on who holds the camera. As long as Graham controlled the camera he could lie to himself (and others) about his moral superiority. When Ann turned the camera on him he fell apart, and in a moment of catharsis revealed who he really was. Thus the female eye sees more than the male eye, for Ann was able to unlock a part of Graham that he refused to allow himself to see.

By engendering his camera, Soderbergh created a new space for the female voyeur. Ann's eye to power, unlike Jane's, escaped, if only for a moment, the grip of the masculine gaze. She does this, in part, because she has exposed the voyeur-pornographer's deepest fear which, as noted earlier, occurs when the voyeur is unable to maintain a separation between the object of his desire (his fantasy) and the real person. Ann shatters this separation, hence her power. She overwhelms Graham with her honest intimacy.

With its echoes of *Peeping Tom* (see Moore, 1989: 44; also the discussion in Chapter 8, pp. 194–5), *sex, lies and videotape*, in droll, comic fashion exposes the male voyeur-pornographer's gaze for what it is; a feeble, passive, yet demeaning attempt to wield power over the feminine subject. By having Ann take control of the camera, the film suggests that males are ill-equipped to use this new video technique for anything but shallow purposes. In this move the text, like Patricia Rozema's *I've Heard the Mermaids Singing*, opens new doors for the female voyeur who seeks to use her camera for sexual, personal and political purposes.

However, these moments of visual freedom are few and far between for Hollywood's female voyeur. The all-pervasive presence of the masculine way of seeing is again clearly evident in the next film.

Blue Velvet (1986)[14]

Blue Velvet is filled with voyeurs and their multiple gazes: Jeffrey Beaumont's sexual and aggressive investigative looks; Sandy's passive, supplemental gazes; Dorothy's aggressive sexual gaze; Frank and Ben's perverted sexual gazes; and the investigative looks of the police. Filled with pastiche and parody, *Blue Velvet* returns to the classic-modernist film noir image of the voyeur who looks with lust, violence, guilt and fear.

The story-line, by now all too familiar, need not be elaborated here. Suffice it to say this black comedy, coming of age film is a put down of 1950s middle-American popular culture. Handsome young man meets beautiful young woman. Young man becomes involved with a sexually attractive older woman, becomes implicated in and solves a series of violent crimes, and returns to the arms of his young love.[15]

My concerns focus on the voyeur's shifting presence in *Blue Velvet* and less on the narrative structure of the film. A single, but complicated thesis, anticipated earlier, organizes my comments. Lynch's film serves as a pivotal transition between two film and cultural moments: high modernism-early postmodernism, and contemporary late postmodernism. His text reaffirms the centrality of the voyeur in contemporary culture, while it mocks and makes fun of earlier high modernist, and early postmodernist treatments of this figure (late Hitchcock, De Palma). *Blue Velvet*'s voyeurs reassert the primacy of a traditional gendered system of looking and gazing. A dangerous text, because of its uncritical cult following, the film is patriarchal and sexist to the core.

But it is a multi-levelled text which challenges the spectator's relationship to what is seen. As such it complicates, even as it replicates, traditional conceptions of the voyeur and his or her gaze. In this it is, as Biga (1987: 47) argues, a 'case study of how women watch men and how the relation of a person looking and a person looked at may depict formulations other than control and power (scopophilia and fetishism, as Laura Mulvey has described them)'. Seen thusly, underneath his sexist text, Lynch creates multiple subject positions for the male and female voyeur. His film contains meanings that challenge conventional theories of the male and female gaze.

Three extended key scenes, Jeffrey in the closet, Sandy looking up at the building where Dorothy lives, and Sandy and her mother gazing on naked, hysterical Dorothy in their living-room establish the film's traditional, albeit complex, treatments of the voyeur.

Jeffrey in the Closet

Sandy starts all of this ('You shouldn't do this. It's crazy and dangerous. My God I should never have told you'). We first meet her through her portrait hanging on the wall of her family living-room. Minutes later, she emerges out of the evening darkness, her voice first, 'Are you the one who found the ear?', then her image, full screen confronts us, the mirror-image of the portrait hanging in the living-room. She is the immediate object of the spectator-voyeur's gaze, a gaze suddenly shifted to Jeffrey, who asks, 'How did you know?' A natural voyeur herself (her father is Detective Williams), eavesdropping Sandy sends inquisitive Jeffrey to the address of Dorothy ('I don't know if you are a detective or a pervert'. Jeff: 'That's for me to know and you to find out').

The extended closet scene begins and ends as a dark dream sequence, defined throughout by violence, perverse, sado-masochistic sexuality and reflexive voyeurism: Jeffrey staring at Dorothy, Dorothy staring at Jeffrey, Frank gazing on Dorothy, Jeffrey watching the two of them in violent sexual intercourse, Jeffrey as voyeur going through Dorothy's private documents (her marriage certificate), Dorothy watching Jeffrey search through her belongings, and Dorothy imploring Jeffrey to touch, feel and look at her body, and the audience as spectator, gazing nearly always over Jeffrey's shoulder, or into his eye.

The voyeur's hiding place: a closet (an intimate space) with a slatted door one can peer through, shadows cast back on the face from the slats, the face now a reflection of what is being peered through. From this vantage point Jeffrey looks out into a darkened room, onto a near-naked Dorothy (black bra and black panties). Jeff makes a noise in the closet. Dorothy goes to the kitchen and returns with a butcher knife.

It happens in a flash, the voyeur's degradation. Roaring, dangerous music fills the soundtrack. Light from the living room shines on Jeff's eye as he looks through the slats. Discovered by Dorothy, forced, at knife point to undress, Jeffrey is turned immediately into a sexual object. The voyeur now becomes the one who is looked upon. She touches his penis and caresses his inner thighs ('Do you like that?'). He reaches out to touch her: 'Don't touch me or I'll kill you. Don't look at me. Get over there. Lie down.' She climbs on top of him on the sofa and they begin to kiss.

This is only the beginning. Frank arrives, pounding on the door: 'Let me in!' Naked, Jeffrey, sent scurrying back to the closet like a rodent, clothes-in-hand, hides again. Fearfully assuming the voyeur's stance, spying through the door, he witnesses Dorothy playing the part of the sexual slave. Frank starts in on Dorothy: 'Don't you fucking look at me. Don't you fucking look at me' (the camera cuts to Jeffrey's lighted eye peering through the slats). Frank continues. 'Baby wants to fuck. Baby wants to fuck. Don't you fucking look at me.' Inhaling bourbon, face attached to a mask, he continues, 'Daddy's coming home. Don't look at me!'

It doesn't end here. A second scene of degradation completed, Lynch now brings Jeffrey out of the closet. The third scene begins, taking its own turn into reciprocal voyeurism and sado-masochism. Jeffrey attempts to help Dorothy. She pleads, 'Hold me, I'm scared.' They embrace. She asks, 'Do you love me?' 'Yes,' Jeffrey softly replies. The camera turns to her face, red lips highlighted: 'Do you like the way I feel? See my breast. You can knead it. See my nipple. You can touch it. Do you like the way I feel? Hit me. Hit me!' He refuses. In near darkness he retreats, dressing, making preparations to leave. She moves away.

Drawn back into his investigative role, Jeffrey now searches through her papers under the sofa as she watches quietly in the corner. Escaping from her apartment, we watch him descend the dark staircase into the night, where, standing in the blackness, his fearful face is suddenly illuminated by a street light. The soundtrack once again fills with roaring sounds. Frank's injunctions and screams are heard. Dorothy screams, 'Hit me, hit me.' From a dream Jeffrey awakens, quivering like an animal in his darkened bedroom. The next evening he recounts part of the story to Sandy who tells him of the dream she had the first night they met. This is her robin dream, an account of evil in the world, and how the robins were set free and there was the blinding light of love.

The closet scene is thus bracketed by two dreams, the one Sandy had the night before Jeff entered the apartment, and the dream Jeff has after being there. Told out of temporal order (we should have heard Sandy's dream first), the juxtapositioning of the two dreams within the film's narrative serves to underscore the dream-like world Jeffrey, as voyeur, has entered. This world is defined by the opposing forces of evil (violence, Dorothy, Frank) and good (Sandy and her loving robins). It is mediated by the voyeur who sees both evil and good.

Take up the three sequences of voyeurism in reverse order. Third scene first:[16] gendered voyeurism moves between the active and passive poles in this scene. Here Dorothy directs Jeffrey to be the sexual voyeur who explores, sees, touches and feels her body. He becomes the object who furnishes the touches she desires. In their reciprocal voyeurism they turn one another into sexual objects, although it is her body, not his, that is explored. When she exhorts him to hit her he refuses. Her request shatters and challenges the passive voyeurism he has assumed for himself. She takes voyeurism to Frank's level of sado-masochism. Jeffrey is afraid to follow. He will look, but not be violent, not understanding that looking is as violent as being physically violent. The voyeur can look and touch, but not hit; only later will Jeffrey be seduced into Frank's violent version of voyeurism. As the scene closes Dorothy has the last look, so to speak, for it is her gaze which defines the illicit nature of Jeffrey's search through her documents.

Now the second scene: active male voyeurism defines the primary action. The audience either looks through Frank's eyes or sees what he prohibits Dorothy from seeing. Reconsider Frank's injunctions, 'Don't you fucking look at me!' and then, in his moment of climax, 'Daddy's coming home. Don't look at me!' A moment of privacy at the centre of violence. Dorothy cannot see Frank come. She cannot enter his world of private ecstasy, yet his eyes and body can control her movements and her experiences. She is his slave. 'Show it to me!' he shouts. 'Lay down!' he commands. And she does, her eyes become vacant, her red-lipped mouth opens, expressing sexual pleasure and fear. She sucks the blue velvet cord that connects her mouth to his. Like blind Double Ed, the elderly black employee in Jeffrey's father's hardware store, Dorothy knows, without seeing, where things ought to be. She becomes the blind voyeur. Jeffrey is the impotent male-child viewing this primal scene, and like a child his voyeurism is guilt-ridden and full of fear. He knows he is viewing a taboo scene.

Finally the first scene: Dorothy's phallic knife (Biga, 1987: 46) dramatizes the connection between looking, power and sexuality. With her knife she controls his gaze, which cuts to the core of his sexuality. By denying him his look, she 'turns the tables on him . . . [and] appropriates a male gaze and [its] sexuality' (Biga, 1987: 46). She becomes the sexual aggressor, the identity previously held by Jeffrey. She needs a knife to do this; apparently the female gaze cannot command without supplemental force.

In its raw, brutal connection of looking with violence, domination and power, this extended closet scene shows, as Sartre argued, that the power to control the look of the other defines their presence in the situation. More deeply, when the other is told not to look, they are stripped of their own subjectivity, for they are unable to see their own presence reflected back in the face and actions of the other. They become an object, not a subject, and in that transformed visual status, their bodies (and minds) become objects to be manipulated by the other, a slave to the master who controls their gaze. The closet scene, then, reveals what happens to the person when the power to look is denied. Here that loss of control over the look is directly connected to the violent, erotic side of the voyeur's project. Fear, submission and self-degradation are produced.

This complex sequence transforms Jeffrey from naïve, investigative voyeur, to sexual predator. Intoxicated by Dorothy's violent sexuality, his subsequent journey is into a world of darkness made visible by the violent voyeur's desires. He will love and then fear what he learns to see and feel. His visual journey will lead out of this darkness into the sun-lit worlds of robins and Sandy.

Sandy's Investigative Journey

Sandy's investigative, voyeuristic journeys will parallel Jeffrey's; her gaze, like his, will first see the blackness of evil and then the sunny side of goodness. However, while she initiates his project, her gaze will soon become supplemental to his active investigative project. Furthermore, she will see what his actions have produced. In this her gaze contrasts to the violent, aggressive looks of Dorothy. Sandy moves, then, from the standpoint of the ineffectual gazing bystander, to the gazing participant who reacts with horror to what the wayward and temporarily evil male has created.

Her journey also starts outside Dorothy's apartment house. Resisting his directions to leave and go home, telling him, 'I'm gonna wait here til she comes. I'm gonna honk four times. Then you'll hear it and know she's on her way up.' She waits patiently. Observing Dorothy return home, she honks four times, just as Jeff, inside the apartment, flushes the toilet. He doesn't hear her honking. Her looking, like water down the drain, was for naught.

This will not be the case the next time she sees Dorothy. Chased by Frank and his friends to his parents' house, Jeffrey and Sandy step out of the car to see a naked, hysterical, Dorothy, emerge centre screen from the darkness. Sandy, bewildered, speaks, 'Dorothy Vallens?' Battered and bruised, Dorothy falls from the front porch into Jeffrey's arms. Sandy, looking puzzled and pained, lowers her eyes as Jeffrey helps Dorothy into the car. Sandy then covers Dorothy's breasts with her shawl. They drive to Sandy's house. Entering the front door, Sandy fearfully backs across the living room, calling for her mother (Mrs Williams) as Jeffrey and naked Dorothy follow. Her mother enters the room, and daughter and mother, in the lower left-hand part of the screen, stare at naked Dorothy, who is centre screen. Evil has entered the living room.

Dorothy hugs Jeffrey, turning to Sandy, who continues to look pained, she screams 'Don't get the police!' and then to Jeffrey, 'I love you!' and then to Sandy, 'He put his seed in me!' Sandy's mother turns her head away as Sandy pulls back, mouth twisted in agony, and attempts to catch her breath, as if she were about to faint. Sandy's mother gets a coat to cover Dorothy. Sandy, 'Jeffrey. What's going on here?' A silent, Edvard Munch like scream on her face, softly sobbing, she nearly collapses in her mother's arms. Her immediate, aggressive reaction, a slap across Jeffrey's face, after Dorothy is taken away by the ambulance, is supplemented in the next scene.

Shot over her shoulder, her voice on the phone, her face reflected in her bedroom mirror, Sandy tells Jeffrey, 'You lied to me.' Jeffrey replies, 'Forgive me. I love you'. Sandy, 'Jeffrey, I love you' (the camera pulls back to reveal her softly lighted, pink and white bedroom), and then, positioning her centre screen, sobbing, 'I couldn't watch that.' The scene closes with Sandy caressing the phone, which rests on her breast, crying, she speaks, 'He's my dream'. Two scenes later she is on the phone to the police, angrily demanding that they find her father so he can help Jeffrey.[17]

Women Staring at Women

The Dorothy-Sandy-Mrs Williams (mother) sequence reveals a complexly gendered social interaction. The feminine space the three women occupy, and the gazes they deploy, constantly move back and forth between the active and passive poles. They each take turns recoiling at the other's presence. The centre of the screen is pulled in two directions at the same time. Dorothy and Jeffrey on one side, mother and daughter on the other. The space in the middle of the scene cannot be crossed, the distance between the voyeur and her subject must be maintained lest she become overwhelmed by her subject (see Metz, 1982: 60; also Creed, 1988: 107).

The typical controlling male gaze is absent, as Jeffrey is visually coded with passive-evil Dorothy. In this he occupies the space usually reserved for the passive-female subject (on this space see Creed, 1988: 103). Dorothy, on the other hand, is presented as a threat, her naked body taints the pure feminine space occupied by mother and daughter. It is not endowed with fetishistic qualities, instead it is treated with abhorrence. She has violated a deep social code; appearing naked and bruised in public.

At the same time, Sandy and her mother are accorded the position of active voyeurs, Dorothy being the passive subject of their gaze. After all she (and Jeffrey) have invaded their private space. But they refuse to take up this active, aggressive position, reacting first with 'traditional' feminine alarm and shock to this untoward scene, and then with fear, disdain, disgust and anger.

Always their desire is to clothe the naked Dorothy, thereby stripping her of her contaminating, but at the same time sexual-erotic appeal. Their passive-aggressive reaction to her presence is, accordingly, aligned with Dorothy's own passive-intruder identity in the situation. They refuse to be the bearer of the voyeur's look. Yet their refusal to look, and their vocal reactions to Dorothy's presence, succeed in keeping her locked in the passive, gazed-upon position; the audience now shares the horror of the mother and daughter as they bear witness to this scene.

This sequence's summary meaning is given in Sandy's statement 'I couldn't watch that'. This statement signals both her purity and her unwillingness to be a voyeur. Her journey into looking has taken her too far. Fittingly, we last see her gazing on the robin on the kitchen window ledge. She will only look at goodness.

Blue Velvet's Voyeur

The multiple subject positions Lynch creates for his voyeurs undermine, while they support, taken-for-granted theories of the male and female gaze. The four principal voyeurs in Blue Velvet are organized in terms of two dyads, Jeffrey and Sandy, Frank and Dorothy. These dyads enact, as Creed (1988) argues, Freud's three primal scenes: sexual origin (Frank raping Dorothy), castration (Dorothy threatening Jeffrey) and sexual difference (Dorothy seducing Jeffrey). Their respective participants engage in their own versions of the sadistic-masochistic, passive-active gaze (the extended closet and living-room scenes).

It works thusly. Jeffrey deploys the active and passive sadistic and masochistic gazes in his interactions with Dorothy, Frank and Sandy. Frank is never passive in his gazing activity. His looks are constantly aligned with the active-masochistic gaze. Dorothy's looks are both active and passive, sadistic and masochistic. Sandy, in contrast, is the constantly passive voyeur, who only becomes aggressive in her scenes of sexual interaction with Jeffrey.

By creating multiple viewing positions for his women Lynch opens up the female voyeur's field of vision. At the same time he closes this field down by consigning Sandy to the traditional, passive identity. Importantly the wild looks of Dorothy are only present when she is under Frank's control. At the end of the film she has reassumed the traditional looking identity of the passive, maternal female (watching Little Donny walk toward her in the park).

Thus in, and through, its film noir, comedy-like comedy structures (the exaggerated violence, Ben, the 'drag queen', Aunt Barbara, Double Ed) *Blue Velvet* creates new problems for the female spectator. She is free to gaze wildly, actively and violently, but only when she is under the control of a violent male.

By weaving these various gazes through his dark comedy Lynch turns back on and mocks the comic voyeur's project. Bumbling, slightly irrational Jeffrey discovers what is hidden from normal view, mocks the police force in its investigative work, creates embarrassing situations for himself, becomes erotically attached to an evil woman, loses his innocence and ends up back in the arms of pure, innocent Sandy. Secure in its mocking conclusions, *Blue Velvet* keeps the high-modernist-Hitchcock version of the voyeur alive, and ends by endorsing a very traditional, conventional view of this film figure. In this conclusion he is, with all his pastiche, less daring than Carl Reiner in *Dead Men Don't Wear Plaid*, the last film to be considered in this chapter.

Dead Men Don't Wear Plaid (1982)[18]

Unlike *Blue Velvet* Reiner's film is all parody. While it mocks the film noir tradition that it steals from, it does so with reverence and a sympathy for the 18 or more 1940 and 1950 film noir originals that it steals from, including *Double Indemnity*, *The Lost Weekend*, *The Killers*, *The Bribe*, *The Big Sleep*, *In a Lonely Place*, *Dark Passage*, *Suspicion*, *Notorious*, *Deception*, *The Postman Always Rings Twice*, *The Glass Key* and *White Heat*. As a comedy in the noir tradition, *Dead Men Don't Wear Plaid*, repeatedly deploys noir's visual and narrative codes, as discussed in the Introduction (wide- and high-angle, shot-reverse-shot, and close-up camera shots, a preoccupation with the illicit gaze, the reflexive use of off-screen space, scenes lit for night, action defined in male terms, women as the object of investigative activity, the noir heroine filmed for her sexuality, etc., Gledhill, 1978: 19).

In praise of the investigative voyeur's gaze, *Dead Men* dovetails footage from the above films into its narrative, as Steve Martin, the hero (Rigby Reardon), is shown interacting with the likes of Ava Gardner, Ingrid Bergman, Veronica Lake, Bette Davis, Ray Milland, Barbara Stanwyck, Cary Grant, Humphrey Bogart, Lana Turner, Fred MacMurray, Charles Laughton, Brian Donlevy, Edmond O'Brien and Vincent Price. He even plays a torrid love scene (in drag) with Fred MacMurray (the Stanwyck role in *Double Indemnity*).

The narrative is really irrelevant. It is a spoof, a vehicle for paying homage to the film noir tradition. The story is told largely through Martin's voice-over narration, flashback scenes, and scene upon scene consisting of shots from the above films, fitted to Martin's current situation.[19] Played straight-faced, the story-as-a-comedy on the surface reinscribes noir's patriarchal treatment of women, including the *femme fatale* (the Stanwyck clips from *Double Indemnity*), the hysterical female (the Stanwyck bedroom scene in *Sorry, Wrong Number*), and the loving, luscious female associate (Bette Davis fixing Bogart a meal in *Deception*). The tough-guy noir male is also kept alive through Rigby's dialogue ('She was real all right', 'Kissing Juliet I thought of nothing but hanging up my gun and spending the rest of my days in that ivy covered cottage'), his violent, courageous acts (sucking bullets out of his shoulder), and the Cagney, Kirk Douglas, Burt Lancaster and Bogart clips.

By comedically honouring the film noir tradition *Dead Men Don't Wear Plaid* preserves, while it challenges and criticizes, the visual and narrative codes of the genre. This is the promise of high modernist and early postmodernist parody, but it is a risky business, for in so doing it also maintains the stereotypical sexual conventions of the genre (Gledhill, 1978: 14–16). By celebrating, while laughing at, and with, the classic elements of the genre, the film destabilizes its own possibilities of critique.

But it should be read as critique. Three key scenes support this reading. Two minutes into the film Juliet walks into Rigby's office and faints. He picks her up and lays her on his couch. He asks, 'Was she real? Only one way to find out. I remembered Marlowe's words (cut to a sign on the wall) "Never fall in love with a client." What the hell does Marlowe know? She was real all right.' He then caresses her breasts. She asks, 'What are you doing?' He replies, 'Adjusting your breasts. They've shifted. All out of whack.' Juliet, 'Thank you'. In this dialogue Rigby and Juliet play to, while distancing themselves from, the Marlowe canon. Rigby's actions are de-sexualized, and accepted by Juliet as something that needed to be done.

In two drag scenes he secures valuable information about the case, and uses that information to protect another character. In the first scene he plays a beautiful blond (Barbara Stanwyck) who seduces Fred MacMurray (as Walter Neff) and finds the passenger list to the SS *Immer Essen* (the

cruise ship that destroyed Carlotta). In the second drag scene he plays
Jimmy Cagney's mother from *White Heat* and tells him that 'The friends
of Carlotta are after you'.

Martin's in-drag impersonations make heroines of famous noir *femme
fatale* characters. In this reversal of tradition he undermines the negative
sexual identity assigned this flawed female character. He uses her presence
(and identity) to positive ends, suggesting that her presence can be
deployed for positive, active investigative purposes. More deeply, he gives
a camp, homo-erotic twist to his impersonations. He suggests that the
male playing the female has power that would not be given if the straight
female, or male role were played. In this move he further defines and
elaborates the noir tradition (for example, making a bad woman good).
He thereby challenges the tradition's negative treatment of females and
homosexuals. In this he goes beyond Lynch, for his women, even as they
are played by men, are free to go places that Lynch's women would never
dare.

Reiner seems to be saying that there is more to these old films than
previously thought. By reworking and redefining the tradition he
'periodizes' its patriarchal biases and fits those stereotypes to the contemporary moment. Marlowe will never be the same again. Reiner's
reflexive text thus turns noir's voyeur into a comic figure. In laughing at
this long Hollywood tradition of filmic representation Reiner seems to be
saying that this version of the voyeur can no longer be taken seriously. But
comedy-as-parody is high praise. In exposing the visual and narrative
conventions that underlie this tradition Reiner brings it to a new level of
development, a level that has yet to be transcended.

Laughing Matters

Back to the beginning and multiple versions of the voyeur: Jane Craig and
Ann Bishop Millaney with their cameras, Dorothy and her knife and blue
velvet robe, Jeffrey looking out of the closet, Sandy outside Dorothy's
apartment, wild Frank, Detective Williams, Graham hiding behind his
camera, Rigby Reardon interacting with all those famous detectives from
the past and Rigby Reardon, voyeur in drag.

And multiple subject positions: active, passive, supplemental reciprocal,
sadistic, masochistic. Always gendered, these positions shift and take on
various levels of comedy in the hands of each filmmaker. Laughing matters
seem to involve the degree to which the female character is able to
transcend the patriarchal gaze and its all-encompassing power. The voyeur
exposed by the comic text is thus a figure who is both less and more noble
than his or her more serious filmic counterpart: less noble because comedy
smashes the sombre conventions that prop up the serious business of 'real'
voyeurism (the norms of rationality, truth and objectivity); more noble
because in laughter reflexive distance is gained from these same

conventions. In that distance the viewer sees the mythic ideals this figure aspires to, and sees also just how dangerous, powerful, generous and self-aggrandizing this character really is.

The following chapter circles around this figure from another standpoint. I turn next to the serious and comic versions of the gaze of the minority group member, in this case the Asian eye which moves from *Charlie Chan at the Opera* (1936) to Wayne Wang's *Chan is Missing* (1981).

Notes

1 I have offered earlier readings of *Blue Velvet* and *sex, lies and videotape* in Denzin, 1991a, Chapters 5 and 8. These readings did not focus, as I do here, on the voyeur's place in the film's text.

2 In order of treatment, I begin with *Broadcast News*, then turn to *sex, lies and videotape*, then *Blue Velvet*, and end with *Dead Men Don't Wear Plaid*, a film which leads logically into the investigative, private eye, detective films discussed in Chapters 4 and 5.

3 Krutnik (1991: 16) also locates *Blue Velvet* in the recent (last two decades) return to the film noir tradition by mainstream Hollywood (e.g. *Chinatown* (1974), *Farewell, My Lovely* (1975), *Taxi Driver* (1976), *Someone to Watch Over Me* (1987) and *Blue Steel* (1989)).

4 Fainting becomes a convenient marker for loss of vision, for with it comes the loss of consciousness.

5 *Shot In the Dark* offers a mocking catalogue of these conventions: cameras blow up in the detective's face; Clouseau's self-inflicted injuries bear no relationship to the usual violence detectives receive; his misplaced erotic attachments lead him to misperceive the identity of one of the murderers; his supervisor's insanity produces violence usually confined to villains or heroic voyeurs; Clouseau's irrational commitment to one solution to the crimes finally proves to be correct.

6 A film Brooks dedicated to 'the master of suspense, Alfred Hitchcock'. It is described, on the video rental box as 'another satire from the comic mind of Mel Brooks, the story spoofs classic mystery/suspense director Alfred Hitchcock'. The film makes a parody of many Hitchcock films, including *Psycho*, *Birds*, *Frenzy* and *North by Northwest*, as well as *Blow-Up*.

7 Stowe discovers his telescope and the blown-up, topless photo of her that he and his fellow-officers have nailed to a wall. She observes the 'exclamation' marks they have placed on her breasts.

8 Written, directed and produced by James L. Brooks; released by Twentieth-Century Fox; cinematography by Michael Ballhaus; cast: William Hurt (Tom Grunick), Albert Brooks (Aaron Altman), Holly Hunter (Jane Craig), Robert Prosky (Ernie Merriman), Joan Cusak (Blair Litton), Jack Nicholson (Bill). Academy nominations for Best Actress (Holly Hunter), and Best Supporting Actor (Albert Brooks).

9 In the interest of space this story will only be glossed. One of Tom's last stories at the Washington Bureau involves an interview with a young woman who was raped on a date. This interview elicited high emotion and tears on the part of the woman and Tom. Aaron questioned the story's accuracy and suspected that Tom, contrary to his claim, used two cameras, not one, for the story. (The first camera shot the woman from the front, leaving Tom off-screen as the interviewer. The second camera shot Tom after the story was done. In the second shot he produced tears which were then spliced into the final story.) Aaron conveys his doubts to Jane who replays the tapes of the interview. She confirms Aaron's doubts. Tom in fact used two cameras and manufactured the tears after the interview had been shot. She nearly cries when this discovery is made. She confronts Tom with this discovery in the airport as they are about to leave on a week's vacation. Jane: 'I'm not going. I saw the taped out-takes of the interview with the girl. I know you acted your reactions after

the interview . . . . It's terrible what you did. . . . You could get fired for things like that.'
Tom: 'I got promoted for things like that.' Jane: 'Working up tears for a newspiece cut-away.
You totally crossed the line between what is news and what is garbage. It's incredible. You
commit this horrible breach of ethics, and then you act as if I'm giving you a hard time about
nothing.'

10 This commitment to authenticity produces the comic scene over Aaron's story
about the soldier returning home from Angola. At the last second Jane races to splice
into the footage a shot from Norman Rockwell's painting of a homecoming. This
Rockwell shot is contrasted to the shot of the lonely, angry soldier stepping off the bus
in Omaha. This produces a sense of irony and sadness that would otherwise not be
present in the story. Pure dramaturgy, Jane's story however had an honest, human touch.
It was a good story.

11 Jane secures all the facts, nothing is staged or inauthentic. She organizes and inserts
into the story historical information on the bombing site, first-hand reports from participants,
actual footage of the crisis, reports from the White House, an interview with the pilot shot
down in 1981, shots of Gadaffi, footage of the planes in action, a shot of the actual area
bombed, its name and the name of the base commander. The emotional, personal touch is
given in the interview with the pilot. Repeating Jane's lines, Tom asks, 'What's it like to be in
a real dog fight? How do you know when you are hit?'

12 Written and directed by Steven Soderbergh; produced by Robert Newmyer and John
Hardy; released by Miramax Films; cinematography by Walt Lloyd; cast: James Spader
(Graham), Andie MacDowell (Ann), Peter Gallagher (John), Lura San Giacomo (Cynthia).
Winner of 1989 Cannes Film Festival Best Picture and Best Actor Awards, and International
Critics Award.

13 I omit a summary of the narrative (see Denzin, 1991a: 109–14), except to note that this
is a study in looking, in gendered voyeurism, in men looking at women on videotape and
women looking at themselves on videotape. The central voyeur, Graham, is sexually
impotent, and compensates by having women tell him sexual stories about themselves.

14 Written and directed by David Lynch; produced by Fred Caruso; released by De
Laurentis Entertainment Group; cinematographer, Frederick Elmes; cast: Kyle MacLachlan
(Jeffrey Beaumont), Isabella Rossellini (Dorothy Vallens), Dennis Hopper (Frank Booth),
Laura Dern (Sandy Williams), Dean Stockwell (Ben), George Dickerson (Detective Williams),
Hope Lange (Mrs Williams). Winner of National Society for Film Critics Best Film Award,
Best Director, Best Supporting Actor (Hopper) and Best Cinematographer (Elmes), 1986;
Academy nominations for Best Director.

15 In American popular culture, and in contemporary cultural and cinema studies
literatures, Blue Velvet has achieved almost canonical status as the postmodern film of the
1980s, and its director David Lynch has been accorded the distinction of being one of
America's leading postmodern filmmakers (see Denzin, 1991a, Chapter 5 for a review of this
literature. See also Jameson, 1991: 287–96; Brunette and Wills, 1989: 139–71; Connor, 1989:
178–80; Graham, 1991: 117–18; Creed, 1988; Biga, 1987).

16 Lynch's text throughout this sequence, may be read, as Creed (1988: 96, 112) argues, as
presenting three primal/sexual fantasies involving the origins of individuals (parental love-
making), their sexuality (seduction) and their concept of sexual difference (castration). Creed
(1988: 112) connects each of these fantasies to a particular version of the voyeuristic gaze:
castration with the sadistic look, parental love-making with masochism and seduction with an
exchange of looks of both forms. She also suggests that these looks may not be
'deterministically linked to gender' (1988: 112); passive and active gazes can shift from female
to male, and back again.

17 Sandy will appear three more times in the film. Frightened, she will appear, with her
father, in Dorothy's apartment just after Jeffrey shoots Frank, then she will be seen
embracing Jeffrey in front of Dorothy's apartment house. Finally, she and Jeffrey will appear
in the family kitchen, looking at the mechanical robin on the window ledge eating a bug.

18 Directed by Carl Reiner; screenplay by Carl Reiner, George Gipe and Steve Martin;
produced by David V. Picker and William E. McEuen, for Aspen Film Society, released by

Universal; cinematographer, Michael Chapman; cast: Steve Martin (Rigby Reardon), Rachel Ward (Juliet Forrest), Carl Reiner (Field Marshall VonKluck).

19 Rigby is hired by Juliet Forrest to find her father, John Hay Forrest, who, prior to his disappearance, had been experimenting with a number of dangerous cheeses. Aided by his assistant Philip Marlowe (Humphrey Bogart), Rigby goes on the trail of a mysterious woman, Carlotta. It turns out that Carlotta is a South American island which strangely dissolved while a cruise ship was sailing by. In South America Reardon discovers that Forrest is being held captive by a group of Nazis, led by Field Marshall VonKluck (Carl Reiner), who wants to use Forrest's deadly cheese to dissolve the United States (Slide, 1983: 135). Rigby shoots VonKluck and the film closes with he and Juliet embracing.

4

THE ASIAN EYE: CHARLIE CHAN AND MR MOTO GO TO THE MOVIES

Thunder crashes. The wind howls. Sinister shadows play across the landscape. Lightning divides the black sky. The camera cuts to a darkened asylum, light reflects from a single large room. Boris Karloff, hair askew, is madly pounding the piano, singing grand opera. Rain batters the shoulders of a shivering night-watchman who gazes at Karloff. Shutters bang against stone walls and Karloff's wailing voice carries, like a pained scream, into the night wind. These are the opening shots and sounds which establish *Charlie Chan at the Opera* as part 'whodunit, part horror [and part Gothic] film' (Hanke, 1989: 83).

The story is old and straightforward enough, although unravelling what happens is not so easy. A woman murders her unfaithful husband and his lover. These are not ordinary people: they are opera stars. The city is Los Angeles: the date, 1936. A partial reworking of *The Phantom of the Opera* (1925), the film stars Warner Oland as Charlie Chan and Boris Karloff as Gravelle, a 'crazed' operatic baritone, and the first husband of Lilli.[1]

In the following dialogue Charlie solves this murder-mystery:

> Proof most elemental. Fact in deduction . . . if Gravelle guilty, must have both knives on person before singing . . . Previous examination of costume disclose no tell-tale blood stains. Madman not use Barelli's knife, having one of own . . . Method devised by re-murderer born in rational mind. Use presence of maniac in theatre as perfect alibi to cover own guilt. Conceal murder knife after first crime. . . . Fact that Madame Barelli in wings during final singing final link in chain of evidence [camera shot of Anita]. You are murderess [she jumps up]. You were only one who knew Gravelle planned to sing the Mephisto role tonight . . . so avail self of perfect opportunity to avenge intrigue which cause you so much humiliation . . . you conceal knife on person after murder of husband.

Confronted with the facts, Madame Barelli confesses. The film ends, as it opened, in darkness. Only now Charlie and Number One Son are racing to catch the boat to family and home in Hawaii. With a police escort lighting up the night, sirens shrilling, Charlie and son, the pragmatic voyeurs, have solved another crime. Now it is time for family.

As argued in Chapter 2, the gaze of the voyeur is structured along racial and ethnic lines. Only privileged members of racial and ethnic minorities are allowed to gaze on majority group members. The concept of a colour (see Blumer, 1965/1988: 208; Lyman, 1990b) and gender line (see

Gamman, 1989) operates in this context, assigning to white and non-white males and females different gazing positions in the social order. *Charlie Chan at the Opera* and the other films in the Chan series simultaneously transgress and are confined by this colour and ethnic line.

In this chapter I examine famous racial and ethnic voyeurs, in particular Charlie Chan and Mr Moto. I will contrast the Chan and Moto film series to the experimental, 1981 film *Chan is Missing*,[2] a text which undoes the Asian stereotypes perpetuated by the Charlie Chan and Mr Moto characters. I will take one film from each of the Chan and Moto series (*Charlie Chan at the Opera* (1937),[3] and Mr Moto's *Last Warning* (1939)).[4] Each is representative of their respective series and currently available for video rental.[5] Each is also representative of a particular type of detective/ investigative fiction. The Chan series are 'whodunits', the Moto films are thrillers, and *Chan is Missing* merges the 'whodunit' formula with the suspense format (see Todorov, 1977: 50).[6] This examination of the privileged, minority male gaze in the pre- and post-classic periods should help to establish my argument that Hollywood's treatment of this figure has moved from a repressed voyeurism, through parody, to a blatant voyeurism characteristic of the contemporary period.

While the Oriental sleuth was virtually ignored in silent film, he became a staple of the Hollywood screen with the third Chan movie, *Behind That Curtain* (1929) (Everson, 1972: 72–3; Hanke, 1989: xiii). Until the Chan figure, the concept of an Oriental hero was unthinkable. For the American audience the ultimate 'Yellow Peril' was the insidious Dr Fu Manchu, Sax Rohmer's Oriental master criminal (see Penzler, 1977: 43).[7] Indeed, Asians were generally missing in early cinema, or if present only as laundrymen or lowly paid workers (for example, *Chinese Laundry Scene*, 1894; see Musser, 1991: 43–4, 76, note 13).[8] However, Chan's third appearance opened the door for America's unique version of the Oriental sleuth.[9] Over the next 20 years there would be more than 60 films starring Charlie Chan, Mr Moto and Mr Wong (48 for Chan, 8 for Moto, 6 for Wong).[10]

To study this figure is to study ourselves, for through his persona are filtered all the arguments we as Westerners give ourselves for looking and gazing upon others.[11] We are the Asian voyeur. But today 'Chan is missing'[12] and the warrant to look the way Charlie once looked is no longer automatically given. How did this come to be? What happened? Or has anything really happened?

A single, yet complicated, thesis drawing from Jameson (1990), Said (1979, 1989), Stam (1991), Bakhtin (1981, 1986), Shohat (1991) and Hall (1981) organizes my discussion. Modifying Edward Said (1979), I suggest that between the years 1929 and 1949 Hollywood aided in the containment of America's Asian-American population through the production of the more than 60 films featuring the Chan, Moto and Wong characters.[13] These Oriental sleuths neutralized previous negative images of the Asian-American, and offered to Asian-Americans (and Americans) a particular Americanized version of who they were and who they should be. In this

Hollywood operated as an 'Orientalizing' agency for the larger American culture. Hollywood cinema worked, that is, as an institutional apparatus which described, taught, and authorized a particular view of Asian culture, Asian men, women, and Asian family life. It created a system of discourse which constituted the 'Orient' and the Asian as 'imaginary others' who were simultaneously categorized, exteriorized, excluded and included within the Western framework.[14]

These films contained a kernel of utopian fantasy (see Jameson, 1990: 34; Shohat, 1991: 222). As such they may be seen as sites of ideological struggle for they projected a world where Americans and Asians could happily interact within a unified culture where the facts of bigotry, racism and discrimination were, if not absent, at least easily negotiable (see Desser, 1991a: 383). In this they operated as ethnic allegories which, even when 'narrating apparently private stories, managed to metaphorize the public sphere, where the micro-individual is doubled by the macro-nation and the personal, the political, the private and the historical, are inextricably linked' (Shohat, 1991: 234; see also Jameson, 1990: 32–3). Chan, Moto and Wong became positive stand-ins for the negative Asian other, and the 'Yellow Peril', even as their characters critiqued and made a parody of the ethnocentric, Eurocentric, racist stereotypes[15] which were ascribed to them (see also Shohat, 1991: 238).

These texts and their heroes, however, were in Bakhtin's terms (Stam, 1991: 253) complex discursive constructions. A polyphonic play of voices, from the ethnic margins and the centres of white society, interact in each film to produce characters who are not just unitary essences, but rather three-dimensional, flesh-and-blood entities (see Stam, 1991: 253, 257–8). The characters cannot, that is, be read as flat stick figures. Charlie, Wong and Moto were always at the centre of 'conflicting and competing voices' (Stam, 1991: 257), voices which constituted them as subjects within clashing racial and ethnic contradictions. At different moments within any of these films the heroes could be 'traversed by racist and antiracist discourse' (Stam, 1991: 257). Each figure became a complex construction whose dialogical angle of vision on the American-Asian ethnic order was always at the very core of the 'American experience' (Stam, 1991: 259). By being folded into the centre of crises produced by Americans, they were able to live racism from within, inside looking out, as they were outsiders brought into the inside.

On the surface Hollywood's Orientalist discourse distinguished the Oriental/Asian from the Western/European figure, in terms of cultural and racial stereotyping (K. Lee, 1991: 1). The European/American was presented as the culturally-known, familiar comfortable other; the Asian as the unknown, dangerous, devious other. The European/American other was rational, virtuous, mature and normal; the Oriental was irrational, depraved, fallen, childlike, immature, a danger to society (K. Lee, 1991: 1; Said, 1979: 300). In these ways American cinema perpetuated its version of Orientalism, which, Said reminds us, is the 'corporate institution for dealing with the Orient . . . by making statements about it . . . ruling over it: in short Orientalism is a Western style for dominating, restructuring and having authority over the Orient' (Said, 1979: 3; see also Barthes, 1982; Kristeva, 1977; Doane, 1991, Chapter 9).

In the Chan, Moto and Wong movies Hollywood offered the American audience a superficial, stereotyped image of the neutered, slant-eyed, greased-down hair, thin moustached (the Fu Manchu moustache), calm, implacable Oriental detective. (The three series seldom dealt with other Asian stereotypes, including the Asian drug kingpin and the exotic China doll – see, for example, Cimino's *Year of the Dragon* and Marchetti's (1991) discussion of these stereotypes.) This figure would work in the service of law and order, peace and justice. He would protect the world from sinister criminals, and take pleasure in solving crimes and catching criminals who eluded the dimwitted police.

It is no accident that the Asian male would find acceptance in American culture as a voyeur and a sleuth, for there is a long tradition connecting Orientalism with voyeurism and at times scopophilia (see Doane, 1991: 180). His earlier image, after all, was as the sinister master criminal Dr Fu Manchu. It remained to capture this Oriental gaze and to put it to Western uses. As Foucault (1980: 155) implies, twentieth century regimes of power and surveillance turned the observed into the observer, the deviant into the one who studies and controls deviants. Consequently, a major power strategy involved the state's recruitment of minority group members as surveillance agents. In the guise of these three male figures (Chan, Moto and Wong) the master Oriental criminal was turned into a master sleuth, a person who could use his sinister qualities for positive purposes.

He was then invested with all of his culture's negative and positive characteristics. He carried the weight of being Asian upon his investigative shoulders, using his oriental eyes as a way of being (and seeing) the truth that others could not see. He was forced to rely upon his wit as a vehicle for disarming cultural criticisms of his ethnic origins. While self-deprecating ('All my life I study to speak fine English words. Now I must strangle all such in my throat, lest suspicion rise up. Not a happy situation for me') his wit was always barbed, and passively aggressive ('Silence big sister of wisdom', 'Tongue often hang man quicker than rope'). (Penzler, 1977: 47). Thus did he attack with words his Western aggressors.

However, in its representation of the Oriental sleuth, Hollywood inverted the usual stereotyped picture of the Asian male. It gave this figure precisely those Western/European/American traits which had been previously denied the Asian other. Chan, Moto and Wong were rational, virtuous, mature, normal men who were paired and pitted against irrational, depraved, childish, violent, immature Westerners.[16] In this move the Asian male was simultaneously excluded from, and included inside, a Western-Orientalizing discourse which made him stranger and friend at the same time.

The comedy format of the Asian detective series facilitated this textual displacement, for these films must be read as comedy. In this they took their place in a long Hollywood history, for as Musser (1991: 43) argues, 'ethnic-based comedy has been a feature of American cinema from its beginnings until the present'. Ethnicity – being Asian – is presented in this series as a 'constraint and a construction from which characters and audiences can be at least temporarily liberated' (Musser, 1991: 43). Thus Charlie, Wong and Moto, in key moments in every film, are momentarily released from their Asian identities and turned into serious sleuths, often preceded by their movement into a disguise (for example, clown, shop-keeper, etc.). (The comedy basis of the Chan series is obvious, of course, given in the usual capers of Number One Son.) In the movements back and forth between serious detective film and comedy, the Asian detective films exaggerate ethnic stereotype through speech and dress patterns, and through dialogue directed to the Asian detective (for example, chop suey).

Through these comedic gestures the filmmakers exercised a form of social control over the non-Western figure, arguing that he should be made to accommodate the central features of Western culture. Thus these texts operated in an assimilationist manner, wiping out in a single stroke all of the distinctive, positive features of Oriental culture. Indeed, the fact that each Oriental detective was a master at disguise further reinforced the cultural message that the Oriental should be made to fit into American culture (see Musser, 1991: 55). This demand would be most evident in those situations where the detective would be forced to assume a 'false mask of politesse when waiting on the condescending and self-absorbed' Westerner (Musser, 1991: 57).

It is clear that the Oriental voyeur, unlike Sherlock Holmes, Bull Drummond, Nick Carter, Mike Hammer or Hercule Poirot, had to overcome an ethnic identity before he could be a detective. So Chan, Moto and Wong had to be given ethnic identities that Americans could feel comfortable with. These identities had to be, on the surface at least, firm and certain. They could not threaten the identities of others. Thus Chan, Moto and Wong first appear as wooden, cartoon characters with little depth. Their private lives were apparently irrelevant, all that needed to be known about them was that they were good at solving crimes. However each carried a history from one film to the next, a history of previous crimes solved. This history gave substance and depth to their personal biographies.

As a consequence they were never presented as personal, or sexual threats to the white other. They became feminized Asian men, even eunuchs (see Marchetti, 1991: 290 on the stereotype of the Asian male as sexual threat). Still, as Eugene Franklin Wong argues (1978), and Marchetti repeats (1991: 289), ethnicity is never neuter. Images of race, ethnicity and sexuality are always intertwined. Indeed racial and ethnic hierarchies are often maintained 'through fantasies which reinforce those differences through references to gender. Thus fantasies of threatening

Asian men, emasculated eunuchs, alluring Asian "dragon ladies," and submissive female slaves all work to rationalize white, male domination' (Marchetti, 1991: 289). Sexually passive Charlie, Mr Wong and Mr Moto reinforced the sexually dominant position of the white males in the text. (Only Number One Son would be permitted to flirt, and his sexual games were harmless, written off to his adolescent genes, not his ethnicity.)

In these ways the series would foreground and then displace and repress ethnic identity and ethnic difference. Audiences could accept the Oriental detective as a familiar 'white' other, who was at the same time different. (Mr Moto would often disguise himself as a 'white man'.) In these ways the films played different ethnic and racial identities off against one another, even Charlie had a black chauffeur! But in so doing it maintained a rigid ethnic hierarchy, which placed whites above non-whites.

A double spectacular structure organized these texts. The centre of any given film in the series would often unfold around, and be marked by, moments of spectacle. There would be operatic performances, vaudeville acts, the unveiling of new archaeological discoveries, carnival displays of dramatic violence, murders on stage and so on. The ethnic hierarchy of selves would then typically be realized through a 'spectacle of discovery' wherein Chan, Moto or Wong would ceremoniously unmask the murderer or villain. This would often occur in a group situation, where all of the suspects were brought together (sometimes in a locked room). The detective would then create anxiety by pointing out how each suspect could have been the murderer. (Typically the anxiety was sufficient to lead the 'real' murderer to confess.)

The spectacle of criminal discovery would occur within this larger specular (and spectacular) structure. It would allow for the 'contemplation of the racial and ethnic Other as an object, separated from and under the visual control of the viewer positioned with the camera, in power, as the eye of the dominant culture' (Marchetti, 1991: 287). In the moment of discovery Charlie, Wong or Moto would invariably be distanced from the Westerners in the film, simultaneously object and subject of his own (and ours) investigation. In this way the films would reinscribe racial and ethnic difference, and usually sexual difference as well. In his spectacular moment of discovery the Oriental detective became spectacle and, by implication, his ethnicity became spectacle too.

Thus were the Asian detectives orientalized. Their ethnicity was ubiquitous, yet textually submerged, as they were given fixed, yet mutable, ethnic identities. Never really pitted against the culturally dominant group, they were always outsiders on the periphery who were brought into the cultural centre when a crisis appeared (see Shohat, 1991: 217 on the centre-periphery issue). Once they entered this inner, sacred space of the culturally dominant group they performed their function with dispatch, humour and grace. Their ethnic identities were submerged and stitched into the dominant colonialist discourse which was itself turned into the discourse of crime, punishment and discovery. Through a dialectic of presence and absence (Shohat, 1991: 222), the Hollywood films on the Asian detective allowed this Asian other to be both present and absent at the same time. As he moved from disguise to disguise he became first you, and then me and then someone else. In this way the investigative and comedic codes which contained these narratives undertook to speak for the marginalized Asian culture.

A superficial form of cultural integration was thereby produced. At one level these films simply inserted new heroes, 'drawn from the ranks of the subaltern, into old functional roles' (Stam, 1991: 263). The implication was clear. By playing the part of detective, or law enforcer, Chan, Wong and Moto had an Asian link to the American and international 'power structure' (Stam, 1991: 263). But of course this was 'quite out of keeping with the actual configuration of social power' (Stam, 1991: 263).

The hegemony of the comedy and investigative narrative codes included and excluded the Asian spectator. It gave such viewers only one subject position to assume – the position of seeing themselves through the larger, dominant culture's eyes. These viewers, like their American counterparts, thus learned quickly how to master the 'presumed codes of a foreign culture, shown as simple, stable, unself-conscious, and susceptible to facile apprehension [and representation]' (Shohat, 1991: 225). The Asian eye thus read its culture through the codes developed by the dominant culture. The oppositional nature of ethnic and cultural life was minimized, as a fixed, stereotypical picture of an isolated minority group was pitted against a fixed, 'white-American power structure' (Shohat, 1991: 217). The image of overlapping, conflicting de-centred circles of ethnic identities was never considered (Shohat, 1991: 217). Such an image of the Asian-American identity would not appear until 1981 with Wayne Wang's *Chan is Missing*.

This is how the Asian detective movie series worked. It simultaneously contained and released the Asian eye to be just like you and me, while he was always different, foreign, strange and somewhat distant from our own experience. Now *Charlie Chan at the Opera*.

Charlie Chan at the Opera

Lilli Rochelle and Gravelle are famous opera singers who were married to one another. They have a daughter Kitty. Lilli has an affair with Enrico, also an opera singer. She and Enrico plot to kill Gravelle in a fire. Gravelle is trapped in the fire, loses his memory and is confined to an asylum. It is now 13 years later. Gravelle's memory returns when he sees a picture of Lilli announcing her upcoming performance in *Carnival*. Gravelle escapes, vowing to kill the two of them. Charlie is brought in by Inspector Regan to help find Gravelle. Lilli has since married Whitely, a wealthy businessman. Enrico is married to Anita (also an opera singer). Enrico and Lilli have continued their affair. Lilli refuses to acknowledge her daughter Kitty. Anita hates Lilli for stealing her husband and Whitely hates Enrico for stealing his wife. During a performance of *Faust* Gravelle knocks out Enrico and dons his costume, playing the part of Mephisto. Immediately after the performance Lilli and Enrico are stabbed to death. There are four suspects: Gravelle, Phil (Kitty's boyfriend, who is found with blood on his hands), Anita, and Whitely who sent his wife a note (along with flowers) saying she would die that evening at the opera). In a spectacle of discovery (Gravelle and Anita re-enact their roles in the opera), Charlie eliminates every suspect, until he comes to Anita, who finally confesses. Gravelle is reunited with his daughter. William Demarest plays the part of Sergeant Kelly, an anti-Chinese policeman.

Reading the Opera

An investigative Oedipal tale with racist and anti-feminist overtones, this is a story of love, betrayal, vengeance and justice. Three strong women, Lilli, Anita and Kitty, paired with weak men,[17] structure the narrative. Two, Lilli and Anita, are *femme fatales*, *divas*, and suffer the fate of being such (see Doane, 1991: 2). Lilli and Anita are the carriers of power, symptoms of 'male fears about feminism' (Doane, 1991: 3), for each, in her way, embodies the threat of castration. Each is also the antithesis of the maternal, mothering figure (see Doane, 1991: 3). Denying their reproductive functions, they are both carried and moved by out-of-control sexual desires.

The three women each want something the other has, or won't give up. Kitty wants her mother back. Lilli wants Anita's husband. Anita wants Lilli to give up her husband. Lilli dies because she betrayed her two husbands and rejected her daughter, Kitty ('she was afraid a [grown] daughter would hurt her career'). Anita goes to prison because she did what a weak husband (Whitely) 'was not man enough to do anything about'. Their 'textual eradication involves a desperate reassertion of control on the part of the threatened male subject' (Doane, 1991: 2). Charlie functions as the arbiter of justice who also reunites a father with his daughter. He is the paternal figure, the law of patriarchy. The only male unafraid of, and unmoved by, the sexually threatening figures of Lilli and Anita.

At the anti-feminist level the story is direct. Women should not reject their daughters and betray their husbands, nor should they attempt to get even. A woman's place is at home, caring for husband and daughter. When she relinquishes these responsibilities and pursues work at the expense of marriage, she gets what she deserves. On this point the story is firm. Kitty, the only woman to completely embrace the traditional female identity, finds happiness. She, the weakest woman of the three, faints and becomes hysterical when danger approaches (when Gravelle confronts her), and willingly allows her husband-to-be to take on his new job of making her happy. The strong women, in contrast, are punished.

In their fates and their fatal strategies, Lilli and Anita anticipate the famous *femme fatale* figures of film noir. In their roles as *divas* of Italian opera, they connect to nineteenth-century representations of the *femme fatale* who was associated with the styles of Decadence, Symbolism Art Nouveau and popular Orientalism (see Doane, 1991: 1). At this level the film joins two versions of Orientalism, namely female decadence and male voyeurism.

The Opera as a Whodunit The film's opening shots (thunder and lightning, the Gothic insane asylum) immediately locate it within the Gothic thriller, horror genre. Within minutes the thriller will be further defined as a murder mystery of the whodunit variety (although a murder has not yet occurred). Karloff's escape from the asylum (newspaper headlines: 'Madman eludes dragnet', 'Madman in Los Angeles') sets the police on his trail and brings Charlie in as the person who will find this maniac before he kills.

The film merges genres, or investigative forms, the (Charlie Chan) whodunit with the thriller (on these forms as literary conventions see Todorov, 1977, Chapter 3). The film contains (at least) two stories, the murders of the two lovers (Enrico and Lilli), and the story of Charlie's investigation which leads to the discovery of the murderer. (Todorov calls these the story and the plot.) The two stories run alongside one another, coinciding finally when Anita confesses as the murderess. As the stories come together and merge, it becomes apparent that the first could not be present without the second. (Charlie's presence is so tightly stitched into the text we do not realize that he is there to tell us what is happening, and why. As the action coincides with the narrative, the film shifts from being a whodunit to a thriller.)[18]

The first story, the film as it presents itself to the viewer, is the story of what 'appeared' to have happened. The second story (plot), the story of investigation, is the story of how the investigator (Charlie) and the viewer (you and I) come to know what 'really happened' (Todorov, 1977: 45). In the second story Charlie (the narrator) re-presents to us what actually happened (for example, re-playing the opera scene). The first story follows the natural progression of time, effects follow causes (see Todorov, 1977: 45). The second story inverts time, with results (dead bodies) coming before causes (the real murderer). Charlie serves as the mediator between these two stories, explaining to us what we did and did not see when we saw what we thought we saw.

In classic fashion the film has a geometric architecture: two murders, four suspects, four sets of clues and four interrogations. In order: two dead bodies (Enrico, Lilli); four suspects (Phil, Whitely, Gravelle, Anita); four clues (blood on the hands of Phil; Whitely's fingerprints on the card to Anita; Gravelle's oiled knife with no blood stains; Anita's second costume belt which has blood stains, and the second, hidden knife, with blood on the handle); and four interrogations, wherein, following the hypo-deductive method, Charlie systematically eliminates each suspect until he comes to Anita.

This geometric structure builds on an earlier architecture, involving Charlie's discovery of Gravelle's real identity and the relationship between Phil, Kitty, Gravelle and Lilli. Two clues are the key to each puzzle. For Gravelle this involves the wirephoto sequence and the earlier prediction that the heel on the photo signalled a relationship between the escaped maniac and Lilli. The discovery of the family relationship involved Charlie observing Phil and Kitty asking to see Lilli and overhearing Gravelle's discourse to Kitty about a lost daughter. When Charlie puts these two pieces of the puzzle together he is able to exclude Phil and Gravelle as murder suspects.

The film's geometric structure, including Charlie's use of the hypo-deductive method, serves to place reason and rationality on the side of this particular Oriental eye. It underscores the text's commitment to the position that every event has a cause, every cause an effect, and every effect is the cause of another effect (see Haycroft, 1972: 249; Todorov, 1977: 49). But, like a pragmatist, Charlie always works from consequences back to causes.

Everyday Pragmatic Voyeurism

He could not do this if he were not a voyeur. But Charlie is a particular kind of voyeur. His are not the secretive and hidden gazes of the criminal. His looks do not carry violent, sexual, or erotic overtones. His looks are sudden, quick, done in the immediate presence of others, focused always on small physical details (an unburned cigar in an ashtray, a note card in a wastebasket) overheard words, untoward gestures, footprints, smells and odours. Like Sherlock Holmes, he deduces information from the traces left by human actions (see Truzzi, 1976: 65; and earlier discussion in Chapter 2, pp. 53–4). In this he makes the ordinary, immediately at-hand, taken-for-granted, physical world problematic and visible. He is a voyeur of the visible, of the could-be-seen, but not noticed, everyday world.

His commitment to the pragmatic investigative method leads him to be constantly alert to clues and traces of action which would point to meanings that others want to suppress. His method of inquiry is progressive, processual and transformative (on the pragmatic method see Farberman and Perinbanayagam, 1985: 8–9; Farberman, 1991: 480). The entire point of any one of Charlie's investigative activities is to produce an interpretive account of past action which squares with the facts. Facts are based on the consequences of actions. For example who could have been present in this room at this time and have had the motive and method to kill this person?

Charlie's pragmatic method becomes hypo-deductive when he hypothesizes motives for action. Doubt and scepticism operate at every step of the way. Charlie doubts any individual's account and he is sceptical of his own interpretive procedures. Every hypothesis (and account) is fallible, 'since it is open to future experience that may well refute it' (Farberman and Perinbanayagam, 1985: 9). Charlie's pragmatic theory of truth assumes that 'the best hypothesis is the one which best explains past experience and most comprehensively predicts future consequences' (Farberman and Perinbanayagam, 1985: 9). In this he aligns himself with the pragmatism of Charles S. Peirce. But his pragmatism goes beyond Peirce, and merges with that of William James who argued that what is meaningful is what is true for the individual (see Farberman and Perinbanayagam, 1985: 10). Charlie understands that each person's interpretation of a situation works because it gives an account of actions. But this account may be false, hiding the real facts of the situation. The real facts of a situation can only be uncovered by creating an emotional situation which shatters the deceiver's false account.

Here is how this works in *Opera*. Charlie has all the suspects (except Gravelle) in the same room. (Gravelle has been shot by the police and taken off by the medics.) Sergeant Kelly has charged Charlie with endangering the life of Anita, 'Egg foo yung! The guy who pulls rabbits out of the hat sends a woman out there to let a guy stick a knife in her. Well Chief, that about closes the case.' Charlie contradicts him: 'Contradiction please. Case still wide open, like swinging gate . . . will demonstrate with hypothesis.' He then lays the two knives side by side on a table. He continues:

> Proof most elemental. Fact in deduction . . . if Gravelle guilty, must have both knives on person before singing . . . Previous examination of costume discloses no tell-tale blood stains. Madman not use Barelli's knife, having one of own . . . . Method devised by re-murderer born in rational mind. Use presence of maniac in theatre as perfect alibi to cover own guilt. Conceal murder knife after first crime . . . Fact that Madame Barelli in wings during final singing final link in chain of evidence [camera shot of Anita]. You are murderess [she jumps up]. You were only one who knew Gravelle planned to sing the Mephisto role tonight . . . so avail self of perfect opportunity to avenge intrigue which cause you so much humiliation . . . you conceal knife on person after murder of husband.

Confronted with the facts, Madame Barelli confesses: 'You're right. I used it on Lilli when I came back with the smelling salts and found her alone'. Then, turning to Whitely, she states, 'You knew what was going on, but you weren't man enough to do anything about it'.

Charlie's investigative method is in full presence in this scene. Facts, deductions, motives, methods and opportunities for crime are all assembled. Gravelle is logically eliminated as a suspect because he did not have both knives on his person. Whitely is excluded because he did not know Gravelle and his presence during the performance could be accounted for. Phil was earlier excluded because of Kitty's account about wanting to see her mother. (Phil got the blood on his hands when he attempted to move Lilli.) Only one suspect remains, Madame Barelli. By having her recreate her role in the opera Charlie created the emotional scene which would lead her to confess.

For all practical purposes the film ends with the above speech, although the obligatory last scene with Number One Son who rushes in with the missing clue (no longer needed) must be inserted into the finale. Just before this occurs Sergeant Kelly apologizes to Charlie, 'You're alright. Just like Chop Suey, a mystery, but a swell dish. By the way, I didn't get that Chinese lingo you sprung on us before you asked Madame to sing'. Charlie, 'Ancient Chinese proverb meaning when fear attack brain, tongue wave in distress'. Kelly, 'I get it. You made her sing with Gravelle just to scare her into talking'. Charlie, 'Yes'.

With these lines the film closes, as it opened, in darkness. Only now Charlie and Number One Son are racing to the harbour to catch the boat to Hawaii. With a police escort lighting up the night, sirens screaming in the air, Charlie and son, the pragmatic voyeurs, have solved another crime. Now it is time for their Oriental family.

Racial Overtones

Consider the following lines, they are all spoken by the William Demarest character, Sergeant Kelly, or his immediate superior, Inspector Regan (Guy Usher). They reference the film's underlying racism. *Kelly*: 'You haven't called chop suey in on the case have you Chief?' *Regan*: 'No, but it's not a bad idea and take your hat off. You can learn a little politeness from the Chinese'. *Kelly*: 'I can pick him out, he's Chinese'. *Kelly*: 'If that Chinese dick knows where he is . . .' *Kelly*: 'He's [in reference to Charlie] hitting the pipe again'.

These lines occur in those pivotal investigative moments when Charlie's methods and techniques are contrasted to those employed by Sergeant Kelly. In each sequence Charlie's methods are shown to be superior to those employed by Kelly. For example, in the film's opening sequence, when Charlie enters Regan's office, Kelly attempts to keep him off the case. Charlie immediately shows Kelly to be a fool when he establishes a link between the photo found in Gravelle's room, and the picture of Lilli. Charlie continues to establish his superiority when he suggests that Kelly has been criticized by Regan. Charlie: 'Small things sometimes tell large stories. For instance, very obvious here that many men indulge in nervous tic. Perhaps unfortunate assistant receiving dressing-down on carpet . . . when policeman on small pay discard large cigar after two puffs, sure sign of distress'.

These barbed exchanges serve four functions. They establish Charlie's superior investigative powers, while allowing him to speak his famous lines, which embody kernels of Chinese wisdom. These signature lines mark the film as a Charlie Chan movie. But most importantly they allow the racial subtext to be continually present. Even as Charlie rebuffs each of

Kelly's charges, the charges, and their bigotry still stand. Thus the film is able to superficially transcend its own racism at the same time as it depends on these racist lines to establish Charlie's superior skills. In these conversational exchanges the film simultaneously places Charlie inside and outside mainstream America. It aligns him with Asian stereotypes, while using these same stereotypes as a means of overcoming the stereotypes and their negative moral implications. I turn next to Mr Moto, another Oriental sleuth who also confronts racist bigotry.

Mr Moto

There were eight Mr Moto films made in the two years, 1937–9. Peter Lorre starred in all of them, which were based on the four John R. Marquand novels (*No Hero, Thank you Mr Moto, Think Fast, Mr Moto, Mr Moto is So Sorry*). *Mr Moto's Last Warning* (1939) is the seventh in the series, which took its initiative from the highly popular Charlie Chan films. The series was finally dropped because Lorre went on to bigger and better roles, and the World War II situation made 'acceptance of a Japanese hero dubious' (Everson, 1972: 82).

Unlike Chan, Mr Moto, who was Japanese, worked under cover, was a master of disguises, often used doubles (or persons who looked like him so he could hide in disguise), was between 35 and 40, a ju-jitsu expert, adept at magic, and worked for the International Police. Like Chan, Mr Moto's syntax was distinct, immediately conveying Hollywood's stereotype of an Asian speaker, 'I am so very, very happy' or 'You must not make sound, please'.

Mr Moto's Last Warning (1939) is set in the Mediterranean, in Port Said, in the midst of World War II. The visual style has much in common with the film noir tradition, including the use of lighting, shadows and off-screen space to suggest distance and danger. France and England are allies against the German army and navy. A group of foreign conspirators (led by Ricardo Cortez (Mr Fabian) and George Sanders (Eric Norvel)) are attempting to sabotage the French fleet as it steams through the Suez Canal and blame this on the English, thereby breaking the alliance. Mr Moto has been dispatched by the International Police to avert this disaster. Sending a Japanese look-alike on board the *SS Himilay*, Moto identifies Norvel as a member of this gang, and suspects that Mr Fabian, who is passing himself off as a ventriloquist, is its leader. Duped by Moto's double, whom he has killed, Fabian thinks that Moto (who is disguised as a small shop owner named Mr Keroke) is out of the picture. Yet he begins to suspect Moto, who disguises himself as a clown and listens in on Fabian giving his gang directions. Moto identifies himself to Danforth (John Carradine), a member of Fabian's group, who is a secret British agent. Fabian begins to suspect Mr Keroke when his girlfriend Connie describes 'a little bitty Japanese man who played ping pong with a couple of bruisers'. Fabian has Danforth killed. He then bombs Moto's shop, but fails to kill him. Moto is subsequently captured by Fabian, dropped in the canal, escapes in time to save the fleet and wrestles with Fabian, who is shot by his girlfriend Connie. This is the story. The publicity for the film described it as follows:

'The indestructible pint-sized detective fights his greatest battle'
'Mr Moto, the crafty, implacable operative of the International Police'
'Mr Moto with more lives than a cat, works within a colourful Egyptian background to avert disaster and uncover the sinister plot'

Moto embodies mid-century Asian male stereotypes. He is short (pint-sized), good at ju-jitsu (indestructible), dignified in appearance (implacable), deferential to everyone and a person who upholds the law. He has no trouble with English but can speak a broken dialect if required to do so. He is always more than he appears to be (crafty, more lives than a cat), hence giving the illusion of being duplicitous. He has no sex or love life, work is everything. He is devoted to international law and justice (averting disaster and uncovering sinister plots). He is the sinister Oriental other, animal-like, smaller than ordinary humans, yet indestructible. He exists for, and his existence is justified because he can deploy his sinister skills in averting disaster for the white world. He can protect this world against its own kind (foreign master spies like Fabian). Mr Moto's ability to use disguises is thus deliberate, for he must pass himself off as a white other in order to use his 'oriental' skills of crime detection.

Moto's investigative, voyeuristic activities involve furtive looking, eavesdropping, often with technological aids (hidden microphones), the use, as noted above, of look-alikes and disguises as he passes himself off as an ordinary human being. He is not above violence and is able to put his martial arts skills to good use when required to do so. His voyeuristic skills, which allow him to see what others cannot see, are contrasted with the skills of the police and the military. The generals in the film are bumbling caricatures of British and French ineptness. These protectors of law and order need the Mr Motos of the world, as long as these foreign others are kept in their place.

The world of 'otherness' that Mr Moto inhabits, like Chan's world, is filled with upper, middle and lower class non-Orientals, for example, French, British, German and Egyptian men, women and children. These people are either in the leisure class, the military, the police or the entertainment or service occupations (vaudeville performers, bartenders, bar owners). This is a world of strange foreigners, united in their dislike of strangers and foreigners. (At one point a British sea captain refuses to drink with Moto because he 'can't stand strangers and foreigners!'.) Moto's foreignness thus stands out in this group. He is the only Asian and the only person called foreign, suggesting that the Asian other is the only foreigner to the British or the English in this film. Thus his being Asian places him in a permanent outsider and subservient position to this world of white others who know who they are.

The Mr Moto character, unlike Charlie Chan, had no personal or family life (Pitts, 1979: 195). A mystery character, he went from film to film changing identity: a Japanese merchant and amateur detective (*Think Fast, Mr Moto*), in the employ of a Chinese princess (*Thank You, Mr Moto*), a Japanese detective running a school of criminology (*Mr Moto's Gamble*), a ju-jitsu expert posing as an archaeologist (*Mr Moto Takes a Chance*) and, finally, a member of the International Police.

Mr Moto's Last Warning *as Thriller*

The Moto films are thrillers, not whodunits. In the thriller, as Todorov (1977: 49–51) argues, the detective's life is placed in danger, killers are professionals and action focuses on danger, pursuit and combat. There is little mystery, only suspense; that is, will the villain kill the protagonist? A story's climax typically involves a final battle between the protagonist and his or her arch-enemy. The protagonist, having already solved the crime, emerges a double victor. The person or persons who attempted to kill the protagonist are killed, and in that act law and order are restored to the situation. Vengeance and justice are merged in this single, violent act. In such stories (and films), investigation takes a second place to violence.

Mr Moto is a violent voyeur. While he will, on occasion, deploy investigative methods, he does not routinely use the pragmatic and hypo-deductive logics of Chan or Holmes. His project is never one which leads to the non-violent solving of a crime. Indeed the narrative structure of the Moto films is one which minimizes the detective project. The audience typically knows, even before Mr Moto, who the criminal is, and what dangers he poses for our protagonist. The films, then, make violence and danger their topic.

As an Oriental expert in the martial arts, Mr Moto represents one of the first of many Oriental, and later American, martial arts experts that Hollywood would present to American society. These figures, from Mr Moto to Modesty Blaise, James Bond, Bruce Lee, Chuck Norris, and most recently Steve Seagal, keep the Chinese-Oriental and Asian connection alive in American culture. These violent figures, who use Asian methods of combat, continue the Orientalizing project started with the Chan series. The Asian Eye, now deployed and taken over by Norris and Seagal, fights the worldwide communist and Asian conspiracy associated with terrorism, drug cartels, white slavery, pornography and pro-Vietnam fantasies concerning veterans who return to Vietnam to free American POWs. These same right-wing cultural icons also take stands against drug pushers, underclass violence toward the police and sexual violence against middle-class American women. These films, as Ryan and Kellner observe, represent a 'curious mixture of anti-authoritarian individualism and extremely conservative law and order moralism that characterizes the populist American male' (1988: 227). This was the door that Charlie Chan and Mr Moto opened.

To summarize, while Mr Moto's identities changed from film to film (and within films), underneath each of these changes was a firm understanding. This tiny Asian male knew who he was, knew his place in society and felt pride in his ability to always right a situation that had gone wrong. Of these things he was certain. In this certainty he shared with Charlie Chan the belief that he occupied a particular and special place in American society. All of this is undone in *Chan is Missing*.

Chan is Missing

Several Chans are missing in this film. Mr Chan Hung, a Taiwanese businessman who owes Jo (a humorous, soft-spoken, sweet-tempered middle-aged Chinese American cabdriver)[19] and his young Freddie Prinze-like, 'Americanized' nephew Steve, $4,000, cannot be found. He has been missing for 22 days. (Jo and Steve decided to sublease a licence from an independent owner. Mr Chan Hung was to deliver $4,000 to finalize the deal.) Charlie Chan and the Chan mystery series are missing, although the series is ridiculed by Jo, who says, 'Those old films are a source of cheap laughs'. Charlie and Number One Son are not here, but their absence is several times noted, and their presence mocked. Laughingly, Jo and Steve, for example, introduce themselves to Mr Chan's daughter as Charlie Chan and Number One Son. In this film no clue leads anywhere and a mystery, in the conventional sense, is never solved. What's not here seems to have just as much meaning as what is here. Nothing means what it seems to mean.

But these easily identifiable absences are not what the film is about. Self, in its Asian-American versions, and its empty centres, are the topic at hand. On the surface this is a 'whodunit', but more deeply it is a 'whoisit'. Its topic is epistemological. 'How do we know the self and its meanings' and are these meanings ever certain? The film first.

The city is San Francisco: the setting, Chinatown: the time, now. The style is cinema verité, film noir, grainy screen, dark shadows, back-lit scenes, voice-over narration. Mosaic-like, *Chan is Missing* is a collage of over-laid images, pictures, and close-up camera shots, many viewed through the front windscreen of a cab which glides through the streets of Chinatown, its window reflecting the scenes that pass by: stoop-shouldered, aged-Asian males and females shuffling along the sidewalk, young Asian-American children holding their parents' hands waiting for a bus, Kung-Fu warrior posters outside movie houses, pagoda roof tops in the distance, Chinese and Italian restaurants, smoked chickens hanging in cafe windows, signs in Chinese, a Christmas decorated Buddha with tinsel and flashing lights, Chinese rock and roll ('Rock Around the Clock') and suspense music in the background, as a Pat Suzuki version of Rogers and

Hammerstein's 'Grant Avenue' plays over the film's credits. A voyeur's film from start to finish, the text is filled with shots of Jo gazing either directly into the camera, or slightly off-screen into the distance. His voyeurism yields nothing.

Jo and Steve set out to find the missing Chan. Steve wants to go to the police, but Jo resists. Their journey brings them in contact with four clues and more than 12 persons who know, or knew Chan. Although he is never found, by the film's end the $4,000 is delivered to Jo and Steve by Mr Chan's teenage daughter, Jenny.

What is missing is the firm and steady, easily assimilated Chinese-American character embodied in the Chan films. Indeed the film offers a virtual dictionary of contemporary Asian-American identities: Chinese Richard Pryors, Chinese cooks who wear 'Samurai Night Fever' T-shirts and sing 'Fry Me to the Moon', FOBS (fresh off the boat), Kung-Fu warriors, China dolls, Chinese scholars with hot tubs and their Loy Fong girlfriends, jade-faced rich old men, young Asian males with the GQ look, two-faced schizophrenic Chinamen, Oakland Hill Wah, Ho Chi Minh look alikes, young Asian males who eat US certified food (cows ears and mushrooms from Des Moines, Iowa), PRCs (People's Republic of China), Pro-Taiwan rich men, Asian males who sell Chinese-American apple pie, young Asian women who dress like American women, old Asian men and women who look like mainland peasants, young, streetwise Asian males wearing baseball caps, and so on.

These multiple images add up to one conclusion: there is no single Asian-American identity. The film's mystery seeks to unravel and find a solid core to this identity. The voyeur's project thus lies in the discovery that there is no Chan who can be missing, for every Chan (Asian-American) has an identity, even the three Chans, as Jo notes, who everyday appear on the missing person's list in the Police Department. What is missing is a centre to this identity.

Jo summarizes this struggle to define self. To Steve, he states, 'It's hard enough for guys like me who've been here so long to find an identity. I can imagine Chan Hung's problem, somebody from China coming over here and trying to find himself'. Steve protests, 'That's a bunch of bullshit man! That identity shit. That's old news. Man that happened 10 years ago'. Jo retorts, 'It's still going on'. Steve argues, 'Shit! I ran into this old friend from high school down town. We used to run together. He's all dressed up in his fuckin' GQ look with his Lo Fong girlfriend. He didn't want to talk to me man. He knew who I was. He's playing a game man. Fuck the identity shit. He knew what he was doin', I know what I'm doin'. I coulda kicked his fuckin' ass. Chinese all over this fuckin' city. Whatdaya mean about identity? They got their own identity. I got my identity!'

This absence of a singular identity is itself political, for the Asian-American must take a stand on the American experience that is either Pro-Taiwan and assimilationist, or anti-American and pro-People's Republic of China. But this politicized identity is also mocked. For every character in the film has been deeply touched by the San Francisco version of the Asian-American experience, even the 83-year-old Asian male who murders his 79-year-old Asian neighbour over which flag should be carried in the Chinese New Year's Parade.

The film, then, mocks these popular culture, standardized, stereotypical Asian-American identities. It also mocks social science and those scholars who point to language as being central to cultural differences. The following Lily Tomlin-like monologue is a key to this position. The speaker is a female Asian-American attorney. She is attempting to find Mr Chan, who had an automobile accident, just days before he disappeared. She is speaking to Jo and Steve. They are at Chester's Cafe. The young attorney is dressed in a black masculine-style suit, with a white shirt and dark tie.

> You see I'm doing a paper on the legal implications of cross-cultural misunderstandings [nods head]. Mr. Chan's case is a perfect example of what I want to expose. The policeman and Mr Chan have completely different culturally related assumptions about what kind of communication about communication [shot of Steven, then Jo] each one was using. The policeman, in an English speaking mode, asks a direct factual question – 'did you stop at the stop sign?' He expected a 'yes or a no' answer. Mr Chan, however, rather than giving him a yes or a no answer began to go into his past driving record – how good it was, the number of years he had been in the United States, all the people that he knew – trying to relate different events, objects or situations to what was happening then to the action in hand. Now this is very typical . . . . The Chinese try to relate points, events or objects that they feel are pertinent to the situation, which may not to anyone else seem directly relevant at the time . . . . This policeman became rather impatient, restated the question, 'Did you or did you not stop at the stop sign?' in a rather hostile tone, which in turn flustered Mr Chan, which caused him to hesitate answering the question, which further enraged the policeman, so that he asked the question again, 'You didn't stop at the stop sign, did you?' in a negative tone, to which Mr Chan automatically answered 'No'. Now, to any native speaker of English 'No' would mean 'No I didn't stop at the stop sign'. However to Mr Chan 'No I didn't stop at the stop sign' was not 'No I didn't stop at the stop sign' [Jo shakes head, looks away]. It was 'No, I didn't not stop at the stop sign'. In other words 'Yes I did stop at the stop sign'. Do you see what I'm saying? [camera pans room]

Jo (voice-over) 'Chan Hung wouldn't run away because of the car accident. I'm feeling something might have happened to him'.

As Jo and Steve go looking for Chan, no two individuals describe him the same way. To his wife he is a man who never properly assimilated to the American way of life. To his daughter he is an honest and trustworthy man. Presco, the manager of the Manilla Senior Citizen's Center calls Mr Chan 'Hi Ho' and thinks he is an eccentric. George (who is marketing a version of Chinese apple pie), thinks Mr Chan is too Chinese. Amy thinks he is a hotheaded political activist. Frankie thinks he returned to the mainland. Mr Fong thinks Chan is a genius because he invented a Chinese word processing system. Mr Lee says he is dim-witted and an old man in Chan's hotel says Chan is a paranoid.

The film itself refuses a single identity. Reviewers called it a gumshoe thriller (Rickey, 1982), an original, eccentric, anthropological comedy (Gelmis, 1982), not a neatly-plotted Oriental mystery (Winsten, 1982), a detective mystery that becomes a meditation on Chinese-American identity (Denby, 1982), a Chinatown mystery (Thomas, 1982), a dark comedy, a light melodrama, and existential mystery (Sterritt, 1982), a re-make of *Citizen Kane*, (Studlar, 1983: 115; Ansen, 1982), a film in the tradition of the French New Wave (Horton, 1982), a very Chinese mystery (Thomas, 1982) and a 'homely and funny cousin to *The Third Man*' (Denby, 1982). These descriptions point to the film's refusal to present a stereotypical picture of the Asian-American community. In its attempts to deconstruct and criticize previous images of the Asian-American subject, *Chan is Missing* suggests that the Asian-Oriental other will no longer stand still and allow itself to be seen and understood through Western eyes.

Four key clues organize Jo and Steve's investigation. In Chan's jacket, which was left at the Manilla Senior Citizen's Center, they find a newspaper story about a fight which occurred between pro- and anti-communist supporters during the Chinese New Year's Parade. In Chan's hotel room they discover a photo clipped from the paper showing the fight itself. Along with this photo is the story of 82-year-old Sun Kim Lee who was charged with murdering his 79-year-old neighbour, Chung Wang. Also in his room they observe a missing picture on the wall, a picture which later turns out to be of Chan. In Chan's car they find a gun and a letter from mainland China. The letter leads them to an address where they learn that Chan had separated from his wife and daughter six months ago to live with another woman. These four clues take them back and forth through the streets, piers, shops and cafés of Chinatown and San Francisco.

The clues add up to nothing. Chan is never found. This is a Chinese mystery, so says Jo. 'The murder article is missing. The photograph's not there. The other woman is not there. Nothing is what it seems to be.' Disclaiming his own identity, Jo states, 'I guess I'm not Chinese enough. I can't accept a mystery without a solution'. He returns to lines spoken earlier in the film by Presco. An old Chinese piano player who went crazy had reported that the only person who could fix him was the man who looked at him in the rain puddle on the ground. Presco tells Steve and Jo, 'Well, you guys lookin' for Mr Chan, why don't you look in the puddle?' As these lines are spoken the screen dissolves into a shot of glimmering water, ripples overlapping one another, to be replaced by a kaleidoscopic sequence of scenes which repeat the film's main narrative moments: the interviews with Presco, Mr Lee, Mr Fong, Mrs Chan, Amy, Henry, Frankie, George, Jenny, the old man.

Jo continues speaking. He is back in his cab. The windscreen reflects street scenes. 'The problem with me is I believe what I see and hear. If I believe that with Mr Chan, I'll know nothing because everything is so contradictory. Here's a picture of Chan Hung'. We see a photo of a somewhat overweight Asian male, smiling, a second man in the shadows, then a shot from Chan's apartment where the missing picture once hung. With these lines Jo stops speaking. Pat Suzuki begins to sing 'Grant Avenue' and the screen once again fills with images from Chinatown (old men and women on the sidewalk, haggard, faded brick apartment buildings, torn curtains blowing through broken-out windows):

> They call it Grant Avenue, San Francisco, California, USA. Look for Chinatown. You travel there in a trolley, up you climb, dong-dong, you're in Hong Kong, having yourself a time. Sharkfin soup, beancake fish, the girl who serves you your food is a dish, you know you have a Grant Avenue way of living. That's where it's at. San Francisco, California, USA. A western street with eastern manners, tall pagodas with golden banners, you can shop for precious jade, or silk brocade, or see a bold and brassy night club show on the most exciting thoroughfare I know they call it Grant Avenue, San Francisco, USA.

The viewer's ears are flooded with the sounds of these American Chinatown stereotypes, which are undercut by Wang's old men and women staring into the camera. Leaving these contradictory images in the viewer's field of vision, the film cuts to its credits.

Biting parody and pastiche, this film satirizes what it imitates and critiques, the 'neatly plotted oriental mystery' (Winsten, 1982), the 'Charlie Chan Orientals' (Rickey, 1982). Its jumbled, collage- and pastiche-like mosaic structure refuses to imitate the Chan mystery tradition which it draws upon. *Chan is Missing*, with its absent protagonist, is like Welles' *Citizen Kane* (1941), Reed's *The Third Man* (1949) and an Antonioni philosophical puzzle (*Blow-Up, The Passenger*). The 'mystery evaporates in the face of the uncertainty of knowing anything for sure' (Denby, 1982: 72). Jo, like the investigative protagonists in *The Third Man* and *Citizen Kane*, is more interested in discovering who Chan *was* than in either getting his money back or finding the real missing man. With *Citizen Kane* the film is a story of contradiction. 'The riddle, not the solution is the point' (Gelmis, 1982: 11), the 'whodunit' dissolves into a 'whoisit' (Horton, 1982), a discourse on the mystery that lies behind every life and the faces people wear. This is not a TV mystery, Jo muses, for if it was 'an important clue would pop up at this time and clarify everything'. Yet much is revealed, for the many-sided Chan Hung becomes the perfect metaphor for the many-sided, complex Chinese-American community (Denby, 1982: 72).

It matters little if the plot reveals a murder, a gun, a missing photo and set of clothes that may or may not have been connected to Chan's disappearance. These absences and occurrences tell us, as Jo says to Steve, to 'use the negative to emphasize the positive', and to look into the puddle to find ourselves. What is absent is present, and what is present lacks substance, and hence is absent.

As parody and spoof *Chan is Missing* refuses the utopian fantasies of the Orientalizing Chan series. Its multi-voiced (polyphonic) text isolates

Chinatown from San Francisco's version of American society, and offers no assimilationist solution to the Asian-American experience. Indeed the film suggests that Chinatown has enough problems of its own. It does not need to be part of the larger society which demands conformity to America's version of the Asian other. Racism is right here, at home, with Asians who hurl racist epithets at one another (two-faced schizophrenic Chinaman, jade-faced rich old men, FOBS). No heroes or heroines are here. There are no stars, no cultural models, for every model is a stereotype and every stereotype itself a stereotype. Here in Chinatown there are no perfect Western others who would stand as a measure of the Asian self. This self has become so thoroughly westernized no otherness is any longer possible. That is why 'Chan is missing'.

At the centre of the film are multiple images of overlapping, conflicting, decentred circles of ethnic Asian-American identities: Chinese Richard Pryors, Chinese cooks singing 'Fry Me to the Moon', GQ-dressed young Asian males, young women dressed like American teenagers, sad old Asian men and women, brass Steve, philosophical Jo, quizzical Presco, and Chinese-American apple pie salesman George. These multiple identities do not cohere into a single structure, for every Asian-American finds him- or herself only by looking into Presco's puddle of muddy water. And this self which is reflected back is always missing, always different, for the next time I look I will look different. It's always a different puddle.

No successful sleuths, no masters of mystery, but a mystery is solved. In the film's odd, idiosyncratic way it confronts its own spectacle of discovery. This occurs when Jo realizes that he is 'not Chinese enough'. He can't accept a mystery without a solution. He now understands that his problem is that 'I believe what I see and hear. If I believe that with Mr Chan I'll know nothing because everything is so contradictory'.

Three puzzles are solved. Jo discovers that you cannot be Chinese enough. You can no longer use the negative to emphasize the positive. And, you must believe more than you can see or hear. If you only believe what you can see and hear then you are confined, like Charlie Chan's pragmatic voyeur, to a world of solid facts. In Jo's 'pure' Oriental-Chinese world there are no solid facts, only mysteries, puzzles and things that are not there. By not being Chinese enough, Jo recognizes the failure and poverty of the Charlie Chan orientalizing project. This project, which uses the negative to emphasize the positive, creates a world where Chinese men make American apple pies, and, as George argues, 'take the good things from our background, and the good things from this country to enhance our lives'. This produces Steve's world where that 'identity shit becomes old news, something that happened 10 years ago'.

That old news was not news to Rogers and Hammerstein. On their (and Ethel Merman's) Grant Avenue, San Francisco, USA you can still have yourself a time, sharkfin soup, China dolls, precious jade, and silk brocade. And so the film, *Flower Drum Song* (1961), which contained Rogers and Hammerstein's song, is now critiqued in Wang's last gesture.

There are no flower drum songs, wise Asian patriarchs, obedient sons and daughters and arranged marriages in his Chinatown, or on his Grant Avenue, San Francisco, California, USA.

Here at the end of the film as viewers stare at the blank space on the wall where Chan Hung's picture once hung, they are told to accept a mystery without a solution. The old world that Charlie Chan inhabited no longer exists. Chan is not missing. Chan is dead. And in that death dies the Oriental sleuth, the ever-present Oriental eye, always ready to solve a crime for the Western other. Wang's message is clear. To the Americans in his audience he says, 'We have enough problems of our own. Stop asking us to help you solve your crimes. We did that for too long and look at where it got us'.

Leonard Zelig and Charlie Chan

Just minutes into Woody Allen's supremely reflexive and historical film *Zelig* (1983) Irving How informs the audience that Leonard Zelig's story 'reflected the nature of our civilization, the character of our times, yet it was also one man's story. Zelig's case reflected the Jewish story in America – he wanted to assimilate like crazy' (Sobchack, 1991: 344). In making this point Allen presents Leonard in a variety of different human disguises. We are told that this 'curious little man spoke with the Boston accent of Coolidge and the Republicans . . . later the same year he turned up on the southside of Chicago as a tough looking coloured boy playing a trumpet, and two months later Eugene O'Neill traced his whereabouts to Chinatown, where a strange oriental fitting Zelig's description tried to pull off a disguise. This man was taken to the hospital where he spoke authentic Chinese'.

The end of Zelig's story is of course familiar. Cured by the love of his psychoanalyst-wife, Eudora Fletcher, Leonard and Eudora lived full happy lives together. Leonard's episodes of character change grew less and less frequent, and eventually his malady disappeared completely. On his death-bed he announced that 'the only annoying thing about dying was that he had just begun reading Moby Dick and wanted to see how it came out'.

Psychoanalysis cured Leonard's character disorder, for the desire to assimilate, is, according to Woody Allen, a disorder, or a disease of the self. In it the unique, personal, sacred structures of the self are destroyed. This destruction of self is, he claims, the disease of our culture, for the desire to fit in has produced a nation of chameleons, persons constituted and shaped under the Orientalizing, surveillance gaze of a homogeneous, all-seeing, powerful other.

Being a detective in the Western mould cured Charlie, for his illness was the one of being different, being the alien, the Oriental other who was cured by Orientalism. All of those old films taught him how to fit in, to become a chameleon, an American imitation of the wise Asian patriarch. What those films taught was clear. In order to fit in the Asian-American was asked to assume a very specific identity, the identity of the rational, investigative other who solved crimes committed by the superior American.

It is no accident that the sciences of psychoanalysis and criminal detection come together at the end of this chapter. The practitioners of each are committed to an agenda of assimilation, to helping troubled, violent, crazed, pained individuals find their proper place in the social order. Each practitioner is committed to making rational sense out of the irrational, and as pragmatic voyeurs, each is committed to restoring order and sanity out of disorder, insanity and violence. Each of these sciences is predicated on the assumption that nothing is without meaning: the skilled voyeur can discover meaning where others see none.

Wayne Wang will have none of this. He destroys the Chinese mystery which has assimilated the Western assumption that all mysteries can be solved, that all things mean something. When Jo finally accepts that mysteries may not be solved he comes to understand that it is possible to live in a world which is irrational, disorderly and without closure. In such a world assimilation becomes an impossible dream. The self that dreams of fitting-in loses itself, and in the end, while seemingly alive, is not only missing, but also dead.

I turn now to the obsessive male gaze in the classic period. The classic mid-century male voyeurs had no need for Charlie Chan's pragmatic voyeurism. Their investigative gaze was repressed, sexual and aimed, almost always, to personal, not social ends. And this phobia of the mid-century voyeur, which would be carried over into the postmodern period (see Chapter 7) is narcissistic. It flees from its own image which shatters in the reflection from the mirror. Re-doing Narcissus's flight from reality, this voyeur returns to the mirror, hoping to find there the reflection of a unified self that will tell the truth about identity and the world (the face in the puddle of water). But this flight from reality is doomed. Undone, perhaps like Narcissus, by the lost gaze of the mother, the postmodern voyeur retreats into fragmentation and illness. Nothing is any longer certain, except uncertainty.[20]

Charlie Chan, the epitome of the pragmatic voyeur, is indeed dead. In his place emerges the uncertain, tentative new voyeur, Wayne Wang's Jo. A voyeur who understands that all mysteries are really about identity and the inability to ever know oneself, or the other. The male voyeurs studied in the next chapter have yet to learn this lesson.

Notes

1 Hanke (1989: 83) also suggests that the film was an attempt to 'cash in on the then prevalent vogue of operatic subjects brought on by the brief popularity of Grace Moore and Lily Pons, not to mention *A Night at the Opera* with the Marx Brothers'.

2 Directed by Wayne Wang; screenplay by Wayne Wang, Isaac Cronnin, Terrel Seltzer; cast: Wood Moy (Jo), Marc Hayashi (Steve), Laureen Chew (Amy), Judy Mihei (lawyer), Peter Wang (Henry), Presco Tabios (Presco), Frankie Alarcon (Frankie), Ellen Yeung (Mrs Chan), George Woo (George), Emily Yamasaki (Jenny), Roy Chan (Mr Lee), Leong Pui Chee (Mr Fong); Wayne Wang Productions, 1981, New Yorker Films, 1989.

3 Directed by H. Bruce Humberstone; produced by John Stone; screenplay by Scott Darling and Charles S. Belden from a story by Bess Meredyth, based on the character Charlie Chan created by Earl Deer Biggers; Twentieth-Century Fox release. Cast: Warner Oland, Boris Karloff, Keye Luke, Charlotte Henry, Thomas Beck, Margaret Irving, Gregory Gaye, Nedda Harrigan, Frank Conroy, Guy Usher, William Demarest.

4 Directed by Norman Foster; produced by Sol. M. Wurtzel; screenplay by Philip MacDonald and Norman Foster; cast: Peter Lorre, Ricardo Cortez, Virginia Field, John Carradine, George Sanders. Released by Twentieth-Century Fox, 1939.

5 According to Hanke (1989: 82–3) this is the Chan film most admired, even 'by people who are not fans of the series on the whole', while the Moto film is an 'exceptional example of the "B" mystery film' (1989: 255–6).

6 To repeat, the *whodunit* contains two stories, the crime, and the story of its detection. The killer kills for personal, not professional, reasons. The detective is seldom in danger. The *thriller* merges the crime with its detection, has little mystery, the detective's life is in danger and the killer kills for professional reasons. Violent passions and violent crime are the subject matter as the story moves through the phases of danger, pursuit and combat resolution. *Suspense* fiction merges the mystery with the whodunit, focuses action on the past and the future, and may deal with a vulnerable detective (his or her self-weaknesses) and even make the detective a suspect (see Todorov, 1977: 51). The thriller often merges into the *adventure-spy story*, with action located in the marvellous, or exotic, locale.

7 A figure who would be reincarnated as the evil *Dr No* (1962), the first of the James Bond movies. In an effort to traffic in the attention given to 'Yellow Peril' fears of the 1920s Warner Brothers introduced Torchy Blane, the 'Yellow Haired Peril' who starred in some nine films between 1937 and 1939, including *Torchy Blane in Chinatown*. Glenda Farrell played Torchy in all but two of these films (see Pitts, 1979, Chapter 17). Stanford Lyman (in correspondence) argues that Chan would emerge as the reverse mirror image of Fu Manchu. While each is possessed with uncanny oriental cunning, Charlie represents, at one level, the tamed Oriental spirit working in the service of the Occident, while Fu Manchu is the 'Yellow Peril' to the Occident. On another level, when compared to his sons, Charlie is the unassimilated oriental, and his sons caricatures of assimilation. Lyman also suggests that Chan's sons are really social isolates, seeking to be recognized as fully-fledged Americans, who also possess their father's oriental skills. Significantly, the sons are often aligned with Charlie's African-American chauffeur who embodies the 'coon' image of the black male.

8 Higashi (1991: 124) and Lyman (1990a: 154–9) present critical interpretations of the forms of institutional racism applied to Asians in the United States. As Higashi notes, racism merged with nationalism 'in hysteria about the Yellow Peril. Japan's stunning victory in the Russo-Japanese War in 1905 threatened America's investment in an Open Door policy in China and impelled novelist Jack London . . . to preach white supremacy. California legislation segregated Japanese students and prohibited the Japanese from becoming naturalized citizens or landowners. Anti-Asian riots erupted all along the West Coast' (1991: 124). Chinese wives were prohibited from entering the country. Chinatowns emerged as racial ghettos, slums, 'whose tinseled streets and brightly lit shops barely camouflage a pocket of poverty in the metropolis' (Lyman, 1990a: 158).

9 In the early 1970s the Chan movies would become staples on American television and 'suddenly found themselves the center of a new cult, part of the general craze for nostalgia of the thirties and forties. As a result they were repackaged [and] their television licensing fee skyrocketed' (Everson, 1972: 80). David Desser (in conversation) reports that during the 1970s these films were not shown in Los Angeles or New York. I watched them in the San Francisco Bay Area in the late 1960s. During the years 1972 to 1974 CBS-TV ran a 30-minute Hanna-Barbera cartoon, *The Amazing Chan and the Chan Clan* which involved Charlie and

his ten children who had a rock band (Chan Children's Rock Band), solving crimes and playing rock music (Pitts, 1979: 66). In the 1990s the Chan films are routinely available in any of the large chain video rental stores, often as a set. The Key Videos Charlie Chan Collection, for example, includes seven Chan films (*Murder Over New York, Charlie Chan in Rio, Charlie Chan at the Opera, Charlie Chan in Paris, Charlie Chan at the Wax Museum, Castle in the Desert* and *Charlie Chan's Secret*) 'with special case dossier packaging, including a list of suspects and their motives, allowing for interactive video viewing'.

10 There were 45 Charlie Chan movies made between the years 1929 and 1949 (see Penzler, 1977: 50–1). Stanford Lyman (in correspondence) notes Chan was played once by a Japanese actor in a silent film in the 1920s, but subsequently the character was given to a white European or American actor. However, Charlie Chan's sons were always played by Chinese-American actors (Key Luke, Benson Fong, Victor Sen Yung). Warner Oland starred as Chan, the famous Chinese-Hawaiian sleuth, in 16 of these films (1931–8), Sidney Toler in 22 (1939–46), Roland Winters in six (1947–9) and Warner Baxter in the first (1929). Keye Luke and Benson Fong alternated playing Charlie's Number One Son in the series while Mantain Moreland played the part of the traditionally scared negro chauffeur (Everson, 1972: 79). The series was based on the character of the same name developed by Earl Derr Bigger in a series of six novels beginning in 1925 (Penzler, 1977: 50). The Mr Wong series was based on the 'exploits of Chinese sleuth James Lee Wong, who was created by Hugh Wiley in a series of stories in *Collier's* magazine' (Pitts, 1979: 207). Boris Karloff played Mr Wong in five of the six films in the series (1938–40). I will not discuss the Mr Wong series, except to note that the character was modelled after Sherlock Holmes, in his ability to deduce a great deal from a small number of clues. He conducted all of his interrogations 'with flawless good manners. His only concession to Oriental characteristics was a minimum of slant-eye make-up, blackened and greased-down hair, and . . . a calm imperturbability in the face of all disasters' (Everson, 1972: 82). He was paired (after Holmes) with a brash, bumbling, loud detective (Captain Street).

11 To my knowledge neither crime fiction nor Hollywood has created a female version of the Chan figure, who was satirized (finally) by Peter Sellers (as Sidney Wang) in Neil Simon's *Murder by Death* (1976). Richard Narita played Number Two Son, Willie Wang (Pitts, 1979: 67). The series was also spoofed in the 1981 release, *Charlie Chan and the Curse of the Dragon Queen* with Peter Ustinov's 'decidedly Roland Winters-styled Charlie' (Hanke, 1989: 260). Also see Goode (1982a, b; 1983 a, b, c) for a history of the Asian in mystery fiction, and Hanke (1989: xv–xvi) for a brief discussion of attacks on the Chan series from Chinese groups. Lyman (in correspondence) notes, however, that Anna May Wong played the title role in the 1932 film, *The Daughter of Fu Manchu*.

12 The title of Wayne Wang's 1982 film, to be discussed below.

13 It is relevant, in this context, to examine the history of modern Chinese cinema during this time, and to compare Hollywood's representations of the Asian-other with those produced by Chinese filmmakers. Chinese cinema during the 1929–49 period was committed to a humanistic, social realism 'motivated by a concern for the plight of the Chinese people' (K. Lee, 1991: 8). Hsiung-Ping (1991), in an interesting comparison of the Hong Kong and Taiwanese film industries, observes that by the 1980s Hong Kong filmmakers were committed to making films based on the American version of the violent, urban, macho male cop, skilled in kung fu and the martial arts. In contrast, Taiwanese filmmakers were more committed to films reflecting a nostalgia for China's rural, pastoral past (see also Lau, 1991). Two early American films (noted by Stanford Lyman) that are relevant for the study of Asian imagery in American films are *Broken Blossoms* (1919) and *The Bitter Tea of General Yen* (1933).

14 Springer (1991: 168) suggests that this system persists to the present day, in what she calls 'third-world investigation films' which merge the action-adventure genre (the Indiana Jones series) with the reporter-film genre (*The Year of Living Dangerously, The Killing Fields*). In such films the hero is surrounded 'with cliched signifiers of the third world as mysterious, inscrutable, exotic, sensual, corrupt, and dangerous' (Springer, 1991: 168).

15 This is a version of what Stuart Hall (1981: 36–7) calls 'inferential racism'.

16 Of course in the Chan series Number One Son played the part of the immature,

irrational, childish Asian, yet even this conduct was neutralized, by having Charlie act as the traditional-white-paternal father figure.

17 Lilli with Gravelle, the crazed maniac, Whitely, the ineffective upper-class male, and Enrico, the effete canary (so labelled by the Demarest character); Anita with Enrico the betraying husband, manipulated by Lilli; Kitty with Phil, the traditional compliant, nurturing husband-to-be.

18 Typically, the thriller insists on fusing story and plot, crime and investigation, the criminal and the investigator (Todorov, 1977: 47).

19 'There's a game I play [a man gets into his cab] "Hey, what's a good place to eat in Chinatown?" Under three seconds, that question comes up under three seconds 90 per cent of the time. I usually give them my routine on the difference between mandarin and cantonese food and get a good tip.'

20 This reading was suggested by an earlier reviewer of this chapter. On narcissism and the gaze of the voyeur see de Lauretis (1987: 51–69), Silverman (1992: 127) and Clough (1992: 38).

5

FLAWED VISIONS: THE OBSESSIVE MALE GAZE

To see you is to love you, and I see you everywhere. To see you is to want you and I sce you all the time . . . and you're never out of sight . . . and I'll see you in the same old dreams tonight.

Bing Crosby, lyrics from 'To See You is to Love You' in *Rear Window*

We've become a race of Peeping Toms.

Stella to Jeff, in *Rear Window*

The camera hidden behind a keyhole is a tell-tale eye which captures what it can. But what about the rest? What about what happens beyond the limits of vision?

Antonioni, *Blow-Up, a Film by Michelangelo Antonioni*, p. 11

They don't mean anything when I do them (his paintings) – just a mess. Afterwards I find something to hang onto . . . . And then it sorts itself out. It adds up. It's like finding a clue in a detective story.

Bill, the painter, describing his paintings to Thomas, the photographer, in *Blow-Up*

In this chapter I examine the obsessive male gaze of the photographer, the photo-journalist and the amateur detective during Hollywood's classic and postwar period (1946–66). I focus on two key texts, Hitchcock's *Rear Window* (1954),[1] and Antonioni's *Blow-Up* (1962),[2] which offer (respectively) modernist and late modernist conceptions of this figure.

The voyeurs (Jeff and Thomas) are both photographers who set out to document and solve crimes discovered through their unwarranted, voyeuristic activities.[3] One of the two (Jeff) is called a Peeping Tom, and the other's name (Thomas) is clearly connected to this voyeuristic label (see Rifkin, 1982: 107, 187; also Huss, 1971a, b). Each suspects (and uncovers) a crime through photographic enlargement. The two photographers each 'shot' a murderer (and his victim, or traces of the victim) with their camera. Both men are bored and distracted by everyday life. Jeff, like Thomas, resists commitment to a permanent, intimate relationship. Thomas, like Jeff, desires to be elsewhere (Thomas: 'I've gone off London this week. Doesn't do anything for me . . . . Wish I had tons of money, then I'd be free'), and neither appears able to complete a project or a task.

Both men discover that the search for visual truth can be dangerous, and wrestle with the problems of involving themselves in the lives of those they photograph. Each man faces his own impotence. Jeff ultimately acts to save his own (and Lisa's) life, but Thomas remains unable to involve himself in his own, or another's life (Samuels, 1971: 18). Each uses his photographic skills to see more than the human eye is supposed to see. They both confuse reality with fantasy, and each resists going to the police. The two photographers violate the private space of others (including the private space of an intimate couple in the public spaces of a park) and are overly cocky concerning their right to do this. Each pays a price for this obsession, including doubting his own sanity.

Here the similarity ends, although Antonioni's film has been connected to Hitchcock's project and one reviewer (Crowther, 1967) explicitly recalled *Rear Window* in his review (see also Alpert, 1967: 303; and Samuels, 1971: 17 for a rebuttal of this reading). Hitchcock's voyeur captures reality and proves a crime. Antonioni's photographer finds reality slip through his fingers and all proof of a crime disappears and he is left with the conclusion that reality is but an illusion. Jeff finds his worst fears confirmed. A murder really did occur. Thomas learns that reality will always elude him. Real murders can occur, but never be proven. His photographic art can never be more than an illusion (see Rifkin, 1982: 106).

The Voyeur's Agenda

As argued earlier (Chapter 2, pp. 55–7), the early and late modernistic voyeur pursues a personal, often sexual, agenda, which may have positive, altruistic investigative overtones. The goal is first personal and then social. If a crime is solved that is fine, but the initial impulse for the gaze is personal desire. This desire must be controlled, or suppressed and re-coded in acceptable, social terms. The modernist gaze is, accordingly, shrouded in noble terms, but underneath it is prurient and self-serving. The personal (sexual) desires it brings are repressed and guilt rides alongside the pleasures derived by this gaze. In some instances the voyeur is presented as a diseased, or disturbed individual. The persistence of this gaze, in all its forms (journalistic, photo-journalist, detective, erotic, psychoanalytic), reveals a commitment to a larger cultural project.

Mid-century American politicians were obsessed with Communism, the 'Red' scare, spies and subversive internal threats to democracy (see Bell, 1960).[4] The FBI and the police (social scientists and journalists too) were granted (and seized) greater authority to pry and probe into the private lives of American citizens. This gaze was organized under the premise that no citizen should have anything to hide. Hence those who resisted the gaze must be guilty of something. Guilt about being gazed upon was generalized back to those who did the gazing. The gazes of the official surveillance agents of the society were repressed, furtive, indirect and laden with guilt. The person who gazed could also be the gazed upon.

In film after film Hollywood implemented this reciprocal guilt-ridden, repressive surveillance structure of looking. Film noir detectives, J. Edgar Hoover FBI agents, psychoanalysts, journalists, cold war spies, and not-so-innocent citizens looking on their neighbours each embodied the repressive 1950s surveillance code.[5] Voyeurs were everywhere, and nowhere. Hollywood normalized this gaze. At the same time the eye of television entered American homes and gazing into the lives of others became a primetime recreational family activity.[6]

Hitchcock's Voyeur

This is the space that the mid-century voyeur enters. Hitchcock is the voyeur's director (see Spoto, 1983; Modleski, 1988: 1; Leitch, 1991: 169). He was obsessed throughout his career with the gaze (Rothman, 1982) in all its forms: erotic, illicit, investigative, political, psychoanalytic, accidental. In film after film he took up the gaze of the innocent bystander (*The Man Who Knew Too Much*, 1934, 1956), the spy (*The Thirty-Nine Steps*, 1935; *The Secret Agent*, 1936; *Sabotage*, 1936; *Foreign Correspondent*, 1939; *Saboteur*, 1942; *Notorious*, 1946; *North by Northwest*, 1959; *Torn Curtain*, 1966; *Topaz*, 1969 (see Simone, 1982)), the young child (*Shadow of a Doubt*, 1943), the sexual predator (*Shadow of a Doubt*; *Psycho*, 1960; *Frenzy*, 1972), the murderer (*Strangers on a Train*, 1954; *Rear Window*, 1954; *Dial M for Murder*, 1954), the innocent man (*The Wrong Man*, 1957), the obsessed detective (*Vertigo*, 1958), the psychoanalyst (*Spellbound*, 1954), the priest (*I Confess*, 1952), the 'paranoid' woman (*Rebecca*, 1940; *Suspicion*, 1941), and the 'Peeping Tom' (*Rear Window*; *Psycho*).

Perhaps the most cinematic, and most imitated, of directors (Sharff, 1991: 7), Hitchcock's gaze was murderous (Rothman, 1982), violent (*Psycho*), patriarchal (*Shadow of a Doubt*, *Vertigo*), and incestuous (*Psycho*), his voyeur both predator (*Strangers on a Train*) and preyed upon (*Rear Window*, *Notorious*). His topics: sin, confession, guilt (Rohmer and Chabrol, 1979/1988: 8), murder and marriage (Jameson, 1990: 103–4), violence, and the contingent dangers that define daily life in urban America (see Jameson, 1990: 110), San Francisco (*Family Plot*, *Vertigo*), Quebec City (*I Confess*), Phoenix (*Psycho*), Bodega Bay (*The Birds*), small town Vermont (*The Trouble with Harry*), Harlem (*Topaz*), London (*The Man Who Knew Too Much*), East Germany (*Torn Curtain*), Chicago (*North by Northwest*), or the French Riviera (*To Catch a Thief*). At this level his films may be read as allegories, philosophical treatments of basic ontological issues concerning life and its deeper meanings (see Jameson, 1990: 103–4).

His films follow a predictable format, typically combining the elements of a thriller, including chase scenes, with a male–female romance (see Brill, 1988: 5), where the male may have to prove his worthiness (and love) to the female. The police and the legal system function as sources of anxiety for the Hitchcock protagonist who is always pursuing something (a clue, a document, a secret plan, the identity of a killer, etc.), what Hitchcock (Truffaut, 1984: 138) called the 'MacGuffin'. The Hitchcock plots hinge on suspense and coincidence, the protagonist happens to be in the wrong place at the wrong time, and this twist of circumstance (and fate) places him or her in danger, often a figure chased both by the police and the villains.

Tension and anxiety fill every Hitchcock frame, where a delicate balance of apprehension, anxiety and certainty turn on what the protagonist (and audience) knows and does not know. The dramatic locus of many of the Hitchcock films made between 1940 and 1964 is, as Weis (1982: 107) notes, concerned less with external reality and more with the mind, a character's subjective point of view and how it distorts and misinterprets reality and its events. This introduces a high level of emotionality into the text, as the audience is inevitably drawn into the protagonist's visual situation, his or her misinterpretations of that situation, and the seen and unseen dangers that lurk there.

The text, with its frequent separation of what is heard (the soundtrack), from what is seen, produces, as in *Rear Window*, a richly 'asynchronous and subjective' (Weis, 1982: 108) experience for the viewer. Indeed, in many of his films (but especially *Rear Window*) all of the music is source music, although 'the source [other sounds as well] is not always identified' (Weis, 1982: 110). The Hitchcock camera, every cut, gives information, barely supplemented by dialogue. But the information, which is conveyed by purely visual means, is often coded through the masculine eye.

The subject of considerable controversy within feminist film theory, Hitchcock has been read (correctly) as a misogynist (Modleski, 1988: 5, 120–1; Keane, 1988: 231–2) and a director who inevitably turned women into 'passive objects of male voyeuristic and sadistic impulses' (Modleski, 1988: 1–2; Mulvey, 1989; Wood, 1989). His films are widely regarded as texts which present women as subjects who fulfil the desires of 'and express the anxieties of men in the audience' (Modleski, 1988: 2). By implication Hitchcock only offers women a masochistic relationship to his films. Hitchcock's articulation of 'patriarchal consciousness' often creates the image of the female as victim, predator, or monstrous other who devours the male subject.

Re-Reading Hitchcock's Gaze

Read thusly, the Hitchcock film, and *Rear Window* specifically, are seen as presenting a single, solitary gaze, the gaze of the predatory, sexual male voyeur. This is a simplistic reading, for multiple gazes and glances operate in the Hitchcock text, glances which not only shift from voyeur to voyeur (spy, child, victim, villain), but vary by gender (*Vertigo, Marnie, The Trouble with Harry*), level of psychic consciousness (for example, the Dali dream-sequences in *Spellbound*), the technological-visual apparatus that is deployed (cameras, telescopes, the naked eye), and the relationship between the voyeur and the subject gazed upon (*Vertigo* versus *Shadow of a Doubt*). Hitchcock's gaze is loving, predatory, violent, inquisitory, innocent; not just sexual and sado-masochistic.

More centrally, multiple 'scopic regimes', as discussed earlier (see Chapter 1, note 32; also Foster, 1988: 1) structure Hitchcock's gazing camera. These regimes range from the realist, coldly analytic Cartesian look of the camera as it circles Jeff's apartment in the opening moments of *Rear Window*, to the fragmented, Baconian empiricist glances around Marion's hotel room in Phoenix, to the rich, Baroque, soft-focused depictions of the bedrooms and homes in *Marnie*, to the hysterical, nightmare visions of *Marnie*, *Rear Window*, *The Birds* and *Spellbound*. These multiple visual regimes complicate the voyeur's gaze, making it multi-dimensional, creating many, often contradictory, visual spaces for the spectator. These multiple spaces complicate Hitchcock's depiction of women and contribute to his simultaneously sympathetic and misogynistic treatments of them (see Modleski, 1988: 5).[7]

These visual regimes display Hitchcock's simultaneous commitment to two principles and two pleasures. The camera must fulfil the spectator's desire to indulge in the pleasures of scopic gazing (the Peeping Tom's desire) but these desires must be channelled into a larger project, the extraction of moral truth from a situation. Hitchcock's camera, as Gunning (1988: 41) observes of early cinema, must stand as an authority, a 'means of ascertaining truth . . . the camera as detective unmasks villainy, or impropriety through an explosion of truth, providing the film with narrative closure in which punishment is more than a comic attraction'. Thus do Hitchcock's films simultaneously punish, please, reveal truth and act as a moral authority.

His visual texts are complex fields. They embody and extend prior treatments of the voyeur and the ideological practices surrounding the point-of-view (POV) shot. These practices, as noted in the Introduction, moved from the simple non-diegetic POV shot directed to the spectator, to the classic POV shot in the service of scopic pleasure (Gunning, 1988: 41), to the POV shot which is entangled with the causal structures that organize an unfolding narrative. Hitchcock's use of the POV shot encompasses each of these visual traditions.

Into *Rear Window*

Answering Lisa, who said to Jeff, 'Tell me what you see and what you think it means' I read *Rear Window* as an ode to voyeurism. At the same time it speaks to the impoverished, anomic character of mid-century urban American life. In this world there are no neighbours, only strangers who live in the same buildings with one another. Prescient in its vision, it announces the further extension and elaboration of Foucault's panopticon into urban American culture. It enunciates a postmodern epistemology where things are real if they appear to be real (Baudrillard, 1983a: 146).

The voyeur's gaze in *Rear Window*, like Foucault's panopticon, functions in this private prison as a warden's look, protecting people from each other and discovering private crimes that would otherwise remain hidden (see Stam and Pearson, 1983: 197). This gaze is cold and analytic, it reads surfaces not depths. It has no need to probe the inner subjective life of the people who are gazed upon. It presumes that visual knowledge produces, and is even the same as, intersubjective understanding. In this world of dramaturgical appearances people are who they appear to be: Miss Lonely Heart, Miss Torse, Lars Thorvald the murderer, the sex-crazed newly weds, the heart-broken composer, the bickering, unhappy couple with the daughter, the sad childless couple with the little dog who knew too much.

In answering Lisa's question I argue against other interpreters (Stam and Pearson, 1983: 205; Weis, 1982: 121; Leitch, 1991: 173) who read *Rear Window* as a cautionary tale for voyeurs, even a whole-hearted condemnation of prying and voyeurism. I agree with Wood (1989: 100–1) that the final effects of Jeff's voyeurism 'are almost entirely admirable'. After all, through Jeff's looking a murderer is discovered and a woman who might have committed suicide doesn't. But I dispute the widely-held argument (Wood, 1989: 101; Weis, 1982: 121; Stam and Pearson, 1983: 205) that the voyeur's voyeurism moves him out of a spiritual deadlock, which at the film's beginning had him confined to an anti-marriage, anti-community point of view. Instead I suggest that Jeff's apparent (and initial) anti-marriage position is purely ironic. Thus his statement to his editor, 'If I don't get back to the job soon, I'm going to do something drastic like get married', should be read as his having already begrudgingly accepted (or capitulated to) his real-life situation, namely he and Lisa are engaged. Bored, and tired of being confined to his apartment, he has no intention of getting married before he gets back on the job and into the field where danger lurks. Accordingly he brings danger into his apartment, through his living-room window.

At the film's end he is not where he was at the beginning, bored, unsettled, and anxious about making any commitment to Lisa. He has experienced danger. He has seen Lisa go into a life-threatening situation and come out alive 'I'm so proud of you, If anything had happened to you . . .'. He also proved that a murder happened. Granted, both legs in a cast, back turned to the courtyard, smile on his face, he appears to have given up his voyeurism for marriage to Lisa. In actuality he has kept his voyeurism and got a wife in the bargain. (His last words in the film are to Doyle (the detective), 'Now do you have enough for that warrant?') His smile is at least two-faced. Like the cat that caught the canary, he trapped Thorvald: no loss of face here. His smile also reflects Lisa's capitulation to his position. She is willing to become a woman of danger, even a woman who will read *Beyond the High Himalayas*! He has the best of both possible worlds.

Under this reading Jeff did not undergo a spiritual journey, and he did not experience a movement from passive voyeurism to emotional involvement. He was always emotionally involved with Lisa. His four-day rear window episode was merely a diversion from that commitment. His preoccupation with the bad marriages and relationships that exist in the apartment complex must be read ironically. They do not reflect deformed, sick relationships which are mirrors of what could happen were he to marry Lisa. These relationships, Hitchcock says, are what life is made up of: lonely people unable to communicate with one another. The little dramas across the way are ironic, bitter, sarcastic little Hitchcock jokes on the viewer. He tells men that they are lucky if they have a Lisa walk into their life, and any woman can be a Lisa if men will let her and if men will but hold up their end of the bargain.

This Jeff does, for in discovering a murdered woman across the way he issues a warning to all women trapped in relationships with violent men. But he learns that he cannot do this alone. (When he screams for help it is Lisa he calls for.) It takes a woman to save a man. This Lisa and Stella do. Jeff's smile at the film's end thus reflects Hitchcock's final joke on men. He was saved by Lisa, and her final smile represents her triumph over him.

It is this framework that structures my interpretation of *Rear Window* (for other perspectives see also, Bellour, 1977; Durgnat, 1974; Rothman, 1982: 206; Stam and Pearson, 1983; Weis, 1982: 107–24; Wood, 1965, 1989; Spoto, 1983; Jameson, 1990). I will argue that the film goes beyond a simplistic treatment of women as the passive object of the male gaze (for example, Mulvey's reading, but see Modleski, 1988: 77, 85). It is also more than a reflection of marriage from the male's point of view (Truffaut, 1984: 223) and it transcends Modleski's (1988: 85) argument that Lisa (as woman), has the last gaze.

This against-the-grain reading of *Rear Window* is supported by the following pivotal moments in the film. Ode to Voyeurism first: in order to support the above reading it is necessary to dismantle the argument that Jeff is the sole, or primary spectator (and voyeur) in *Rear Window*.

Through the Lens: But Where is the Rear Window?

Regarded by many as Hitchcock's most reflexive and cinematic text (Stam and Pearson, 1983: 193), *Rear Window* has been interpreted as a text which turns the voyeuristic protagonist (Jeff) into a reflexive stand-in for the spectator. That is, the Stewart character is a spectator who makes his own cinema (Stam and Pearson, 1983: 193). Read in this way the spectator is confined to seeing what Jeff sees. This naïve reading (see Spoto, 1976: 241; Wood, 1965: 65; 1989: 103) has been undermined by Modleski and Stam and Pearson, who emphasize those moments when Lisa, as aggressor, defines the visual field for the spectator. Furthermore, as Stam and Pearson note, 'Lisa, Stella and Doyle are all granted some point-of-view shots' (1983: 201).[8] Of course, as they note, Jeff's point of view does predominate in those shots 'correlated with the binoculars and telephoto lens, but many of the other shots might be more accurately described from the point of view of the rear window rather than Jeffries himself' (Stam and Pearson, 1983: 201).

But there is no rear window in *Rear Window*, the title is a typical, two-sided Hitchcock joke on the viewer; it teases and warns at the same time. Gazing at Jeff from across the courtyard the viewer discovers that his window, like all the windows, is a front window. The window we (and Jeff) look through is an eye, a camera obscura, 'what unfolds in the room on this side of the window is precisely the inverted image of what unfolds beyond the window of the flat on the opposite side of the courtyard – the Thorvald's flat' (Bozovic, 1992: 162). Jeff is trapped behind this giant eye, this window. He inhabits a world of imitations, copies, photographs of the real thing, never the thing itself (Bozovic, 1992: 163). 'The external world has become a spectacle in his eyes' (Bozovic, 1992: 162–3). As Lisa says, while lowering the shades, 'Show's over for tonight' and the show is being staged on both sides of the window.

It is apparent that Hitchcock titled his film *Rear Window* for at least two reasons. Peering through a rear window immediately implies voyeurism and Peeping Tomism. Jeff is given a visual standpoint which is absolute: he cannot see himself seeing himself, only we as viewers occupy this position. Jeff can only be a voyeur. The eye that looks cannot see itself looking. 'The eye can only see itself in the third eye's pupil.' Heeding Stella's advice, 'people ought to get outside their own house and look in for a change', Jeff seeks out a third eye that would return his gaze. And he is terrified when this happens.

Through his film's title Hitchcock asks the viewer to appropriate the identity of voyeur. But we are particular voyeurs, we return Jeff's gaze and see him as he cannot see himself. He becomes us when we are pure voyeurs. Hitchcock is subtle here. On the surface the viewer-as-voyeur looks out over the courtyard through Jeff's gaze: we see what he sees. In fact, though, the viewer (like Jeff) does not look through a rear window. With Jeff, the window shopper, we look out of his front window onto the doings across the way. At the same time we look (and eavesdrop) through his front window (so to speak) hearing and seeing the battles he and Lisa are having over marriage and career. The viewer, in this respect, follows Stella's injunction to Jeff, 'I smell trouble right in this apartment . . . . Look out that window, see things you shouldn't see'. The title, at this level, refers to the spectator's identity – we are the rear window. We are looking into the mirror called the rear window.

But the 'rear' in the title has other meanings as well. It also refers to 'raise up', to 'stir up', 'to dislodge from the covert'. What Hitchcock does is stir up and make overt what is covert (hidden) behind the front windows of the people who live in the apartment complex. Jeff's window, like a rearview mirror, is a mirror that shows what is behind the window-mirrors in the other apartments. His window is also perhaps the window of cinema, the lens of the camera, the window of the projection booth, where the eye, like film, is a window on the world (Stam and Pearson, 1983: 195). This window does more than reflect the world. It activates the world, stirs it up, makes it problematic.

What is really stirred up and made overt by this particular rear window are the arguments between Lisa and Jeff over marriage and Jeff's settling down and living the kind of life Lisa imagines for him.[9] Interpreted in this way, the title *Rear Window* describes the multiple, moving images and pictures of reality that originate, are erected, occur and come into being when one lifts the veils or curtains (blinds and shades) that separate the private from the public in daily life. As with the message on an automobile's rear window, Hitchcock cautions, 'objects in mirror are closer than they appear'.

The text is a multiplicity of last (and first) gazes, and a multiplicity of POV shots which adhere to Hitchcock's two rules and two principles. This multiplicity is given, then, not only in Lisa's last look, but also in the lives (and exchanged gazes and looks) of the people who inhabit the apartment building that Jeff gazes into. The building is itself the site of the three types of POV shots just outlined (non-diegetic, visual pleasure and mediated-narrative causality). Indeed, the subject of Jeff's gaze, I will argue, is really the apartment building and the multiple dwellings and lives it contains, especially Miss Torse and her body. (He just happened to focus on, and then become obsessed with Thorvald's apartment.)[10]

A Voyeur's Playground

It is necessary, then, to read Hitchcock's multiple gazes in *Rear Window* through a rear window, projecting ourselves into the building he gazes upon, and thereby seeing him through this reverse reflection (on this reversal of point of view see Gunning, 1988: 33). Looking back at Jeff, his apartment window, and ourselves as viewers-spectators, we see some 15 people whose lives and gazes define the Peeping Tom activities of Jeff. At the same time these individuals are also Peeping Toms, gazing at one another openly and furtively, confined inside the tiny worlds of experience Hitchcock has given them.

In the right-hand building are the composer and the couple with the daughter, all of whom are seen gazing out into the courtyard. In the building to the left are the newlyweds (who pull the shade on the voyeurs outside) and the lady with the pet bird. In the centre building are the sculptress, who attempts to chat with her neighbours, and her neighbour Miss Lonely Heart who entertains and engages men picked up at local bars. Miss Torse and the Thorvalds are on the next floor, and are repeatedly observed looking out of their windows, sometimes directly at Jeff. On the top floor are the two carefree, sunbathing party girls, the objects of a gaze from a helicopter which flies over the building. Immediately below them is the unhappy couple with the little dog that is killed.

This closed community, an anonymous little urban village which Hitchcock has created, is the antithesis of neighbourliness. Every neighbour is a potential threat (Stam and Pearson, 1983: 203). Fear of the alien, outside other unifies this fractured community into a whole, into an interactional structure where each person asks of the other (as Thorvald does of Jeff), 'What do you want from me? Tell me what you want!' At the same time each person exclaims, 'Leave me alone! Let me live my life alone. Keep out of my affairs!'

The voyeur's unwarranted gaze penetrates the fragile membrane that protects this community from itself. Jeff's passive and active gazing, while validated because he discovers a crime, are ultimately punished, for the voyeur, in the end, is trapped with a broken leg inside Lisa's spider web: and thus Hitchcock's ironic moral. Community has disappeared in mid-century American life. The voyeur contributes to that disappearance, but without this figure things would be even worse. At least he (or she) discovers crimes that would otherwise go unpunished.

As rear window, the spectator sees Jeff, even when he can't see himself. The spectator has the perfect, omniscient, omnipresent point of view. As all-knowing, objective observer we see everything, even Thorvald leave his apartment with the woman in black (Jeff is sleeping). Jeff's solitary control over the camera is shattered when the other figures in the film become drawn into his voyeuristic project. The authority of Jeff's visions (and his warrant to gaze) are also challenged on multiple occasions.

The Immoral Gaze

Stella and Lisa's early conversations with Jeff about being a 'Peeping Tom' represent the usual, normative and disapproving attitudes toward this activity. Stella tells him that we 'are becoming a race of Peeping Toms', and that 'such persons should have their eyes put out with red hot pokers'. Lisa suggests that people in his occupation think of themselves as a 'private little group of anointed people'. She calls him diseased, and says that he scares her, as she challenges his interpretations of what has happened in Thorvald's apartment, 'You could see all that he did?' She mocks Jeff's conduct, invoking the concept of 'Girl Friday' from the pulp private eye literature to describe how he wants her to help him. Later, as she embraces his project, she calls the two of them ghouls, 'We are two of the most frightening ghouls I've ever seen. We should be happy that the poor woman is alive and well. There is an old saying "Love Thy Neighbour"'.

Tom Doyle also challenges Jeff's project, offering perfectly plausible accounts of Thorvald's activities, including evidence that his wife is alive and well in Merrittsville. 'You've got a lot to learn about homicide' Tom tells Jeff, even suggesting that he is hallucinating, and uses the Bill of

Rights to deflect Jeff's requests for a search warrant. Rebuffing Jeff at another point, Doyle comments, 'Lars Thorvald is no more a murderer than I am. That's a secret private world out there. People do things in private that it wouldn't be possible to explain in public'.

Gazing at Miss Lonely Heart, as she prepares to host a male visitor, Jeff begins to doubt his own project, 'Pretty private stuff going on out there. I wonder if it's ethical to watch them with binoculars and a long-focused lens. Do you suppose it's ethical if you prove that he didn't commit a crime? Course they could do the same thing with me. Watch me like a bug under a glass'.

Displacing Jeff's Gaze: Stella and Lisa as Active Voyeurs

Stella and Lisa become progressively involved in Jeff's voyeuristic project. As this occurs they take turns using his binoculars and telephoto lens. They cannot resist the pull of Jeff's binocular gaze. The morning after the murder Jeff asks Stella to get his binoculars for him. Gazing into Thorvald's apartment he sees him with a knife and newspaper. Thorvald looks out his window and Stella tells Jeff to back up. The viewer sees Thorvald reflected in the lens of Jeff's binoculars. Feeling that he is safe, Thorvald removes his own glasses, stretches and lies down. Stella shares Jeff's gaze.

It is now the day after the little dog has been murdered. Jeff, Lisa and Stella take turns using the binoculars watching Thorvald wash down his bathroom walls. Jeff then has the two of them examine his slides of the yellow zinnias in the flower bed in the courtyard. Lisa and Stella go exploring and Lisa enters Thorvald's apartment. Back with Jeff, Stella watches Lisa, and then lowers her gaze to Miss Lonely Heart who has just laid out a series of pills to take. Stella sees a suicide in the making and tells Jeff to call the police, as Miss Lonely Heart hears the composer's finished song ('Lisa') played for the first time.

Stella and Lisa become co-investigative voyeurs, who displace, not supplement, Jeff's gaze. It is their feminine intuitions concerning Mrs Thorvald and her ring that lend authority to Jeff's interpretation of Thorvald's project. The female voyeur interprets what Jeff only sees. In this way their gaze comes to carry more power (and authority) than his. In this move Hitchcock shifts the power of Jeff's look into female hands (and eyes). Without Stella and Lisa's looks, Jeff's project could well have evaporated into fantasy, along with Thorvald's projected late-night exit from town.

Thorvald's Window

Jeff knows that those across the way could do the same to him, watch him 'like a bug under a glass'. And this is what Thorvald does. He reciprocates Jeff's gaze. A burning cigarette in the centre of Thorvald's window suddenly announces that someone is looking back at Jeff. This is not a perfect self-mirroring. Jeff does not see himself reflected in this third eye, he only sees 'the point of the gaze of the other, at the point from which the window itself looks back at him' (Bozovic, 1992: 169). And seeing this window looking at him, he reacts in terror. Until this point he has been the predator, the entomologist studying other bugs. He has been outside the frame of his own gaze. Now Thorvald's window looks back and Jeff is in the frame of that gaze, now he is the subject of another's look.

The window sees him, but he cannot see (only imagine) the look that lurks behind the glare of the burning cigarette. The other has seen him, or so he supposes, a gaze has suddenly appeared on the other side of the keyhole. ('Stella refers to Jeff's long-focus lens as a "portable keyhole"' (Bozovic, 1992: 170)). 'Being-seen-by-the-other is the truth of seeing-the-other' (Sartre, 1943/1956: 260; Bozovic, 1992: 168) and Jeff sees himself because somebody sees him.[11] This gazing eye, which is Thorvald's window, traps him, he has become the bug under the glass. He is now part of his own picture, spectator to his own spectacle. He has stepped into Thorvald's picture of him, the tables have turned. And soon Thorvald will throw him out of the window and as he falls he tumbles into the picture he has created, a defenceless voyeur falling into the arms of two women and the police.

No Neighbours

While Lisa reminds Jeff of the old saying, 'Love Thy Neighbour', it is clear that there are few, if any, loving neighbours in this neighbourhood. Hitchcock makes this point on many occasions. The newlyweds keep their blinds pulled. The bird-lady is never seen. The sculptress attempts a friendly overture to Thorvald and is rebuffed. The unhappy couple never talk to anyone. Miss Lonely Heart, until the very end of the film (when she listens with the composer to his completed song), has no friends. Jeff knows none of his neighbours, only Thorvald's name, address and telephone number. Indeed in this imaginary community, which Jeff has named, there are no friends.

Hitchcock dramatically makes his point about this absence of community on two specific occasions. The second scream in the night occurs when the wife of the childless couple discovers that their little dog is dead. She screams to the community, as persons look out of their windows, 'He's dead. Strangled! His neck is broken. Which one of you did it?' As she screams a voice is heard from a distant apartment, 'Something happened to the dog'. Another voice speaks, 'Somebody fell out of the window'. The wife continues, 'You don't know the meaning of the word neighbour! Neighbours like each other, speak to each other, care for each other, care if somebody lives or dies. But none of you do! I couldn't imagine any of you'd be so low you'd kill a helpless, friendly dog'. (Her husband hoists the dead dog up to their balcony as she speaks.) She continues, 'Did you kill him cause he liked you? Just because he liked you'. As she speaks people withdraw back into their apartments. The party in the composer's apartment continues, and a voice is heard, 'Let's go back to the party. It's only a dog'.

In this startling sequence Hitchcock is making a bitter point. Community has disappeared in America, and no one cares if a little dog is killed: no friends, no love here.

This conclusion is repeated in the film's penultimate scene. Jeff is hanging by his fingertips from his window ledge. Thorvald is trying to kill him. Jeff has just screamed, 'Lisa! Doyle!' In a quick sequence of shots Hitchcock cuts from Lisa and Doyle and the police, to the sculptress, the dog couple, Miss Lonely Heart and the newlyweds. A voice off-screen asks, 'What was that?' and another announces, 'Over in that apartment'. And still a third, 'Look at his leg, it's in plaster'. And Jeff falls to the ground, his fall partially blocked by Lisa, Stella and the police. The voices in the background return to their respective apartments. No more interest in Jeff's situation is evidenced.

Living and dying in Greenwich Village, Hitchcock's metaphor for modern urban America, here your friends (and lovers) don't live where you do, and if you have no friends (or lovers), nobody cares what happens to you. Your only hope is for that isolated, lonely, bored voyeur out there who might be keeping an eye on (and out for) you. But he (or she) will only know you as he sees you, for he will never talk to you and share in your intimate life details, except as he can see them through your kitchen, living-room, or bedroom window.

The Empty Eye: All-seeing, but Understanding Little

Rear Window is about reality and its misrepresentations. Jeff, as photographer-voyeur, carries Hitchcock's message that what we see may not be what we see, and we get ourselves in trouble when we think that the situations we have defined as real are in fact real in their consequences (Thomas and Thomas, 1928). The film, then, is a study in misperceptions, an analysis of the trouble we get into when we misinterpret events in terms of our own preconceptions (Weis, 1982: 107). The text is set up to prove and disprove Jeff's perceptions of reality. At the same time the story that is told involves the argument that visual knowledge does not equal understanding. A certain symmetry unites the stories that are told.

Each of the stories that Hitchcock's camera tells are given meaning through Jeff's interpretations. On the surface they are stories of love, death, illness, and the male–female relationship. Jeff and Mrs Thorvald are both invalids (ill) and victims 'of their mobile partners' (Bozovic, 1992: 162). Jeff doesn't want to marry Lisa, who nags him and Mrs Thorvald nags her husband. Miss Lonely Heart longs for a man in her life, as does Lisa (and apparently Miss Torse). The newlyweds make love all day and at the film's end are bickering, like the Thorvalds, and Jeff and Lisa. Thorvald wants to be rid of his wife, just like Jeff, on the surface, wants to be free of Lisa. This symmetry can be extended. Lisa 'crosses the courtyard to enter Thorvald's flat, and it is Thorvald who has come from the opposite side to Jeff's' (Bozovic, 1992: 162). Death also unites the stories. Miss Lonely Heart is about to commit suicide. The childless couple's dog, which is treated like a child, is killed, like Thorvald's wife. Jeff's gaze, supplemented by the work of Lisa and Stella, coincides with the happy endings that come to the other individuals in the film. Voyeurism is justified in the name of love, law and order.

The voyeur's project has been vindicated. But what does he know? Jeff knows, and has proved, that Thorvald killed his wife. He suspects a girlfriend in the background and explains the murder by reference to Mrs Thorvald being a nagging, invalid wife. But he does not know why Thorvald killed his wife. He thinks the composer is blocked with his new song because of a broken heart. In fact he finishes his song before a new love appears in his life – Miss Lonely Heart. Miss Lonely Heart is lonely because there is no man in her life (music not a man saves her). The newlyweds are sexual animals, doomed to failure once the erotic lure wears off. (In fact the bloom wears off when it is discovered that Harry quit his job.) Men can't keep their hands off Miss Torse, and she seems to desire, as an exhibitionist, constant male attention. (In fact she has a husband who returns at the end of the film.)

Each of these situations refute or undermine Jeff's prior interpretations of them. He has seen what he wants to see. While his visual perception has been invested with the power of truth (and justice), underneath it all he knows nothing. Hitchcock is quite explicit on this. As Jeff sleeps, back turned to the apartment complex, we as viewer, get one more look into the lives Jeff has constructed. In this last, final look, we see what he could not see. Here lies the truth of Hitchcock's text. Reality is constantly changing and surface appearances cannot reveal deep, inner truths about human relationships and human experience.

The camera and its lens can produce knowledge but not understanding. The voyeur's gaze endangers while it saves, and, as danger approaches, the voyeur's only recourse is in the technology that produced his voyeurism in the first place. This gaze, Jeff's feeble flashbulbs glaring off Thorvald's glasses, blind both him and his attacker. They cannot protect him from the consequences of having broken into the life of another. This technology simply exposes the Peeping Tom's ultimate vulnerability. As the flashes go off they finally expose Jeff, in his invalid status, to Thorvald. In this, Hitchcock says, in his demonic way, the voyeur deserves what he gets.

More is involved. Hitchcock is not content to conclude his argument with these simple observations. He wants us to understand that understanding is not seeing, and knowing something is not understanding it. Moreover, objects paraded before spectators, like the puppets in the little windows across the way, cannot be understood unless you enter directly into their lives. If you do not do this the truth that you proclaim will always be unstable and subject to error. Hitchcock's final message is not appealing. Gazing out at his version of mid-century America he argues that there is no way out of this situation. We have become a nation of strangers, dependent on anonymous voyeurs to save us from one another. Victims of a complex and sophisticated visual technology, we can see but not understand.

As voyeurs we have fooled ourselves. We are already in the pictures we create. In looking for, and at, the other, we look at ourselves. We are ceaselessly fascinated by our own presence, as given in the presence of the other. We seek, like Jeff, that moment when the other's gaze is announced behind the blank, dark window. That gaze defines our selfsame presence in the world, and herein lies Hitchcock's critique of voyeurism. As voyeurs we have no objective, external vantage point. We are already always in the picture. If we want to see ourselves, we only have to look at the object of our own gaze (see Bozovic, 1992: 175–6). This is Hitchcock's ode to voyeurism.

Out of the Window

This disturbing, reflexive, pivotal film closes the modernist period, even as it begins. Little more can be added to Hitchcock's project after *Rear Window*. He saw, through the rear window of this film, the complex, hyperreal, mass-mediated world that would become the topic, 30 years later, of the so-called postmodern theorists (see Denzin, 1991a). He saw a world where images would replace lived experience, and understandings would be produced by those who controlled the information technologies of a culture.

At the same time he transgressed the gender stratification system and made women co-equals and co-victims in this new social order. Stella and Lisa, pro-active feminists, women on the move, would not take a secondary, supplementary investigative position in their relationship to Jeff, the lone wolf male voyeur. They pushed him aside, and, unlike Sandy in David Lynch's *Blue Velvet*, would not lurk in the shadows honking the horn to alert their male hero of approaching danger. (Indeed Jeff performs this duty when Lisa invades Thorvald's apartment.)

So here at the end Hitchcock confronts a crisis that has yet to be resolved, by either cinema theory, social theory, or the contemporary filmmaker.

Enter *Blow-Up*

Now *Blow-Up*, an influential text (see Huss, 1971a; Rifkin, 1982), which can be interpreted as pushing Hitchcock's obsession with the camera's gaze to new levels.[12] As noted above (pp. 114–15) Thomas's camera records a real event (a murder), which at the film's end exists only as a memory, an image, a copy of the real thing. The real dead body has disappeared. The film, in part, is a series of photographs about a series of photographs (Freccero, 1971: 118). It is a self-reflexive text that meditates on its own textuality, asking what is real, and how is the real represented? It is a study of reality and its representations ('I'm really questioning the nature of reality', Antonioni, 1971: 14). It thus belongs to a long literary tradition, extending from Petrarch to Joyce and beyond, its subject is itself and 'the portrait of the artist is his [or her] act' (Freccero, 1971: 119). Antonioni's film is also a critique of a historical moment and its members, especially those voyeuristic members who have been given the right to make records of reality.

Filmed in 'Mod' London, in the halcyon days just before the Vietnam war protests, *Blow-Up* examines the manners, sexual morals and customs of the 'pre-hippie generation', the lifestyles of the young artists, models, trend-setters, dress designers, musicians and fashion photographers who partially inspired (and recorded) this international movement. Drug use and free love are recurring images in the film, but Antonioni's characters (Thomas, Jane, Patricia, Ron), like those in his other films (*L'Aventura, La Notte, L'Eclipse* and *The Red Desert*) (Samuels, 1971: 14–17) are trapped, in tiny, lonely existential dramas. Loveless, bored, exhibiting a paralysis of will, a loss of faith in anything, they are on an indifferent modernist quest for new experience. Few (if any) undergo radical self-changes.

Antonioni's project represents an attempt to go beneath the surfaces of action that define this superficial world. His focus is on the visual and psychic meanings that exist beyond faces, masks and images. Here he differs from other directors who emphasize dramatic action and character development embedded in critical, life-threatening situations (for example, Hitchcock). In an Antonioni film events occur and are interpreted, not in dialogue, nor dramatic action, but in gesture, movement, a flicker of the eye, a grimace, a sudden turn up a hill, the interaction of background and foreground in carefully composed scenes (see Samuels, 1971: 14).

Colour is the key to his visual method. *Blow-Up* carefully modulates, and contrasts the black and white visions and world of the photographer with vivid, dramatic, deeply saturated colour sequences which bring depth, meaning and action to the pivotal scenes that move the story forward. But colour is seductive, and in its realism may gloss what to the eye are brutal and cruel experiences. The film dialectically moves back and forth between the stark, black and white empirical world of Thomas and his blow-ups, and the sweet, distracting world of colour (Rifkin, 1982: 106). Thus the scenes with the teeny-boppers are suffused with blue-greens, pink and purple. The scenes in the park give off a green, serene ambience, which contrasts with the violence that is occurring in front of Thomas's camera. When Jane enters Thomas's studio, attempting to steal his camera, her black and white clothing contrasts with the white room of the entrance area (Rifkin, 1982: 105). As Thomas re-enters the dark, black spaces of the park to check on the body he passes a wall painted bright red. The film's last extended scene reveals Thomas, in black and white against a field of green. The film's title is superimposed in black, rather than cut-out of the field of green, as had been the case in the beginning of the film (Rifkin, 1982: 108). Thomas appears as an insubstantial figure against this larger green field, a victim of his own obsession with surfaces rather than substances.

Antonioni's heroes are peripatetic anti-heroes. They undertake frenzied searches for things that are never found (no MacGuffin's here), and the conclusion to their stories is given only after they have recognized their own impotence, finally understanding that their life has no sense or purpose (Samuels, 1971: 18). So it is with Thomas. When faced with the challenge of uncovering the murder and re-examining the dead body in the park he succumbs to the temptations of a party. There he gets stoned awakening the next morning, debauched and hung-over, only to return to the park to find nothing.

Antonioni's camera, unlike Hitchcock's, is not an authority, a means to the truth. For Antonioni there are no ultimate truths, only stories that can be told. There are things that happen beyond the field of vision that this tell-tale eye of the camera cannot record. These are unrecordable, they can only be alluded to, suggested through the careful use of colour and the composition of scenes.

But like Hitchcock, Antonioni in *Blow-Up* creates multiple 'scopic regimes', alternating between the cold, analytic gaze of the camera on the photographic enlargements, the lush, baroque glimpses of the objects that fill the antique shop, and the hysterical gaze that circles the room during the riot at the disco. Women are the frequent objects of Antonioni's gaze and Thomas exhibits a viscous misogyny.[13]

I focus on four sequences in the film. Thomas's initial pictures in the park, when the photographs in question are taken, his blow-up of these pictures, and his two returns to the park, the first which reveals the dead body, and the last, its absence.

What Does a Photograph Mean?

Unlike the paintings of his friend Bill, which mean nothing when he does them, Thomas knows what his photographs mean. Finishing a book of photos on human suffering, poverty and loneliness, Thomas (wearing white pants, white shirt, dark jacket) is in search of a happy picture ('something fab for the end'), something peaceful to contrast with the violence of the other photographs in the collection. He chances into a park which is bathed in a beautiful, soft light. Camera in hand, he squints through his viewfinder, adjusting the lens, snapping shots of a flock of fluttering pigeons on the grass. He glimpses a man (dressed in a conservative, grey suit) and a woman (Jane, short dark skirt, plaid, checked shirt, dark scarf around her neck, pulled forward like a tie) climbing up the wooded slope, holding hands and laughing, they tease and flirt with one another.[14] This is pure love, the perfect ending for his book on the human condition.

The camera follows Thomas's gaze, as he watches the couple. The woman is doing her best to get the man to follow her into the park. He pulls back. The camera turns and follows Thomas coming up the steps. This slight friction between the two strangers catches his attention. He discreetly trails them, peering between branches, focusing his camera. A gentle breeze moves the leaves on the tree, and off in the distance, unaware of his presence, the attractive and graceful woman is laughing, pulling the man by the arm. Thomas leaps over the fence and aims his camera. He takes pictures from all angles. He moves closer, hiding behind a tree near to the couple. The woman brings the man out into the middle of the meadow. She kisses him. Her eyes wander across the landscape. Thomas moves closer to his prey. The woman draws the man farther out into the meadow. She embraces him and they kiss again. Thomas leaves his hiding spot, then stops, snaps another shot of them, and then turns making his way back down the path. The woman and the man see him. The woman runs after him. Thomas hears her, stops, holding up his camera he takes more shots.

The silent scene is broken by Jane's words, 'What are you doing? Stop it! Stop it! Give me those pictures. You can't photograph people like that'. Thomas lowers his camera, gives her a friendly smile, and replies, 'Who said I can't? I'm only doing my job. Some people are . . . bull-fighters. Some people are politicians. I'm a photographer'. Jane replies, 'This is a public place. Everyone has a right to be left in peace'. Thomas mocks her concept of peace in a public place. 'It's not my fault if there's no peace. You know most girls would pay me to photograph them'. She answers, 'I'll pay you'. Then he mocks her, 'I overcharge. There are other things I want on the reel'. He turns back to the meadow, looking at the spot where the man was standing. The woman follows, 'What do we do, then?' Thomas, 'I'll send you the photograph'.

She rejects this proposal, 'No, I want them now'. She snatches at the camera, bites at his hand. He pulls back, and shouts, 'No! What's the rush? Don't let's spoil everything. We've only just met'. She moves away, looking him in the eye, 'No, we haven't met. You've never seen me'. Thomas retrieves the lens cap to his camera. He looks up into the meadow. The man has disappeared. The woman runs across the park, to join the man. Thomas snaps more shots of her as she disappears on the other side of the hill.

This ends the film's perhaps most important scene. It will be replayed many times as Thomas comes to realize that his photographs of the couple mean more than they appear to mean on the surface. Already Antonioni has introduced a harsh irony into his text. What Thomas at first sight thought was love ('It's very peaceful. Very still' he tells his friend Ron), is in fact murder, and, with his friend Bill, he has a mess on his hands. He will have to return to these photographs over and over again to sort out their meaning and as he does this he finds clues, as in a detective story. Thomas the fashion photographer, like or not, has trapped himself. He will become an unwilling sleuth, unravelling the clues buried in his prints.

A certain, firm hubris organizes his work. He has the right to photograph anything ('It's my job'), and he feels no guilt about invading the privacy of others ('It's not my fault if there is no peace'). Here he is both like and unlike Coppola's Harry Caul, the wire tap expert of *The Conversation* (1974, see Chapter 7). Like Harry, Thomas invades the privacy of an intimate couple in a public space, but Harry suspected his couple was up to no good, and feels great guilt about his work. Thomas's arrogance leads him to believe that surface appearances are true, there is nothing malevolent in his recording of the scenes he photographs, and besides most girls would pay him to take their picture.

A rapid sequence of events shatter Thomas's insolent attitude toward the park pictures. Over drinks with Ron he pats himself on the back about the perfect ending to his book, glancing out the window he spies a man in black watching him. Back at his studio he is confronted by the woman from the park, 'I've come for my photographs'. She evades his question, 'How did you manage to find me?', but in response to 'What's so important about my bloody pictures?' she replies, 'That's my business'. Thomas resists, 'The light was very beautiful in the park this morning. Those shots should be very good. Anyway, I need them'. Jane persists, 'My private life's already in a mess. It would be a disaster if . . .' Thomas's arrogance rears its head once more, 'So what – nothing like a little disaster for sorting things out'.

The Blow-Up Begins

Jane attempts to steal Thomas's camera and to seduce him. Her efforts are interrupted by a delivery man and she leaves with a fake roll of film, after giving Thomas a false telephone number. Within minutes Thomas develops the film from the park. He studies the negatives, one catches his eye, which he enlarges, the shot of the couple on the top of the hill. He hangs two blow-ups from the beam in his studio. He kneels closer to the prints. What looks like a peaceful scene now changes for the look on the woman's face appears tense. She seems to be looking away, as she kisses the man, at something outside the picture. Antonioni's camera moves back and forth between the two blow-ups. Thomas produces another enlargement of the couple embracing. Now there is no doubt about the anxious expression on the woman's face. Thomas attempts to identify the object of the woman's gaze, which ends in the forest at the edge of the park. He picks up a magnifying glass and brings it to the blow-up. The viewer's eyes gaze through Thomas's magnifying glass, watching him draw a square around an area at the distant edge of the picture's frame. This square is enlarged. The camera focuses on what appears to be a man's face emerging from the trees, staring back at the couple.

Thomas returns to the darkroom and develops another set of blow-ups which he hangs on the wall. One print shows the woman looking at Thomas as she embraces the man and another shows the man looking at Thomas. The third blow-up reveals the man looking at that point in the meadow after the woman has disappeared.

Thomas interrupts this work to place a call to the woman ('Knightsbridge one-two-three-nine'), discovering it is a wrong number. He returns to the darkroom, producing an enlargement of the man hiding in the trees. He is holding a pistol. Thomas arranges the blow-ups in sequence on his wall, reproducing the entire episode: the long-shot of the woman pulling the man into the park, the enlargement of that shot, the long-shot of the two embracing, the close-up of the two of them, the woman looking at the clump of trees, the blow-up of the man with the gun, the object of her gaze. Another blow-up exposes the gun, which is fitted with telescopic sights and silencer. Next we see the woman and the man seeing Thomas, and successive frames enlarge upon her anxiety and fright, as she realizes she has been captured on film, and attempts to cover her face.

A self-satisfied smile on his face, Thomas moves around the last two blow-ups, putting together and interpreting the story he has just created through this blow-up, editing process. He places a call to Ron, 'Something fantastic's happened. Those photographs in the park . . . fantastic . . . . Somebody was trying to kill somebody else. I saved his life'.

But there is more to be told. After a sexual interlude with two teeny-boppers, the photographer returns to his blow-ups. He looks at the last enlargement, the picture of Jane walking away. A dark patch is visible on the ground. He blows this up, the dark patch turns into a picture of a corpse. Thomas returns to the park, enters its deserted, silent dark spaces, he stops near the bushes and the trees at the edge of the meadow. A dead man, his eyes still open, his face white, stares up at him. Thomas touches his eyes (reality touches its representation, Freccero, 1971: 126). A twig snaps, leaves in the trees move, Thomas looks around, frightened, and makes a rapid retreat from the park, looking back to see if anyone is following.

What was, at first blush, the Garden of Eden, a site for a photograph of love, has turned into a site of death and murder, love and sex, Eros and thanatos cannot be escaped. A cruel blow to Thomas who wanted to end his book with a peaceful photograph. The dead man is the 'dead-end conclusion of Thomas's book' (Freccero, 1971: 121). No cinematic sleight-of-hand will bring him back to life and instil joy in this death march into the park. A *double entendre*, the oldest theme of erotic art, death coupled with the orgasm, for Thomas discovers the dead lover in the park only after his debauch with the teeny-boppers (Freccero, 1971: 121).

A Record of Death?

Back in his studio he discovers that all of the blow-ups and the negatives are gone. All tangible evidence of the murder seems to have vanished, but he finds, behind a storage cabinet, one final blow-up, the close-up of the corpse. His friend Patricia urges him to call the police, after he tells her, 'I saw a man killed this morning'. She asks, 'How did it happen?', and he answers, 'I don't know, I didn't see'. He shows her the blow-up, 'That's the body'. 'Looks like one of Bill's paintings' she replies.

Thomas now sets out to confirm the death. He fails to get his friend Ron to go with him ('I want you to see the corpse. We've got to get a shot of it?'), and only returns to the park the next morning. He retraces his path from the night before. The only sound is the wind moving through the trees. Camera in hand he walks to where the corpse should be. There is no body, no bent blades of grass. He moves to the edge of the meadow, to where the murderer was hiding. Again, no record of anything.

He moves to leave the park. A jeep speeds to the far end of the park and stops at the tennis courts. A group of students (seen in the film's opening sequence) gather around the tennis court. A man and woman mime a tennis game, they have neither rackets nor balls. Thomas watches the game. The imaginary ball sails over the fence into the meadow near Thomas. The camera follows its imaginary arc as it hits the grass. The woman looks at Thomas, imploring him with her eyes, to return the ball. He hesitates, perplexed, the students watch as he moves to the ball. He drops his camera, picks up the imaginary ball, tossing it up and down in his hand. He then runs forward, and hurls the ball back into the court. He smiles, watching the game, and slowly the 'shots themselves begin to be heard, above the rustling of the wind in the leaves, until they can be recognized as the typical sounds of a tennis ball . . . Toc, toc. Toc, toc' (Antonioni, 1971: 112).

So ends Thomas's search, which had actually ended earlier, with the final blow-up of the dead body. Here there is no equivocation. The technical process of the blow-up was the real search (Freccero, 1971: 123). Antonioni is testing his artist who knows that 'beneath the revealed image there is another, more faithful to reality, and beneath this still another, and once more another. Up to the true image of reality itself' (Antonioni quoted by Freccero, 1971: 123). But there is a moral truth behind this final image, a truth which requires action. Thomas lacks access to this final moral truth.

So Thomas's most creative act occurs, not with the camera, but with the enlarger, another technological apparatus. Thomas is a wizard with this tool, a self-cast hero saving a man from death. Once again the filmmaker plays a trick. Not only did Thomas not save a life, but the object of his search will not be unravelling a whodunit (Freccero, 1971: 123). This is not a murder mystery and Thomas is not a real detective. His only desire is to establish the truth of his simulacrum: is there a real dead body in the park? Having established that, his journey is over.

Thomas lives in a world where he is king of the image: he creates reality. In this Mod world of staged theatre, where make-believe is reality (Slover, 1971: 115), his models are puppets in his hand. They only come to life when he tells them to. 'Close your eyes' he shouts, 'stand still', as he moves off to load his camera for another shot (Freccero, 1971: 123). Only his eyes and his vision count.

What was Seen?

Blow-Up's criticisms of the voyeur and his (or her) society move in two directions at the same time. On one level it is about what happens beyond the limits of the field of vision. It is a critique of a visual, technological society that bases its assumptions about reality on photographic and visual records. There is more to reality than the records we make of it, Antonioni says. And the visual field only gives up surface representations, not images and understandings of a deeper reality that lurks behind the visual record. The eye cannot be trusted. It sees reality and its shapes in terms of colour, motion, distance and space. Antonioni deconstructs this visual field and the technological apparatuses that bring it into play, arguing that the underlying meanings of 'reality' are best given when it is stripped of colour and reduced to stark black and white images. This empirical attitude leads Thomas to examine his blow-ups without the 'distraction of color' (Rifkin, 1982: 106). When he does this he discovers the murder.

But Thomas cannot rely on what he saw because his camera restricted his field of vision. Furthermore, he only sees what he thought he saw. His 'perceptions of the moment were colored by his own perceptions of what he wanted to see' (Rifkin, 1982: 106). Even when Thomas discovers the hidden gunman, he clings to his subjective interpretation of this objective image: he thinks he saved a life! (Rifkin, 1982: 106). The technologies of visual reproduction only create, as Hitchcock also argued, one view of reality. The artist must uncover the hidden meanings given in these representations of reality. Here Antonioni becomes bitter and ironic.

For *Blow-Up* is also a scathing analysis of the objective, aloof, exploitive, technically-skilled artist-expert who feels little obligation towards, nor any feelings for, 'those who come into the view finder of his camera' (Scott, 1971: 90). Thomas's art does not connect him to the community he photographs. This aesthetic detachment makes him the pure spectator. Unlike Jeff in *Rear Window*, Thomas's autonomy allows him to escape from life. But Antonioni asserts that artistic autonomy is necessary because an artistic work only indirectly asserts its meaning (Scott, 1971: 91). The real is always subjective, never objective. The artist must stand back from a painting or photograph, only then, as with Bill's paintings, will meaning emerge. Here the message is clear. The real subject of art is 'distinct from the conscious designs of the artist, to which it often does violence' (Scott, 1971: 91). Thomas learns this lesson, when he reassembles his blow-ups and discovers the real meaning of the pictures in the park.

But Thomas is a victim of his historical moment. He cannot connect to the images and their meanings. Even though he photographed the death he does not know why it occurred and he has no real interest in bringing a murderer to the police. Thus does Antonioni make his most important moral argument. The technologies of vision are without morality, and when they do permit the reproduction (or capture) of violence, they can do so in a way that only 'embellishes and often sweetens that which, to the eye, seems harsh and aggressive' (Antonioni, in Huss, 1971b: 10). The moral argument thickens. The experts who deploy these artistic technologies of vision are also without morality. Even when deeper meaning can be discovered in these records of reality, artists like Thomas are unmoved to action.

'After such knowledge is there forgiveness?' (Scott, 1971: 95). Confronted by the reality of a violent death Thomas is unable and unwilling to act. He is not asked to play the part of a hard-boiled private eye, hunting down, like Jeff, the guilty woman and man. Nor does he have any desire to do so.

And so he enters the silent, Fellini-like tennis game at the end of the film. Several things are going on in this move. Thomas is telling us that he wants, at some level, to reach out to others. He even states that he knows the difference between reality and illusion, but it is doubtful that he regrets his inability to take action in this new, Mod world which is cutting itself off from the past. After all he sought out, not the murderers, but the dead body, the real object of his art.

And, more importantly, Antonioni is disassociating himself from those technological experts, those cinematic and photographic virtuosos, those 'talented perpetrators of illusion' (Freccero, 1971: 127) who have taken control of the new visual media. Here the filmmaker is quite firm. He does not condone Thomas's actions. Technology has turned the world into a series of images where 'sender and receiver stare blankly as though their transaction at some point still touched the solidarity of the ground' (Freccero, 1971: 128). This is the game where everyone loses, and Antonioni refuses to play.

Conclusion: An Ode to Voyeurism?

The pre-Vietnam War society that Antonioni enters continues the post-World War II assault on civil society and its concept of public place. Hitchcock anticipated this assault. Jane and her accomplice used a park as a scene for a murder, a private matter taken care of in a public place. (Lars Thorvald used the privacy of his bedroom to take care of his private problem.) Jane uses the ideology of the public place ('Everyone has a right to be left in peace') to rebuke Thomas, who knows that nothing is any longer private. And Thorvald deployed the reverse of this ideology when he attacks Jeff for invading his apartment. There are no private places left, everything is public. Not only is the 'visual essentially pornographic', as Jameson will report (1990: 1), having as its end 'rapt, mindless fascination', the public and the private have also become pornographic.

Antonioni, like Hitchcock, announces the end of privacy in the early postmodern age.

Several lessons can be drawn from *Rear Window* and *Blow-Up*. Hitchcock's modernist camera answered to two principles and two pleasures. The camera must indulge scopic desire, reveal moral truths, act as a moral authority, and punish those who transgress the law. Antonioni's late-modernist camera begins to doubt these principles. While willing to engage in voyeuristic, sexual looking, Antonioni undoes Hitchcock's moral agenda. His camera acts neither as a moral authority, nor as an agent of the law: it can no longer be assumed that the voyeur will answer to a higher good.

Both filmmakers make their voyeurs part of the spectacle that is produced, the age of the objective voyeur is dead. Furthermore, both directors understand that reality is never totally objective: what is seen is determined by one's angle of vision. There is more to reality than the viewfinder can capture. And while Hitchcock still believes that the image can be matched to a firm object in the real world, Antonioni knows that this law that connects the image to its referent is finally dead. But in the end sex and death will remain the voyeur's obsession, for these are, perhaps, the only eternal realities. And the violent truths (and lies) that his (and her) camera reveal are always only partial and inconclusive.

These insights will be taken to new levels by the next generation of high modern and postmodern filmmakers. Now the malevolent uses of the camera by the state and its agents will be thoroughly explored, as the age of the postmodern simulacrum finally arrives. But before exploring these transformations, it is necessary to take a detour through the fatal female vision, the topic of the next chapter. Late and high modern female voyeurs embrace violence and desire in ways that Jeff and Thomas never imagined. David Lynch's (*Blue Velvet*) Dorothy is not a cinematic aberration.

Notes

1 Directed by Alfred Hitchcock; studio: Paramount; screenplay by John Michael Hayes from a novelette by Cornell Woolrich; cast: James Stewart (L.B. Jeffries), Grace Kelly (Lisa Fremont), Wendell Corey (Thomas J. Doyle, the detective), Thelma Ritter (Stella, the nurse), Raymond Burr (Lars Thorvald), Judith Evelyn (Miss Lonely Heart), Georgine Darcy (Miss Torse).

2 Directed by Michelangelo Antonioni: produced by Carlo Ponti, released by Premier Productions; screenplay by Michelangelo Antonioni and Tonio Guerra, inspired by a short story of Julio Cortazar; cast: David Hemmings (Thomas), Vanessa Redgrave (Jane), Sara Miles (Patricia), John Castle (Ron), models (Verushka, Jill Kennington, Peggy Moffitt, Rosaleen Murray, Ann Norman, Melanie Hampshire), the tennis players (Julian Chagrin, Claude Chagrin).

3 Only Jeff attempts to solve the crime, Thomas is content to have documented (if only momentarily) its occurrence.

4 Stam and Pearson (1983: 203) suggest that Hitchcock's *Rear Window* can be read as a political essay on surveillance which 'echoes the historical ambiance of McCarthyite anticommunism . . . Jeffries is an anonymous accuser whose suspicions happen to be correct,

but the object of his hostile gaze might as easily have been innocent as Father Logan in *I Confess*, or Christopher Emmanuel Balestrero in *The Wrong Man*, to cite two other fifties [Hitchcock] films with anti-McCarthyite resonances'.

5 A number of post-1990 'retro' films have returned to this historical period and its repressive, destructive gaze. Examples include, *Shining Through*, *JFK* (by implication), *Guilty By Suspicion*, and the late 1980s *The House on Carroll Street* (1988).

6 Barry Levinson's 1990 film *Avalon* lovingly details this mid-century domestic project.

7 Weis argues, for example, that *Rear Window* is 'the film that quintessentially presents a subjective point of view within an apparently realistic style' (1982: 107).

8 This conclusion is supported by a simple count of the point-of-view shots that occur from the time Lisa enters the film until the murder of Mrs Thorvald. Of the 140 (approximate) shots in this sequence 36 are from Jeff's POV.

9 Hence the readings of this film which emphasize the marriage theme.

10 This is meant to supplement, not contradict, the argument that Jeff's fixation on Thorvald reflects a desire to justify not settling down with Lisa (see Leitch, 1991: 170). Each apartment that Jeff gazes into reflects back on an uneasy picture of the male–female relationship (see Stam and Peterson, 1983: 199).

11 Bozovic (1992: 166–9) interprets Thorvald's window and its implied gaze from the standpoint of Lacan and Sartre. Sartre argues we cannot see the other's gaze, only apprehend its presence, for the gaze is not on the object manifesting it, not in the window, but in front of it. The other's gaze, for Sartre disguises his (her) eyes. According to Sartre we cannot simultaneously apprehend the other and their gaze, we can do either one or the other, but not both (Sartre, 1943/1956: 258). For Sartre Thorvald's window is an eye, not a gaze. Lacan (1988: 215; Bozovic, 1992: 167) disagrees. 'I can feel myself under the gaze of someone whose eyes I do not see . . . . All that is necessary is for something to signify to me that there may be others there. This window . . .'. For Lacan, Jeff sees both the window (as an eye) and the gaze behind the eye.

12 De Palma's 1981 *Blow Out* borrows directly from *Blow-Up*, as does Oliver Stone's 1991 *JFK*. For prescient connections between these three films see Ebert (1989c: 79–80). Coppola's *The Conversation* (1974), an influence on *Blow Out*, also borrows from Antonioni's film. *Blow-Up* received, or was nominated for, a number of important awards, including Best Achievement in Directing (Academy of Motion Pictures), Best Picture (National Society of Film Critics, New York Film Critics), and it was on the 'Ten Best List' of 1966 films for *Saturday Review*, *Newsweek*, *New York Times*, *Commonweal*, and the *New York Post*. It remains a popular video rental and is regularly assigned and discussed in cinema classes.

13 Antonioni's use of POV is primarily diegetic, emphasizing shots which define the unfolding narrative structure of the film. There are, however, non-diegetic POV shots directed to the spectator (the opening shots of the students in the jeep), and shots strictly in the service of scopic pleasure (when Thomas photographs Verushka).

14 Jane and Thomas never exchange names. The viewer learns their names only after the credits are run.

6

WOMEN AT THE KEYHOLE:
FATAL FEMALE VISIONS

What happens when women are situated on both sides of the keyhole?
The question is not only who or what is on either side of the keyhole,
but also what lies between them, what constitutes the threshold that
makes representation possible?

> Mayne, *The Woman at the Keyhole: Feminism and
> Women's Cinema*, p. 9

Hello Dan . . . . Part of you is growing within me . . . . I feel you. I
taste you. I think you. I touch you . . . . You're a cocksucking
sonofabitch. You don't even like girls. I scare you. I know I do. You
are a gutless, spineless sonofabitch, a fucking faggot.

> Alex to Dan, on tape, *Fatal Attraction*

Like her mid-century counterpart, Hollywood's contemporary female
voyeur has fallen on hard times. Her gaze is still defined by the masculine
eye, even as recent texts expose the limits of the male look and give women
the power to gaze on themselves and the male figure. Multiple viewing
positions for the female were opened up, as argued in Chapter 4, by the
end of the 1980s in films like *Broadcast News*, *Blue Velvet* and *sex, lies and
videotape*.

The female investigative and erotic voyeurs in these texts exposed the
power of the feminine gaze as it appropriated the eye of the camera, and
turned that eye back on the powerful male. These texts made women
active, aggressive voyeurs. They were able to transcend the supplemental,
passive, gazing positions cinema had traditionally assigned to women. But
in the end, each woman (Jane, Dorothy, Sandy, Ann) found her gaze and
her body coded in patriarchal terms, she remained the object of the male's
look (see Gamman, 1989: 12).

In this chapter, borrowing my title from Mayne (1990: 9), I examine
two highly influential and controversial late 1980s films, *Black Widow*
(1986)[1], and *Fatal Attraction* (1987)[2]. These texts reverse conventional
imagery by placing women on both sides of the keyhole. With Mayne
(1990: 9) I ask what 'happens when this occurs?' Alexandra Barnes (*Black
Widow*), is a Justice Department investigator who pursues husband-killer
Catharine, and Alex Forrest (*Fatal Attraction*) is a successful book editor
who pursues Dan Gallagher, a happily married lawyer. Alexandra Barnes
(she prefers Alex) and Alex Forrest are simultaneously voyeurs and the
subject of a woman's (and man's) gaze.

Both texts struggle to give women a powerful gaze which overrides the male's look, thus continuing the struggle within mainstream Hollywood cinema to create a space for the aggressive, voyeuristic female.[3] Each film is simultaneously panoptic and panauditory. Alexandra and Alex create scopic and ocular observational regimes as they spy upon their victims, thereby merging vision and sound as the primary sites for their surveillance conduct. Both films have overtones of Hitchcock and De Palma (see Konigsberg, 1988: 118; Hoberman, 1987: Denby, 1987).[4] Each recalls earlier texts, including the violent female voyeur of *Play Misty for Me* (1971), and the women investigators in *Shadow of a Doubt* (1943) (Charlie), *Spellbound* (1945) (Ingrid Bergman as the psychiatrist), and *Persona* (1966) (Alma the nurse). Each film follows the film noir tradition of creating a *femme fatale* (see Katovich and Haller, 1993; McLean, 1993; Gledhill, 1978).[5]

Following Mayne (1990: 9) and the Bakhtinian analysis of the Asian Eye given in Chapter 5, I investigate the multiple subject positions both women play in these voyeuristic dramas. I argue that the cinematic screen, the narrative logic, and the visual fields in each text complicate the feminine gaze and the image of woman that is thereby produced. She becomes something more than a simple object of male desire. The two women, both named Alex, occupy ambivalent, ambiguous sexual positions *vis-à-vis* the objects of their gaze, Catharine for Alexandra, Ann, Ellen and Dan for Alex.

Four propositions organize my analysis. The first is not new, merely supplementary to earlier arguments (Mayne, 1990: 8; Doane, 1991: 3; Clover, 1992: 8). These two films superficially present the feminine gaze, on both sides of the keyhole, as being fatally flawed. Even when it takes up the traditional, masculine investigative project, the female look is never benign. It is always coded in obsessive, neurotic terms, and this look is inevitably anchored back in sexuality and sexual desire. But underneath this gaze shifts and takes on multiple forms, making it impossible to clearly define who is subject and who is object, who is sane and who is insane. (On two occasions Dan loses control, bulging-eyed, red-faced he nearly strangles and kills Alex.) Thus, when given the power to look, the female voyeur unleashes a gaze which disrupts the social order, erasing the boundaries between male and female, law and order, investigator, criminal and victim.

My second proposition elaborates the conclusions of Chapter 6 concerning the essentially pornographic features of the contemporary visual field. Antonioni and Hitchcock (also De Palma) took violent sexuality to new levels, exposing the transgressed sacred boundaries of the public and the private in the late modern age. Filmmakers in the late 1980s and 1990s exploited this rupture, erasing forever these sacred boundaries. Not surprisingly, women took the lead here. Their bodies and their gaze would now be the site for this final deconstruction, the place where the female gaze, feminine sexuality and murderous violence finally flow together as a single unity. Under the sign of family, law and order, female voyeurs would usher in a new era of soft pornographic, investigative cinema. The female investigative voyeur becomes the queen of pornography.[6]

The third proposition, drawing from Bakhtin (1981, 1986), Derrida (1982), and Irigaray (1985) thickens this interpretation. The gaze of the female voyeur is multi-perspectival, or multi-sensual. It goes beyond pure vision and specularity to privilege the other senses, including touch, hearing and taste.[7] On the other side of the masculine looking glass, on the 'other side of the mirror, behind the screen of male representations, is an underground world' (Jay, 1993a: 533). This is the 'dark night of [the feminine] soul' (Irigaray, 1985: 103, quoted in Jay, 1993a: 533). If women only identify with the narcissistic subject created by the masculine, flat mirror, 'they are imprisoned in a male specular economy in which they are always devalued as inferior versions of the male subject, as mere objects of exchange, dead commodities' (Jay, 1993a: 533). The two Alexes reject this monolithic, narcissistic identity. Deploying all of their sensibilities, they move to the dark side of the feminine and masculine soul.[8]

The fourth proposition elaborates the third. It is utopian. This dark side of the feminine soul calls into question the power of the masculine gaze. This harkening exposes and illuminates the need for an empowering, multi-sensual feminine subjectivity. This subjectivity embraces a field of experience that is more than just visual. When released into society, this multi-sensual field of experience threatens the status quo. But this is an unstable threat, for the feminine gaze must always fight to resist the masculine pull, which is the pull of law and order and family.

Black Widow and *Fatal Attraction*, accordingly, are complex discursive constructions. A polyphonic play of voices and gazes from the sexual margins and the centres of patriarchal society interact in each film to produce women who are not just unitary, sexual objects. Both women are at the centre of conflicting, overlapping and competing voices and gazes; each is simultaneously defined by sexist and non-sexist discourse. Both women are given the power to gaze on the other, while both become the passive (and active) object of the gaze of this selfsame other.

Each woman becomes a complex discursive and visual construction. Their contradictory angles of vision virtually define the contradictory core of the late 1980s feminist and anti-feminist American sexual order. By being folded into the centre of the sexual crises produced by the 1980s (Alex and AIDS, see Williamson, 1988; Hoberman, 1987; Petley, 1988), the two women live sexism from within, struggling at all times to escape the pervasive presence of patriarchy and the male gaze.[9] Inside looking out, like Charlie Chan, they are outsiders brought into the inside. Their battle is to define a woman's place within, or alongside the edges of the inner structures of marriage and the family, within the visual, panoptic apparatuses of law and order.

On the surface, Hollywood's visual, sexist discourse (like its Orientalist discourse) distinguishes the violent *femme fatale* from the normal, sane, feminine figure (see Doane, 1991: 1). The sane feminine figure is presented as the culturally-known, familiar, comfortable other. Her vision is defined as stable and aligned with law and order, family and truth. She is superficially contrasted to the stereotyped image of the sexually alluring, erotic, dangerous and violent female (Sharon Stone of *Basic Instinct*, Beth versus Alex, Alex and Catharine). The violent woman is the unknown, devious, unstable, secretive, deceptive other obsessed with scopophilia. The tamed woman is rational and virtuous; the violent, predatory woman is irrational, depraved, fallen, a danger to society. The good woman is the sexually unthreatening Girl Friday, neutered, the sometimes calm, implacable female detective or voyeur who works on the side of law and order (from Miss Marple to TV's Emma Peele of 'The Avengers' to Angela Lansbury of 'Murder She Wrote' and Maudie of 'Moonlighting'). This woman works in the service of law and order, peace, family and justice. She protects the world from sinister women (and men). She takes pleasure in solving crimes and catching criminals who elude the police. In these ways American cinema perpetuated its version of an Orientalizing, visual sexism which serves to keep women in their proper place, on the right side of the keyhole.

Unlike her Asian counterpart, it has been difficult for the female to find her place in American culture as an investigative voyeur and sleuth. While her white male counterpart (Marlowe) virtually defined law and order through his voyeurism, the female voyeur either had to take a supplemental part to this figure (Sandy in *Blue Velvet*), or be defined totally outside the sexual mainstream as a frumpy, unattractive, but intelligent woman. Not surprisingly, then, the female voyeur would occupy the position of *femme fatale*, aligned with the Oriental, foreign other, the dragon lady of the East (see Doane, 1991: 3). Only recently has she been invested with positive attributes, but typically her strengths would be used to bring down the sinister figure of another woman, not a male.

The investigative female voyeur carries the weight of being a woman upon her shoulders. She uses her female intuition (like Chan's Oriental eyes) as a way of seeing the truth that others cannot see. She is forced to rely upon her wit, charm and sometimes her beauty as vehicles for disarming cultural criticisms of her sexuality. Thus the female voyeur embodies a double negativity: she must overcome her sexuality in order to use it in a positive way. She can never escape sexual desire but it must never be seen as a threat to the established social/sexual order. She becomes a masculinized woman (Ingrid Bergman in *Spellbound*), only on call sexually when a 'real' man seeks her pleasures. She is more brother (or sister) than sexual lover.

As with the films containing the Oriental sleuth, films about the female voyeur are organized around double spectacular structure. Inevitably this structure is focused on sexuality, where the female body is a site of multiple gazes. (Beth and Alex in Beth's bathroom, Alex and Catharine's image in Alex's bathroom.) This gaze is anchored (usually) in an erotic or investigative spectacle which is aligned with family, or the law, a wedding, lovemaking, the police station, a bath, the dinner table. The sexual battle between the good and the bad woman is then realized through a 'spectacle of discovery' and violence wherein the good woman overcomes her evil counterpart. This often occurs in a group situation, where the representatives of proper, civil society are present. (Exhausted Dan passively watches as Beth murders Alex.)

This spectacle of law and order occurs within a larger specular structure which isolates the sexual other as a threat to society. The *femme fatale* falls under the visual control of the camera and she is presented as an alien, fatally flawed, dangerous figure, a victim of her own sexuality and desire. (Alex stabs herself as she attempts to kill Beth.) In this decisive moment of justice the positive virtues of the investigative voyeur are celebrated. She has saved the day, and at the same time reinscribed the value of sexual difference.

Thus are female voyeurs sexualized and orientalized. With Charlie Chan, they are outsiders brought into the centre of civil society when a crisis appears. Their sexual identity is submerged, in the moment of justice, stitched into a larger sexual discourse connected to family, crime, law and order. This produces a superficial form of cultural and sexual integration. Women voyeurs, if they play their cards right, really do have a place in this culture. Now the films: *Fatal Attraction* first, for here the aggressive, sexually charged, female voyeur creates the crisis that must be resolved by the good woman and the law.

Fatal Attraction

Set in the late 1980s first in Manhattan, and then in the Connecticut countryside, it is a fairy-tale story, straight out of the Brothers Grimm (Raschke, 1988). Family man and successful lawyer, Dan Gallagher, 10-years married to beautiful Beth, with five-year old daughter Ellen, has a weekend fling with a frizzy-permed Medusa named Alex, the archetypal witch, the murderous phallic mother (Taubin, 1987). The wicked seductive woman won't go away. What for Dan was a one-night stand ('Two adults saw an opportunity and took advantage of it') for Alex is the beginning of a family. Refusing to let him go, she begins a relentless visual and auditory surveillance attack, phoning him at all hours, at work and home. She happily announces her pregnancy to him ('you are alive in me'), spies on him, harasses his secretary over the phone, shows up at his office, visits his wife and attempts to buy their old apartment, leaves a tape cassette for him at work, kidnaps Ellen for an afternoon, boils Ellen's rabbit in a pot on the kitchen stove, invades the family house, attacking Beth in the bathroom with a large butcher's knife, finally to be killed by Beth, a bullet to the heart. The bad witch from the West, the lovelorn psycho, is annihilated. Alex, the bad virus that threatened to infect and kill the family, has been destroyed. Order and peace can be restored. Damaged father Dan is reunited with his vigilant, strong wife (they embrace) and loving daughter (he tucks her in). The police leave the house as the camera lingers on the family photo, Ellen, Beth and Dan, the perfect threesome of the 1980s. There is a clear message, the application of Murphy's law to the extramarital fling, everything that could go wrong did (Hoberman, 1987).

Alex is not a passive voyeur. From her first gaze which settles on Dan's body at a cocktail party (Jimmy, 'I think she tried to undress me'), to her final look, the violent, volcanic eruption, knife in hand, from the family bath tub, she is the sexual predator, using her eyes, her body and her voice to control, manipulate and finally destroy Dan. Alex's aggressive voyeurism, her intrusive surveillance and constant intrusions (the ringing telephone) creates an ominous presence in Dan's happy domestic life. She is everywhere and nowhere.

Here Howard Atherton's (the film's cinematographer) camera functions as an extension of her gaze. Even when she is not present we sense her lurking presence. She has got inside Dan's head and turned him into a voyeur who can't escape his own life, let alone hers. Indeed he is driven to spy on her. The voyeur's ultimate victory.

The Looks of Fatal Attraction

Thus, on the surface, the film's seduction lies in its vivid portrayal of the victim who becomes the voyeur. But underneath, *Fatal Attraction* is a study of the late 1980s yuppie gaze and its multiple forms. The text isolates, interrogates and distinguishes the gaze, or look, attached to the loving, nuclear family formation, the impassioned gaze of lustful sexuality, the insane look of the mad woman (and man), the murderous and investigative gaze of law, order and family. Four pivotal and extended scenes (and sequences) fitted to the film's three main acts (seduction, harassment, murder) illuminate these four looks. Each scene focuses on Alex's aggressive gaze and its progressive, destructive effects on Dan.

The multiple looks of the text are cinematically accomplished through clever editing, the skilful use of subjective and POV shots (zooms, close-ups), as well as a mobile camera, which becomes an extension of Alex's omnipresent gaze. The camera seeks out its subject and isolates Dan, Beth, Ellen and Alex in tightly framed scenes, cutting them off from the outside world. Bathrooms, water, heat, fire, telephones and knives are central to the story's visual and auditory symbolism.

Act One: The Loving, Lustful Look

Like *Rear Window* the story begins inside the closed walls of an apartment. The camera pans the evening skyline of New York City, slowly approaching a lighted window in a large building, where the shade is pulled, and the action begins. We cut back and forth from Daddy Dan (in underwear), daughter Ellen and family dog Quincy in the living-room, and

mother Beth (T-shirt and panties) in the bathroom, water running in the
sink, fixing her face for a party, checking panties and bras hanging on the
shower bar. She and Dan are about to go out, leaving Ellen with the
friendly teenage babysitter. The film will begin and end (for all practical
purposes) in the family bathroom, recalling *Psycho* and *Dressed to Kill*.

This loving, graceful, cluttered, chummy, romantic look of the perfect
family is quickly shattered. Minutes later at a publisher's party (a Japanese
author has just published a Samurai cookbook), after assuring Beth that
her hair looks fine, Dan and Jimmy (one of Dan's law partners) are
visually inspected by sexually alluring Alex, who, overhearing their
discussion, scorns them with a withering look of disgust. Side-by-side at
the bar, Dan finds Alex looking at him, introductions over, he is caught by
Beth's look that says they have to leave. As the perfect couple moves
through the crowded room, Alex holds them in her gaze.

Dan is called to work on Saturday morning[10] where he is introduced to
Alex. Caught in a rainstorm after the meeting, Dan finds himself under
Alex's umbrella. Together they seek a cab. Over drinks and lunch Dan
accepts Alex's invitation ('How discreet are you?') to come and play in her
loft apartment (bare and white), set in the smoke and fire-illuminated
(flames leap out of barrels), rainy and dank meat-packing district. ('A
nocturnal landscape of carrion and fire' (Hoberman, 1987).) Atherton's
camera circles the coupling duet as they make love in the kitchen (against
the sink, water running behind them), the bedroom and the elevator. Dan
sneaks home the next morning, taking a shower, the phone rings. Alex
wants him to come back and spend the day. The camera cuts to the
Connecticut countryside, Beth's mother watering bright flowers in a
greenhouse. Beth won't be home until the next day. The new couple play
in the park with Quincy, dine to the sounds of Madame Butterfly, and,
attempting to leave, Dan is confronted by an Alex who has slashed her
wrists. Her blood stains his white shirt. The camera lingers on the blood,
on the bathroom floor, the knife, and the sounds of the thunder storm
outside. Rain pounds against the bedroom window and Dan places a call
to Beth after showering. A dazed bedridden Alex, wrists wrapped, white
telephone on bedstand, listens to his proclamation of love to Beth.

Act Two: The Insane, Harassing Gaze

The violent virus has entered Dan's life, it lives in Alex's womb, carried
now along telephone wires, erupting in ringing phones, embodied in her
physical presence in Dan's life world. He becomes a vigilante, a man out
to save his safe family from this destructive threat. He spies on her
apartment and enters one morning after she leaves for work. The hand-
held camera follows his investigations of her personal life, creating the
sense that we as viewer have invaded this insane woman's home
(Konigsberg, 1988: 119). As if in retaliation, she spies on him in his
parking garage. We see her lurking behind posts and just as he approaches

his car she throws acid on the hood. The car bursts into smoke and flames. She tails him to the country as he listens to her tape. He joins his happy family in front of the burning hearth (we look through the picture window). Alex is behind us, also looking in, *Stella Dallas*-like, turning away in revulsion at the sight of the perfect family, vomiting on the green spring grass.

Her gaze, which we share, has penetrated the protective walls of Dan's house. It remains for the virus to now enter the family home and make its presence known. And so we get the boiled rabbit, the trip to the amusement park with Ellen, and the final bathroom scene.

The meaning of the boiled rabbit goes beyond a dead bunny. It produces Dan's confession to Beth, who asks him to leave. The confession gives the virus to Beth. Her happy family is shattered, faithful Dan is sick, he has betrayed her.[11] Home from the hospital, now reconciled with Dan, Beth will tell Alex (over the phone) that she will kill her if she ever comes near her family again. Thus the virus strengthens Beth, while it continues its destructive effects on Dan.

Act Three: The Murderous Gaze

Denouement. Doors locked, Ellen tucked into bed, police alerted about Mad Alex, solicitous Daddy Dan leaves Beth in the steam-filled bathroom, water running over the plugged drain (*Psycho*). He and Quincy are off to the kitchen to fix her a cup of tea. Downstairs the kettle boils on the stove. Upstairs water fills the bathtub, Beth examines her face in the steam-covered mirror. We glimpse first her bruised eye and, as she wipes the mirror clean, Alex's face appears. Beth screams, pulls back, knocking bottles and pictures to the floor. The kettle whistles in the kitchen. Water from the tub drips through the ceiling, sleepy-eyed, thirsty Quincy on the floor of the dining-roon licks it up. Alex, butcher's knife in hand, punctures her right thigh with the knife point, blood flows, Beth screams again. Alex asks, 'What are you doing here? Why are you here? He tried to say goodbye to me last night, but he couldn't, and I feel the same way about him'. She pokes her leg with the knife. 'You meet somebody for the first time, and you know they are the one'. The camera cuts to the kitchen. Dan is looking at the fire. Quincy is still drinking. Alex continues: 'I understand what you are doing. You thought you could move him to the country away from me and play the happy family'. Water runs over the edge of the tub. Quincy gets up. Mad-eyed Alex continues speaking, 'You are so selfish. He tells me about you. You are so stupid'. The kettle whistles. Beth screams again. She and Alex fight for the knife. The kettle screeches. Alex stabs Beth. Boiling water erupts from the kettle. Beth and Alex fight on the floor. Beth screams again.

Dan races upstairs, crashing into the bathroom, knocking Alex against the mirror which shatters. Alex stabs Dan. He begins to bleed, falling back against the wall above the bathtub. More pictures fall to the floor. Dan

grabs Alex and submerges her in the bathtub. Her bloody feet kick above
the end of the tub. The water turns blood-coloured. He holds her under
the water, her beautiful hair fans out in the water framing her face (shades
of Charles Laughton's *Night of the Hunter*), air bubbles gurgle out of her
mouth, water drips above her head from the faucet. The camera gives a
close-up of Alex's hand on the bottom of the tub, still holding the knife.
Dan's face is seen looking through the bloody water. Dan slumps against
the wall and wipes his face. Water drips over Alex's head. Only the sound
of dripping water is heard. Suddenly Alex erupts out of the tub (shades of
Friday the 13th), knife in hand. A shot rings out, blood appears in the
centre of her chest, she slumps against the wall, smearing blood against the
tile. The camera turns. Beth is standing in the doorway, gun in both
hands. Alex slides down the wall. Her head slips into the polluted bloody
water in the corner of the tub.

The camera cuts to the front of the house. The police leave. Dan is
framed in the middle of the garden gate. He enters the hallway of the
house. Beth embraces him and they exit into the kitchen. A close-up of the
family photo merges with the credits, the screen darkens, white on black,
like Alex's apartment.

The Female Voyeur's Watery, Bloody Look

The panoptic structure of *Fatal Attraction* enfolds the murderous, bloody
gaze of the mad, female voyeur into the inner fabric of the loving, nuclear
family. This gaze-as-a-virus follows the treacherous pathways of lustful
sexuality, coding illicit sex with violence and death. But Beth's violent
sexual gaze is not, in the usual sense, pornographic.

Turning back on itself, the film creates two victims, Alex who is
transgressed by Dan, and Dan, who is transgressed by Alex. But never
wavering, the text makes itself clear. Dan, not Alex, is the victim. This is
so because he has more to lose (Ellen and Beth). Refusing to keep her
place in society, Alex, this pregnant SWW, must be given a gaze that
moves from casual, sexual lust, to visual and vocal harassment, to
murderous rage. Alex's gaze will move along each of these dimensions, as
it is progressively coded as insane and out of control. So she is given a
special violent sexual gaze, and it is not the gaze of the soft pornographic
(*Basic Instinct*).

Alex's is the watery look of hysterical female insanity. It is everywhere
and nowhere, constantly flowing, erupting, taking new forms, like an out
of control mountain stream, darting in one direction and then taking a
sudden turn elsewhere, following its victim in and through the routinized
channels of his life. This watery gaze follows its victims to its own source,
the cleansing, purifying waters of the family bathroom.

The film is firm on this. Alex's gaze is repeatedly associated with water:
the spring rainstorm that joins her and Dan on the weekend of their affair;
the water that flows in the sink as they make love; the thunderstorm that

follows her slashed wrists; Dan's shower that washes her effects from his body; the early morning rain that falls on her shoulders as she leaves her flat the day Dan breaks in; the night time fog that hides the family home when she spies on Dan, Ellen and Beth; Dan peering out into the rain as he confesses to Beth; Alex's final watery grave in the Gallagher bathtub.

Alex embodies the two tensions, creation and destruction, that together form the cluster of symbolic meanings historically brought to water (see Eliade, 1958: especially, 188–90, 204–5, 212–13; Biedermann, 1991: 372–5).[12] She is creation (fertility, birth) and its antithesis (the flood, death). She is a water nymph who dwells above fire and water, a dangerous nymph given to stealing children and driving men crazy with her sexual charms. She has nymphomania, a madness connected to her uncontrollable sexual desire. A nymphomaniac, she infects Dan with nympholepsy, a violent emotional state, a state of frenzy caused by her presence. She is the goddess of night, a nymphaid butterfly who traps, smothers and attempts to kill her prey.

Dan's initial contacts with Alex are rejuvenating and regenerating. He comes alive sexually, and the rain and the water that flows over and into the two lovers is generative, and in Sumerian (ancient Babylonia) water means sperm (Eliade, 1958: 190). The spring rain impregnates the water nymph, but the foreboding thunder storm that follows the act of creation signals the violence that will come from this transgressive sexual act. The rains and storms that follow reinscribe this original sin. Dan cannot be washed clean and Alex's polluted waters follow wherever he goes. She grows into a monster, the monster who guards sacred waters.

Her invasion of the family country bathroom, where the film ends (just as it began in the bathroom in Manhattan), pollutes the clear, clean water that washes over the bodies of the Gallagher family. This virus from the city must be killed, immersed in water, drowned, as in the flood (and the tub floods over), submerged in her own polluting waters. Her immersion in the tub signals Dan's doing away with this ugly part of his recent past. He must kill what he has created in Alex's body. And she must die, but she rises from the water, not purified but defiled by her own bloody water. She must be shot by a gun held by Beth and fall back into the bloody tub.[13] And so Dan is absolved of his crime against family and nature, purified by Alex's final submersion. Healed, he arises from out of this watery maze, a forgiven and new man. The mad, untamed nymph has been killed.

And so the cycle of life and death is replayed in the Gallagher bathtub. It is the fate of all forms to be dissolved, in order to reappear anew, cleaned and cleansed of past sins. Water takes back that which it created. Dan is reunited with the rhythms of an ancient universe, Alex's death a site for springtime ritual bathing that brings health and fortune to the Gallagher family.

Thus the film confirms the usual, stereotypical picture of the *femme fatale*, contrasting this figure with the sane, rational, safely erotic Beth. Alex's gaze, in its many forms, is never presented as being rational, or socially acceptable. The looks of a 'Single Working Woman' have no place in the late 1980s yuppie world. They are always associated with calamity and destruction (see also Faludi, 1993: 121).

Black Widow

The viewer enters this retro film noir through the feminine eye. The film opens with a shot of two feminine eyes, a split screen, a mirror, a hand applying eye-liner to each eye, comparing one eye to the other. A loud roar intrudes into the soundtrack. A helicopter hovers close to the ground, its searchlight casts a glowing circle (a large eye) on the rain-covered runway, a glamorous woman steps to the ground, enters the dark night and quickly slides into a waiting limousine. The black widow, sultry serial murderess Catharine (Theresa Russell), has just returned from the funeral of her Mafioso husband.[14] Days later 31-year-old tomboy Alex Barnes (Debra Winger), a top-notch Justice Department investigator, rushes to work, two hours late. She's been studying obituaries, noting an odd pattern. Several wealthy, late-middle-aged men have died recently of a rare disease, Ondine's Curse, caused by the lack of oxygen to the brain during sleep. Soon another death appears (Dennis Hopper), again with Ondine's Curse, and Alex suspects that these deaths are caused by the same woman. (When they later meet, Catharine will share with Alex her history of dead husbands, 'I was a professional, I loved every one of them deeply, honestly'.) Alex follows Catharine to Seattle but is too late to prevent the next murder (Nichol Williamson). (Bruce (Alex's boss), 'She's obsessed with killing and you're obsessed with her. You're as whacky as she is'.)[15] The chase moves to Hawaii where Alex hires a private eye to track down Catharine, whom she soon meets. The two women go scuba diving together and share the same lover, Catharine's next victim, Paul. Catharine murders the private eye and marries Paul, provoking a jealous outburst from Alex, who gives her a black widow brooch as a wedding gift. (Catharine: 'The black widow. She mates and she kills. Your question is does she love? It's impossible to answer that question unless you live in her world'.) Catharine poisons Paul's wine and frames Alex who is charged with Paul's murder. Visiting Alex in jail, Catharine is confronted by Paul and blurts out a confession. Alex leaves prison, fashionably dressed, into the full sunlight of a bright Hawaiian day, and the film ends.

A double plot structure operates here, two female voyeurs spying on one another, two stories, a series of crimes and their investigation. A woman's story told by a man (Bob Rafelson). *Black Widow* is an examination of the feminine voyeuristic self and its obsessions with work, duty, appearance, femininity and masculine ideals of beauty (see Heung, 1987; Sweet, 1987). Narrated from the feminine point of view (with hints of erotic, lesbian attraction; see Mayne, 1990: 46–8; Heung, 1987), this is a story of a female investigator wanting in 'feminine' qualities who chases, becomes obsessed with, and captures a *femme fatale*, a beautiful creation 'of male fantasies and fears' (Heung, 1987: 54; see also Hogan, 1988; Sawyer, 1987; Benson, 1987; Williamson, 1987; Denby, 1987; Ebert, 1989d; McGrady, 1987; Combs, 1987; Edelstein, 1987). Thus is the good, but unattractive, female who is wedded to her job, with no man in her life ('a problem of timing'), pitted against the dangerous, inscrutable other woman, who throws off wealthy husbands once she has trapped and married them.

The Looks of the Black Widow

Catharine and Alex are both on both sides of the keyhole; each is spied upon, and each spies on the other. *Black Widow*'s superficial appeal lies in this voyeuristic exercise which makes the woman the object of the female gaze. But the gazes that structure the text are neither simple nor pornographic. They go beyond one woman looking at another. Film director Bob Rafelson (*Five Easy Pieces* (1971), *The King of Marvin Gardens* (1972), *The Postman Always Rings Twice* (1981)) and cinematographer Conrad L. Hall (*Harper* (1966), *Marathon Man* (1976), *Tequila Sunrise* (1988), *Class Action* (1991)) enter *Black Widow* through the eye of Catharine, the evil reflexive eye looking at itself. This narcissistic gaze is quickly complicated. In rapid sequence the film articulates feminized panoptic and panauditory surveillance regimes that move from the purely technological, through the predatory, the erotic, to the traditional masculine looks of the law and the state.

Alex and Catharine are inside each of these gazing structures. Alex's looks are aligned with law and order, Catharine's with the circumvention of this order. Yet as Alex becomes Catharine, her gaze is progressively connected to the erotic and the narcissistic. Her passion for Paul and her obsession with Catharine displace the looks of law and order. Only in the end, as she leaves the courthouse, after Catharine's confession (in full glare of the photographer's camera) is her gaze returned to the side of justice and the state. Thus the film is a study of the trajectory of the feminine gaze, a gaze which struggles to find its own subjectivity and subject matter within the confines of family, law, personal intimacy and masculine defined feminine beauty.

This trajectory unfolds through the film's three main acts: suspicion, confirmation and seduction and entrapment. *Black Widow*'s investigative journey is set by Catharine's project which is to find a new victim, kill him and then move on to the next. Catharine's project defines Alex's, which is to catch this woman before she kills again. In each act the narcissistic, technological, predatory, erotic, and legal gazes entangle and inform one another. Each woman takes up each of these looks, and in the film's final act these multiple gazes come together to place each woman on the other side of the other woman's 'keyhole'.[16] The message is clear. The feminine investigative gaze, unlike its male counterpart, is always subjective and fatally narcissistic. The female voyeur cannot separate herself from her prey. She becomes the erotic object of her own gaze. And so Catharine and Alex are both losers, both doomed to pay the cost of their feminine narcissism. Six extended, interconnected scenes support this conclusion.

Act One: The Technological Apparatus and the Narcissistic, Suspicious Look   Alex is a surveillance expert, displaying the standard set of private eye investigative and technological skills which quickly allow her to zero in on Catharine as the black widow. She assembles newspaper photos of the weddings of the victims of Ondine's Curse. She does computer runs on the statistical likelihood of single women in Catharine's age bracket being married to wealthy middle-aged men. She does blow-ups of Catharine's wedding pictures. She tracks down and interviews the living relatives (female) of Catharine's dead husbands. She stakes out Catharine in Seattle, hides behind posts and in parked cars and even rides the same boat with her.

Act One ends with Alex's inspection of a series of wedding slides of Catharine and her previous husbands. The scene opens in Alex's bare living room, a white wall, a table on which sits the slide projector. The glare of the projector's light defines a white, empty screen. Alex moves into the white screen, a full shot of her face framed by the white wall. The slide projector clicks into motion, a scene is projected, a male (left side of screen) and Catharine (right side of the screen) who is holding his arm. Alex's image blends with Catharine's, whose head is turned. Another male (Dennis Hopper) enters the screen. There is a shot of Alex's face, then a split screen with two images of Catharine. Alex once again enters the screen, blocking out Dennis Hopper. Alex reaches up and touches Catharine's face as the camera turns back to the slide machine which hides in the dark, its orange and black lips pulsing like a breathing mouth. The next shot is of Hopper, Catharine and Alex in the far left hand corner of the screen. Catharine's head is covered with a wedding veil. Alex enters the screen and touches Catharine's face. The lips of the projector continue to breath and pulse, in and out. Alex shifts position, covering the man in the slide, now the screen projects Alex and Catharine side by side. Now Catharine's face covers Alex's, who is standing in front of her. Catharine's face and eyes are projected through Alex's back which is to the screen. Her face blanks out Catharine's gaze. Alex moves to the side of the screen, her image still on the wall. Catharine's arm is slightly lowered, her hand and wrist are crossing her waist. Alex pulls back the bottom of her night shirt placing her hand on Catharine's arm, which crosses Catharine's waist, nearing her genital area.

The camera suddenly moves to Alex's bathroom, a small lighted room at the end of a short hallway. Alex stands in front of the mirror, touching her nose. The camera shifts back to the living room. Catharine is projected on the wall, then there is a split screen shot of Catharine on the wall and Alex in the bathroom mirror. The next shot shows Alex pulling her hair back in front of the mirror, as the slide projector is heard in the background. Alex slumps, arms on the sink, darkness behind her, the slide projector clicking.

Several things are operating at the same time in this slide sequence. One female surveys another. This selfsame female surveys herself surveying another woman. The object of this gaze (Catharine), in turn is seen looking back on the voyeur, for when Alex turns from her bathroom mirror back to the living room screen, there is Catharine on the wall, gazing at her. In this enlivened space, this tiny screen play within the film, Alex's investigative gaze turns erotic, she is drawn to Catharine.

And here Alex assumes a variety of subject positions in relationship to Catharine. She stands in the position of husband, she touches Catharine's image 'in a way strikingly similar to the boy at the beginning of *Persona*' (Mayne, 1990: 47) and she blends her image with Catharine's. As Mayne observes, this screen play 'isolates and combines with dizzying rapidity three modes of desire: substitution (for the husband), merging (in the child's fantasy of fusion), and the narcissistic identification' (1990: 47). Alex-as-husband wants to be captured by Catharine. She wants, at the same time, to protect Catharine, even as she desires to show her off as a possession.

Alex-as-Catharine wants a man at her side. Alex-as-Catharine desires to be beautiful, alluring, strong, confident. She wants all that Catharine has. But it is not to be, she is not beautiful Catharine. This is what the bathroom scene establishes. The mirror scene reflects Alex's tarnished self-image back against the beautiful face of Catharine. Alex becomes the surveyed female, the object of the voyeur's gaze, and she is the dirty, tainted, inadequate voyeur.

But Alex has become Catharine. She identifies with Catharine, she desires Catharine. What started out as an investigation of Catharine's multiple looks in her many marriages has suddenly turned into a narcissistic experience. Alex has become the object of her own gaze, and the subjectivity she perceives in the gaze is lack, emptiness. Catharine is full woman, Alex, empty woman. Still, Alex has something Catharine lacks. Alex has a moral conscience. She knows what is right and what is wrong. The law is on her side. And the law may not be beautiful, but it is right. Or so Alex believes.

Act Two: The Predatory Gaze Meets the Legal Look   Certain now that Catharine is a killer, Alex sets off for Seattle, and in an extended scene in the Seattle Police Department her predatory look confronts the legal gaze of the police. A police training film is projected, slightly off-centre, on a screen in front of a group of policemen. A man fires a gun on screen. Someone shouts for Lou to fix the screen, as the title of the film, 'Survival Shooting Techniques' flashes on the wall. A voice from the film is heard, 'Just because you can't see a suspect doesn't mean he can't see you'. The screen now divides, the men watching the film on the one side, and Alex in front of the desk of a detective with a map of Seattle on the wall behind him. The two scenes go on at the same time. Alex is on both sides of the law. She has placed her newspaper clippings and photos of Catharine on the policeman's desk. While admitting there is a resemblance in the photos, the detective refuses to take action. Alex moves, walking into the screen of the film playing on the other side of the room. Her image is on the wall, slightly off-centre, as a policeman fires a shot at a suspect. The detective explodes, 'You want me to go to one of the five richest men in the state and tell him some ding-bat thinks his wife's a murderer when nobody else thinks there's been a homicide!?' Alex retorts, 'I just spent the whole morning showing you the God Damned evidence . . . . I know I'm right'. Two days later Catharine kills her next victim.

This brief screen play projects two versions of the law, the masculine and the feminine. Male law is violent, certain and quick, guns, bullets, survival techniques that will take out hidden suspects. This is not the law that Alex projects. Her villain is a woman who poisons her husbands. Her villain is in full sight. Alex's off-centred screen image aligns her with this unacceptable version of the law.

This, of course, is a traditional theme, the private eye confronting the stupid police (see Symons, 1985: 54). But here it is given a new twist, for the private eye works for the Justice Department and he is a woman. But the police will not accord her the status of a man, she's a ding-bat. Thus in this second play within the film Alex experiences herself as lack: a double failure, neither an attractive female, nor an acceptable officer of the law. She must now pursue her villain alone, and so she takes off, undercover, for Hawaii, in pursuit of the elusive black widow. Two extended water scenes erotically and violently draw the two women together.

Act Three: The Violent Erotic Gaze   Under an assumed name, Jessica Bates, Alex meets up with Catharine (now named Remi Walker) at the poolside in a scuba diving lesson. As partners they must share an air regulator and give each other mouth-to-mouth resuscitation. It is in this first of two water scenes that Alex draws closest to Catharine, pretending that her watery kiss during mouth-to-mouth resuscitation is not a real kiss. (Alex: 'You aren't taking this seriously, are you?' Catharine, 'Don't worry'.) So, a kiss is not a real kiss, this is a joke, no sexual desire here.

The poolside scuba scene is soon extended to the real thing. Days later Alex and Catharine, air tanks on their backs, are underway, off-shore, swimming in and around coral reefs and schools of colourful fish. Alex picks up a black coral. She and Catharine play catch as Catharine swims behind her and dislodges her air hose. Alex struggles for air. Catharine looks back. Alex panics. Catharine reappears and suddenly gives her an air hose. The two women struggle to the top of the ocean. Unaware that Catharine nearly killed her, Alex thanks her, 'Scared the shit out of me back there! Thanks for not having your back turned back there'.

Violence displaced, erotic attraction still beneath the surface, Alex continues her surveillance of Catharine. Catharine, in turn, is spying on Alex, breaking into her room, smelling the scent on her handkerchief, holding it tenderly to her cheek. Watching Paul and Catharine from afar, across the pool, at their wedding, Alex approaches Catharine, giving her the black widow brooch, Catharine abruptly grabs her and kisses her violently on the mouth. Alex coldly pulls back, turning the kiss into an act of hostility (see Heung, 1987).

The film's penultimate scene brings the two women together in the jail. Alex is behind the screened partition, a policeman stands nearby. Catharine gloats, 'Are they treating you OK? You know they think you were obsessed with me . . . . I killed him [Paul] to frame you . . . . You know of all the relationships I look back on in 50 years time, I'll always remember this one'. As Catharine turns to leave Paul steps into the room. Catharine gives him a kiss and is taken off by the police.

Here the viewer is asked to accept the reciprocal attraction between the two women (Heung, 1987), an attraction mediated by the law, for Alex's gaze is finally vindicated. Her obsessive lapse into narcissism and her erotic attraction to Catharine are now justified.[17] The crack Justice Department investigator has trapped her victim. In the process she has been feminized, made beautiful, suggesting that the ends do justify the means. After all we've got a complete woman here at the end.

Two Voyeurs: Catharine as Retro Femme Fatale

Black Widow traces the investigative journeys of two female voyeurs. The story line moves back and forth between Alex's surveillance of Catharine, Catharine's surveillance of her next victim and Catharine spying on Alex. These three investigative structures privilege Alex's project, displacing the deceitful means Catharine uses to trap her next victim. Her methods are not that different from Alex's. She studies newspaper clippings and stacks of books which allow her to bone up on her next victim. She clips photos, fabricates identities, tries on new identities, breaks into rooms, searches Alex's luggage, uses a private eye, spies on and tails Alex, and uses her feminine wiles to trap her next victim.

As a retro femme fatale Catharine is outside the law, even as she uses the surveillance methods of the law to accomplish her next violent act. But unlike Alex of Fatal Attraction, her sexuality is secondary to her predatory purposes. Erotic, sensuous love is not central to her project. She traps her victims with her mind, not her body. Eroticism, and erotic voyeurism only appear in her relationship with Alex, where her seductiveness proves to be a trap. As the black widow she in fact mates with Alex, their obsessions coalesce into a single attraction, each wants to trap the other.

Here the film departs from its traditional male counterpart, where the detective's only goal is to bring the criminal to trial. Like Persona,

Catharine merges with Alex, perhaps desiring to be a strong woman who doesn't need a man, just as Alex merges with her. By placing Paul and Alex together, Catharine substitutes herself for Paul in the relationship, as she narcissistically identifies with Alex in the handkerchief scene.

Both women become the surveyed woman for the other. Each places herself on the other side of the other's keyhole. Each surveys herself from the vantage point of the other. In these moves the film delineates, but refuses to endorse, lesbian attraction (Mayne, 1990: 48). At the same time the multiple screen scenes within the text function as a 'trope for women's cinema that refuses to be married to the law' (Mayne, 1990: 48). These screen scenes, that is, complicate the feminine gaze and the gazes that are directed at the figure of the woman. She becomes more than pure spectacle for male pleasure. Her voyeurism yields more than scopic pleasure: it produces positive self-fulfilment.

Fire, Rain and the Violent Female Gaze

As with *Fatal Attraction* water is everywhere and clearly associated with the feminine self, sexuality, creation, destruction and death. Rain and water are repeatedly present, from the film's opening shot of Catharine leaving a helicopter in the rain, the cemetery scene in the rain, overcast Seattle, ferry rides across Seattle's waterfront, the scuba diving lessons in Hawaii, Catharine and Alex's underwater scuba diving adventure that nearly ends in Alex's death, Catharine and Paul's lovemaking in a swimming pool, to Catharine's using the bathroom sink as the site for destroying all evidence of the poisons she inserts in her husbands' toothpaste, brandy and wine.

While Catharine and Alex appear as water nymphs, it is dangerous Catharine who dwells both near and in water and fire. She even takes Alex to the top of the volcanic mountain which erupts in red smoke and fire. And it is in the water scenes where Alex draws closest to Catharine, pretending that her watery kiss during mouth-to-mouth resuscitation is not a real kiss.

Primal nature, the rain forests of Hawaii, earth, sea and sky, are contrasted to civilized (artificial swimming pools) nature, where water and its forces are controlled and carefully managed. The two female characters embody these contrasting views. More natural Alex clashes with contrived, superficial Catharine. Natural Alex makes love with Paul in a rain forest. Artificial Catharine seduces Paul in an indoor swimming pool. Thus are the negative features of nature and water symbolically associated with the *femme fatale*. And while Alex Forrest will go to a violent, watery grave, the iron grasp of the law (in the form of Alex Barnes) will take Catharine off to jail. Thereby aligning this properly feminized Alex with patriarchy and the state. Two parallel solutions to a domestic crisis.

Retro Noir Femme Fatales

Black Widow seeks to recast the noir tradition while invoking many of the expected noir themes including, role reversals, transferences, doublings, double-crosses, misplaced guilt and innocent persons charged with the crimes of others, betrayals, murder and violence. Following, and elaborating, the lead of recent films (*Body Heat, The Jagged Edge, Prizzi's Honor*) where *femme fatales* and Single Working Women are intellectual superiors to the men they victimize (Williamson, 1987; Combs, 1987), *Black Widow* pits two strong women, both neurotic about men, against one another. (Heung, 1987; Combs, 1987). Catharine, like Alex Forrest, is a virus. She infects and then destroys the men who fall in love with and marry her (see Williamson, 1987). A threat to society, she must be stopped. But Alex's neurotic, obsessive identification with Catharine (shades of *Persona*, see Benson, 1987), the man's woman (Heung, 1987), makes her the victim, not the aggressor. Thus, like *Jagged Edge*, the strong professional woman on the side of the law falls under the spell of the evil other.

Alex and Catharine are doubles, both are skilled at what they do. (Catharine: 'You never really figure you're quite there . . . . Well, I used to think of it as my job . . . I was a professional'.) As Alex gets closer to Catharine (her new prey), the two women share dresses, are clothed in the same colour scheme (red, blue, black), go to the same hairdresser, exchange erotic kisses, fall in love with the same man and in the end Alex is charged with Catharine's crimes (see Heung, 1987). Alex is feminized by her erotic identification with Catharine, she seeks Catharine's beauty (Alex: 'We spent most of the day in the pool: you come out looking like that and I look like this . . . . Can I borrow your hair?') The dedicated female investigator is unfulfilled woman (*femme manquee*): the *femme fatale* is all-woman, a man's woman (Combs, 1987). So, in the end, this noir experiment fails. It 'exploits the full-blown iconography of the *femme fatale* based as it is on the fetishism of the female body and the mythology of woman's unfulfilled sexuality and her willingness to control men' (Heung, 1987).

The Worldly Feminine Look

Back to the beginning and the four propositions. Mayne (1990: 227) speaks of the ambivalent threshold that is created when women are on both sides of the keyhole. As both subject and object of another woman's look, the figure of the gazing (and gazed upon) woman is multiply coded: as fatally flawed; as supplemental to the male look; as the object of erotic desire; as multi-sensual; as maternal; as narcissistic, and obsessive; as an affront to the male look; as a threat to the law, family and the state; and as embodiment of family and traditional femininity.

Each of the women voyeurs (the two Alexes, Beth, Ellen) work against and within a male specular economy. Each seeks an empowering, feminine subjectivity that transcends the visual. Here mirror scenes become critical (see La Belle, 1988: 179). Each woman struggles to find a mirrored self-image that is not controlled by the male mirror. Each seeks a multifaceted specularity that is uniquely feminine. And they cannot find this gaze in the look of the male other.

Alex Forrest sees and feels her reflection in Dan's seed that grows inside her womb. Beth sees a maternal and erotic self reflected back from her dressing table mirror. (Even as Dan hangs over her shoulder.) Alex Barnes sees herself in Catharine's photographs and rejects her own mirrored image. Each time Catharine approaches the bathroom sink and pours poison down the drain she avoids her own mirror image. It is as if this poison which kills her husbands were a vile bodily fluid.

The look and the subjectivity that is sought by each woman is given, in the end, by another woman. This gaze and its feelings are born out of violence. Beth's fully maternal love gaze (and self) return only after she has done battle with, and killed, Alex in her bathroom. Alex Barnes's complete turn away from Catharine occurs only after the violent under water scuba scene and her gift of the black widow. Two acts of violence (near death) and the betrayal of affection, produce this resolute change in self (and gaze). Alex Forrest's final violent, maternal screams echo from the acoustical mirror in the Gallagher bathroom. Out of the fog and the steam her face displaces Beth's. Alex's murderous intentions are clear. She must kill Beth who has taken her place with Dan.

In turn, Catharine must act to kill Alex Barnes. Alex has become Paul's lover and she knows what the black widow has done. But more deeply, for a moment, Catharine has become Alex. She has been touched by this unattractive woman who has chased her to Hawaii. Tables turned, now the hunted, not the hunter, Catharine opens up to Alex, sharing her past history, shedding her masks, revealing a version of herself that has never been shared with a man. She becomes a whole woman, near-naked in front of Alex in her skimpy bathing suit, touching her in the water, sitting next to her as the sun sets on the beach: two lovers – two women in search of the same thing, wholeness, self-unity.

On the surface these self-changes are produced by the voyeur's gaze, for it is the gaze that brings each woman to the edge of the other's keyhole. And it is the gaze that startles and catches the other off-guard, exposing them in their interactional, intimate and primal pursuits. But these changes are not produced by the exposure of the other. Such exposure is the traditional province of the investigative, erotic or illicit gaze.

Instead, confrontation with the other produces self-awareness and fuels self-desire. This transcends narcissistic identification, obsessive involvement in the other. The feminine gaze produces its own self-understanding. In the speculum of the other woman each woman finds herself. But this is not the concave speculum used by gynaecologists to investigate the female genitalia, for what is found exceeds sexuality. Each woman's body and self is beyond 'the tain of the mirror, outside of any specular representation' (Jay, 1993a: 534; Irigaray, 1985: 146).

Each woman is excess, more than her corporeal self. Yet she has always previously defined herself within the structures of that corporeal self-body image. She has not understood that she is outside specular representation, more than what the silver backing of the mirror reflects. So in the moment of self-discovery each woman does more than take the mirror, which reflects the other, into her own hands. She remakes herself inside the self-understandings awakened by the reflected, refracted images of herself which collide with those of the other woman. She does more than see herself through the eyes of the other. She discovers herself through her own eyes. Thus the mirror that is used neither reflects nor contains her specularity. It creates specularity which knows no reflected boundary.

Bergman's *Persona* provides an example. Alma is speaking to Elisabeth Vogler, 'That evening when I had been to see your film, I stood in front of the mirror and thought, "We're quite alike". Don't get me wrong. You are much more beautiful. But in some way we're alike. I think I could turn myself into you if I really tried. I mean inside. Don't you think so? And you wouldn't have any difficulty, of course, turning into me. You could do it just like that' (Bergman, 1972: 57–8). That night, after this speech, Elisabeth enters sleeping Alma's room and 'caresses her cheek with her lips. Her long hair falls forward over her forehead and encloses their faces' (Bergman, 1972: 60–1). Days later Elisabeth begins her recovery which will return her to her husband and her work. Elisabeth recreates herself through this concave mirror that Alma has given her.

This is a new form of specular self-knowledge, a knowledge that feels its own self-understandings and transcends the immediate present. This awareness arises precisely at that moment when each woman renounces male specularity. Thus it can be seen that Alex Barnes begins to awaken in that pivotal living-room scene when she inserts herself next to Catharine, displacing the husband who marks this place and relationship in masculine terms. But this is only the beginning of the journey that Alex Barnes must take. She is still defined within the male mirror.

Her rejection of this mirror begins at the poolside in Hawaii when the relationship with Catharine takes shape. Still seeing herself through male eyes, when she compares her hair and body to Catharine's, Alex begins her transformation when she and Catharine leave civilization and enter the primal sea or sit on the beach near the rain forest. Gazing into the setting sun, the male mirror is burned away and replaced by the calm reflection of the ocean waters. Together Catharine and Alex discover a feminine subjectivity that is not defined in male terms. This is given by the mirror of nature.

In this act of renunciation, each woman embraces the 'dazzle of [a] multifaceted speleology, a scintillating and incandescent concavity, of language, also, that threatens to set fire to fetish-objects and gilded eyes'

(Irigaray, 1985: 143). She passes through the tain of the mirror (Irigaray, 1985: 149) to the other side of language and self-imagery. She burns away 'the fetishized woman-as-object seen in [and created] by the [masculine] glass . . . the "gilded eyes" of [male] mirror-mindedness [are] replaced by eyes that search deeply into the hidden caverns of female selfhood' (La Belle, 1988: 179–80).

Thus do Catharine and Alex experience conflict. They have burned through the male looking-glass and discovered a form of being that has never before been experienced. Under water, and now beside the sea, they have been united by the sun's rays and the water's gaze. But each remains trapped by what the male body can give. And so they fight over Paul. Self-discovery has only been partial. The male mirror still reflects back on their shared consciousness. And now their journeys go in different directions.

Alex Barnes seeks to be united with an embodied, felt self-image that is 'nothing less than a state of consciousness defined through its constant commingling with corporeal being' (La Belle, 1988: 180). And this being embraces the world, becomes one with the world. In this new world that Alex embraces there are two mirrors, the law/mirror of the father, the state, the law, and the newly emerging law/mirror of feminine subjectivity.

Catharine has betrayed this first law. She cannot transcend the masculine mirror and its flawed reflections so she must be destroyed, captured, brought behind the mirrored bars of prison. The trap is set. But all is not lost, for Catharine learns too. Full feminine self-awareness is finally announced in the film's penultimate moment, when she confesses, and then tells Alex that she will never forget this relationship. What she has taken from Alex can never be given by a man.

Alex triumphs, exults in her moment of victory. She has learned a new law, the law of the feminine mirror, and this law is fully compatible (for her) with the law of the father and the state. She hasn't thrown away the mirror of the world, she has remade it in her own collective self-image. The mirror is no longer tyrant, the dominant male/mirror. She marches proudly through the glare of the lights from the photographers' cameras into the full glare of nature's sun, whose rays reflect back against the courthouse, the site of the law of the father. Thus does the feminine worldly mirror transform itself.

These are some of the things that can happen when women are on both sides of the keyhole. In the next chapter I explore what happens when males take up this position. The lessons are less promising.

Notes

1 Directed by Bob Rafelson; Studio: Twentieth-Century Fox; screenplay by Ronald Bass; cast: Debra Winger (Alexandra Barnes), Theresa Russell (Catharine); Sami Frey (Paul), Dennis Hopper (Ben), Nicol Williamson (William), James Hong (Shin).

2 Directed by Adrian Lyne; studio: Paramount; Screenplay by James Dearden; cast: Michael Douglas (Dan Gallagher), Glenn Close (Alex Forrest), Anne Archer (Beth Gallagher), Ellen Hamilton Latzen (Ellen Gallagher).

3 For example: *Gilda, Rebecca, She's Gotta Have It, Blue Steel, Prince of Tides, Desperately Seeking Susan.* Here my focus differs from Mayne's (1990) who analyses the female voyeur in non-mainstream, 'women's films', including *I've Heard the Mermaids Singing,* and *Illusions.*

4 Both *Fatal Attraction* and *Psycho* begin with the camera panning the skyline of a large city (New York and Phoenix respectively), then switch to the inside of an apartment. The Close character locates her father in Phoenix (see Konigsberg, 1988: 118). *Fatal Attraction* draws on horror film techniques (knives, shower-bath room scenes, à la *Psycho*). The obsession Winger's character displays mirrors that of earlier Hitchcock and De Palma characters (Scottie of *Vertigo*; Cliff Robertson in *Obsession*). Winger's voyeurism is matched, in part, by Charlie's gaze in *Shadow of a Doubt,* while Russell's character, in a play on De Palma, *is* dressed to kill. Hitchcock's investigative, female voyeurs (Charlie in *Shadow of a Doubt,* Doctor Constance Petersen in *Spellbound*) were comfortable in their female identities. Charlie, the female, attractive, inquisitive, thoughtful adolescent complements the attractive, dreamy, maternal Constance Petersen, a psychoanalyst who leads Gregory Peck (John Ballantine) out of his amnesia and frightening nightmare. Both women use their powers of feminine intuition and compassion to save lives and discover a real murderer. Their foes are males. They are females on the masculine side of the keyhole. Their gazes are not flawed. They are supplemental to the male gaze. Each deploys the traditional masculine look of law, order and/or psychiatry. Their gazes are not sexual, and they are seldom spectacle for the male gaze. They embody the classic image of the female voyeur. She is not a threat to self, society or other. She is the good woman. Hitchcock reverses this imagery in *Psycho*. The object of Norman Bates's gaze is doubled back through the look (and exhortations) of his dead mother, producing the famous shower scene where the watery eye of dying Janet Leigh is mirrored in the floor drain.

5 Katovich and Haller (1993) distinguish the *femme fatale* of the 1940 film noir tradition (*Double Indemnity, The Postman Always Rings Twice*) from the retro *fatale* of the retro noir nostalgia (*la mode retro*) tradition (Jameson, 1991: 190) of the 1980s and 1990s (*Body Heat, Black Widow, Fatal Attraction*). Noir's *femme fatale* manipulated men without committing violence. The retro *fatal* is obsessive, fanatical, violent, acts out of self interest, breaks the law and in her subversive identity (*Thelma and Louise*), flees from male authority.

6 This is taken to a new level in Paul Verhoeven's 1992 highly controversial, erotic, soft pornographic, anti-gay and lesbian thriller, *Basic Instinct*. Here the bisexual retro *femme fatale* (Catherine Tramell), played by Sharon Stone, is a man-eating, sadomasochistic, nymphomaniac, serial murderess. Stone blatantly exploits the latent bisexuality perfected by Marlene Dietrich in *Blue Angel* (1930). The Stone character writes mystery novels, her most recent being about a violent, damaged cop. Other films in this recent tradition include *Final Analysis, The Temp,* and to a lesser degree *Single White Female.*

7 Hence Alex's taped message to Dan 'I taste you, part of you is growing in me'.

8 Not surprisingly in *Basic Instinct* this merger produces a violent bisexual.

9 Williamson (1988) speaks here of the 'Single Working Woman' (SWW) stereotype, a recent representation in American movies. This woman, recently played by Debra Winger and Glenn Close, has permed-crinkly hair, is good at her job, is neurotic about men and, in films like *Fatal Attraction* and *9½ Weeks,* is fitted into a text that deals, on one level with yuppie sex life and on another with body-horror (*The Fly*). The SWW becomes the AIDS virus, the 'Horror' that will destroy the yuppie nuclear family. According to Faludi (1993, Chapter 5) these films display Hollywood's 1980s backlash against the women's movement. Richard Bradley called my attention to Faludi's analysis.

10 A client of his firm, a publisher, is being sued. A Congressman who has had a number of affairs is claiming that the female author of a new book has written about him.

11 The confession follows an earlier erotic scene between Dan and Beth where Dan nestles his face next to hers in the mirror as she sits in panties and bra at her dressing table.

12 I thank Joanna Bradley, Rachel Denzin, Richard Bradley, Katherine E. Ryan and Nate Stevens for their assistance in this discussion of water and its symbolic meanings.

13 In the original ending of the film Beth commits suicide (see Faludi, 1993: 117–23). The second ending, which audiences preferred, exploits the *Friday the 13th* cliché with the villain who is never really dead (Ebert, 1989c: 249).

14 Theresa Russell's character takes on several names in the film: Catharine (the wife of a Mafioso); Marielle (the wife of a toy manufacturer); Margaret (the wife of an anthropologist); Remi Walker (a playgirl who romances a hotel developer in Hawaii). Winger's character takes on the name of Jessica Bates (after *Norman Bates* of Psycho?) when she goes undercover to investigate Russell's character in Hawaii. Following Heung (1987) I will refer to Russell's character as Catharine.

15 The film mocks psychoanalytic explanations. Just before she leaves her job to work full-time on Catharine's case, Alex recounts to Bruce the story of her father who was violent and who keeled over one day after beating Alex with a steel spatula. 'This woman [Catharine] has the same deep resentment against older men. Ha! Ha! A lot of crap. Nobody knows why anyone does anything!'

16 The gazes of *Black Widow* (like those of *Fatal Attraction*) are cinematically produced through clever editing, split screens and subjective and selective POV shots. Also, like *Fatal Attraction*, bathrooms, water and fire play central parts in the story's visual symbolism.

17 Even to the point of making love with Paul, raising the question, is she Paul or Catharine in this relationship?

7

PARANOIA AND THE
EROTICS OF POWER

I have no interest in human nature. I listen. I'm not responsible. I just run the tapes. It's a business.

Harry Caul, *The Conversation*

The American people have yet to see the Zapruder film.[1] Why? The American people have yet to see the real photographs and X-rays of the autopsy. Why? There are hundreds of documents that could help prove this conspiracy. Why have they been withheld or burned by the Government?

Jim Garrison, *JFK*

In this chapter I examine paranoia and the erotics of power, the paranoic obsession with the gaze, the belief that one is being gazed upon, the desire to contain the other within a 'new and more generalized sensory space in which there are no longer any . . . hiding-places of any kind' (Jameson, 1992: 66). This obsession presumes the malevolent uses of the panoptic and panauditory gaze by the state and its agents in the contemporary, postmodern period. The paranoid gaze merges with the erotics of power, those scopic pleasures derived from the power of the look. These pleasures go beyond the purely sexual. But they always work outward from the body, its containment, its presence in the situation, its sights and sounds, its erotic appeal, its sensuality, the flesh.

Building on the analysis in Chapters 5 and 6, I continue my investigation of the male mirror, the masculine gaze and the obsessive desire to capture political and everyday life in all their plenitude. I look at men on both sides of the keyhole, men watching men (and occasionally women). Again I select two texts for intensive analysis, Francis Ford Coppola's brilliant and disturbing 1974 film *The Conversation*[2] called by some critics 'one of the darkest and most disturbing films ever made in this country' (Farber, 1974: 13) and Oliver Stone's equally controversial and disturbing 1991 film *JFK*[3] (see Zelizer, 1992: 201–14; also Stone and Sklar, 1992, Part II: 187–529). Stone's film, of course, is a re-telling of the Kennedy assassination, what Don DeLillo (*Libra*, 1988) calls 'The story that won't go away, the seven seconds that broke the back of the American century'. Stone's film, as noted in Chapter 1, turns on the use of other visual texts including newsreels and photographs and, most importantly, the Zapruder film to establish its own theory of the assassination. Thus is history rewritten within another version of the cinematic simulacrum. Fittingly, I end this study with *JFK* for it documents the final spasms of the cinematic apparatus in the twilight of the twentieth century.

The following propositions organize my argument. The first elaborates arguments given in Chapter 5. Hitchcock and Antonioni brought the voyeur into the early postmodern period. Their projects provide the backdrop for Coppola and Stone. Hitchcock and Antonioni delineated the spaces the cinematic voyeur could inhabit. Both directors rejected the notion of the objective observer and each made the voyeur part of the spectacle that was witnessed. Both directors also announced the end of privacy in the early postmodern age. Each told 'classic' detective stories (as elaborated in Chapter 4) involving a victim, a lone detective and a villain. Their stories would turn on two tales, the murder (what appeared to happen) and its investigation (what really happened).

Hitchcock's camera, as argued in Chapter 5, was guided by two principles and two pleasures. The camera indulges the spectator's desire for scopic pleasure, which is joined with the need for the revelation of moral truth. At the same time the camera must act as a moral authority (revealing final truth) and the film must tell a story that shows how those who violate these moral laws are punished and brought to justice. Antonioni rejected these principles. His camera, while courting the sexual gaze, does not answer to a higher moral truth, and his voyeur is not an agent of the law.

As leading filmmakers of the generation that built on Hitchcock and Antonioni, Coppola and Stone explore the misanthropic, malicious, conspiratorial uses of the cinematic apparatus in the late postmodern surveillance society. Stone adheres to Hitchcock's moral principles, his camera is an agent of political truth, the narrator of history for a post-Vietnam generation. Coppola is more closely aligned with Antonioni's project, wrestling with the moral dilemmas produced by the new information technologies, worrying about the higher truths to which these technologies must answer. Stone seeks certain truths, Coppola wonders if such truths are any longer possible.

My second proposition concerns the emergence and meanings of the reflexive cinematic text in the postmodern period. Stone and Coppola produce versions of what Jameson (1992: 3) calls the 'conspiratorial text'. Such texts, as allegorical film narratives, attempt to discover the truths, or lack thereof, that are embedded in the late twentieth century American histories surrounding Vietnam, Watergate, the political assassinations of John and Robert Kennedy, Martin Luther King, the Nixon tapes, and, by implication, the political cover-ups of the Reagan/Bush Presidential administrations (Irangate, etc.).

The conspiratorial text takes as its subject matter the new surveillance society, or what Marx (1986; 1988: 221; 1992) calls the maximum-security society, a society filled with undercover agents, human and computer informers, computer hackers, and sneakers (*Sneakers*, 1992), vigilantes and for-hire paramilitary networks attached to multinational corporations who ignore the geo-political boundaries of nation-states, hidden video and audio cameras in public places, electronic leashes, electronic article surveillance (EAS) systems, personal truth technologies (body fluids, DNA matches), anticipatory and high-tech surveillance systems, computerized mailing lists and dossiers, electronic, stalking on public and private E-mail systems (Compuserve, Internet and Bitnet, etc.), wiretaps, hidden microphones and video cameras in the walls of private homes (*The Firm*, 1993; *Sliver*, 1993), automatic telephone switching systems (*Three Days of the Condor*, 1975; *Sneakers*, 1992), satellite surveillance systems (*Patriot Games*, 1992), chemical tracking, hidden beepers, a mandatory national ID system (Marx, 1988: 216), an electronic leash implanted in the brain of every person (*Clockwork Orange* (1971) and in the film of Orwell's *1984*), private and state security guards outside every door.

This is the stuff of the conspiratorial film. Examples include *The Manchurian Candidate* (1962), *Z* (1968), *Klute* (1971), *Executive Action* (1973), *The Conversation* (1974), *The Parallax View* (1974), *Three Days of the Condor* (1975), *Taxi Driver* (1976), *All the President's Men* (1976), *Who'll Stop the Rain?* (1978), *Blow Out* (1981), *Missing* (1982), *The Year of Living Dangerously* (1983), *Under Fire* (1983), *Salvador* (1986), *Betrayed* (1988), *JFK* (1991), *Sliver* (1993), *In the Line of Fire* (1993), *Ruby* (1992), *Love Field* (1992). Such films are preoccupied with attempts to re-tell and come to grips with contemporary history and the cover-ups and symbolic meanings attached to this history (Vietnam, Kennedy's assassination, Watergate, toxic and nuclear waste sites, Latin American guerrilla wars of national liberation, etc.).

Third, these texts reflexively interrogate the new information technologies and those who control them. They argue that these technologies, in conjunction with the media and a private and public power elite (Mills, 1956), conspire to tell only one version of history. This is a self-serving version of history which perpetuates the power elite. Reflexive, conspiratorial cinema is premised on the belief that a true history can be uncovered, a true reality lies beneath the simulacrum. Reality is more than it is presented as being. There is a real truth to history. A reflexive paranoia is at work here. These films are preoccupied with the belief that those in power always lie and distort the truth.

Thus these films reproduce the camera theory of reality discussed in Chapter 1. They argue that there is a body of fixed truths in the social world that can be dug out and verified by the reflexive filmmaker. These truths are aligned with the doctrines of a free, open, democratic society. They must be told, if democracy is to persist. So Oliver Stone has Kevin Costner (as Jim Garrison) speak the following lines in his closing speech in *JFK*. 'The truth is the most important value we have because if the truth does not endure, if the Government murders the truth . . . then this is no longer the country in which we were born and this is not the country I want to die in . . . . And this was never more true than for John F.

Kennedy whose murder was probably the most terrible moment in the history of our country'.

If the viewer didn't get the message, Stone repeats it, minutes later, in the film's closing moment. This following slogans appear on screen: 'STUDY THE PAST', 'PAST IS PROLOGUE', 'ETERNAL VIGILANCE IS THE PRICE OF LIBERTY', 'DEDICATED TO THE YOUNG, IN WHOSE SPIRIT THE SEARCH FOR TRUTH MARCHES ON' 'THE END'.

Fourth, conspiratorial films follow, while radically altering, the traditional model of the detective story (see Jameson, 1992: 33–9, 45–7). In these films (and stories) a reporter, photo-journalist, innocent bystander, private investigator, war veteran or public defender takes on the establishment. Here the victim becomes both the slain public official and the public-at-large (having been denied accurate facts). The villain is no longer a solitary individual, as it was in the modernist and high modernist age of Hitchcock and Antonioni. The villain becomes a collectivity, a faceless Firm, the Director, the Parallax Corporation, the White House. This collectivity functions both as detective, in search of the detective who seeks to expose them (*The Conversation, The Parallax View*), and as villain, they have perpetuated a crime against society and history. The solitary detective is then recast as villain or psychotic, often an alcoholic outsider who threatens the status quo (for example, the Warren Beatty character in *The Parallax View*).

These films pass judgement on society, working their own magic with the so-called facts of the current historical moment. Hence they are usually discredited by the media (see Zelizer's (1992: 201–14) review of the criticisms of *JFK*; also Stone and Sklar, 1992). At the same time the impulse for the attack on 'official history' that these texts launch comes not from the social or the collectivity *per se*. It is lodged instead in the psychology of the individual. That is, collective critiques and investigations arising from the status quo are seldom undertaken. Jameson (1992: 56–7) observes, drawing on the arguments of Lukacs: 'the dramatic . . . what shakes the status quo and produces crisis . . . is difficult to derive . . . from out of the status quo . . . and must therefore be housed, as a disturbing and unsettling force within the individual'.

There are six reasons for this. They all involve the politics of narrative. First, in the absence of a grand meta-narrative that would move a collectivity on its own behalf, North American literary and filmic tradition resorts to stories inscribed at the mythic, individual level (see Jameson, 1992: 56). Hence we have the story of the rebel, the outcast, the pathologically obsessed individual who selflessly and dangerously acts on some 'insane' altruistic need to save the social from itself (again the Warren Beatty character in *The Parallax View*, the Frank Sinatra character in *The Manchurian Candidate*, Jim Garrison in Stone's *JFK*, Harry Caul in *The Conversation*, Bernstein, Woodward and 'Deep Throat' in *All The President's Men*, and so on). This narrative system reinscribes the myth of the solitary, male individual in the anonymous mass society who acts also with honour, grace and self-sacrifice in the name of a higher good. Thus does the classic detective story of mid-century Raymond Chandler reproduce itself in the late twentieth century.

Second, however, the revolutionary, political rebel is a dying species in the postmodern, bureaucratic and multinational corporate world. Of course the utopian political ideology of protest movements still seeks to channel anti-social violence and revolutionary impulses to productive social ends. But this seldom succeeds. These movements have failed to find a way that would join the anti-social rebel with corporate utopian ends. There are few positive social heroes left, universal cynicism is the norm (see Jameson, 1992: 58). Consequently, the pathology of the protagonist is taken as a measure of their inability to be fitted into a larger utopian project.

Third, the social has been lulled into complacency by the official history that the power elite has written. There is no reason to challenge this history, for it is working. Only the lone detective, because of his or her pathology and social circumstance, is in a position to undertake this deconstruction. This search for truth must be more than an epistemological journey, it must go beyond 'reportorial curiosity' (Jameson, 1991: 56). The detective's project must be ontological, for he or she believes that conspiracy is the fundamental law of the social (Jameson, 1992: 56). Thus the messiness of 'protagonist's psyche somehow corresponds to the messiness of the social (Jameson, 1992: 56). In 'nailing' the story of the truth, the protagonist achieves personal redemption (and perhaps sanity), puts his or her life back together and saves society for another battle further on down the line. Or the detective dies for this higher truth.

Fourth, by placing the protagonist outside the social, outside the passive collectivity, these stories sustain the fiction of a division between the public and private, perpetuating the myth that they are incommensurable and mutually antagonistic. Two allegorical processes are at work here. The public and private lives of the public official (the assassin's victim) are distanced from another, even as his death (always a man) negatively influences the private lives of the members of the social (*JFK, In The Line of Fire, Love Field*). This gap between the public and the private is bridged by the private life of the detective. The protagonist's pathology signals the fact that only the disturbed person would attempt to make public what is irremediably private. The conspiracy to kill the public figure is thereby marked as a public concern. It is (and has been) properly dealt with by the public, and is of no legitimate interest to the private sectors of the social.

And there are no longer any hiding places, the conspiracy always wins, 'simply because it is collective and the victims, taken one by one in their isolation, are not' (Jameson, 1992: 66). Thus are conspiratorial tales always individual stories.

Fifth, the conspiratorial film presents its own carnival of specularity, a dizzying display of electronic, panoptic wizardry, and this carnival is without a director. Foucault (1980) observes that the machinery of the contemporary panopticon is diabolical. It is a 'machine in which everyone is caught, those who exercise power, just as much as those over whom it is exercised' (Foucault, 1980: 156). (Even Nixon was trapped by his own tapes.)

Sixth, summarizing the above arguments, and extending the analysis of Chapter 6, the male on the other side of the keyhole, like his female counterpart, embodies a fatally flawed gaze. Still, despite its reliance on the most sophisticated of surveillance technologies, the masculine gaze (unlike the feminine look), is unable to produce a depth and form of understanding that goes beyond the violent, narcissistic subject created by the flat masculine mirror. The postmodern male voyeur is a prisoner in a house of visual and ocular mirrors, a victim of his own power and deception. Now the films . . .

The Conversation

Noon, December 2, Union Square, San Francisco. An attractive young couple, Ann and Mark, clandestine lovers, weave in and out of a crowd, having what appears to be a banal conversation about Christmas presents. A man with a hearing aid and a shopping bag follows them. He in turn is followed by a mime in white face. High above the square another man with a telescopic lens watches their every movement. A fourth man, Harry Caul, the best bugging expert on the West Coast, enters a van where tape recorders play fragments of the couple's conversation (Farber, 1974: 13). The sounds of other conversations, mingled with a saxophone solo, fill the air as the couple walks around the square and an off-screen band plays 'When the red, red robin comes bob, bob, bobbin along'.

Thus opens Frances Ford Coppola's *The Conversation*. Started in 1966 and finished in 1974, the film's history spans the Vietnam War years, the shattering revelations of the Pentagon Papers and the Watergate scandals (Einstein, 1981: 515). This is a political text. It remains ominous in its devastating statements about the unchecked new communication technologies which threaten to destroy our democratic heritage by eroding our fundamental civil liberties concerning the right to privacy (Einstein, 1981: 515). Clearly influenced by Antonioni's *Blow-Up*, *The Conversation* demonstrates that technological prowess can only detect, it cannot comprehend or feel or form moral judgements. It produces a pornographic ecstasy of communication in which the invisible (the private) becomes visible (public) and nothing is any longer secret or sacred.

Harry Caul, his name a play on 'call' for he monitors telephone calls, is a voyeur, an anti-hero.[4] Forty-two years old, single, a Catholic, his birthday is December 2.[5] He abhors profanity ('Stan, don't use those words!'). He has no valued personal possessions, just the key to his apartment and his saxophone. He takes morbid pleasure in spying on others, in wire-tapping their phones and using the latest technologies to capture their private conversations which occur in public places. He works for anyone. He espouses no moral conscience: 'I once placed a bug in a parakeet. I don't care what they're talking about, all I want is a nice, fat recording. You get a better track if you pay attention to the recording, not what they're talkin' about. Just do the job. Never ask questions. Do it right. Keep your eyes and your mouth closed'. But he is haunted by a prior case where at least one murder occurred as a result of his bugging.

Harry is a man of contradictions. An expert on recording the conversations of others, he is unable to communicate with anyone. Rain or shine he wears a transparent plastic raincoat, 'as if for prophylactic protection against society' (Canby, 1974: 11). His universe is defined by sounds and their recordings. He is riddled with guilt, yet feels disconnected from the three murders that resulted from one of his jobs. 'I just turned the tapes.' He is alone and paranoid, triple locks the door to his sparsely and cheaply furnished apartment (alarms go off when he opens the door), makes love with his shoes on, listens to the sounds in his girlfriend's apartment before he knocks on her door and is unable to feel or to trust other people. His fear of 'being overheard is as intense as his compulsion to eavesdrop on others. His favourite position is "outside the door"' (Silverman, 1988: 88). His only release comes from playing his saxophone 'in accompaniment to a jazz album – a live recording which ends with a cheering crowd' (Einstein, 1981: 516).

Undoing The Conversation

Like David Lynch's *Blue Velvet*, Pakula's *Klute* and DePalma's *Blow Out*, Coppola's film enters reality through the ear, through the sounds of the human conversation, itself an acoustic mirror which 'permits the speaker to function at the same time as the listener' (Silverman, 1988: 79) to the sounds of their own and the other's voice.[6] A story about auditory and visual surveillance and what the listener shouldn't hear (and see), *The Conversation* moves quickly. His tapes in hand, Harry goes to his workshop and shapes the sounds into a coherent conversation. The young couple's words form full sentences.[7] Harry places a phone call (pay phone) and asks to speak to the Director. A male assistant tells him to bring the tapes the next afternoon. That evening Harry visits his girlfriend, Amy, who begins to ask him questions about what he does. He tells her that he has no secrets. The next day he goes to the Director's office, where the assistant attempts to take the tapes, warning Harry that they are dangerous. Leaving the office Harry sees Ann and Mark. He returns to his workshop and listens to the tapes again. More information is heard. Something sinister is going to happen on Sunday at 3.00 p.m. in room 773 of the Jack Tar Hotel. Harry deciphers a line spoken by Mark, 'He'd kill us if he got the chance'.

The next sequence of scenes takes the viewer to the annual surveillance convention, a national meeting, a carnival of the nation's top wire-tappers and security men. In this group Harry is a legend. He learns that his best assistant (Stan) has left him and his girlfriend has changed her telephone number. That night he sleeps with a woman (Meredith) who steals the tapes. His intimate talk with her is recorded and broadcast as part of a practical joke. In a flashback, Dali-like dream sequence, he relives the recording sequence in Union Square. He then follows Ann through a fog up a hill, recalling his childhood, he tells her that he is not afraid of death, only murder. Unable to let go of the information about what is going to happen in Room 773 of the Jack Tar, Harry goes to the hotel at the appointed time. Entering the empty hotel room, he hears water running in the toilet. As he flushes the toilet blood flows out and covers the bathroom floor. Ann and Mark have killed the Director, Ann's husband. Reading the newspaper headlines he learns that the death has been disguised to look like a car crash.

Harry is now implicated in the murder. He becomes the hunted, not the hunter. Through a sequence of flashbacks he sees the dead Director's body on the bed in the hotel room. His life begins to fall apart. He is the only man outside the Company who knows the real details of the death. His own life is now in danger. He returns home to find that it has been bugged. The telephone rings and the Director's assistant tells him 'We know that you know. For your own sake don't get involved any farther. We'll be listening to you'. In a manic, paranoid rage he destroys his apartment, looking for the bug, pulling the floor apart, board by board, even smashing a statuette of the Virgin Mary. A victim of his own craft, he is unable to discover how the bugging was done. In a final, dismal, nightmare-like scene, Harry sits in the rubble of his possessions, playing his saxophone, as the camera pans the destroyed apartment.

Structures of Surveillance and Harry's Nightmare

The Conversation is one long study in the surveillance of the other. Its subject is the act of observation itself (Kolker, 1980: 196): Harry recording and bringing meaning to the taped voices of Ann and Mark; the Director's firm tailing Harry; Harry's co-workers taping his voice; Harry's landlady reading his mail and letting herself into his apartment; Harry spying on Amy; Amy getting a new unlisted telephone number so Harry can't call her; Harry confessing to the priest; Ann and Mark watching themselves being watched, trying to escape surveillance; Harry attempting to live a totally private life where nobody can observe or know him. At the same time the film parades before the viewer the latest techniques of audio and video surveillance, including voice and motion activated recording devices.

Four gazes are central to the film's surveillance system: Harry's technological, auditory gaze which weaves sentences and stories out of sound bites; the organizational gaze of the Director's firm, which penetrates closed walls; the gaze of intimacy, which joins Ann and Mark in the park, Harry and Amy in her bedroom, Harry and Meredith for one night in his work place; and finally the moral gaze of guilt, the church, a heavenly surveillance system 'which might at any moment be turned against [Harry]' (Silverman, 1988: 89).

These multiple gazing structures are united in a single roving eye, the eye of the viewer, for we are the central voyeur in the film. We are studying other voyeurs, as if they were in captivity, insects or mice chasing around inside the glass walls of a contained, anonymous space. However, underneath this visual system of surveillance lurks the always present human voice and its recording, the voice of Ann as she calls out to Harry. Haunted by her description of the drunk on the park bench ('He was once somebody's baby boy'), Ann's maternal voice speaks through him, calling him back to his own childhood ('I was very sick when I was a boy'). Her voice awakens his moral conscience and sets him on his journey to stop a murder ('I'm not afraid of death. I am afraid of murder'). Thus does *The Conversation* give control to the female voice, more control than it is usually granted (see Silverman, 1988: 97).

Ann's voice activates a reverberating acoustical mirror which allows Harry to project himself into her situation with Mark. As he re-listens to the tape, the word *us* in 'He'd kill *us* if he had the chance', is reinterpreted to include Harry, thus does he insert himself into this murderous plot (see Silverman, 1988: 90; Kolker, 1980: 198). He thinks he can save them, and if he can save them, he can save himself. (At the same time by preventing the death of Ann and Mark he can achieve some relief from the guilt that he feels from the earlier murders that occurred because of his tapes.)

Ann's voice and her presence structure each of the four gazes that define the film's surveillance system. These four forms of looking are each filtered through Harry's eyes and ears.

Harry's Technological Gaze   Ann's description of the drunk on the park bench occurs in the middle of her conversation with Mark. Her words take shape for Harry as he sits at his workbench, replaying the sounds from the three hidden microphones. The equation is complete (Einstein, 1981: 516). Harry is the man on the bench, he was 'once somebody's baby boy, and he had a mother and a father who loved him'. These lines become part of Harry's conversation with himself as he puts this conversation together. The next day the line 'He'd kill us if he got the chance' emerges from the tape.

That night, after the party, as he stretches out on a mattress (again like the drunk on the bench), he replays the tapes. Meredith makes love to him as we again hear Ann's description of the drunk and the lines, 'He'd kill us'. The film segues into Harry's dream sequence. He recounts his childhood and his fear of murder to Ann who remains beyond his grasp atop the hill in the fog. This dream sequence moves forward in time. Harry is outside the door to room 773 of the Jack Tar Hotel. Harry sees Ann standing against the glass doors leading to the balcony, a noiseless scream is seen as the Director attacks her. A reverse shot shows the curtain smeared with blood which also stains the walls of the bathroom (see Silverman, 1988: 92). Harry has failed to save Ann.

Days later Harry actually goes to the Jack Tar. He rents the room next to 773. Underneath the sink, next to the toilet, he drills a hole through the wall, inserting a microphone into the next room. He hears excerpts from the Union Square tape, including the words 'I love you'. For Harry these words come from room 773, for the listener they come from the tape. As Silverman (1988: 93) notes, Harry's psychic auditory apparatus is now confused with the film's cinematic and sound apparatus. His mind has become this exterior apparatus. The machinery of Harry's mind has created the sounds he wants to hear, the call of Ann's maternal voice, the 'I love you'. Her voice is inside Harry's head. The 'voices of Ann and her friend have been produced by Harry all along — we have never heard them except through either his technological or psychic "apparatus"' (Silverman, 1988: 93).

Harry climbs out on the balcony and looks towards room 773. He now sees another 'imaginary' scene, a replay of the earlier murder scene, only now Ann's back is to the camera and someone else is being murdered. An electronic scream drives Harry back to the bedroom. He huddles under the covers in the darkness of the room. When he opens his eyes a Flintstone cartoon is playing on the television screen. Fred is taking his wife to the hospital to have a baby. Another retreat into childhood for Harry.

Undaunted, he now actually enters room 773, flushing the toilet an electronic scream wells up as blood and tissue spew onto the floor. Harry escapes from the room. He enters a crowd of people (reporters, work associates of the Director) who are asking Ann about the future of the Corporation. Harry now mentally replays the conversation from Union Square. Ann is heard, 'I don't know what to get him for Christmas', and Mark says, 'He doesn't need anything anymore'. As Harry listens to the imaginary tape he 'sees' the Director's corpse on the bed, wrapped in a plastic body-bag, and next he sees the bloody struggle that he had dreamed twice before. Once again he hears Mark, 'He'd kill us if he had the chance'.

Ann's maternal voice drops from the tape. She has betrayed Harry, and now she will kill him if she has the chance. He retreats to the shelter of his room, only to receive the ominous phone call, 'We know that you know'. He has no recourse other than to destroy his own room, seeking the bug that has bugged him, forgetting to ever look inside his saxophone, his last site of solace, lonely music played inside a destroyed room.

The camera zooms in on Harry, now the man inside the room, no longer outside the door. Trapped, the voyeur in the corner. The message is clear. The film began from the outside, the exterior shots of Union Square, Harry in control of hidden cameras and tape recorders. At the end we now see and hear Harry through someone else's eyes and ears (Silverman, 1988: 98). Harry has no auditory control over anything. He has created everything he heard. This psychic apparatus, his mind and his imagination, have manufactured his own destruction. He is not exterior to the sounds he records and manipulates. He is deeply implicated in them, indeed he has created what he wants to hear (Silverman, 1988: 96).

The Organizational Gaze   Harry has been duped from the outset. He was being bugged and tailed from the time the Director hired him to tail and record Ann and Mark. He was followed by Martin Stett (Harrison Ford) and Meredith was sent to steal the tapes from him. Bernie Moran's dirty little trick of recording Harry's intimate conversation with Meredith also played into the Director's hand, for it heightened Harry's paranoia, and made him the victim, not the voyeur, the not-so-good-natured subject of another hidden surveillance system.

So *The Conversation* inverts the traditional work relationship that Harry finds so comfortable. The usual triangular structure of voyeur, subject and client no longer operates here. The client, the Director, is also a voyeur. The traditional voyeur (Harry) is now the subject of the client's gaze, and the subject, Ann and Mark, are the real villains. Their villainy merges, in the end, with the Corporation, who is, it appears, complicitous with them.

The Look of Intimacy   There are four moments of voyeuristic intimacy in the film: the intimate conversation of Ann and Mark that is recorded, Harry's bedroom scenes with Amy, and Meredith, and Harry's dream sequence with Ann. Each sequence draws out Harry's need for, but fear of, intimacy. He will not tell Amy what he does, she does not know that today is his birthday, he will not reveal his age, she doesn't know he is planning to visit her, he won't let her call him, and he challenges her for asking him 'all these questions'. He must be in control of his visits to her, even as she listens for him listening outside her door.

When Amy changes her phone number and withdraws from Harry he approaches Meredith, 'Would you go back to a man who never tells you anything?' Seduced by Meredith, prostrate on his mattress, inside his wire work cage, Harry plays his tapes and drifts off into his dream of Ann and the impending murder. He only knows intimacy through the sounds he creates in his own mind. These are the intimate sounds that others make.

The Moral Gaze   'I have sinned' Harry says as he steps into the confessional booth. 'It's been three months since I confessed my sins. I took newspapers without paying. I've had impure thoughts. My work's been used to hurt people, two young persons. Before, people have been hurt by my work. But I just listen. I'm not responsible.'

In the presence of this omnipresent heavenly surveillance system, Harry expresses his guilt. A haunted, moral man, Harry seeks solace in another voyeur's place, the confessional of the priest. He wants another voyeur to hear his sins, to be the site of his confession. So he brings the silent sounds of his internal conversations to the priest. But once here, he cannot go beneath the surface of his own thoughts, he is not responsible for what happens to his tapes. He cannot share with the priest the conversation he has taped.

So this study of dreams and surveillance systems comes to an end. Without intimacy, no one to confess to, heard by unseen ears, this lonely loveless man, a guilty victim of his own nightmares and the nameless surveillance systems of others is beyond redemption. Betrayed by his own technology, he is led, like a lamb to the wolves (*The Silence of the Lambs*), by the meanings he brings to Ann's words, 'I love you . . . . He was once a baby boy . . . . I was very sick when I was a boy . . . [my mother] put holy water . . . on my body'.

And here the film plays one more trick, for surely, as Silverman (1988: 95) observes, Harry's last name (Caul) is a word play on amnion, or the inner membrane protecting the foetus before birth. And surely he is drawn to the maternal voice and the spaces it inhabits. In addition, he desires to control that voice, to manipulate it, to make it bring the words 'I love you' into his life. Most certainly he fails to either recover or control that voice.

But it is inappropriate, as Silverman proposes, to solely read *The Conversation* as a text 'which attests more powerfully than any other to the ways in which the female voice becomes the receptacle of that which the male subject throws away and draws back toward himself' (1988: 87). Such a psychoanalytic reading ('Harry attempts . . . to make good his symbolic castration' (Silverman, 1988: 95)) aligns the film's treatment of Ann with 'an unpleasurable and disempowering interiority' (1988: 100). At the same time this reading connects the film to the 'larger cultural disavowal of the mother's role both as agent of discourse and as a model for linguistic (as well as visual) identification' (1988: 100).

Harry's relationship to the maternal voice is complicated by the moral guilt he brings into this situation from his earlier case where people were murdered because of his work. He seeks to prevent another murder. Ann's remarks about the drunk on the bench reminds Harry of his own childhood, his own (presumably) lost mother and father. He seeks to neither control nor manipulate Ann's voice, only to understand it so he can stop the murder.

Ann betrays him. In the end he has nothing. He did not stop a murder. Amy has left him and the woman he wanted to save is a murderess. His apartment is bugged, and he has nowhere to hide. The more he tries to withdraw from the world, the more he is seen. The more he 'attempts to look into the privacy of . . . [Ann and Mark], the more he traps himself in his guilt and his vulnerability' (Kolker, 1980: 197).

Harry's suffering reflects a larger cultural situation that Coppola wants to identify (Kolker, 1980: 198). Harry is not to be pitied, vilified, or dismissed. He is not an agent of evil. His plight is to be read as symbolic of the 'destructiveness of the act of surveillance for all concerned' (Kolker, 1980: 198). This is an allegory, a tiny moral tale. Harry's infatuation with Ann's voice is but one small part of that larger story. To focus solely on Ann and her voice is to miss this larger picture.

A Tiny Moral Story

Like *Blow-Up* and later *Blow Out* (1981), which also have their murders, *The Conversation* leaves the protagonist-investigator without proof of his secret, guilty knowledge. In a variation on Antonioni's photographer, Coppola's Harry anticipates a murder before it occurs. He is 'like a filmmaker, putting together bits and pieces to make a whole. But what he puts together is the wrong movie' (Kolker, 1980: 198). However, unlike Antonioni, Coppola keeps a moral focus on his voyeur (Kolker, 1980: 198). And, unlike the Hitchcock of *Rear Window*, Coppola does not 'morally implicate the audience in its voyeuristic role' (Kolker, 1980: 196). Coppola's voyeur has heard and seen the truth, but his tapes are now gone and what he has heard and seen no longer exists. His technology turns against him. The legendary wire-tapper has been bugged by someone even better than he is. We as audience merely watch. We are not called to action.

Here Coppola extends Antonioni's project. His subversive effects involve more than just saying the new technologies of listening are evil. This is not news (see Carey, 1989; Couch, 1990). At one level, as Ebert notes (1989b: 154–5), *The Conversation* is about 'paranoia, invasion of privacy, bugging – and also about the bothersome problem of conscience. The Watergate crew seems, for the most part, to have had no notion that what they were doing was objectively wrong. Harry wants to have no notion. But he does, and it destroys him'.

This is the level of meaning that is easily gained by the viewer's identification with Harry's plight. This interpretation suggests that if the wire-tappers had moral consciences, they would only use their craft in those situations which were morally correct. But whose morals? Good people, as Everett Hughes (1963) observes do dirty work. Harry is a good person who does dirty work. His values are ours, the Watergate crew thought they were good people doing good work.

But Coppola's movie is about more than good people and their moral consciences. It is about a world where there is no longer any privacy, a world where 'everything that's ever been said . . . might still be echoing somewhere . . . [a world where one day] there will be equipment sensitive enough to retrieve and record humankind's oral history. In 24 abridged volumes it would make a perfect introductory offer to a book club. Or even a book club all of its own' (Canby, 1974: 11).

No, this is not what the film is about, although this is surely one of its stories. *The Conversation* is a moral tale about the human gaze, the voyeur and the fundamental inability to ever unmask the simulacrum, 'the truth which conceals that there is none' (Baudrillard, 1983a: 1). Coppola explodes the myth which holds that the simulacrum 'conceals the truth' (Baudrillard, 1983a: 1). There is no truth other than the truth that there is no truth. The new information technologies are predicated on the assumption that the real, when captured, will convey the truth of the event in question. The actual conversation when recorded or the life event when telecast is the real conversation or event in question.[8]

But suppose that these recordings have no status beyond the moment of their recording. Assume that the recording is an assembled, dramaturgical production. It then becomes a recording, not of the real, but of an assembled simulation of the real; the real has become the hyperreal, 'that of which it is possible to give an equivalent reproduction . . . the real is always already reproduced' (Baudrillard, 1983a: 146). If this is the case then Coppola's story is not about morals and the human conscience, it is about life in a world where nothing any longer has any status beyond its symbolic representation on a sound disk, a video tape, in a photograph or on a printed page. The social has not only become the text, it is the text.

That text is only a construction, like Harry's tapes which reconstruct the conversation between Ann and Mark. This construction makes a difference only when it is heard, seen, touched, felt or read. It can be erased, destroyed at a moment's notice. With its erasure goes that moment of reality it reflected. When this is done all we are left with are the keening sounds of a wailing saxophone and Satic-like piano accompaniments, just sounds and sights, nothing permanent, only the visible text that disappears in the next frame.

The conversation, that mundane form of human communication which has become an area of specialization in ethnomethodology (see Boden, 1990: 203), becomes, in Coppola's film, nothing more than something that might have been heard, but maybe wasn't.[9] This artful, ordinary form of human exchange, called here *The Conversation*, is a conversation about a conversation that made a difference, but what was the difference?

Here is where the text begins its own undermining, for, by burrowing deeply into the fabrics of human talk and its recordings, Coppola shows that talk no longer matters. This is why Harry is so silent, why he speaks in short sentences, why he never reveals who he really is. What would his talk reveal? A conversation that could be recorded? What does it matter? Talk is a commodity, an object that can be bought and sold. An object that can be copied and recorded. An object that can be dubbed, fashioned into a sound-track, into a cluster of sentences that mean something, even something like 'He'd kill us if he got the chance'.

Playing off talk that makes a difference and talk that is a commodity, Coppola shows how everyday life has become an art form, an aesthetic experience, talk turned into a good recording. This process of turning the everyday and the mundane into a commodity, wherein the most human of human experiences, 'the conversation' now becomes something that kills and drives you crazy. At the same time it is something that is produced and sold, like any other everyday object or commodity. It is not the talk that drives Harry crazy, it is the fact that somebody else has bugged his apartment: he has been turned into a commodity, into the producer of a set of experiences that somebody else can capture and sell.[10]

This is what Coppola's film is all about: the commodification of the everyday. No wonder, then, that his narrative resists all of the conventional devices of melodramatic realism. Harry's dilemma is not neatly resolved at the end of the film. He does not return home to the arms of a loving woman. We don't know if he will be killed, or if he will just go crazy. We don't know who bugged his apartment. We don't know if he will continue in this line of work. He just is at the end of the film. This picture of him playing his saxophone lingers in the memory: no talk, just painful, woeful music. The conversation has ceased, talk is replaced by music and images.[11]

This process of commodifying human experience, of turning the voice and its talk into something that is bought and sold, has produced a deeper anxiety, an anxiety revealed in the film's final sequence when Harry destroys his apartment. Anticipated earlier when Harry discovers that his landlady has a key to his apartment, we now learn that this man cannot stand to have anyone invade his private space. His telephone number is unlisted. He now gets his mail at a box in the Post Office. No one has ever entered his apartment. But the Company has successfully bugged his phone and his home, 'we will be listening to you'.

The new information technologies have stripped Harry of his private, sacred self. The private and the public no longer exist as separate domains (see Meyrowitz, 1985; Lengermann and Niebrugge-Brantley, 1990: 334). A pornography of the visible now visits each of us. Even our own telephone answering machines can record our and others' conversations. (Dick Gregory, describing the White House Tapes, 'Imagine feelin' so lonely and insignificant that you'd bug your own phone' Sayre, 1974: 44.) We have turned each other into recordable commodities. What is now sold is private life. The voyeur has won. We have each interiorized the ominous, investigative gaze of the other. To repeat Foucault's words: 'Just a gaze. An inspecting gaze, a gaze which each individual under its own weight will end by interiorizing to the point that he is his own overseer, each individual thus exercising this surveillance over, and against, him-[her] self' (1980: 155).

Always in the service of others, Harry now learns that the voyeur's eye points in two directions, inward to self, and outward to the other. Harry has become the other who bugs himself. He has nowhere to go. There is no privacy, no site for the sacred self. All is visible: nothing can escape the new technology. This is Coppola's message. Harry, the anti-hero, the voyeur with a conscience, self destructs at the end. Part evil and part good, his tapes might have stopped the murder of the Director. Pessimistic in its world view, *The Conversation* undermines the traditional values of law and morality. But we have difficulty identifying with Harry, even his lover left him. Who can love a man who never talks?

Coppola's film is filled with irony and desolation. His visual style, which highlights spectacle over narrative (the bareness of Harry's workplace, the empty San Francisco streets) refuses the traditional narrative impulse of realist melodrama. There is no closure to this story. Harry's story does not end with him in the arms of a gentle, good woman. The police do not enter the situation and arrest the murderers. All that is clear at the end is that Harry has nowhere to go. In this he is you and me, the universal voyeur unmasked.[12]

It would be reductive, as Kolker (1980: 202) suggests, to simply conclude from *The Conversation* that 'we are all being watched and are powerless to control [those who observe us]'. Such a reading would place Coppola's film entirely within the conspiratorial, paranoid genre, to liken it to *Three Days of the Condor*, or *The Parallax View*. Such texts, as suggested above, presume impotence in the face of a massive, 'nameless governmental or corporate power' (Kolker, 1980: 202). As such, as Kolker (1980: 202) notes, they reinforce our fears by relieving them. At least somebody will tell the story of our powerlessness.

Coppola resists this easy path. His is the story of the terror of surveillance, the terror that 'the phenomenon of surveillance can create' (Kolker, 1980: 202). Harry's is the story of a character who cannot hide from himself, and who, by his very work, exposes himself to the spying he practices. Coppola exposes the 'fragility of the politics of surveillance through the fragility of his character' (Kolker, 1980: 203). This fragility is seldom explored by Foucault, Marx, and other students of the maximum security society.

So *The Conversation* is a political film that transcends the paranoia, conspiratorial genre. It does not remind us of a golden time when power was innocent (Kolker, 1980: 203). Its point is blunt. Surveillance destroys, it always traps 'the victim and the agent who wishes to control the victim' (Kolker, 1980: 103).

JFK

Now *JFK*. Stone disagrees with Coppola. He wants more than a simple conspiratorial film. More than paranoia, although it is paranoia that drives the story he tells. Stone is after the truth, the truth of JFK. The truth that will halt the steady, silent march of fascism in America. His conspirators are everywhere: within the power elite; the CIA, the FBI, the National Security Council, the Defense Department, the Secretaries of State and Defense, paramilitary organizations, Cold Warriors in the Pentagon, the Dallas Police Department, the White House, President Lyndon Johnson. The murder of John Kennedy was a *coup d'état*, backed by Lyndon Johnson and executed at the highest levels of the American government. Kennedy wanted to withdraw from Vietnam, was soft on communism. Billions of dollars in defence contracts were at stake. No one liked the Kennedy brothers. It had been done before: Lumumba in the Congo, Trujillo in the Dominican Republic, attempts on Castro's life.

Contextualizing Stone's Story

Stone is the detective. He had already re-written the 1960s and its aftermath (*Salvador, Platoon, The Doors, Born on the Fourth of July, Wall Street*). It remained to write the history of Kennedy's assassination. He will track down the killers, reveal the plot against the American people, show that they, like JFK, have been victims of a murderous plot. After all, if JFK had not been killed there would have been no Vietnam, no slayings of Robert Kennedy and Martin Luther King, the racial conflict of the 1960s would not have happened. The politics of the counter-culture would have prevailed and the new frontier would have been reality.

Set primarily in New Orleans, beginning in 1963 with the assassination, and ending in 1969 when Jim Garrison brings Clay Shaw to trial, the film is a dramatic reshaping of history, a piece of cinematic history. (Stone: 'I consider myself a person who's taking history and shaping it a certain way, like Shakespeare shaped *Henry V*' (Stone quoted in Anson, 1992: 221)). *JFK* is Oliver Stone solving the big mystery of the 1960s, 'Who Killed JFK?', Kevin Costner *Dancing with the Facts*, a Jimmy Stewart-like character goes to Washington and discovers the truth about his corrupt government.

There are three interconnected stories here: the re-telling of the assassination by Stone, which blurs with Stone's telling of Jim Garrison's version of the assassination, which blurs with the private story of Jim Garrison, his life with Liz and his children and the effects of this story on their shared lives. Thus we see Stone's version of JFK's story through Garrison's eyes. This is a personalized tale, part mystery and part detective story, that shows how Garrison inserted his own biography via Stone into this national nightmare.

In keeping with the format of the conspiratorial film (detective, villain, victim), *JFK* pits Garrison and his team of stalwart investigators against the American government (the conspiratorial villains), as they open up this unsolved mystery (we know who was killed, but not why) which had been investigated many times before. Jim and his men (and women) are the detectives. Soon they must confront the conspiratorial enemy, the press, the FBI, the CIA, as they attempt to bring the government to trial. On trial is Garrison's quickly evolving theory that Oswald did not act alone, that JFK's murder was organized by persons high in American government.

Thus the film is a story of one of the many conspiracy theories about the assassination. It unfolds in three parts: the assassination, the *Warren Report*, and Garrison's investigation which results in the trial of Clay Shaw. The text remains entirely within the conspiracy genre, attempting to prove that a conspiracy exists, and that none of us can be free from those who control the gaze that radiates throughout the surveillance society. At the same time the film is utopian. Like a Capra film, Stone imagines a time when no conspiracy exists, the new frontier. And so it is part of the conspiracy discourse that it attempts to explode and discount.[13]

The film is based on two key texts, Garrison's (1988) *On the Trail of the Assassins* and Jim Marrs's (1989) *Crossfire: The Plot that Killed Kennedy*, as well as the *Warren Report* (1964), public sources on the assassination and its investigation and interviews with key participants and conspiracy experts. The story is both a whodunit and a whydunit. Stone describes the project, '*On the Trail of the Assassins* read like a Dashiell Hammett whodunit. It starts out as a bit of a seedy crime with small traces, and then the gumshoe district attorney follows the trail, and the trail widens and widens, and before you know it, it's no longer a small-town affair . . . . The D.A. [is] somewhat like a Jimmy Stewart character in an old Capra movie' (Stone quoted in Anson, 1992: 213).

More than a mystery, like Kurosawa's *Rashomon*, Stone creates a kaleidoscope of possible realities, a complex montage, cinema verité in the grand Hollywood manner. He re-creates history, transposes scenes, presents composite characters (Willie O'Keefe), creates imaginary situations (the three marksmen who fired at Kennedy), weaves real newsreel texts and documentary footage with flashbacks, constructed events and dramatic re-stagings (some in sepia-tone, others in black and white). JFK's assassination is shown over and over again, in slow motion, on the Zapruder film, in news footage, in simulated form, 'from the vantage point of different witnesses and possible participants' (Denby, 1992: 50). Alternative versions of history, what might have happened, are shown (Oswald in the movie theatre, in his landlady's house). Witnesses report odd occurrences (the hobos, the man with the umbrella, the phony Secret Service men). The motorcade rounds Dealey Plaza, one more time and this time we see the three teams of trained shooters. All of these pieces of visual (and auditory) information are knitted together, creating a story that comes to a single conclusion: the single assassin theory will not stand up.

Into the Film

JFK begins on an ominous and allegorical note. All of the symbols that collectively define the early 1960s are brought before the viewer. A seven minute sequence of documentary images set the stage for JFK's presidency: President Dwight D. Eisenhower's farewell address, warning Americans about the growth of the military-industrial complex; news clips from Kennedy's early presidential days; schoolkids reciting the Pledge of Allegiance; WPA farmers harvesting the Texas plains; shots of J. Edgar Hoover, Marilyn Monroe, families leaving church; voice-overs detailing Kennedy's 1960 Presidential election; Bay of Pigs, Secret War and Nuclear Test Ban imagery; the Cuban Missile Crisis; shots of Martin Luther King, Teddy, Rose and Joe Kennedy; John Kennedy campaigning; Jackie in San Antonio, Houston, Fort Worth, in the plane/descending on Love Field, coming toward the Dallas/Fort Worth plain.

A dramatic black-and-white sequence suddenly appears on screen. Out of a moving car carrying two Cuban males, a screaming woman, Rose Cheramie, tumbles to the ground, bleeding in the dust. In the next shot Rose is pleading with a policeman, 'They're going up to Dallas . . . to whack Kennedy. Friday the 22nd, that's when they're going to do it. In Dealey Plaza . . . . You gotta call somebody'. Rose's warning is discounted by a doctor, 'Higher'n a kite on something'.

Documentary images reappear, close-ups of Kennedy on Love Field, the downtown streets of Dallas, people lining the sidewalks. A voice-over reports on Kennedy's efforts to establish a dialogue with Castro, his civil rights bill in Congress, Bobby Kennedy's prosecution of the Mafia, Jack's fight with the steel companies, a Kennedy dynasty, Bobby Kennedy in 1968, Teddy in 1976. Archival footage carries the Kennedy party to the dreaded Dealey Plaza. Documentary tapes intersect with dramatic restagings, as Stone sets up what is to come, the murder of Kennedy. We hear sirens, screeching tyres, the crowd runs towards 'The Grassy Knoll'. We see a glimpse of the Zapruder film. Mrs Kennedy reaches for help. An agent climbs into the car. JFK slumps forward and then is hit by another shot. Mrs Kennedy silently screams.

In a crowded neighbourhood bar people are gathered, watching the news coverage of the assassination. Walter Cronkite is talking, 'President Kennedy died at 1.00 p.m. Central Standard Time . . . some 38 minutes ago'. Two drunken men, former FBI agent and right-wing militant Guy Bannister and his part-time assistant, Jack Martin, argue and fight, expressing hatred of Kennedy. Oswald is arrested in Dallas and charged with the murder of Kennedy and Dallas police officer J.D. Tippit. Jim Garrison is in his office. Lou, his chief investigator, enters the room, 'Boss, the President's been shot. In Dallas. Five minutes ago'.

And so begins the story. In quick order the key players are in place: Oswald, Ruby, Bannister, Martin, David Ferrie, Clay Bertrand/Shaw, Willie O'Keefe. Garrison immediately learns that Oswald was in New Orleans during the summer of 1963 handing out pro-Castro leaflets. He begins an investigation to determine Oswald's New Orleans connections. Two days later Jack Ruby kills Oswald. David Ferrie is brought into the office. He is questioned about his knowledge of Oswald. We see the Kennedy funeral.

It is three years later. The *Warren Report*, which concluded that Kennedy was killed by a lone assassin, has been published. On a plane Senator Russell Long confides to Garrison that Oswald was a patsy. In an epiphanic experience Garrison burns the midnight hours reading the 26-volume *Warren Report*. This report (as presented by Stone) argued that Kennedy was killed by Lee Harvey Oswald, who acted alone and who fired three shots in 5.6 seconds from the Book Depository at the Presidential limousine as it entered Dealey Plaza. One shot missed the car entirely. Another shot hit Kennedy's head, killing him. Still another shot produced seven wounds on the bodies of Kennedy and Connally. (Garrison calls this the magic bullet.) After firing these three shots

Oswald left the Book Depository, returns to his rooming house, kills Officer Tippit, and then entered the Texas Theatre where he was arrested. Two days later, acting as a patriot, taking vengeance on the man who killed his President, seeking to spare Jackie from having to testify at a trial, Jack Ruby, a Dallas nightclub owner, kills Oswald as he leaves the underground garage of the Dallas Police Station. Ruby is convicted of killing Oswald. He dies under unusual circumstances (which Stone re-dramatizes) just after he is granted a retrial for his conviction.

Convinced that something is fishy with this official story, Garrison backtracks to Jack Martin, who places Ferrie and Oswald in Bannister's office in the summer of 1963. Garrison lunches with Dean Andrews, the attorney Clay Bertrand allegedly asked to represent Oswald. Later Willie O'Keefe, a convicted male prostitute, tells Garrison that he and Bertrand partied with Ferrie (and a right-wing, kinky sex group), where Ferrie openly discussed killing Kennedy. Here Stone takes artistic licence as he dramatizes this homosexual party (leading to homophobic charges against Stone, see Yarbrough, 1992).

Garrison and his staff travel to Dallas and re-enact the assassination. They conclude, given Oswald's shoddy marksmanship skills and the age of his rifle that he could not have fired all the shots in the allotted time. They now see the plaza as an ideal site for a crossfire shooting by a team of marksmen. Back in New Orleans Garrison's investigators discover that Bertrand is actually Clay Shaw, a businessman with CIA connections. They plan to bring Shaw to trial, charging him with conspiracy in the Kennedy assassination. Suddenly everything unravels. Garrison's offices have been bugged. His investigation is leaked to the news media. His staff is harassed by the FBI. Ferrie, a key witness, turns up dead. Liz, Garrison's wife, becomes disgusted with his obsession with the case.

Garrison meets 'X' in Washington DC. X, a former member of a secret Pentagon military-intelligence unit, tells him (à la Deep Throat) that Kennedy was killed by a conspiracy involving the CIA, the military and others in government who wanted Kennedy out of the way. (Flashbacks recreate secret meetings with high ranking Pentagon officials.) Garrison returns to New Orleans, convinced that he has a case. He brings Shaw to trial. A network television special discredits Garrison's investigation. Liz takes the children and leaves him.

And now the moment everyone has been waiting for. The Zapruder film. The camera cuts to a movie screen in the courtroom. A hush comes over the room. The film lasts 25 seconds. We see JFK's body lurch forwards and backwards as it is hit by bullets. Garrison begins his argument, noting that the Warren Commission thought it had an open and shut case: three bullets, one assassin. But facts, he argues, disprove this theory. The Zapruder film leaves no doubt (Garrison argues) that four shots were fired. Garrison moves to his discussion, complete with charts and a pointer, of the magic bullet theory. This bullet, he says, 'enters the

President's back, headed downward at an angle of 17 degrees [he illustrates its downward movement], then moves upward to leave Kennedy's body from the front of his neck'. The bullet waits 1.6 seconds. It then turns right and continues into Connally's body 'at the rear of his right armpit'. It then 'heads downward at an angle of 27 degrees, shattering Connally's fifth rib . . . [and] then enters Connally's right wrist [wound number six] – shattering the radius bone. It then enters his right thigh . . . from which it falls out and is found in "pristine" condition on a corridor of Parkland hospital. That's some bullet.'

Garrison then calls key witnesses who attest to hearing one or more shots being fired from behind the picket fence. Flashbacks reconstruct doctors examining Kennedy in the Dallas hospital. Another flashback cuts to the Bethesda autopsy room, where an army general orders an end to the examination of Kennedy's head. Garrison next recites details concerning the autopsy photos (never released to the public), President Johnson ordering the blood-soaked limousine to be washed and rebuilt and the disappearance of Kennedy's brain. He then takes the jury through his version of the assassination, with mock-ups and flashbacks, and the three teams of shooters.

The camera moves in on Jim then a shot of Liz, who is sitting behind him. Oswald's actions are reconstructed and more witnesses are brought forth. Oswald's capture in the theatre is shown and then his murder by Jack Ruby. Garrison offers his summation, 'Official legend is created and the media takes it from there . . . . Lee Oswald, a crazed lonely man who wanted attention and got it by killing the President, was only the first in a long line of patsies. In later years Bobby Kennedy and Martin Luther King . . . . We have all become Hamlets in our country, children of a slain father . . . . The ghost of John F. Kennedy confronts us with the secret murder at the heart of the American Dream'.

He concludes, 'Do not forget your young President who forfeited his life. Show the world this is still a government of the people, for the people, and by the people . . . . It's up to you'. The jury returns with its verdict, 'We find Clay Shaw not guilty on all counts. We believe there was a conspiracy, but whether Clay Shaw was part of it is another kettle of fish'.

The screen turns black, information is given on Garrison, his marriage, the Vietnam War and the mottoes chiselled on the walls of the National Archives in Washington DC: 'Dedicated to the Young, In whose Spirit the Search for Truth Marches On. THE END'

Whose Gaze? Whose Story?

Within the first year of its release, Stones $40 million budget film was viewed by over 15 million people (Mankiewicz, 1992: 189). It was immediately devoured by the popular culture. Publishers re-issued assassination related literature. Trading cards appeared. A five-part series on the 'Today Show' examined alternative conspiracy theories. A movie about Oswald (*Libra*) began production in 1992 and another film, *Ruby*, appeared in March of 1992 (Zelizer, 1992: 210).[14]

JFK is the story that will not go away, and this is so, because, as Zelizer points out, from the beginning, 'the assassination record lacked closure' (1992: 111). This lack of closure surrounding 'the assassination tale [has given] rise to an on-going contest for authorization, by which different groups attempted to promote their version of what happened in Dallas in order to promote themselves' (Zelizer, 1992: 201).

Indeed, each decade since Kennedy's murder has had its competing versions of what took place on November 22, 1963 in Dallas, Texas, from the *Warren Report* in 1964 and the immediate criticisms of that report in the mid-1960s (see Zelizer, 1992: 106–11) to the House Select Committee investigation in 1976, the Rockefeller Commission study in 1977, the Department of Justice inquiry of 1988, and most recently, the 1992 Joint House and Senate Resolution to open the files of the assassination.

Journalistic, historical and popular culture texts exist alongside these governmental inquiries, each telling one or another official (or unofficial) version of what happened. *Life* would re-publish stills from the Zapruder film in 1966. As noted above, p. 162, this film would be re-shown by Geraldo Rivera in the mid-1970s on 'Good Night, America', and also in the mid-1970s the Assassination Information Bureau would draw 'thousands of people to Massachusetts for the first major public showing of [the] film' (Zelizer, 1992: 113). Soon after the *Warren Report* was released Dan Rather would offer his verbal description of the film on CBS News and later admit to a mis-reading of the text (Zelizer, 1992: 242).

Contradictory accounts, for and against the conspiracy theories, would be offered from the mid-1960s onwards by celebrity politicians, news-makers, journalists, historians, novelists, filmmakers and assassination buffs including Gerald Ford, Dan Rather, David Halberstam, Theodore White, Walter Cronkite, Michael Kurtz, Mark Lane, Tom Wicker, Gary Wills, Robert MacNeil, Daniel Boorstein, William Manchester, Jim Marrs, Jim Garrison, Sylvia Meagher and Gary Owens, Tom Petit, Harrison E. Salisbury, Arthur Schlesinger, Don DeLillo, Nora Ephron, Barbara Walters, Ellen Goodman, Pete Hamill, Dwight MacDonald, Martin Scorsese and Alan J. Pakula.

Stone's film enters this discourse, it feeds on it, criticizes it and takes its own stance on who killed Kennedy and why. Of course Stone brought considerable stature, advance media interest, money, and celebrity talent to the project (Zelizer, 1992: 202). Predictably, the movie met with immediate negative reaction. It was called 'Dallas in Wonderland'. The *New York Times* carried over 30 articles, op-eds, letters, addenda, editorials and columns criticizing the film. Attacks were launched by CBS, Dan Rather, Tom Wicker, Gerald R. Ford, Daniel Patrick Moynihan, Arthur Schlesinger Jr and Alexander Cockburn (see Stone and Sklar, 1992; Zelizer, 1992: 201–14). George Will attacked the film when it was still in script form.

Stone's film would be read as a docudrama (Ebert, 1992: 250), and he would be accused of many sins: not having the proper credentials to tell this story, confusing history with fact, endorsing the crackpot theories of Garrison, 'an unscrupulous publicity-seeker who drummed up his celebrated case against Clay Shaw out of thin air' (Ebert, 1992: 250), misusing visual, media materials, taking artistic licence, holding to one true version of history, not respecting the hard facts of history, not using the hard evidence of the journalist, being homophobic and being critical of journalists who had previously written the master narrative of this story (see Zelizer, 1992: 203–13).

These criticisms turn on two questions: who owns the gaze and who will tell the story of how and why JFK was murdered on November 22, 1963? This story, as Zelizer (1992: 51) argues, resolved into five key moments: Kennedy's shooting; the events at the hospital where Kennedy was taken; Johnson's swearing in; the follow-up to the killing, including the arrest and murder of Oswald; and Kennedy's funeral.

The original tellings of Kennedy's killing were hampered from the beginning. There was no original, professional text of the event; all of the photos were taken by amateurs. This meant that all tellings of this story had to be reconstructions (see Zelizer, 1992: 51–5). Zapruder's film thus became the key text, the only 'real' record of the murder. Reporters and journalists would build their reputations on their 'nearness' to the event. Media celebrities were created. Journalists fought over who had the most credibility to report the event. Celebrity-hood was built for those reporters who exhibited the most dedication to the telling of this tragedy, to those who appeared to be the first in telling it and to those who were the best and the most professional in their original tellings (see Zelizer, 1992: 193).

But no one had an actual record of what happened. Everyone missed the biggest scoop of a lifetime. The stories that were told had to rely on secondhand witnesses. Reporters had to address the charge that they (the reporters) had interfered with history and had fallen victim to a failed technology (no photo records (Zelizer, 1992: 67–75)). Hence the stories that were told stressed the reporters' triumph in overcoming these obstacles (being first, the best, the most dedicated). All tellings were based on secondary sources, the usual journalistic criterion of truth could not be applied. Because the event was witnessed by amateurs, not professionals, there was only questionable eyewitness testimony. Journalistic accounts became narrative constructions, involving personalization (nearness to the event), synecdoche (one part of the story stood for the whole story) and the omission of critical information from other media sources (for example, radio (see Zelizer, 1992: 37–45)).

The hospital scene was different. Journalists were present, but direct eye-witness evidence (as there would be for the swearing in) was still difficult to obtain. There was immediate confusion over the nature of Kennedy's head wound and whether or not one bullet could have done all of the damage (Zelizer, 1992: 55–6). The murder of Oswald was equally confusing. Reporters were charged with interfering with events (they convicted Oswald before he was brought to trial). Some contended that the reporters' presence in the Dallas Police Station created the circumstances that allowed Ruby to shoot Oswald (Zelizer, 1992: 91). But at least in this instance, they had the murder on film, for Oswald was murdered in full glare of photographic and television cameras (Zelizer, 1992: 60). The mourning became a national affair. Private citizens came by the thousands to view the casket. NBC News devoted nearly 42 hours to the continuous coverage of this event (Zelizer, 1992: 62).

This five-part story without closure, or a consensual ending, is the national drama Stone re-tells. No wonder it was criticized, for bits and pieces of it were owned by persons who had a personal stake in how it would be told. The following issues (including the story's prior ownership, its lack of closure and the absence of an original record) are at work in this conflict of interpretation.

First, Stone proposed to take the story away from those who had previously controlled its telling. Second, this produced a 'biased reading' of his text. His film was read as a 'factual' docudrama that deliberately got the facts wrong (see Ebert, 1992: 250). Tom Wicker would complain, for example, that when Stone shows the assassination of Robert Kennedy, he makes it look like Kennedy was 'shot at the end of his California victory speech, rather than shortly after' (Ebert, 1992: 250). Ebert comments, 'Does Wicker think Stone was trying to deceive us on this point?' *Newsweek* continued this line of criticism, 'Only the alert viewer will be able to distinguish real documentary footage from reconstructed events' (quoted in Ebert, 1992: 250).

The film is not a docudrama. It is not a historical study or a courtroom presentation of the evidence supporting Stone's thesis. *JFK* is a 'movie that weaves a myth around the Kennedy assassination – a myth in which the slain leader was the victim of a monstrous conspiracy' (Ebert, 1992: 25). *JFK* is a complicated re-telling of this five-part national drama, using all of the tools of Stone's trade, from jump-cuts to flash-forwards, sound and image bites, showing the same events in different ways from different points of view, a mixture of first-hand testimony with flashbacks, possibility and conjecture mixed together (see Ebert, 1992: 252). Stone's myth undoes the long-standing lone assassin myth.

Third, Stone is not telling his story to the members of the JFK generation who can remember, with vivid accuracy, where they were at the moment they learned of the assassination. His telling is a myth for that generation for whom JFK is a paragraph in a high school history text book, a generation with high visual literacy, well-schooled on the hyperreal cinematic techniques (and realities) of television and computer video games. He wants to capture this generation (generation X) and have them demand that the truth of JFK's murder be told. Hence, the critics of the film are speaking for the wrong generation. But they are protecting their own history, a history Stone wants to challenge.

Fourth, in his myth-making Stone has no reservation about inventing history, about putting the facts of history together in new and novel ways. His myth expands beyond the five days following the murder. It tells the story of the generation that was shaped by Kennedy's assassination. His myth encompasses the subsequent deaths of Malcolm X, Bobby Kennedy and Martin Luther King and the tragedies that followed from Vietnam. This is his warrant as a filmmaker and this warrant flies in the face of those who want to stick to the socially reconstructed 'factual' history of the assassination as previously told. Stone will have none of this, hence his dedication of the film (as previously quoted) to 'the young, in whose spirit the search for truth marches on'.

Fifth, Stone believes that the filmmaker can accurately tell history. By taking this stance he challenges the culture's official historians. Cinema can tell the truth of history, and this history, Stone's 'mystory' (Ulmer, 1989), 'his story', can make a difference. This utopian tale believes that conspiracies can be exposed. This myth believes people can make history, that people can overturn the technologies of surveillance that capture all of us within its gaze. Stone believes that we can technologically undo history and make it tell the truth. We can put the apparatuses of surveillance to democratic use, even as we understand that 'media technology, far from providing a hotline to the truth, makes it easier for information to be controlled and disseminated' (Billson, 1992: 35).

This is what the Zapruder film does. This shaky, grainy 25-second 8 mm tape captures the real and in its frames are the truth of JFK. And so Stone's film rests on a firm belief in the cinematic theory of reality. The real can be captured and the truth, made public, will free us.

Stone and Coppola on Both Sides of the Keyholes of History

Stone, like Coppola, is on both sides of the keyholes of history, a voyeur looking at the official voyeurs. Men watching men make history. Men watching men manipulate and control the apparatuses of surveillance that the post-security society has come to rely on. The erotics of power: men taking visual, scopic pleasures in the production of rich, thick, audio and visual documents that record the transgressions of others: men playing God. The paranoid gaze is everywhere, the voyeur is gazed upon, nobody can be trusted. And the truth is always socially re-constructed, events re-formatted to fit a master narrative telling of what really happened on this date, in this place, to this person. The who, what, where, why and how of classic journalism are now re-framed, re-photographed, and re-told. A new (or old) myth argues that no conspiracy operates in this version of history.

Modifying Hitchcock, Stone's camera indulges the scopic pleasures that come from manipulating the texts of history. At the same time Stone's camera searches out the truth and punishes the villains, the men who distort history. He exposes the conspiracy, interrogating, as does Coppola, the new information technologies that seek to discover certain truths about everyday life. Like Harry Caul, Stone-as-Garrison, is a man trapped in a corner of a tiny room. His back to the wall, he throws up on the screen the Zapruder film. 'See', he says, 'the magic bullet theory can't be true. This film proves it.'

And here he rises above Harry's paranoid impotence. Garrison, the publicity-seeking DA from New Orleans, a man branded as crazy by his wife and co-workers, weaves a counter-theory of history. This theory rests on a story that makes Stone-as-Garrison the hero, not the victim of this larger historical conspiracy and its surveillance apparatuses. In a carnival of specularity (the courtroom), using all of the tricks of his cinematic trade, Stone-as-Garrison re-tells history. And even if he lost the case he won the big battle. No despair, alienation or loss of hope here. Truth is on his side.

But what truth? I argued earlier that the male on the other side of the keyhole embodies a fatally flawed gaze. The masculine gaze is unable to produce a depth and form of understanding that goes beyond detailed glimpses of the pathetic masculine subject reflected in the flat historical mirror. He cannot, unlike his female counterpart, plumb the depths of another's soul and discover and understand the rage, the fire, the emotionality, and the meanings that move another to action.

Stone-as-Garrison and Coppola-as-Harry Caul only confront images of the other, representations of them as given on tapes, in photographs, news reels, in dreams. Stone and Coppola's voyeurs seldom come face-to-face with their enemies or those they record. When they do confront the other these males are trapped in their own voyeuristic, investigative identities, staring, talking at the other, affirming prior suspicions and fears.

Here they stand in stark contrast to the female voyeurs examined in Chapter 6. Alex Forrest, Alex Barnes and Catharine directly confront the other who haunts their dreams. Out of this confrontation comes self-awareness, self understanding, a truth about the self and the other that goes beyond mirrored reflections, overheard voices on audio tapes and visual representations given in pictures and photographs. This self discovery, as argued in Chapter 6, is made in that moment when the voyeur re-discovers herself through her own eyes.

This form of self understanding is withheld from the male voyeur. Consequently he can never fully understand the male other he pursues with all of the vengeance and power contained in his apparatuses of surveillance. In the end neither Harry Caul nor Jim Garrison knows why a murder was committed. They don't even know the identity of the murderer. Of course Harry Caul knows he doesn't know. Humility is on his side. Jim Garrison thinks he knows, or could know, and this certain hubris, which inevitably defines the male voyeur's project, always invites disaster. The consequence goes beyond comedy, farce, or tragedy. It points to a fatal flaw in that epistemological framework that says certain truths can always be discovered if one is objective and has the right tools of observation. More on this in the next chapter.

Notes

1 This is the 8 mm, 25-second film of the Kennedy Assassination taken by Abraham Zapruder, a Dallas dressmaker. It is the only live photographic documentation of this event. *Life* bought all rights to the film from Zapruder for $150,000 and ran a four-page photographic spread in its November 29, 1963 issue. The film was then locked up in *Time-Life*'s vaults and not shown publicly until Jim Garrison's 1969 subpoena forced its release. In 1975 *Time-Life* sold the film back to the Zapruder family for $1. In 1975 Geraldo Rivera aired the film on his network television show (see Stone and Sklar, 1992: 151–2; Zelizer, 1992: 38–9, 68–9, 113). Corliss (1991: 66) reports that Stone paid $40,000 for a copy of the film.

2 Directed by Francis Ford Coppola; screenplay by Francis Ford Coppola; cinematographer: Bill Butler; studio: Paramount; cast: Gene Hackman (Harry Caul); John Cazale (John); Frederic Forrest (Mark); Cindy Williams (Ann); Teri Garr (Amy); Harrison Ford (Martin Stett); Robert Duvall (the Director). Although still a popular video rental, it was not successful at the box office and failed to make the Top Twenty list for its decade (Ray, 1985: 328).

3 Directed by Oliver Stone; Screenplay by Oliver Stone and Zachary Sklar, based on the books *On the Trail of the Assassins* by Jim Garrison and *Crossfire: The Plot That Killed Kennedy* by Jim Marrs; cinematographer: Robert Richardson; studio: Warner Brothers; cast: Kevin Costner (Jim Garrison); Sissy Spacek (Liz Garrison); Joe Pesci (David Ferrie); Tommy Lee Jones (Clay Shaw); Gary Oldman (Lee Harvey Oswald); John Candy (Dean Andrews); Jack Lemmon (Jack Martin); Ed Asner (Guy Bannister); Walter Mattau (Senator Russell Long); Donald Sutherland (X); Kevin Bacon (Willie O'Keefe); Brian Doyle-Murray (Jack Ruby); Jim Garrison (Earl Warren). Stone won the Golden Globe for best director and was nominated for the Director's Guild America Award. *JFK* received eight Academy Award Nominations (best director, best adapted screenplay, best picture).

4 As Silverman (1988: 95) notes, 'Caul' is also a play on 'the amnion or inner membrane enclosing the foetus before birth . . . the amnion is the same membrane which subsequently becomes the afterbirth'. Silverman reads this as suggesting that Harry's name conveys his desire to be enveloped in 'pure [maternal] sonorousness' and his desire to control sound, to be exterior to it. She sees Harry as being obsessed with the complete control over the sounds (voices) of others, while he is irrationally drawn to the female voice 'which activates in him the desire to be folded in a blanket of sound' (1988: 87).

5 The date of the first nuclear chain reaction, December 2, 1942.

6 The voice of the acoustic mirror (Silverman, 1988: 80), unlike the gaze in the looking-glass mirror, is perpetually in effect for the subject can always send and receive the sound of their own voice. Alan Pakula's *Klute* (1971) disembodies this relationship between voice and the subject by having Bree's conversation taped by Cable, who then plays it back to her (see Silverman, 1988: 81–3 on this film).

7 In one part of the conversation Ann's words describing a drunk asleep on a bench are recorded, 'That's terrible . . . Oh God . . . he was once somebody's baby boy, and he had a mother and a father who loved him . . . and now there he is half-dead on a park bench. And now where are his mother and father and all his uncles?' (Silverman, 1988: 89).

8 But see Silverman's (1988: 87–98) feminist, psychoanalytic interpretation (footnote 4) which bypasses the above issues.

9 Coppola reflexively and relentlessly turns the concept of the taped conversation back on itself, showing that all of us have something to hide in the talk we take for granted. It is not clear that the ethnomethodologists have done this.

10 As Raymond Schmitt, a reviewer, points out (in conversation) this reflexive turn in Coppola's text treats talk as a cultural and a commodified object, while revealing how dramaturgically produced talk can make a difference in everyday life.

11 Michael Katouich, another reviewer, suggests (in conversation) that Harry has lost all hope of control over 'the response of the other'. His loss of privacy reflects this loss, for now he is under the control of others who are defining his situation for him. Yet, as still another reviewer notes, Harry's terror does not arise from the information revealed. His terror is focused on the intrusion itself, on the form of the invasion, not on the content of what is revealed. Here is Coppola's point. The new information technologies have no respect for content, they are entirely focused on form – pure information. There appears no desire, either within the technological society or academia, to separate these two interests.

12 It is unclear whether Harry's paranoia and anhedonia arise from his work, or whether he was like this before he took up wire-tapping. Silverman's reading (1988) suggests the latter, arguing that he seeks always to get back to the missing maternal figure in his life, a figure who momentarily left him in childhood nearly causing his drowning in a bathtub – hence his obsession with Ann's voice on the tapes. This reading can be easily supported by the dream sequences but it does not put to rest the broader argument that no one is immune to this technology that Harry attempts to master.

13 Within two weeks of the release of the *Warren Report*, conspiracy theories were circulating (Zelizer, 1992: 106). As Zelizer (1992: 34) observes, 'nearly 200 books that were published within 36 months of the tragedy have since been joined by over a thousand periodical pieces and books, dozens of television retrospectives, at least twelve newsletters, and numerous bookstores specializing in assassination literature'.

14 Other Kennedy-related films would also soon appear (*Love Field*, 1992; *In the Line of Fire*, 1993), recalling connections back to earlier JFK-assassination texts (*Executive Action* (1973), *Nashville* (1975), *Taxi Driver* (1976) and *The Parallax View* (1974) which ends with a Governmental Commission concluding that a lone assassin killed a United States Senator).

8

THE VOYEUR'S FUTURE

Basically it was journalism, that capital invention of the nineteenth century, which made evident . . . the utopian character of this . . . gaze . . . .

It was the dream of a transparent society, visible and legible in each of its parts, the dream of there no longer existing any zones of darkness

Foucault, *Power/Knowledge*, pp. 152, 162

surveillance and spectacle may be widely decried, but the power of visuality has certainly survived the attack

Jay, *Downcast Eyes: The Denigration of Vision in Twentieth Century French Thought*, p. 594

today there is a pornography of information and communication . . . it is no longer the obscenity of the repressed, the obscure, but of the visible . . . it is the . . . obscenity of that which no longer contains a secret

Baudrillard, *The Ecstasy of Communication*, p. 22

It remains to return to the beginning, to take up again the task of offering an interpretive framework for the understanding of the voyeur's place in the American cinematic society. A critical, interpretive interactionism (Denzin, 1989b), based on a feminist cultural studies approach (Morris, 1988: 2; Franklin et al. 1991: 175) to the contemporary postmodern situation (Carey, 1989: 46; Denzin, 1991a: 18) requires a framework that analyses the cinematic apparatuses that reproduce and represent society back to itself.

I come back to the cinematic (and ethnographic) version(s) of Foucault's gaze (1980: 155). This is the panoptic and panauditory gaze of surveillance transformed into a self-deterring code, the gaze of power that has also been internalized, the gaze which unveils the private and makes it public. It is the ethnographer's and the fieldworker's gaze (see Rosaldo, 1986: 92),[1] the gaze which seeks to expose the social and reveal the hidden truths that lie therein (Atkinson, 1990: 27).

I seek a reflexive ethnography appropriate to a critical cultural studies project; a project which makes a spectacle of the voyeur, and in so doing objectifies and makes problematic the ideological presuppositions which underwrite the traditional, realist ethnographic and cinematic text (see Van Maanen, 1988, Chapter 3; Rose, 1990).[2] This discussion necessitates a reflection on the preceding seven chapters and the films that have been examined. If interpretive sociology is to gain a stronger, more ethical footing in the next century then the basic elements of a post-visual theory of interpretive understanding and enquiry require presentation.

In this conclusion I offer preliminary observations on the voyeur's place in the cinematic, surveillance society and the human disciplines. I will also discuss vision and alternative ways of knowing and understanding the other and outline the ethics and epistemologies of voyeurism and a post-pragmatist social criticism.

The Voyeur's Place

A single problem, moving in four directions at the same time, has guided this study. I have sought repeatedly to interrogate the gender and ethnic biases, the forms, motivations, costs, consequences and functions of cinematic voyeurism for a post-surveillance society. In this society, each individual has interiorized the hearing and visual gaze of an 'objectified', external, generalized, nameless, often faceless, other. This technological other is everywhere and nowhere, in hidden cameras and recording devices, in telephone answering machines, electronic mail systems and home burglar alarm systems.

Multiple forms of the voyeur's gaze have been discussed: medical, investigative, technological, informational, erotic, accidental, inquisitive, comic, paranoid, obsessive, masculine, feminine, passive, active, direct, indirect, supplemental, legal, illegal, secret, illicit, loving, hostile, aggressive, official, regulated, unregulated, indifferent. Each of these forms of the gaze is engendered, fitted to masculine and feminine codes of looking.

These structures of the gaze have evolved through the major historical and aesthetic phases (realism, modernism, late modernism, postmodernism) of the cinematic society in the twentieth century. This history has come full circle. It starts with the blatant, open voyeurism of early primitive cinema, turning to the repressed gaze of modernism (Hitchcock's camera) and then shifting to the parodies in late modernism (*Body Double*, *Dead Men Don't Wear Plaid*). The rampant voyeurism of the postmodern, contemporary period suggests that the strictures and guilt that operated in primitive and modern cinema are no longer relevant. A pornography of the visible is now everywhere. Nothing is any longer hidden. Guilt connected to illicit, secret looking has all but disappeared. It has been replaced and displaced by the fear that if one's personal surveillance system is not in place, he or she will be attacked by the hidden, invisible other.

In each of its historical phases the cinematic society has systematically elaborated and institutionalized a surveillance and deterrence code that privileged the voyeur's place in public and private places. The tricks of the official, legal voyeur's trade protected the members of the society (the public) from those conspiratorial agents who would do harm to them, their families or the state. Here the moral neutrality of the surveillance apparatuses came into play. Official and unofficial voyeurs used the same surveillance techniques on one another.

In its serious, legal form, the voyeur's gaze has been structured by a set of official norms or conventions which stress rationality, truth, objectivity and compassion. (As argued in Chapter 3, the comic voyeur's text challenges these norms.) Yet the voyeur's eye has always been complicitous with patriarchy and racism. It has been attuned to a form of spectatorship that turns the female and alien ethnic or racial other into a site for the scopic and investigative pleasures of the state and the masculine eyes of the police, the Peeping Ton or the private investigator.[3] The voyeur's gaze is supposedly motivated by these scopic, investigative and personal pleasures, while often answering to a higher truth or morality, defined as justice.

Those who are given (or who take) the warrant to gaze pay a high cost for this privilege. They suffer from what I have called fatal flaws. Some give their lives to it (*Fatal Attraction*), others lose their families (*JFK*), their sanity (*The Conversation*), the ones they love (*sex, lies and videotape, Broadcast News, Blue Velvet*), their personal identity (*Chan Is Missing*). Others find their lives endangered by their voyeurism (*Dead Men Don't Wear Plaid, Rear Window, Black Widow, Fatal Attraction*) or find that they no longer have a firm contact with what is called reality (*Blow-Up, The Conversation*).

These are small costs for a cinematic society that is committed to the belief that voyeurs are needed. These persons reveal the truths others are afraid to expose (*Black Widow, JFK*). They protect our private, sacred spaces from the violence that lurks everywhere (*Rear Window*). They perpetuate the illusion that there are still private places where we can all hide. At the same time voyeurs expose the freedoms that are lost because of the new information, surveillance technologies (*The Conversation*), and they show how certain truths can still be revealed if these technologies are correctly used (*Broadcast News*). And underneath all of this discourse lurks the ever present possibility that the voyeur can never discover the truth about anything, except the truth that no truth can be discovered (*Chan is Missing*). Sometimes we need to be reminded of this.

The voyeur's film, what I have called the reflexive text, reinforces the above assumptions. These films, as 'progressive or subversive texts'[4] (Klinger, 1984/1986: 74–5; Comolli and Narboni, 1971/1976: 27), undermine from within the realist illusion that reality can be unmasked and the truth revealed.[5] They rupture the veneer of their own premises (Klinger, 1984/1986: 77). They subvert the traditional story of investigation wherein the hero discovers a truth that others have not seen (the detective story, the psychoanalytic case-study, the flawed-heroic journalist). These films make a spectacle out of the ideological belief that truth can be discovered, thereby exposing the paucity and the limits of the voyeur's project.

The Cinematic Society and the Voyeur's Epistemology

The cinematic culture made ocular vision an analogue for knowing (see Ong, 1977: 122–3). As argued in Chapter 1, by 1900 the cinematic eye had become firmly engrained in American society (Comolli, 1971–2/1985: 55), which was soon to become a cinematic society; a society, that is, that would know itself through the reflections that Hollywood produced.

To repeat, the cinematic impulse arose out of an attempt to compensate for the imperfections of the human eye. The cinematic apparatus substituted the objective, scientifically accurate eye (and ear) of the camera lens for the imperfect human eye (Branigan, 1979/1985: 133–4). This desire to replace the imperfect eye with the scientific lens reflected the rise to power of the surveillance society. In its twentieth century version this society embraced the ideological demand to see the social world in its entirety, to capture, through a totalizing scientific apparatus, all of the features of modern life. There was an economic demand to make this new form of seeing profitable, to make movies out of what the camera could see. The cinematic eye was thus put to immediate service by the state. It served democracy well as it became an extension of official state ideology, carrying news to the American public about our military adventures abroad (for example, the newsreel coverage of World Wars I and II, the Korean and Vietnam wars, etc.). It is to these impulses that the twentieth century cinematic society owes its being (see Comolli, 1971–72/1985: 55).[6]

Several consequences followed from this commitment to the cinematic apparatus. Visual perception, as argued in Chapters 1 and 2 was invested with the power of truth (Springer, 1991: 177) and the scientific, investigative voyeur became a valued social type. However, human understanding was excluded from this visual paradigm, for seeing does not equal understanding (see Lonergan, 1963/1977: 121–2; Springer, 1991: 177–8).[7] And of course the person doing the looking is not a neutral spectator. Voyeurs see what they want to see, or think they see (for example, *Body Double*).

Hence, as the records of visual perception were invested with the power of truth, and the voyeur elevated to new heights, truth itself became an unstable phenomenon, dependent on the viewer's interpretive framework for its empirical grounding. The very processes that joined truth and perception undermined from within the observer's ability to point with certainty to what was seen, and hence known about the visual world and the subjects who inhabited that world.[8]

Understanding that understanding could not just be given by and through visual knowledge, cinema and the human sciences then turned to a host of interpretive methodologies which would presumably enter the inner world of the subject and render that world meaningful.[9] So were born personal, subjective cinema and *Verstehen*, qualitative sociology. These formations would yield the understandings that the older, objective (cinematic) epistemologies were incapable of producing. But paradoxically, these new methods would themselves yield to the very realist epistemology they were attempting to overcome. Through devices like tables, charts, figures, ideal types and excerpts from transcribed interviews they would reduce the world of sounds, words and interior conservations to visual records.[10] None of these devices made any sound or noise, 'however informative and desirable and useful and indispensable and beautiful and true' (Ong, 1977: 125) they may be. These methods, which deploy terms like cast light on, illuminate, demonstrate, show, draw a conclusion, comprehend, perceive and observe, all reflect a commitment to a position which equates knowledge with vision and visualization (see Ong, 1977: 133–4).[11] In this gesture they would forget that visual constructs and metaphors can supplement, but not replace, an interpretive methodology which plunges into and reveals the interior feeling, hearing, tasting, smelling and touching worlds of subjective (and intersubjective) human experience (see Ong, 1977: 137).[12] And so the limits of the voyeur's classic project are exposed. Certain truths cannot be revealed by this epistemology.

Downcast Eyes: Vision as a Violent Way of Knowing

Recall Michael Powell's troubling, violent 1960 film *Peeping Tom*. This is the story of Mark, a professional cinematographer who moonlights as a photographer for a pornographic magazine. Clever Mark has equipped his tripod with a hidden spike. His camera has a mirror which reflects the faces of the women he photographs. As his light flashes in his victims' eyes the hidden spike penetrates their throat. The mirror reflects the fear that is in the woman's eye as she sees herself murdered. In this way Mark's hidden, magic, killer camera reveals one face of death, the face of fear (see Clover, 1992: 170). We soon learn that Mark was the childhood subject of his father's gazing camera. We are led to believe that he is now seeking vengeance on his father by forcing his female victims to experience the same loss, pain and fear that were forced upon him (Silverman, 1988: 34).

Peeping Tom, of course, reproduces the classic themes of mid-century, modernist cinema, including the masculine, scopophilic desire for a sadistic voyeurism which makes women the object of male violence (Clover, 1992: 177). Furthermore, the film reminds us, as Sontag (1977: 14–15, 24) argues, that photography is a form of death, an act of power and aggression, sublimated murder. But more is suggested, as Clover (1992: 181) observes, for Powell's film is about the eye that is killed, not the eye that kills. *Peeping Tom* turns its eye on the victim, the person who is literally annihilated by the camera's forceful gaze.

Thus Powell's film stands as a metaphor for my study. In the race to capture the visual field in its entirety, the cinematic society has instantiated an apparatus that kills what it seeks to understand. Like Mark's victims we have experienced the violence that comes from the microphones and the cameras that are everywhere hidden in the walls that enclose us. And so we look with humbled, downcast eyes (Jay, 1993a) at the fruits of our labour.

In his stunning study of the denigration of vision in twentieth century French thought, Martin Jay (1993a) repeats themes that have by now become familiar. The list of French theorists who have questioned the truth of the visual (ocularcentrism) is long, from Bergson to Bataille, Sartre, Merleau-Ponty, Lacan, Althusser, Foucault, Debord, Barthes, Metz, Derrida, Irigaray, Levinas, to Lyotard and Baudrillard. Each theorist expresses disenchantment with a visual epistemology, from Bataille's blinding sun, to Sartre's masochistic look, Merleau-Ponty's doubt about vision's certainty, Lacan's illusive ego in the mirror stage, Foucault's fear of the panopticon and the medical gaze, Debord's ridicule of the society of the spectacle, Barthes's connection of photography with death, Derrida's assertion that a specular ideology reproduces a white mythology (light over darkness), to Irigaray's speculum, and Baudrillard's suggestion that postmodernism rests entirely on the simulacrum.

Americans have joined this chorus which expresses extreme doubt about vision as the main path to truth. John Dewey rejected a spectator theory of knowledge, and Rorty has echoed this position. Postmodern anthropologists, like Clifford (1986: 10–12; 1993), Rosaldo (1986: 92), Tyler (1986: 131) and Bruner (1993), have elaborated the media criticisms of McLuhan and Ong which reject visualism as the preferred way of knowing. Sociologists Howard S. Becker (1986, Part Four), and Douglas Harper (1994) have questioned the authority of the visual image, and feminine film theorists from Mulvey (1989), Modleski (1990), Doane (1991), de Lauretis (1987), Clover (1992), to Stacey (1994) have challenged the power of the male gaze.

These are commonplace understandings for many of the directors examined in this study, including Hitchcock, Coppola, Antonioni and Stone. With Ong (1977: 122–3) and Lonergan (1963/1977: 121–2) they would argue that understanding is not seeing. They too would reject the epistemological equation which has converted human knowledge into visual perception.[13]

This assault on visual truth runs deep and wide. It opens the door for a critique of the enlightenment project which privileged vision as the primary mode of knowing the world. The theorists just listed all criticize the cold, analytic eye of Cartesian perspectivalism (Jay, 1993a: 589–90). At the same time these criticisms reinforce the seduction of the visual, its pleasurable side, suggesting that there are also other visual regimes, from the Baconian to the Baroque and the hysterical (Jay, 1988) which undermine the all-seeing objective, Cartesian eye. Thus this discourse simultaneously criticizes while it repositions the centrality of the visual in the postmodern project.

The Interpretive Research Text as a Cultural, Visual Form

This critique of a visual epistemology has direct relevance for interpretive enquiry in the social sciences. A questionable pragmatic epistemology organizes current qualitative enquiry in the social sciences (See Denzin and Lincoln, 1994b; Lincoln and Denzin 1994). Contemporary enquiry is organized under modernist, post positivist ethnographic assumptions (Lather, 1993). Like the modernist novel (see McHale, 1992: 44), the modernist ethnographic text presumes a stable external social reality that can be recorded, photographed and transcribed by a stable, objective, scientific observer.[14] While this external reality may yield to multiple interpretations, the interpretive, mobile consciousness of the researcher-as-observer is able to form certain and conclusive observations about it (see Wolcott, 1994: 408).

The modernist qualitative (ethnographical) text records the many voices, faces and sites heard and seen in the field setting as indicators of how this stable reality is socially constructed and given meaning. The modernist observer-writer then mediates those voices, sites and presences and assembles them into a text that re-orders reality according to a particular interpretive logic. Unlike its postmodern counterpart, this traditional text does not attempt to connect mobile, moving, shifting minds (and their representations) to a shifting, external world. There is no attempt to create a parallax of discourses where nothing is stable. If such were the case there would be discourse on discourse, discourse on perspective, point of view, language itself (see Richardson, 1994; Lather, 1993; McHale, 1992).

Seeking to create a space for the voices and presences of those studied, qualitative researchers attempt to capture and re-present, through photographs, transcribed interviews and audio-tapes, the authentic, original voices heard, seen and felt in the field setting. It is understood that this re-presentation of the voice and experiences of the other requires special skills, a special way of seeing, what Eisner (1991: 1–7) calls the enlightened eye, a form of connoisseurship which goes beyond looking, allowing the scholar to then make public, in a critical way, what has been seen.

The qualitative research text is a distinct form of cultural representation, a genre in its own right. The researcher creates, through his or her textual work, concrete experiences which embody cultural meanings and cultural understandings that operate in the 'real' world. These texts carry news from one world to another. This news is based on three types of discourse: ordinary talk and speech, inscriptions of that speech in the form of transcriptions and written interpretations based on talk and its inscriptions (see Bakhtin, 1986; Barthes, 1985; Duranti and Goodwin, 1992).

This discourse is based on the modernist commitment to study lived experience in the real world. Those who honour lived experience ground their work on the study of flesh-and-blood individuals. This experience, and its materiality, as given on the video tape, the picture or the transcribed text, is taken as the final court of appeal for such researcher. This emphasis on lived presence falters on the following points.

First, the worlds we study are created through the texts that we write. We do not study lived experience, rather we examine lived textuality (Frow and Morris, 1993: xvii). There is a doubling of textuality at work here. The direct link between experience and text can no longer be presumed. Lived textuality transforms lived experience; that is real, live experiences are shaped by prior textual representations and understandings. These understandings in turn are re-inscribed in the transcribed voice and dialogue of the other. They are created in the social text. These texts are dialogical, the site where multiple voices co-mingle. In them the voices of the other, and the voices of the researcher come alive and interact with one another. These accomplishments have a prior life in the context where they were produced.

Secondly, the modernist project privileges visual representation. This representation is a stand-in for real interaction. It is one level removed from the actual experiences studied. Accordingly, scholars find themselves in the position of reading video tapes and transcriptions as cultural texts which represent experience.

This ocular epistemology (like its cinematic counterpart) presumes the primacy of visual perception as the dominant form of knowing. But perception is never pure. It is clouded by the structures of language which refuse to be anchored in the present, the site of so-called pure presence. Presence in its plenitude can never be grasped. Consequently, presence on a tape or in real life is always elusive, shifting, indeterminate, its meanings never final or clear-cut. Visual representations can only be understood as textual constructions. Furthermore, the specularity of the visual image is always problematic, for the image is never a pure copy. Even when two images appear identical, there is always a surplus of meaning, an invisible otherness that disrupts 'specular unity' (Jay, 1993a: 505). The image always splits what it doubles, and is always more than itself.

Derrida (1972/1981, 1976, 1978, 1982, 1993), Jay (1993a: 493–523), Ulmer, (1989), Barthes, (1957/1972, 1981, 1982, 1985) and Bakhtin (1968, 1981, 1986) are useful here, for each reminds us that mimesis is an impossibility. Like the photograph, the inscribed text is a form of mimesis. It copies what has already been (see Barthes, 1985: 355). And so its wonder, which, as Taussig (1993: xiii) argues, lies in that moment when the copy, the representation, assumes the power of the original, more real than the real. The printed text replaces the spoken word, it is more accurate than what was spoken. But in this moment a confusion occurs. The original 'original' changes each time it is spoken. It cannot be copied. Mimesis is a fraud.

The inscribed text, like all copies, is caught between three dangers. Its copies are originals. It cannot copy as well as the cinematic text (which contextualizes the text). And, the referent of what is copied is no longer the subject being quoted/copied. Rather, the subject of the new text, as with the photograph, is the viewer-as-reader. Still the seductiveness of the transcribed text is given in its illusive naturalness. On the surface its referent points to the lived experiences of a real person. But this reality is one-dimensional. It is a construction, one of many possible slices/images of reality selected by the scribe. Its naturalness is a masquerade.

The 'original' voices of individuals in a field setting, and the intentions behind those voices, can never be recovered. There are no original voices, for every instance of a voice being heard is an original, a new hearing, a new voice speaking (and hearing) its mind. Every transcription is a re-telling, a new telling of a previously heard, now newly-heard voice.

The third place where the modernist project falters occurs with those qualitative researchers who give primacy to the voice over writing. Perhaps this is the case because they believe that hearing their own voice defines their presence in a situation. Speech is seen as the window into experience and its meanings. But speech is not transparent. As Derrida (1982: 51) notes, the ear should not be regarded as that organ which best establishes the presence of the other. To privilege the ear as the central communi-cative organ is to misunderstand hearing and listening as interactional activities. The ear is an impediment to common understanding. In the process of hearing the speaker's words are filtered through the hearer's ear (and mind), thereby undermining and transforming the authority of (and in) the speaker's voice. Silverman (1988: 79–80) supports this argument, the acoustical mirror always distorts, and country-singer Willie Nelson reminds me that when 'I hear the sound of your voice in my mind, I hear what I want to hear' ('The Sound in your Mind').

So qualitative researchers' two main methods of enquiry, voyeuristic looking and hearing, on inspection turn into self-fulfilling methods which privilege the theatrical spectacles of sight and sound. These technologies of representation crumble precisely at that moment when the representation is taken to be a measure of pure presence, pure interaction. There are no such measures, they are all textual constructions.

Ethnography, Cinema and Cultural Studies

Baudrillard speaks of the postmodern simulacrum, those media-based apparatuses that produce replicas and representations of the real, what he calls the simulacrum. He reminds us that the simulacrum 'is never that which conceals the truth — it is the truth which conceals that there is none. The simulacrum is true' (1983a: 1). The procession of simulacra that defines the postmodern moment is haunted by the belief that the real in its plenitude can be captured if only the right camera angle and shot can be found.

More is involved here than just theories of knowing or apparatuses of reproduction. The issues go beyond an aesthetics of representation. Reality becomes a political, visual and auditory construction. The person who manipulates the images and sounds of everyday life controls the way everyday life is perceived and understood. This is not news, for a society's storytellers have always constructed the past to fit a particular storied image of human history. Yet these stories were presumed to be true, they followed a law of representation that said an image (a telling) could always be firmly connected to the external world. Objective storytellers could tell objective stories about the world out there. For all practical purposes this world is dead. Today there is only a single truth, the simulacrum, the truth which tells us that there is no truth beyond the image itself.

All of this speaks directly to the intertwined discourses of cultural studies and ethnography. A double crisis confronts this sprawling field of enquiry. In the aftermath of the post-Geertz (1988) writing culture project (Clifford and Marcus, 1986) ethnographers stand frozen in a reflexive moment, hesitant to move the writing hand across the multi-voiced terrains that define the contemporary cultural world.[15] Aware of how their texts produce subjects created in their own image, not knowing which tale from the field to write (Van Maanen, 1988; Geertz, 1988; for example, confessional, realist, impressionist, 'I-Witnessing' 'Us/Not Us') ethnographers now struggle with new metaphors to organize their texts. Attempting to avoid the voyeur label (Rosaldo, 1986: 92), some now describe their efforts in the languages of tourism and travel (Clifford, 1989; Bruner, 1989). Others extend the tourism model, developing the notion of the travelling, nomadic cultural critic (Grossberg, 1988b; Morris, 1988; Taussig, 1990; but see Urry, 1990, who writes both a politics of culture and a politics of criticism). And a few, following the leads of Ulmer (1989), and earlier feminist theorists (see Gluck and Patai, 1991: 4) struggle with new writing forms shaped by the concept of the 'mystory'[16] and the 'auto-ethnography'. In these new writing forms there is an erasure of the ethnographer's status as a scientific observer: classic ethnography disappears to be replaced by a new kind of political text. The ethnographer-as-social-theorist now produces personal texts which express a politics of resistance (Agger, 1991a: x; 1991b).

As this revolution in postmodern ethnography occurs the multi-disciplined field of cultural studies enthusiastically engages the ethnographic project.[17] Corner (1991: 135) observes, '"ethnography" [is] a key methodology of post-theoretical cultural studies'. Franklin et al. elaborate, 'ethnographic work within cultural studies . . . has provided one of the main sources of exploration of "lived cultures"' (1991: 181). The 'new' cultural studies ethnographer simultaneously deploys traditional versions of those identities attached to the covert, ethnographic voyeur (Adler and Adler, 1987, 1994), including the use of informants and 'insider' documents (Radway, 1989: 6), while attempting to avoid those discursive practices that lead the ethnographer to construct 'the other as "difference"' (Grossberg, 1989: 25).

The discourses of ethnography and cultural studies are mediated by the representational structures of the cinematic society. But even as ethnography and cultural studies intermingle and interact with one another, various critics, including Jameson (1991: 68), Ulmer (1989: x) and Baudrillard (1988a: 10) argue that 'culture today is a matter of media' (Jameson, 1991: 68); the dominant cultural form of the twentieth century is, and has been, cinema, and now video. Only modernist formulations argue that we inhabit a print culture.[18] We live instead in a video, cinematic age, where the cinematic apparatus intervenes between the material world and everyday, lived experience.[19]

The challenge now is to think video, to think cinematically, to visualize, not only theory and culture as products of a complex visual cinematic apparatus, but to show how that apparatus entangles itself with the very tellings we tell. To tell a theory visually, like a story or a 'mystory', to use Ulmer's (1989: xi) term, is to argue for a new ethnographic relationship to the old-fashioned writing self. This self disappears behind its own traces as it struggles to articulate, in cinematic fashion, its own literal, visual relationship to itself, inscribing itself within a video, visual culture. The disappearing voyeur is a key to this new visual theorist.

The cinematic apparatuses of contemporary culture stand in a two-fold relationship to ethnography and cultural studies. First, the cultural logics of the post-video, cinematic culture define the lived experiences that a critical studies project takes as its subject matter. Baudrillard describes this cultural logic as it operates in the age of the hyperreal 'the real is no longer what it used to be . . . . There is a proliferation of . . . signs . . . of objectivity and authenticity . . . an escalation of the true, of the lived experience . . . a panic-stricken production of the real' (1983a: 12–13). Television, cinema, ethnography and the panoptic gaze of the cultural voyeur are the keys to the production of these authentic, realistic accounts of lived experience (see Baudrillard, 1983a: 13–14, 49–55). In them there is a sudden switching of surveillance codes, from Foucault's panopticon to a system of deterrence (Baudrillard, 1983a: 53), where the person gazed upon is the person doing the gazing: the voyeur as newsmaker, visual theory, reflective ethnography![20]

These texts (cinematic, ethnographic and video) interact with the worlds of lived experience, creating representations of experience that are then interpreted and acted upon by cultural members.[21] The cultural logics which structure these representations articulate (as argued above, pp. 196–7, and in Chapter 1) an epistemological theory of realism which assumes not only that the real exists, but that it can be accurately represented in the cinematic, video or ethnographic text. Such texts create, as Jameson (1990: 166) notes, the very reality they purport to map and interpret. This theory of realism blurs into, and shapes, the ethnographic texts that are written about the culture and its members.

The foregoing situation suggests two problems. The realist logic of the ethnographic text must be deconstructed. At the same time a new form of ethnography, an ethnography of the video-cinematic text, must be constructed (see Krug, 1992). Such an ethnography will attempt to unravel and undo the cinematic texts that themselves map the lived experiences that ethnographers seek, in some final analysis to interpret and critique.

Still more is at issue. Ethnography will not go away. It remains a requirement for that cultural studies project which directs itself to the analysis of 'lived cultures' and the intersections between cultural texts and lived experience (Johnson, 1986–7; Grossberg, 1989). The unstable relationship between the ethnographer, the cultural subject, the ethnographic text and cinematic-video representations cannot be avoided.

Paradoxically, and despite the literature just cited, current cultural critics of ethnography, cultural studies and cinema theory have yet to seriously interrogate and question their own licence to gaze. They appear, that is, to justify the gazing eye of the voyeuristic cultural critic by appealing to the politics of resistance that they attempt to write: they remain, accordingly, under the protective umbrella the surveillance society has traditionally always made available to the voyeur disguised as ethnographer or theorist.

The Collapse of Epistemologies

The qualitative researchers and ethnographers, like their cinematic counterparts, were unable to escape the epistemologies of realism.[22] They each sought a total cinema or a total ethnographic report which captured everything the eye and writing or recording hand could see and hence inscribe. As a consequence, they take their place in a long tradition which has been simultaneously positivist and post-positivist, or interpretive. From Weber to Durkheim, Mead to Watson, Blumer to Lazarsfeld, Marx to Althusser, this tradition has maintained a commitment to a science which renders the invisible world visible through the production of a series of realist, interactionist, melodramatic, social problems texts which have created an identification with the powerless in society. These works of realism reproduced and mirrored the social structures that needed to be changed. They valorized the subjectivity of the downtrodden individual, while making a hero (or heroine) of the sociological theorist/observer who could write moving texts about the powerless. They created a body of textual work that kept the private/public divisions alive and well in American sociology.[23]

Today social realism is under attack.[24] It is now seen as but one narrative strategy for telling stories about the social world out there. In its place comes poststructuralism and grammatology: new writing and reading styles grafted into the cinematic society, where a thing exists if it can be captured in a visual or printed text. Poststructuralism undermines the realist agenda, contending that things do not exist independent of their representations in social texts. Accordingly, if we want to change how things are, we must change how they are seen and heard. How they are seen (and heard) is itself determined by the older realist and modernist agendas which presumed worlds out there that could be mapped by a realist, scientific method. It is this hegemonic vision that must be challenged. We must let go of the concept of a world out there that proves our theories right or wrong. This is where the voyeur's project re-enters the picture.

Through the Rear Window: Ethics and the Voyeur's Project

I turn again to the central voyeurs in *Rear Window* and *The Conversation*. As an ethnographer and a sociologist, I am L.B. Jeffries and Harry Caul, and you are too. Jeff and Harry embody the iconic postmodern self, the voyeur and Peeping Tom taken to the extreme.[25] To study these two voyeurs, their motives, their actions and their accounts, is to study who we are. We are voyeurs. We take morbid pleasure in looking and seeing.[26]

The selves of Jeff and Harry, like ours, know themselves only through the looking investigative gaze; the gaze which unmasks the other and exposes them in their full interactional nakedness. Jeff's (and Harry's) warrant to gaze, even as it is challenged by Stella, Lisa and Tom, is, like ours, given by our contemporary, post-visual, pornographic culture which values information and knows no barrier between the private and the public spheres of social life.

Like Jeff and Harry I seldom doubt my right to look, to lift the veils of secrecy that shroud the mysteries of human group life. This is my job. It is what I get paid to do. All I want are nice, fat, thick descriptions. I try to do it right and keep my mouth closed. I'm not so different from Harry, although I may make an appeal to a different professional code of ethics to justify my actions, and with Harry I make judgements about what I observe, but some of us, like Harry, do intrude and make secret observations without permission.

Jeff differs from Harry (and other recent cinematic voyeurs) in one important way.[27] He is not getting paid. Jeff is the pure voyeur, the voyeur who simply takes pleasure in looking, and in his gaze are found erotic, sexual and sensual pleasures, as when he looks knowingly at the newlyweds who pull down their window shades. In this he is like Graham in *sex, lies and videotape* (1989). But his pleasures, like the sociologist's, extend beyond sexuality. They include the desire to know and to have power over the other. By peering as a Peeping Tom into the lives of another, Jeff, like the ethnographer, gains power over them. He compares their situation to his own, and feels superior to them. He even applies his theories to their experiences. His, like the sociologist's, is the gaze of pure power, the gaze which desires only to know. This gaze borders on an obsession and leads the central figures in his life to call him crazy, insane and obsessed.

This is the case because his gaze, while producing knowledge of the other, fails to produce any detailed connection between their lives, their actions and their experiences. Here his fate is parallel to the sociologist's who looks, but doesn't understand. Thus Doyle, the detective, is able to counter every one of Jeff's charges against Thorvald by offering concrete material on Thorvald's job, the length of his apartment lease, his financial and marital history, the destination of the trunk sent from the apartment, who picked it up and what its contents were. These rational facts counter Jeff's intuitions and his visual knowledge of Thorvald's situation. Hitchcock unravels the voyeur's epistemology and in so doing speaks directly to the interactionist's ethnographic, voyeuristic project. What gives us the right to secretly (or openly) study the other?

A Voyeur's Ethics

A contradictory set of ethical understandings organize the voyeur's gaze. Understanding that the manners and morals of the public could be tainted by 'immoral' scenes playing on their screens, successive waves of production codes (see Chapter 1), starting in 1909, having shaped what Hollywood's camera could capture. Early production codes excluded scenes showing adultery, rape, prostitution, miscegenation, childbirth, criminal violence, drug addiction and excessive drinking. A middle-class, Christian morality shaped these codes. Today these restrictions do not hold, and only excessive violence and 'clearly' pornographic sexuality are kept from the screens that play before general audiences (but see *Body of Evidence*, 1993; and *Reservoir Dogs*, 1992; also Leff and Simmons, 1990).

The federal government was less timorous, quickly appropriating and using for democratic and criminal justice purposes all the tools of the cinematic apparatus. In keeping with the commitments of a surveillance state, spies and covert observations have been central to the federal government's activities throughout the twentieth century (see Marx, 1988). Indeed Hollywood and the state exchanged secrets and technologies. Hollywood willingly took up the assignment of cinematically representing the latest tools of surveillance used by the FBI, the CIA, the Defense Department, and so on. The gangster and prison films of the 1930s and the urban crime film cycle of the 1940s and 1950s were critical here (as noted in Chapter 1). The conspiratorial films of the 1970s and 1980s took up the problem of presenting the more sophisticated new surveillance techniques, and 1990s films now bring these techniques more directly into the home (*The Firm*, 1993; *Sliver*, 1993).

In addition to deploying hidden surveillance techniques, the federal government was also engaged, as early as 1930, in questionable, disguised scientific, medical research. (The 40-year Tuskegee Project of the US Public Health Service is but one example. Here 399 poor Black males were 'mislead by researchers into believing their ailments were being treated rather than merely observed' (Mitchell, 1993: 27).

The federal voyeur operates under a single code, the ends justify the means. This means that there is no need to protect subjects from harm or loss of reputation, to disclose the purpose of one's enquiry to a subject, to receive informed consent or to report one's findings back to those studied. The federal voyeur can use any method of observation or persuasion to obtain information about the other, including wiretaps, hidden recorders and cameras, tactical secrets, hypnosis, drugs, deception, lies, false intimacy, threats to life, physical injury, blackmail and betrayal.

Compared with Hollywood, social science voyeurs took much longer to develop a code of ethics governing their scientific gaze. It was not until the 1950s that codes of ethics became problematic (see Mitchell, 1993: 25; Deyhle et al., 1992; Hornsby-Smith, 1993; Lee, 1993; Kayser-Jones and Koenig, 1994; Punch, 1986, 1994). Historically, and most recently, one of five ethical stances (absolutist, consequentialist, feminist, relativist, deceptive) has been followed, often these stances merge with one another.[28]

The **absolutist stance** argues that social scientists have no right to invade the privacy of others. Disguised research is unethical. However, social scientists have a responsibility to contribute to a society's self-understanding. Because invasions of privacy can cause harm, social scientists should only study those behaviours and experiences that occur in the public sphere. Mitchell (1993: 25) calls this a version of the liberal position. It dominates much of the secrecy-ethics discussion in many social science disciplines.

Guba and Lincoln (1989: 120–41) review the traditional arguments supporting the absolutist position (see also Kayser-Jones and Koenig, 1994, and Lee, 1993). Professional scholarly societies and federal law mandate four areas of ethical concern, involving the protection of subjects from harm (physical and psychological), deception and loss of privacy. Informed consent, the fourth area, is presumed to protect the researcher from charges that harm, deception and invasions of privacy have occurred. Guba and Lincoln analyse the weaknesses of each of these claims, challenging the warrant of science to create conditions which invade private spaces, dupe subjects and challenge a subject's sense of moral worth and dignity. According to Guba and Lincoln (1989: 120), these guidelines were put in place to support the realist ontology of positivism, because 'whole groups of professionals believe that ethical limits will from time to time be breached, unless we adopt stringent means to enforce them'.[29] (Lincoln and Guba (1989) call (see below, p. 205) for an empowering, educative ethic which joins researchers and subjects together in an open, collegial relationship. In such a model deception is removed, and threats of harm and loss of privacy operate as barriers that cannot be crossed.)

The absolutist model stands in sharp contrast to the **conflict, deception model**, which endorses investigative voyeurism in the name of science, truth and understanding (see Douglas, 1976, Chapter 8; also Mitchell, 1993).[30] In this model the researcher uses any method necessary to obtain greater and deeper understanding in a situation. This may involve telling lies, deliberately misrepresenting the self, duping others, setting people up, using adversarial interviewing techniques, building friendly trust and infiltrating settings. These techniques are justified, this position argues, because frequently people in power, like those out of power, will attempt to hide the truth from the researcher. This model is fully compatible with the governmental, conspiratorial code. It is justified by its practitioners because it exposes hidden power structures in society.

The **relativist stance** assumes that researchers have absolute freedom to study what they see fit, however they should *only* study those problems which directly flow from their own experiences. Agenda-setting is determined by personal biography, not some larger scientific community. The only reasonable ethical standard, accordingly, is the one dictated by the individual's conscience. The relativist stance argues that no single set of ethical standards can be developed, for each situation encountered requires a different ethical stance (see Denzin, 1989a: 261–4). However, the researcher is directed to build open, sharing relationships with those investigated, thereby connecting this framework to the feminist and consequentialist models.

The **contextualized-consequentialist model** (Smith, 1990; House, 1990) builds on four principles. (These principles are compatible with those espoused by Lincoln and Guba.) They are the principles of mutual respect, non-coercion and non-manipulation, the support of democratic values and institutions, and the belief that every research act implies moral and ethical decisions which are contextual. Every ethical decision, that is, affects others, with immediate and long-term consequences. These consequences involve personal values, held by the researcher and those studied. The consequential model requires the researcher to build relationships of respect and trust which are non-coercive and not based on deception.

This consequentialist model elaborates a **feminist ethic** which calls for collaborative, trusting, non-oppressive relationships between researchers and those studied (Fonow and Cook, 1991: 8–9). Such an ethic presumes that investigators are committed to an ethic that stresses personal accountability, caring, the value of individual expressiveness, the capacity for empathy and the sharing of emotionality (Finch, 1993; Collins, 1990: 216). This is the position I endorse.

Ethical Mandates and Public and Private Places

Informed consent, which is intended to protect subjects from harm, deception, and invasions of privacy, is a sham. The liberal solution to the voyeur's code protects the state researcher against the subject. The humanist code, which endorses pure deception, presumably protects the researcher against the state by turning the tables on those in power, while protecting the researcher's sources (but see Scarce, 1994). This is also a sham, for the state inevitably has more power than the researcher, and in practice it leads to the study of marginal groups.

Both the liberal and the humanist ethical mandates work within and against a state-sponsored conspiratorial ethical code. Neither adequately addresses the place of the voyeur in the postmodern age. This voyeur, as this study has revealed, comes in multiple forms (investigative, conspiratorial, medical, scientific, journalistic, legal, accidental, pornographic, tourist). The contemporary video culture absorbs each of these forms of the voyeur into a visual and auditory text. Each type is simultaneously a user of visual surveillance techniques and a product of that use; that is the voyeur is also represented visually as a user of these visual tools.

Whose Private Space?

The liberal and humanistic ethical codes were written (and continue to be rewritten) for a historical moment when it was presumed that there was a firm and steady division between the public sphere and private life. Each code carries the traces of the Panoptic Project outlined in Chapter 1. The disciplinary society required a mobile panoptic eye, an eye that could hear and see everything that was going on in the social world. And so, journalism, the media and a generalized cinematic apparatus came into place. Together these systems of surveillance made visible the dark, hidden worlds of evil and disorder that lurked on the borders and edges of the public sphere. As Foucault (1980: 152) notes, a double dream organized this project, 'It was the dream that each individual . . . might be able to see the whole of society' and the keepers of the gaze could, at the same time, see those who were made visible by this system of observation. Nothing was hidden, and in the public realm reason and democratic politics would be played out. Here justice would be served (see Gaonkar, 1994: 549; Habermas, 1992: 102).

The legacies of this system were 'conceived between the American War of Independence and the French Revolution . . . [which were] the harbingers of a disciplinary society that followed in the wake of democratic revolutions inspired by the Enlightenment' (Gaonkar, 1994: 547). The disciplinary society presumed a social world of autonomous individuals, variously gifted with intelligence, and this gift was stratified by class, ethnicity and gender (Wiley, 1994: 6). A hierarchy of differentially virtuous autonomous selves was put in place. The less virtuous were those who fell under the eye of the panoptic, cinematic apparatus. Their private lives became topics of discourse in the public sphere.

The ethical codes of conduct for the social sciences take for granted the existence of private spaces that science can and cannot invade. Informed consent forms draw subjects out of their private spaces into a public space where science can operate. If subjects know they are being studied, then their private lives are not being invaded.

Of course this was all a myth. There are no longer (if there ever were) any private, sacred places. While the voyeur sustains the illusion that such spaces do exist (and that they should be protected), the twentieth century histories of governmental surveillance and cinematic voyeurism indicate that this myth only operates for the benefit of the state. Oliver Stone is right. A massive conspiracy does operate in the United States, the conspiracy that gives the state the right to observe whatever it wants whenever it wants to.

Contrary to the arguments of Richard Rorty (1989: xviii; 1994), in the postmodern period there is no private sphere, that is, a part of one's life that is irrelevant to one's responsibilities to other people. And so the fiction of the free, autonomous individual lingers. But there is no part of one's life that cannot be observed by others. Nor is there any part of one's life that cannot be implicated in the life of another. Together we are all intangled in an interconnecting web of narrated video images.

We live on a broad horizon of 'voyeuristic otherness' where the other's presence is variously disguised, hidden, obtrusive, noticed and taken into account. I enter the front, or side door of Menards, a national hardware chain-store. I notice a sign, 'We reserve the right to use electronic surveillance techniques to protect against shoplifting'. I have a cup of coffee at a Dunkin' Donuts outlet and my conversation is recorded by hidden microphones (see Kilborne, 1994). I buy gas at my local Amoco service station and watch myself on a video camera paying for my purchase. I come home and replay the taped messages on my telephone answering machine, check my E-Mail and find a dirty message from an angry student. I step onto my front porch and a photographer is taking pictures of my house and the park next door. I answer my phone and a rare coin salesman from the Bronx, who has gotten my telephone number from some list, wants me to buy gold bullion.[31]

Several consequences follow from this situation. Each bears on the ethical mandates that structure the voyeur's activities. It is possible, as Lyotard argues, to 'conceive a world of postmodern knowledge governed by a game of perfect information, in the sense that the data is in principle accessible to any expert: there is no scientific secret' (1984: 52). Take this one step further, nothing is secret. We all have access to all the information that bears on our lives. Make everything public.

Alternatively, uncouple and unplug the existing surveillance devices that penetrate every corner of daily life. This utopian, Luddite proposal turns back the electronic revolution and reinscribes zones of privacy that no one has the right, or power to invade, including the state. This proposal has the virtue of giving teeth to Rorty's liberal utopia, for it would create sacred spaces of personal solitude. Under this model no one would have the right to study life in these sacred places. Public life would then become that activity that occurs under the full glare of the other's gaze, and one would be fully accountable for their actions in this sphere. There would be no closed doors behind which public officials hide. No private spaces for public life.

A third consequence of the above argument lies in the full recognition that a major form of contemporary voyeuristic activity lies in the study of those visual texts which depict and represent the modern voyeur in his or her activities. We are voyeurs of the voyeur's text. We are ethnographers of the contemporary visual culture. We study those visual and auditory representations that mediate, as C. Wright Mills argued, this second-hand world we all live in. Everyday life and our consciousness and interpretations of that life are filtered through and defined by the cinematic apparatus, that structure that brings life, as Noel Burch (1990) argues, to those shadows that define daily existence. Krug (1992: 60) elaborates, 'the intersection of experience and cultural forms is the site where the [postmodern] self is articulated linguistically and formally'. This intersection is aesthetic, talking the self into existence through a cultural form, like a home video, a family photograph, or Oliver Stone's film, *JFK* (see Krug, 1992: 60). As visual ethnographers of the postmodern visual, cinematic culture (see Harper, 1994) we study our own and other's intersections with these visual texts, showing how they give and produce meaning for ourselves and others.[32]

Three additional solutions to the above situation are also suggested. They each move back to the world of lived experience and its study. They also assume that the data banks are not made public and that the electronic surveillance devices are not unplugged. The first solution builds on the state model of surveillance. This would be a state-based ethical system that would give scholars the same rights, privileges and protections that are now given the official agents of the state.

The second solution follows the Hollywood model. Scholars would be obliged to adhere to a production code that prohibits the presentation of materials deemed offensive to a mature audience. In conjunction with the state-conspiratorial model, the Hollywood system would allow researchers to use any necessary method of observation to produce the materials required for the stories they want to tell. These stories would move in and out of the private and public spaces that define the postmodern video culture.

Video Justice

The third solution modifies the Hollywood code. It builds on the liberal utopian model, which seeks to create zones of privacy. I call it the 'new video justice' model. It argues that the new video technology should not be used as a form of social control that operates outside the formal legal system. Altheide (1994, also 1992, 1993) describes two forms of media justice, each a variant on what he calls 'Gonzo Justice'. In each form the print and electronic media identify persons who have been defined as breaking the law. These individuals are then publicly punished and stigmatized, their stories and the evidence supporting their deviance are widely reported in the media. In one form of Gonzo Justice, what I will call, after Nathaniel Hawthorne (1850/1984), 'Scarlet Letter Justice', a person is publicly tried, and then their case is made a public spectacle. For example, a judge orders a man to place a sign in his front yard that says 'I am a thief' (see Altheide, 1992: 70 for other examples). In the second form, what I call the 'pure media' model, a trial never occurs. The individual is tried in the press (see Altheide, 1993, for an example).

The on-going O.J. Simpson case is an example (see Goodman, 1994). Simpson was arrested and jailed on Friday June 17, 1994 for the double murder of his former wife (Nicole Brown Simpson) and a friend (Ronald Goldman) which occurred on June 12. Prior to his arrest Simpson led the police on a nationally televised 90-minute chase through the Los Angeles freeway system. As this chase unfolded a friend read on national television Simpson's suicide letter which was directed to his children and family. As the white Bronco pulled to a stop in front of his house the camera zoomed in on a quivering Simpson, huddled in the back of the vehicle. Within hours of his arrest tapes from his 1989 trial for spousal abuse were played on television. A 911 emergency call from his then wife to the police was broadcast. The transcription of the call was overlayed with the voice of his wife speaking to the police. Background sounds of Simpson shouting at his wife were heard. Simpson's case was read as an instance of classic spousal abuse and experts came forth saying that such men often killed their wives.

By June 19 video tapes were broadcast showing Simpson's mansion, its grounds, his white Bronco, as well as photos from the murder scene. Scenes from Simpson's earlier life were published in national news magazines and newspapers, and reporters discussed whether or not his lawyers would use the insanity plea at the trial. The *National Enquirer* and Paramount's television tabloid 'Hard Copy' quickly got into bidding wars with key informants who could report on Simpson's activities the night of the murder (Toobin, 1994: 35), and one grand jury was dismissed because of pre-trial publicity concerning the 911 tapes.

And the story goes on. This is pure media, Gonzo justice, infotainment as news, cash-for-interviews journalism. Simpson has been given the Scarlet Letter of a spouse abuser and the public label of a man who killed his wife. He is being tried publicly by the print and electronic news media. More importantly, these versions of the cinematic apparatus have invaded every area of Simpson's life. No corner has been left untouched or unphotographed. Media justice without benefit of a trial.

It is apparent that the postmodern age cannot for long tolerate this abuse of the voyeur's talents. This last ethical proposal would prohibit the public broadcasting of such materials. It defines the courtroom as the arena where these private matters are more properly handled. The electronic media, talk shows and tabloid journalism are not the places for justice to be played out. It is no longer appropriate to view the media as the Fourth Estate which advances the causes of a liberal, democratic society (Jansen, 1988: 213). The media, the core structure in the American consciousness industry, have become the arbiters of everyday manners, morals and justice. We have become a nation dependent on information, entertainment capitalism. Paraphrasing Jansen, (1988: 172): neither Liberal nor Marxist critiques of censorship [and justice] adequately explain or provide recipes for resisting the new system of market censorship [and justice] that operates under information-capitalism (see also Smythe, 1981).[33]

The Politics of Textuality

Americans today live with the voyeur's legacy woven through Reagan and Bush's conservative sexual and economic politics. We tell our stories, not to movie-goers, but to science and society. We instantiate the myth that true stories can be told: that masks can be pulled off and real selves revealed. We commodity the self and turn it into an exchange object, into a set of tales told in this text or another. We believe that our truthful stories will make a difference because the truth counts. But suppose this is not the case.

In our alignment with the scientific project of realism, that epistemology which underwrites all social science discourse, we engage in a textual politics which allows our voyeuristic-scientific gaze to be used by others to control those we identify with.[34] This has always been the case.[35] The ethnographic life-story text, that extension of the voyeur's eye, like the cinematic impulse, arose out of a desire to accurately tell stories about the modern self and its dilemmas. This desire was folded into the same structures that located the cinematic apparatus in the centre of the twentieth century disciplinary society (see discussion above, pp. 191–2).

These forces shaped the rise of scientific, investigative sociology, wherein the sociologist, like the journalist, would enter society and return with news (life stories) about the affairs of everyday people. The ethnographer's eye, like the biographer's writing hand and the demographer's life table would become extensions of one another, for each would help society to see itself objectively. Hand-in-hand with the positivists, the qualitative life story/ethnographic researchers entered American society and came back with stories and narratives about life out there. These stories kept alive the myth that in a free democratic society politically neutral, scientific social texts could somehow be written.

But these texts can't be written. Our texts are never without political implications. They are political through and through. Now our assignment is clear. Begin to write progressive, reflective texts which force us to see things differently. Make politics a spectacle. Write works that collapse in upon themselves (see Rose, 1990: 10). Write works which unmask our self-serving voyeuristic project.

More is required. The voyeur will never disappear, only the shape, form and content of the voyeur's gaze can be changed.[36] The cold, analytic, abstract, disciplinary gaze of Foucault's panopticon must be challenged by a newer, gentler, compassionate gaze which looks, and seeks, not technical, or instrumental knowledge, but an in-depth, existential understanding.[37] These will be understandings grounded in the epiphanal moments (Denzin, 1989b: 15) which, in terrifying, existential detail bring the postmodern individual up against the repressive features of contemporary society. At the level of collective lived experiences this epiphanic approach attempts to identify how different social and cultural groupings, for example, gays, the elderly, women, youth, racial minorities, the unemployed and the fallen attach themselves to and come to grips with those traces of the surveillance society that invade and become part of their lives (Denzin, 1991a: 13). Postmodern ethnographies of these experiences will be political criticisms of culture, political texts no longer shrouded in the epistemological guises of scientific realism.

The voyeur's project must be redone if a critical cultural studies perspective is to move forward. In present form the voyeur reinforces the belief that ocular, visual knowledge furnishes the necessary truths about contemporary society. The foregoing has been an argument against that position. However, as Ulmer (1989: xi) and others have observed, America is a society which has become dependent upon visual and video modes of communication and representation. Voyeurs all, we are dependent, for information and entertainment, on the representations furnished by the official and unofficial voyeurs of the surveillance society. These representations, as argued above, p. 193, furnish knowledge about, but not an understanding of, the other. As a consequence, our postmodern culture is built upon a structure of visual mirrors: we see, but never feel or hear, the sounds of the other's mind. Pseudo-understandings are created. Few experiences are shared. Can a culture so heavily dependent on visual representations survive indefinitely?

Recall Freud's retelling of the Oedipus myth: 'Appalled by the abomination which he himself has unwittingly perpetrated, [he] blinds himself and forsakes his home. The oracle has been fulfilled' (Mulvey, 1989: 178–9). Freud's account of this drama unmasks and then blinds the voyeur. Is it unreasonable to assume a like fate for the ethnographer? Whose oracle is operating?

The Voyeur's Future

To return once more to *Rear Window*. Jeff's symbolic death signalled a turn in the cinematic treatment of the voyeur, which would be progressively elaborated by Hitchcock in *Vertigo* (1958), *Psycho* (1960) and *Frenzy* (1972). After these four Hitchcock films this cinematic figure would never again be the same. Voyeurs would experience insanity and extreme personal pain as a consequence of their activities. They would be punished for going against the police, and would learn that the police are the only proper voyeurs in the post-surveillance society. Extreme personal crisis would produce this understanding. Voyeurs would have cathartic experiences, bouts of insanity or alcoholism which would lead them to give up, or drastically alter, their voyeuristic activities.[38]

Hitchcock created the conditions for the subsequent transformations in this figure. As a consequence of the conservative decades of the 1970s and 1980s, the voyeur would be moved in two directions at the same time. No longer an iconic outsider like Harry Caul, who goes insane as a result of his observations, or a genial sport like Jeff, the new voyeur would become either an anti-establishment, at times violent, vigilante figure (*Dirty Harry*, 1971; *Mean Season*, 1985; *Black Widow*, 1986) or a sexual predator, preying on beautiful women and obsessing over his own sexuality (*Psycho*; *Frenzy*; *Dressed to Kill*, 1980; *sex, lies and videotape*, 1989).

These changes reflected the political currents of the conservative decades, but they were also shaped by Hitchcock who was one of the first to question the voyeur's motives.[39] He did this by valorizing the voyeur's activities. That is by exposing the truths that others cannot or will not see, Hitchcock's voyeur functions simultaneously as a social critic and a threat to the existing social order, hence Lisa calls Jeff a madman. Obsessed with looking, detached from others, a perpetual outsider, the voyeur can, however, never be aloof. He or she always gets involved. It is this involvement that Hitchcock questions. This compulsion to be involved stems ostensibly from the altruistic motive to help others, but in the end it is self-serving, for the voyeur seeks only to entertain him- or herself. Driven by an outer morality which often goes against the public conscience, inwardly voyeurs function with a private morality that justifies their every action, including spying on others.

This is Hitchcock's superficial message and the one that he mocks. Unfortunately it is the one that ethnographers have implemented. Underneath, the filmmaker is telling the sociologists that your warrant to look carries dangerous consequences and if you take your project too seriously you, not society, will pay. To this message I add one final point. Society pays too, and pays greatly, for we voyeurs have perpetuated the illusion that looking is not only valuable and worthwhile, but absolutely essential to the functioning of the social order. Is it?

Sociology Meets Cinema

Back to *The Conversation* and the conspiratorial films studied in Chapter 7. As 'progressive or subversive reflexive texts' these films tell us something about the fragile nature of our own investigative practices. The narrative that drives critical, interpretive, interactionist, dramaturgical sociology presumes that this theatrical society-of-the-spectacle can be undone (Lyman, 1990a). It can be unmasked, and behind the mask we will find a solid core of sociality: layers of the real that are more real than the staged versions of the real that now pass for reality. Perhaps this is ideological illusion.[40]

We are back in Harry's apartment, which looks like a bomb site. Here sociology and cinema meet.[41] Coppola has exposed the cinematic society for what it is: a place where nothing is sacred any longer. A place where there are no final truths, only the truth which says there is none. Truth and morality, those ancient Enlightenment signifiers which pointed to ultimate realities where human essence was defined, no longer exist. Here, in the moment of expulsion from our private Gardens of Eden we stand naked before the postmodern simulacrum.

It has not always been so. When cinema first entered American sociology (as argued in Chapter 1), the Chicago Pragmatists, Mead, Park, Blumer, Dewey, thought otherwise (see Clough, 1988: 93–4).[42] They wanted a cinema that would reinforce the traditional values of democracy, family and the school. They resisted the prurient films that Hollywood produced and insisted on Production Codes which would ensure that the movies instilled the proper values in America's youth (see Denzin, 1991a, Chapter 9; but also Vidich and Lyman, 1985: 232).[43]

But the Chicago sociologists could not turn back the forces of cinema.[44] And alongside their desire to make Hollywood tell only certain kinds of stories ran the counter-tendency to value ethnographic research framed by the realistic literary tradition, where naturalism and melodrama went hand in hand (Carey, 1975, Chapter 6; Denzin, 1991a, Chapter 3; Clough, 1988). Such work entered the multiple urban scenes of Chicago and exposed the private enclaves of meaning that gave the city and its inhabitants an inner moral fabric or moral centre (Farberman, 1979). Successive generations of interactionists have displayed a commitment to the production of realist, melodramatic social problems texts which create an identification with the powerless in American society. These works of realism reproduced and mirrored the social structures that needed to be changed. They valorized the subjectivity of the downtrodden individual. They made a hero of the interactionist-ethnographer-voyeur who came back from the field with moving tales of the powerless. What is now called 'classic' Chicago sociology, all of those urban monographs (*The Gang*, *The Jack-Roller*, etc.) told stories framed by the above arguments. They created a body of textual work that kept the private/public division alive and well in American sociology. They served well this ideological goal. They perpetuated two myths. First, that urban, modern man (and woman) still had an enclave of privacy that the complex urban society could not touch. Secondly, the skilled ethnographer could make sense of these worlds of experience.

But now these myths are under assault. Now we know that there are many ways to tell the same story, and maybe it isn't the same story any longer. The myth of a total, realist ethnographic Chicago sociology, like its counterpart, the myth of total cinema, now threatens to collapse. Traditional, realist, narrative cinema, like traditional ethnographic sociology, tells only one version of the story. A version which has a zero degree of textual politics. These texts perpetuate the illusions that stories have happy endings: heroes always prevail; the private is sacred; and in the end man and woman will be joined in peaceful bliss (see Wood, 1977/1986: 60–1 on the ideal structure of these beliefs in classic cinema).

This is what *The Conversation* does. Superficially about morality and the new technologies, underneath the film says that it is not enough to say the new is bad. Instead Coppola says the new cannot be escaped, it has invaded everything, including our dreams and fantasies (Harry's flashbacks). The new cannot be undone. It is a power, like the atom bomb that is now unleashed in human society and can never be withdrawn. The new is a nightmare in daylight. There are no easy solutions, no happy endings. There is no private world we can retreat into.

In undoing the voyeur Coppola undoes us, for we are like the Company, we have invaded the private space of the postmodern. We have perpetuated the ideological illusion that we are keeping the sacred safe from, and for, the public. We, like the Chicago sociologists of old, have contributed to an opiate of the masses, the opiate that says sociological knowledge will protect this democratic society from itself. We can no longer justify our voyeurism in the name of democracy. We must instead, like Coppola, turn this searching eye inward upon our own moral consciences. In so doing we may see how our reflective gazes have contributed to this surveillance society. Then, we may see (and hear), like Harry Caul, that we have perpetuated the illusion that the scientific gaze is politically neutral and really beneficial to all. We turn to the production of progressive, reflective texts and begin the difficult task of unmasking these taken-for-granted ideologies which have for far too long justified our self-serving voyeuristic project.

Contemporary society believes that it needs the voyeur. He or she keeps the illusion of the private, sacred space alive and in so doing this tells us that there is a greater truth which resonates with the great myths of late capitalism. There is, after all, a real world out there and it is structured by recurring truths concerning family, and heroes who dare to take risks and give their lives and their sanity for the rest of us. The deconstruction of this myth of the voyeur, as this figure is implicated in reflexive cinema and traditional ethnography, should serve to further expose the central cultural logic of late capitalism, namely the fiction that there are ultimate, final truths about the dramaturgical, postmodern society, and that these truths are realized in the private spaces the voyeur invades.

Ode to the Voyeur: Towards a Post-Pragmatist Ethical Epistemology

Here at the end I face myself in the mirror. Aligned with the pragmatist's project throughout, it is apparent that a post-pragmatist's project in the postmodern period confronts a series of ethical and epistemological crises. Firm claims about truth, knowledge, consequences, causes and effects can no longer be made. Consequences can no longer be firmly established. Dead bodies disappear, pictures are destroyed and reality, as it was previously known, is erased. The warrant to gaze has been undermined.

A new epistemological and ethical framework is sought, a pragmatism fitted to the globalizing cyberspaces of the cinematic, television age. This will be a media and communication centred pragmatism. It will accept the proposition that the image of reality has replaced reality. It will assume that communication is more than face-to-face interaction and no longer the natural site of cooperation and consensus. Violence, dissent and dispute are the cultural givens in today's multi-ethnic social order. Such a pragmatism will be written against and alongside Habermas's critical theory, perhaps endorsing, after Shalin (1992), the importance of embodied reason, reasonable dissent, and the concept of sane community for any theory of the democratic state.

Little help can be found in classical (Dewey, 1935), and neo-classical (Strauss, 1993; Rorty, 1991) pragmatism. These formations falter at three critical points (see also Wiley, 1994, Chapter 9). First, each stumbles at that precise moment when the phobia for truth confronts the truth that says there is no truth. Suppose, as I have argued throughout, that nothing is any longer certain. All we can count on is uncertainty, and different stories about what makes this uncertainty meaningful. Suppose too that neither science nor public discourse can any longer be used as resources for legitimating one story or account over another. Make one more assumption, the media have become the final site or moral arbitration in the postmodern world. If this is so, then science, narrative and rhetoric are no longer certain, only several among many discourses about reality (see Brown, 1989).

The second stumbling block for traditional and neo-pragmatic theory hinges on the social self and its theories. Rorty (1991: 193) thinks 'we would be better off without' a theory of the self, while Strauss and Dewey disagree. But each articulates a pre-postmodern version of the self, a version that stands outside the structures of meaning produced by the contemporary consciousness industries. And, their theories of the self fail to offer fully dialogic conceptions which are simultaneously reflexive, interpretive and grounded in some sense of internal solidarity that connects the person to a larger moral community. The postmodern mediated self (as argued above, p. 208) finds its moral solidarity in those narrative tales that circulate in the cinematic culture. This self, its meanings, and its freedoms must become a central part of any neo-pragmatic theory of the democratic state (see Wiley, 1994). Only Wiley (1994, Chapter 9), among the neo-pragmatists offers a way out of this impasse.

Thirdly, the classic and contemporary pragmatists fail to show how their theory and method can provide the way for a just society. Dewey's just society was based on rational public discourse and scientific knowledge. Rorty's just society is just because that is the way it is supposed to be. Of course neither solution is workable in a post-visual society which operates on video justice.

Post-pragmatism enters this uncertain discursive field from the vantage point of a radical democratic ethos, a new (but old) form of social criticism, attacking always those structures of political economy and ideology that threaten to take away our most basic freedoms in the name of truth and civil society.

Democracy is not working under capitalism. Dewey anticipated this, understanding that democracy had become a mockery, a simulation of itself (see Antonio and Kellner, 1992: 283). Dewey, like Mills, attempted a critique of American life, attempting to insert that critique, itself subject to critical enquiry, into the political process. He imagined a reconstruction of Jeffersonian ideals, 'without the racism and sexism of the earlier era and with modern forms of organization, media and cultural fragmentation directly in mind' (Antonio and Kellner, 1992: 287).

But today critiques of the post-visual society do not come from Dewey's heirs. The postmodern critiques are located within the cinematic apparatus itself, including radio and TV Talk show celebrities, the hosts of weekly news shows ('60 Minutes', 'America Tonight', 'Hard Copy', 'Nighttime'), and an occasional novelist, angry print journalist, filmmaker, or artist. Here we too frequently have, as Baudrillard (1988b: 30) suggests, instant analysis without benefit of history, or a critical eye that would expose from within the ideological presuppositions that organize the apparatus doing the critique.

Post-pragmatism seeks new conceptions of the state, the nation, civil society, democracy and national identity, seeking to locate these terms within the processes of globalization that encircle all of us (see Calhoun, 1993). The end of history is not here, capitalism and democracy have not won, terrorism at the local and national levels reigns. The discursive spaces of civil society, that public arena historically defined as the place where democracy and capitalism do their work, are now under assault. This sphere has been for too long marred by exclusionary practices based on sexist and racist nationalistic politics. The cultural logics of capitalism erode the civic sphere, turning it into a political economy of signs (Baudrillard) which commodify self, other and valued social relationships.

In the shadows of late capitalism the silent majority eats out under the golden arches of McDonald's. Civic society dissolves into a blur, and on the pathways of the new high-tech information highways spatially dispersed selves communicate in cyberspace. The modernist notion of the autonomous individual no longer works. Pseudo-democracies masquerade within the capitalist world system, and liberal capitalism is 'the main ideological option offered by the West today' (Calhoun, 1993: 403). But this option invokes repressive totalitarian tendencies which celebrate sexist, racist, nationalistic identities (see Calhoun, 1993: 405). A new global politics of identity is upon us, a new public culture that no one understands.

This is the complex, global, negotiated order that post-pragmatism addresses. A radical, reconceptualized theory of democracy, the state and civil society must find its way inside these gendered, culturally and ethnically complex spaces, and their interactional arenas and structural domains. This post-pragmatism will critically attach itself to the post-modern family, the media and popular culture, cyberspace, science, protest movements, national identities and race and gender as the critical sites for interpretive-political work. It will push hard at the boundaries and intersections of public science and the media, seeing science and the media as the dominant discourses of power and control in contemporary life.

This project will build on the pragmatic heritage which has always sought a 'greater mediation between scholarly practices and democratic life' (Antonio and Kellner, 1992: 293). It will follow Dewey's lead of using pragmatically gained knowledge as a tool for social criticism. It will elaborate Clough's call to openly 'engage social criticism as the form of preferred discourse' (1992: 135), thereby distancing itself from the identity of empirical science. This form of criticism will address those certain truths that have escaped the masculine, pragmatic eye.

The Mirrored, Gendered Gaze

The feminine, gay and ethnic gaze, as argued in Chapters 3, 4 and 6, hears and sees things that escape the white masculine eye, the eye that is guided by its norms of objectivity and rationality. Several different versions of truth (and reality) are produced when the feminine (and ethnic) gaze appropriates the masculine tools of looking (Ann Mulvaney with Graham's videocamera, Jane Craig's production of the news, Alexandra spying on Catharine, Dorothy commanding Jeffrey to undress, Rigby Reardon in drag).

The norms of objectivity and final truth are challenged by this unorthodox gaze. For example, Alexandra Barnes (*Black Widow*) believes (quoting again) that 'Nobody knows why anyone does anything'. Jo (*Chan is Missing*), elaborates this argument (to repeat), 'I know nothing because everything is so contradictory'. Jo understands that he must accept a mystery without a solution, no important clues will pop up to clarify anything. There are no neatly plotted Oriental mysteries. All he can do is look into the puddle and see himself, quivering reflections, nothing certain, only uncertainty.

The feminine (and ethnic) eye has the power to dethrone the sexualizing, male gaze. Ann takes the camera from Graham's hands and forces him to tell his sexual story. Dorothy makes Jeffrey undress. Jane takes control of Tom's voice. In these moves a feminine subjectivity redefines the patriarchal narrative. An alternative, more deeply personal way of knowing the other is produced. The male sexual code is shattered, and an equally honourable way of acting in the situation is proposed.

This feminine way of knowing, as argued in Chapter 6, repudiates the male looking-glass as the primary site of self (and other) knowledge. This feminine knowledge transcends masculine, narcissistic identification with the other. In the speculum of the feminine reflecting mirror a new form of self-awareness is produced, an understanding that moves to the core of the other's self. Here, at this core, is reflected back another image of the self, an image that awakens a heightened, liberating self-understanding. This understanding is double-edged. It is able to accept a radically indeterminate universe where there are no final or ultimate causes of anything. At the same time it repudiates the codes of surveillance and deterrence that define the masculine way of looking. These codes are replaced by a feeling, touching, tasting, listening, hearing (not eavesdropping) epistemology that attempts to engage the other (and the self) in their plenitude (see Ediger, 1993, Chapter 8; Clough, 1994).

Thus the mystery of experience. There is no secret key that will unlock its meanings. It is a labyrinth with no fixed origins, no firm centre, structure or set of recurring meanings. All that can be sought is a more fully grounded, multi-sensual, multi-perspectival epistemology that does not privilege sight (vision) over the other senses, including sound, touch and taste.

In The End

It is time to stop using science and technology in the name of a free, democratic society. Such a move will then destroy the fiction that our ethnographic and interpretive efforts are exposing underlying truths about the postmodern social order. Here at the end we confront ourselves and our own voyeuristic projects, understanding finally that the stories we can tell are those which are more than the mere record of the dangers of voyeurism. Our projects must show how human beings endure and prevail in the face of those technological structures which threaten to erase forever the fragile, sacred self and the few remaining spaces it occupies in this horrible and terrifying world we call the postmodern. And it is with downcast eyes that we must now look.

Notes

1 Rosaldo makes the following connection between the ethnographer's and Foucault's gaze: 'the fieldworker's mode of surveillance uncomfortably resembles Michel Foucault's Panopticon, the site from which the (disciplining) disciplines enjoy gazing upon (and subjecting) their subjects' (1986: 92). Atkinson (1990) elaborates this position. The ethnographer 'reports acts of surveillance from the "door of the anthropologist's tent"' (Atkinson, 1990: 28). Van Maanen (1978: 346) is more explicit, calling the participant observer-ethnographer 'part spy, [and] part voyeur'. Fine and Sandstrom (1988: 20–1) elaborate this deceptive identity in their concept of 'deep cover', while Punch (1986: 72–5) calls it into question.

2 The realist ethnographic text, according to Van Maanen (1988: 46–54), adheres to four conventions: an absence of the author from the text, a documentary style, written from the native's point of view, while the author expresses a form of interpretive omnipotence. This is but one form of ethnographic realism (see below, pp. 196–8), which I have elsewhere (Denzin, 1989b: 135–7) called mainstream realism (the other forms being descriptive and interpretive).

3 Recall the gay scenes in *JFK*.

4 Progressive or subversive is Klinger's term for Comolli and Narboni's (1971/1976: 27) category e film, 'films which seem at first sight to belong firmly within the ideology and under its sway, but which turnout to be so only in an ambiguous manner'.

5 My concept of reflective film thus goes beyond the category e films to include Comolli and Narboni's explicitly political texts (categories b and c) which attack ideology, or go against its grain, and category e (live cinema) which attacks the problem of how reality is to be represented.

6 To these two impulses must be added the following, as argued in Chapter 1: the production of a cinematic imagination which would judge everyday life in terms of its cinematic representations; the creation of a new, narrative, spectorial gaze, accompanied by realistic cinema (colour and sound) and new forms of narrative reflexivity which would emotionally draw viewers into the stories films told.

7 Lonergan's distinctions between visual (objective) knowledge and subjective understanding reflects a post-Kantian, post-Merleau-Ponty (1964a, b) phenomenological epistemology which has aroused considerable controversy (see Ong, 1977: 121–3), 143–4).

8 As Ong (1977: 123, 133–4) observes, in elaborating Lonergan's position, visual knowledge is surface knowledge which implies a beneath, interior or deeper structure of understanding; but this deeper, interior structure cannot be given visually. Surface visual knowledge can yield explanation, but not understanding.

9 Words would become the mirror, or window, to the inner world of the subject while vision would give external, objective pictures of the subject's situation. Non-visual knowledge would be coded as non-objective knowledge.

10 Remember that Jeff (*Rear Window*) never hears the words spoken by the persons he spies upon, their sounds are reduced to visual records. We see, but do not hear, them talking. Thus visual sightings give precision, but lacking in intimacy they can only produce abstract, non-intersubjective understanding (see Ong, 1977: 136).

11 The mirror metaphor is revealing in the present context. Silverman (1988: 80) distinguishes between the 'acoustic' and the 'looking-glass' mirror. In the acoustic mirror the sound of the voice and its thoughts are heard, while in the visual mirror only the gaze of the self, reflected back to itself can be seen. The voice, heard in the acoustic mirror, has the property of being sent and heard at the same time; this presence is always in effect.

12 Personal or first-person cinema (for example, Bergman's *Persona*, see Kawin, 1978), explicitly attempts to capture these interior worlds of experience; the social sciences lack a comparable strategy or exemplary text (on Bergman's film see Denzin, 1992c).

13 This proposition is cruelly deconstructed in Jocelyn Moorhouse's 1992 film *Proof* where a blind photographer finds his visual images of the world manipulated by his seeing housekeeper. Jane Chapman's *The Piano* (1993) further inverts this equation where her non-speaking female protagonist becomes the voyeurist subject of the all-speaking (and all-seeing) males in her world.

14 McHale argues that the modernist text is marked by two key textual strategies: mobile consciousness and parallax, or multiple points of view. Such texts attempt to secure a fine-grained interaction between 'consciousness and the world outside consciousness' (McHale, 1992: 45). This internal consciousness may be unreliable, unstable, shifting and digressive, but the world itself is stable.

15 Ethnography has passed through five moments: the first moment, the traditional period, lasted until World War II; the second, the modernist phase, ended in the late 1960s. The third, blurred genres (1970–86), precipitated the fourth; the crisis of representation, which began in the mid-1980s, to be replaced by the fifth period; the present (see Denzin and Lincoln, 1994a; Vidich and Lyman, 1994). Each of these moments and their genres circulate in the present.

16 A form of personal historiography which blends personal biographical accounts with popular and scholarly texts that purport to explain the life in question (see Ulmer, 1989, Part 3).

17 Like ethnography, British and American cultural studies have passed through several historical moments: its pre-World War II Frankfurt School formulations; the mid-century British tradition of Hoggart, Williams and Thompson; Stuart Hall's transformations of this tradition; its recent re-workings in the United States (see Carey, 1989; Grossberg, 1992; 1988a), and contemporary feminist expansions of the approach (Morris, 1988; Franklin et al., 1991). There are also separate Australian (Frow and Morris, 1993), Canadian (Blundell et al., 1993), and critical theory (Agger, 1992) histories of cultural studies.

18 This is Jameson's (1991: 68) argument. A reviewer suggests (Jameson would agree) that such modernists as Joyce (*Ulysses*), Sartre (*Troubled Sleep*) and Dos Passos (*USA*) used cinematic techniques in their works. Perhaps it is only academics who have been slow to come to this understanding.

19 C. Wright Mills perceived this situation in 1963, 'The consciousness of men does not determine their existence; now does their existence determine their consciousness. Between the human consciousness and material existence stand communications and designs . . . which influence decisively such consciousness as they have. The mass arts, the public arts, and the design are major vehicles of this consciousness' (Mills, 1963: 375).

20 This visual relationship between the theorist and ethnography is graphically given in the front cover to *Writing Culture* (Clifford and Marcus, 1986). Sitting in front of his tent, ethnographer Stephen Tyler inscribes fieldnotes.

21 As this chapter is being written the murder trial of O.J. Simpson is being carried by all of the major American television networks. On the night (June 17, 1994) of his surrender 90 million Americans watched the helicopters hover over his automobile (a white Ford Bronco) as it cruised the Los Angeles highways, finally pulling to a stop in the driveway of his Brentwood mansion. And media-video justice unfolds.

22 This epistemology took two forms: positivist and hermeneutic. Positivistic realism assumed a real world that could be objectively studied and re-represented through objective, scientific texts. Hermeneutic realism assumed an interactive, indeterminate, linguistic relationship between the observer and the world observed. Both versions of realism assumed a determinate relationship between knowledge and vision.

23 Social realism in sociology continued the narrative, realist traditions of Romantic and Victorian fiction and in the twentieth century quickly grafted itself into mainstream scientific-positivist realism. However, this realism was short-lived, to be replaced by the new governing aesthetics and philosophies of science peculiar to modernism and postmodernism (see Jameson 1990: 156). While literary modernism (Joyce) attacked the foundations of realism, the modernist turn in sociology (mid-century social theory) merely perpetuated the realist agenda.

24 Realism, as Jameson (1990: 161) suggests and Clough (1992) elaborates, has passed through several phases and forms (ethnographic, cinematic, simulational), reflected in ethnography's moments: naturalistic realism (e.g. the Chicago School case studies), the cold, objective (often statistical) realisms of modernism and the hyperrealism of postmodernism.

25 Jeff lays the foundations for such postmodern voyeurs as Graham of *sex, lies and videotape*, that is, Jeff opened the door that permitted the camera to come directly into the living-room. Jeff, then, is a modernist while Graham is a postmodern voyeur.

26 Raymond Schmitt disputes my use of the word morbid in the context of sociological observation (voyeurism), suggesting that its 'unwholesome' connotations are unsettling when considering the work of the classic interactionists. I agree. Thomas and Park, for example, interpreted their projects (see Baker, 1973) as merely being ones of describing ordinary behaviour. However, the warrant for the investigative gaze of ethnographic positivism/realism may be unwholesomely dysfunctional for society and its members, including the observer (see Guba and Lincoln, 1989: 120, and discussion below, pp. 204–5. For examples of the negative effects of sociological and anthropological investigative voyeurism see Vidich et al, 1964; and Stoller and Olkes, 1987.)

27 See also Warren Beatty, the political reporter in *The Parallax View* (1974), or Richard Boyle, the photo-journalist of *Salvador* (1986), or Russell Price, the journalist of *Under Fire* (1983).

28 This discussion of these five ethical stances draws from Denzin and Lincoln, 1994b.

29 Guba and Lincoln (1989: 120–41) provide a valuable review of the ethical breaches that follow from the positivist paradigm, contrasting that paradigm with the constructionist position which openly brings the subject into the research process and thereby works to nullify the negative effects (invasions of privacy, etc.) of scientific voyeurism. Breaches include the following forms of harm when subjects discover they have been duped, loss of personal dignity, loss of self-esteem and the denial of individual agency. (See also Kayser-Jones and Koenig, 1994; Lee, 1993; and Hornsby-Smith, 1993, for positions which mediate this discourse.) These authors basically side against the conflict, deception mode of Douglas, in favour of the compromise solution of Punch (1994), which seeks a balance between the researcher's obligations and the rights of subjects.

30 Mitchell calls this a version of the humanist position. Mitchell does not endorse deception as a research practice, but points to its inevitability in human (especially research) interactions.

31 Staples (1994) elaborates this argument. He enumerates the small acts of cunning, from Intensive Supervision Programs (ISPs), to electronically monitored home confinement devices, night vision technology and confirmatory drug tests that describe the disciplinary practices of contemporary life. See also Altheide (1994).

32 Krug distinguishes three levels of video textuality: the films and videos produced by native people, home videos, and mainstream Hollywood cinema. Each video form presumes a slightly different version of visual ethnography.

33 Media justice is thus woven through the narrative and normative structures of those multinational corporations that control the media, 'current cultural production is in the hands of privately owned giant corporations, *they* make decisions as to what is mass produced in the cultural area and what will not be produced . . . . It is . . . accurate therefore to refer to corporate decision making in the cultural area as being censorship' (Smyth, 1981: 235, also quoted in Jansen, 1988: 165).

34 A reviewer disputes my association of visual and verbal truth with social realism, arguing that *Verstehen* as a foundation of ethnography directly opposes positivism, making it incorrect to say that realism organizes all social science discourse. This reviewer also suggests that it is an error to equate realism's commitment to the visual with ethnography's emphasis on the linguistic, verbal side of experience. I disagree. To the extent that both versions of realism (see note 20 above) are committed to an 'objective' or 'intersubjective' rendering of a world out there, they both fall under the effects of the transcendent realist epistemology outlined above.

35 It is necessary, however, to distinguish between two forms of hermeneutic enquiry, the anti-foundational hermeneutics of Gadamer, Ricoeur, and Habermas, and the objective hermeneutics of E. Hirsch, and the positivistic ethnographic realism of Blumer (see Baugh, 1990: 92–6).

36 Ben Agger (in conversation) suggests that if the voyeur's gaze is a culturally delimited and socially constructed phenomenon, then in the postmodern moment analytic/visual modes of understanding may give way to a more mythic/oral tradition of understanding. This may occur, but such tellings will still be contained within the voyeuristic extensions of the cinematic apparatus.

37 I am indebted to Ben Agger (in conversation) for clarifying my position, especially the distinction between technical knowledge and existential understanding, which is further distinguished from the surface understandings produced by ethnographic realism.

38 For example, Graham (*sex, lies and videotape*), destroys his tapes after his cathartic session with Ann.

39 He also sexualized the voyeur's motives (e.g., *Psycho*).

40 In challenging this metaphor I am not suggesting that either the classical interactionists, or the dramaturgical theorists (Lyman and Scott, Goffman, Perinbanayagam, Brissett and Edgley) doubted the existence of multiple realities. However, the historical rupture (World War II) that divides the modern from the postmodern period, and the contemporary phase of late postmodernism, with its stress on commodified experiences and staged realities, makes the issue of an obdurate world beneath the multiple layers of the real even more problematic. In such a world the media can overdetermine the meanings brought to cultural objects, even as interactants make choices between the films and television shows they watch and the commodities they buy.

41 This section draws on Denzin, 1992a: 150–3.

42 The following paragraphs draw from Denzin, 1992a: 142–5.

43 They wanted movies that preserved the privacy of the family. In the language of Comolli and Narboni (1971/1976), they favoured category a films.

44 Curiously, few interactionists followed the leads of Blumer's (1933) landmark study of movies and conduct. Still, in their classic text, Lindesmith and Strauss (1949: 211) would point to the movies as sources of fantasy, and criminologists like Clinard (1957: 178–81) would discuss motion pictures and their relationship to deviance. It would not be until the late 1980s, however, that the movies would again become a central focus of interactionist work (see Clough, 1988; Denzin, 1991b, and Fine, 1990: 144–5).

REFERENCES

Adler, Patricia A. and Adler, Peter (1987) *Membership Roles in Field Research*. Newbury Park, CA: Sage.

Adler, Patricia A. and Adler, Peter (1994) 'Observational Techniques', in Norman K. Denzin and Yvonna S. Lincoln (eds), *Handbook of Qualitative Research*. Thousand Oaks, CA: Sage. pp. 377–92.

Agger, Ben (1991a) 'Why Theorize?', *Current Perspectives in Social Theory*, 11: ix–xii.

Agger, Ben (1991b) *A Critical Theory of Public Life: Knowledge, Discourse and Politics in an Age of Decline*. New York: The Falmer Press.

Agger, Ben (1992) *Cultural Studies as Critical Theory*. London: Falmer.

Allen, Robert C. and Gomery, Douglas (1985) *Film History, Theory and Practice*. New York: Knopf.

Alpert, Hollis (1967) 'Review of *Blow-Up*', *Filmfacts* January 1: 302–3. (Originally published in *Saturday Review* January 1, 1967.)

Altheide, David L. (1992) 'Gonzo Justice', *Symbolic Interaction*, 15: 69–86.

Altheide, David L. (1993) 'Electronic Media and State Control: The Case of AZSCAM', *Sociological Quarterly*, 34: 53–69.

Altheide, David L. (1994) 'An Ecology of Communication: Toward a Mapping of the Effective Environment', *Sociological Quarterly*, 35 (4) (in press).

Altman, Rick (1984/1986) 'A Semantic/Syntactic Approach to Film Genre' in Barry Keith Grant (ed.), *Film Genre Reader*. Austin: University of Texas Press. pp. 26–40. (Originally published in *Cinema Journal*, Spring 1984, 23 (3): 6–18.)

Altman, Rick (1987) *The American Film Musical*. Bloomington: Indiana University Press.

Andrews, Dudley (1978/1985) 'The Neglected Tradition of Phenomenology in Film Theory', in Bill Nichols (ed.), *Movies and Methods, Vol. II*. Berkeley: University of California Press. pp. 625–32. (Originally published in *Wide Angle* 2, 1978.)

Andrews, Dudley (1984) *Concepts in Film Theory*. New York: Oxford.

Ansen, David (1982) 'Review of *Chan Is Missing*', *Newsweek*. June 21: 65.

Anson, Robert Sam (1992) 'The Shooting of JFK', in Oliver Stone and Zachery Sklar, *JFK: The Book of the Film*. The documented screenplay, based on 'On the Trail of the Assassins' by Jim Garrison; 'Crossfire: The Plot that Killed Kennedy' by Jim Marris; public sources; Oliver Stone's research notes; compiled by Jane Rusconi. New York: Applause Books. pp. 208–29.

Antonio, Robert J. and Kellner, Douglas (1992) 'Communication, Modernity, and Democracy in Habermas and Dewey', *Symbolic Interaction*, 15: 277–97.

Antonioni, Michelangelo (1971) *Blow-Up, a Film by Michelangelo Antonioni*. London: Lorrimer Publishing Limited.

Athens, Lonnie (1980) *Violent Criminal Acts and Actors*. Boston: Routledge & Kegan Paul.

Atkinson, Paul (1990) *The Ethnographic Imagination: Textual Constructions of Reality*. New York: Routledge.

Austin, Bruce A. (1989) *Immediate Seating: A Look at Movie Audiences*. Belmont, CA: Wadsworth.

Baker, Paul (1973) 'The Life Histories of W.I. Thomas and Robert E. Park', *American Journal of Sociology*, 79: 243–61.

Bakhtin, M.M. (1968) *Rabelais and His World*. Cambridge: MIT Press.

Bakhtin, M.M. (1981) *The Dialogic Imagination*. Austin: University of Texas Press.

Bakhtin, M.M. (1986) *Speech Genre and Other Essays*. Austin: University of Texas Press.

Baran, Paul and Sweezy, Paul (1973) *Monopoly Capital*. London: Penguin.

Barris, Alex (1976) *Stop the Presses! The Newspaperman in American Films*. New York: A.S. Barnes and Company.

Barthes, Roland (1957/1972) *Mythologies*. New York: Hill & Wang.

Barthes, Roland (1981) *Camera Lucida*. New York: Hill & Wang.

Barthes, Roland (1982) *Empire of Signs*. New York: Hill & Wang.

Barthes, Roland (1985) *The Grain of the Voice: Interviews: 1962–1980*. Translated by Linda Coverdale. New York: Hill & Wang.

Baudrillard, Jean (1983a) *Simulations*. New York: Semiotext(e).

Baudrillard, Jean (1983b) *In the Shadow of the Silent Majorities*. New York: Semiotext(e).

Baudrillard, Jean (1988a) *The Ecstasy of Communication*. New York: Semiotext(e).

Baudrillard, Jean (1988b) *America*. London: Verso.

Baugh, Kenneth, Jr (1990) *The Methodology of Herbert Blumer*. New York: Cambridge University Press.

Bazin, Andre (1971) *What Is Cinema? Vol. II*. Berkeley: University of California Press.

Becker, Howard S. (1986) *Doing Things Together*. Evanston: Northwestern University Press.

Bell, Daniel (1960) *The End of Ideology: On the Exhaustion of Ideas in the Fifties*. New York: Viking.

Bellour, Raymond (1974) 'The Obvious and the Code', *Screen*, 15: 7–17.

Bellour, Raymond (1977) 'Hitchcock, the Ennunciator', *Camera Obscura*, Fall 1: 66–91.

Benjamin, Walter (1973) *Charles Baudelaire: A Lyric Poet in the Era of High Capitalism*. London: New Left Books.

Benjamin, Walter (1989) *Gesammelte Schriften VII*. Frankfurt: Suhrkamp.

Benson, Sheila (1987) 'Review of *Black Widow*', *Los Angeles Times*, February 6 (Calendar Section): 1.

Benson, Sheila (1989) 'Review of *sex, lies and videotape*', *Los Angeles Times*, August 4 (Calendar Section): 1.

Berger, John (1972) *Ways of Seeing*. London: Penguin.

Bergman, Ingmar (1972) *Persona and Shame, the Screenplays of Ingmar Bergman*. New York: Grossman Publishers.

Bergstrom, Janet (1979/1988) 'Alternation, Segmentation, Hypnosis: Interview With Raymond Bellour – An Excerpt', in Constance Penley (ed.), *Feminism and Film Theory*. New York: Routledge. pp. 186–95. (Originally published in 1979.)

Biedermann, Hans (1992) *Dictionary of Symbolism*. Translated by James Hulbert. New York: Facts on File, Inc.

Biga, Tracy (1987) 'Review of *Blue Velvet*', *Film Quarterly*, Fall: 44–8.

Billson, Anne (1992) 'Review of *JFK*', *New Statesman and Society*, January 24: 35.

Blumer, Herbert (1933) *Movies and Conduct*. New York: Macmillan.

Blumer, Herbert (1965/1988) 'The Future of the Color Line', in Stanford M. Lyman and Arthur J. Vidich, *Social Order and the Public Philosophy: An Analysis and Interpretation of the Work of Herbert Blumer*. Fayetteville: University of Arkansas Press. pp. 208–22. (Originally published in J.C. McKinney and E.T. Thompson (eds), *The South in Continuity and Change*. Durham: Duke University Press. pp. 220–53.)

Blundell, Valda, Shepherd, John and Taylor, Ian (eds) (1993) *Relocating Cultural Studies: Developments in Theory and Research*. London: Routledge.

Boden, Deidre (1990) 'The World as It Happens: Ethnomethodology and Conversation Analysis', in George Ritzer (ed.), *Frontiers of Social Theory: The New Syntheses*. New York: Columbia University Press. pp. 185–213.

Bordwell, David, Staiger, Janet and Thompson, Kristin (1985) *The Classical Hollywood Cinema: Film Style & Mode of Production to 1960*. New York: Columbia University Press.

Bozovic, Miran (1992) 'The Man Behind His Own Retina', in Zizek Slavoj (ed.), *Everything You Always Wanted to Know About Lacan (But Were Afraid to Ask Hitchcock)*. London: Verso. pp. 161–77.

Branigan, Edward (1979/1985) 'Color and Cinema: Problems in the Writing of History' in Bill Nichols (ed.), *Movies and Methods, Vol. II*. Berkeley: University of California Press. pp. 121–43. (Originally published in *Screen Reader*, 1979, no. 4.)

Brill, Lesley (1988) *The Hitchcock Romance: Love and Irony in Hitchcock's Films*. Princeton: Princeton University Press.

Brissett, Dennis and Edgley, Charles (eds) (1990) *Life As Theater: A Dramaturgical Sourcebook* (2nd edn). New York: Aldine de Gruyter.

Brown, Richard Harvey (1989) *Social Science as Civic Discourse*. Chicago: University of Chicago Press.

Bruner, Edward (1989) 'Tourism, Creativity, and Authenticity', *Studies in Symbolic Interaction*, 10: 109–14.

Bruner, Edward (1993) 'Introduction: Museums and Tourism', *Museum Anthropology*, 17: 6.

Brunette, Bruce and Wills, David (1989) *Screen/Play: Derrida and Film Theory*. Princeton: Princeton University Press.

Burch, Noel (1979) *To the Distant Observer: Form and Meaning in the Japanese Cinema*. Berkeley: University of California Press.

Burch, Noel (1990) *Life to those Shadows*. Berkeley: University of California Press.

Caldwell, Robert G. (1965) *Criminology* (2nd edn). New York: Ronald Press.

Calhoun, Craig (1993) 'Nationalism and Civil Society: Democracy, Diversity and Self-Determination', *International Sociology*, 8: 387–411.

Canby, Vincent (1974) 'A Haunting Conversation: Review of *The Conversation*', *New York Times*, April 21 (Section II): 11.

Canby, Vincent (1990) 'A Revolution Shapes Movies', *New York Times*, January 7 (Section 2): 1, 14.

Carey, James T. (1975) *Sociology and Public Affairs: The Chicago School*. Beverly Hills: Sage.

Carey, James W. (1989) *Communication as Culture*. Boston: Unwin Hyman.

Chandler, Raymond (1950) 'Raymond Chandler's Knight', in *The Simple Art of Murder*. Boston: Houghton Mifflin. pp. 1–22.

Christian Century (1930) January 15.

Clifford, James (1986) 'Introduction', in James Clifford and George E. Marcus (eds), *Writing Culture*. Berkeley: University of California Press. pp. 1–27.

Clifford, James (1989) 'Notes on Travel and Theory', *Inscriptions*, 5: 177–88.

Clifford, James (1993) 'Palenque Log', *Museum Anthropology*, 17: 58–66.

Clifford, James and Marcus, George E. (eds) (1986) *Writing Culture*. Berkeley: University of California Press.

Clinard, Marshall B. (1957) *The Sociology of Deviant Behavior*. New York: Holt, Rinehart and Winston, Inc. (Revised edition, 1963.)

Clough, Patricia T. (1988) 'Movies and Social Observation: Reading Blumer's Movies and Conduct', *Symbolic Interaction*, 11: 85–94.

Clough, Patricia T. (1992) *The End(s) of Ethnography*. Newbury Park, CA: Sage.

Clough, Patricia T. (1994) *Feminist Thought*. Newbury Park, CA: Sage.

Clover, Carol J. (1992) *Men, Women, and Chain Saws: Gender in the Modern Horror Film*. Princeton: Princeton University Press.

Collins, Patricia Hill (1990) *Black Feminist Thought*. New York: Routledge.

Combs, Richard (1987) 'Review of *Black Widow*', *Sight and Sound*, Summer: 220.

Comolli, Jean-Louis (1971–72/1985) 'Technique and Ideology: Camera, Perspective, and Depth of Field', in Bill Nichols (ed.), *Movies and Methods, Volume II*. Berkeley: University of California Press. pp. 41–57. (Originally published in as 'Technique et Ideologie', six parts in *Cahiers du Cinema*, no. 229 (May–June 1971): 4–21; no. 230 (July 1971): 51–7; no. 231 (August–September 1971): 42–9; nos. 234–5 (December–January 1971–72): 94–100; no. 241 (September–October 1972): 20–4. Only Part One appears in Nichols 1985.)

Comolli, Jean-Louis and Narboni, Jean (1971/1976) 'Cinema/Ideology/Criticism', in Bill Nichols (ed.), *Movies and Methods: An Anthology, Vol. One*. Berkeley: University of California Press. pp. 22–30. (Originally published in *Screen*, 12 (1) (Spring 1971): 27–36.)

Connor, Steve (1989) *Postmodernist Culture*. Oxford: Basil Blackwell.

Cook, David A. (1981) *A History of Narrative Film*. New York: W.W. Norton.

Cooley, Charles Horton (1902/1922/1956) *Human Nature and the Social Order*. New York: Scribner's/Free Press.

Cooley, Charles Horton (1909/1956) *Social Organization*. New York: Scribner's/Free Press.

Corliss, Richard (1991) 'Review of *JFK*', *Time*, December 23: 66.

Corner, John (1991) 'Editorial' *Media, Culture & Society*, 13: 131–6.

Couch, Carl J. (1984) *Constructing Civilizations*. Greenwich, CT: JAI Press.

Couch, Carl J. (1990) 'Mass Communications and State Structures', *Social Science Journal*, 27: 111–28.

Cowie, Elizabeth (1979/1988) 'The Popular Film as a Progressive Text: A Discussion of *Coma*', in C. Penley (ed.), *The Future of Illusion: Film, Feminism and Psychoanalysis*. Minneapolis: University of Minnesota Press. pp. 104–40.

Cowley, Malcolm (1950) 'Naturalism in American Literature', in S. Parsons (ed.), *Evolutionary Thought in America*. New Haven: Yale. pp. 300–35.

Creed, Barbara (1988) 'A Journey Through *Blue Velvet*: Film, Fantasy and the Female Spectator', *New Formations*, 7: 95–115.

Crowther, Bosley (1967) 'Review of *Blow-Up*.', *Filmfacts* January 1: 303–4. (Originally published in *New York Times*, December 19 1966.)

Davis, Robert E. (1976) *Response to Innovation: A Study of Popular Argument about New Mass Media*. New York: Arno Press.

de Lauretis, Teresa (1984) *Alice Doesn't: Feminism, Semiotics, Cinema*. Bloomington: Indiana University Press.

de Lauretis, Teresa (1987) *Technologies of Gender*. Bloomington: Indiana University.

Deleuze, Giles (1971) *Masochism: An Interpretation of Coldness and Cruelty*. New York: George Braziller.

DeLillo, Don (1988) *Libra*. New York: Viking.

Denby, David (1982) 'Review of *Chan is Missing*', *New York*, June 7: 72.

Denby, David (1986) 'Review of *Blue Velvet*', *New York*, September 29: 85.

Denby, David (1987) 'Review of *Black Widow*', *New York*, February 16: 72.

Denby, David (1992) 'Review of *JFK*', *New York*, January 6: 50.

Denzin, Norman K. (1987) *The Alcoholic Self*. Newbury Park, CA: Sage.

Denzin, Norman K. (1989a) *The Research Act*, (3rd edn). Englewood Cliffs, NJ: Prentice-Hall.

Denzin, Norman K. (1989b) *Interpretive Interactionism*. Newbury Park, CA: Sage.

Denzin, Norman K. (1991a) *Images of the Postmodern: Social Theory and Contemporary Cinema*. London: Sage.

Denzin, Norman K. (1991b) *Hollywood Shot by Shot: Alcoholism and American Cinema*. New York: Aldine de Gruyter.

Denzin, Norman K. (1992a) 'The Conversation', *Symbolic Interaction*, 15: 135–49.

Denzin, Norman K. (1992b) *Symbolic Interactionism and Cultural Studies*. New York and London: Basil Blackwell.

Denzin, Norman K. (1992c) 'Reading Persona: Setting an Agenda for the Sociology of Emotions', in Carolyn Ellis and Michael Flaherty (eds), *Investigating Subjectivity*. Newbury Park, CA: Sage. pp. 17–30.

Denzin, Norman K. (1993) 'The Voyeur's Desire', *Current Perspectives in Social Theory*, 13: 139–58.

Denzin, Norman K. (1994a) 'Chan is Missing: The Asian Eye Confronts Cultural Studies', *Symbolic Interaction*, 17: 63–89.

Denzin, Norman K. (1994b) 'The Art and Politics of Interpretation', in Norman K. Denzin and Yvonna S. Lincoln (eds), *Handbook of Qualitative Research*. Thousand Oaks, CA: Sage. pp. 500–15.

Denzin, Norman K. and Lincoln, Yvonna S. (1994a) 'Introduction: Entering the Field of Qualitative Research', in Norman K. Denzin and Yvonna S. Lincoln (eds), *The Handbook of Qualitative Research*. Newbury Park: Sage. pp. 1–17.

Denzin, Norman K. and Lincoln, Yvonna S. (1994b) 'Introduction: Locating the Field', in Norman K. Denzin and Yvonna S. Lincoln (eds), *The Handbook of Qualitative Research*. Newbury Park: Sage. pp. 19–22.

Derrida, Jacques (1972/1981) *Dissemination*. Chicago: University of Chicago Press.

Derrida, Jacques (1976) *Of Grammatology*. Baltimore: Johns Hopkins.

Derrida, Jacques (1978) *Writing and Difference*. Chicago: University of Chicago Press.

Derrida, Jacques (1982) *The Ear of the Other, Otiobiography, Transference, Translation*, Christie McDonald (ed.). Translated by Peggy Kamuf and Avital Ronell. Lincoln, NE: University of Nebraska Press.

Derrida, Jacques (1993) *Memoirs of the Blind: The Self-Portrait and Other Ruins*. Translated by Pascale-Anne Brault and Michael Naas. Chicago: University of Chicago Press.

Desser, David (1991a) 'The Cinematic Melting Pot: Ethnicity, Jews, and Psychoanalysis', in Lester D. Friedman (ed.), *Unspeakable Images: Ethnicity and the American Cinema*. Urbana: University of Illinois Press. pp. 379–403.

Desser, David (1991b) '"Charlie Don't Surf": Race and Culture in Vietnam Films', in Michael Anderegg (ed.), *Inventing Vietnam: The War in Film and Television*. Philadelphia: Temple University Press. pp. 81–102.

Deutelbaum, Marshall, and Poague, Leland (1986) 'Introduction', in Marshall Deutelbaum and Leland Poague (eds), *A Hitchcock Reader*. Ames: Iowa State University Press. pp. xi–xvii.

Dewey, John (1934/1986) 'Character Training for Youth', *Rotarian*, 45 (September): 6–8, 58–9. (Reprinted in J. Boydston, A. Sharpe and P. Baysinger (eds), *John Dewey: The Later Works: 1933–1934, Vol. 9*. Carbondale: Southern Illinois University Press. pp. 186–93.)

Dewey, John (1935) *Liberalism and Social Action*. New York: G.P. Putnam's Sons.

Deyhle, Donna L., Hess, G. Alfred Jr and Le Compte, Margaret D. (1992) 'Approaching Ethical Issues for Qualitative Researchers in Education', in Margaret D. Le Compte, Wendy L. Millroy and Judith Preissle (eds), the *Handbook of Qualitative Research in Education*. New York: Academic Press. pp. 597–641.

Doane, Mary Anne (1987) *The Desire to Desire*. Bloomington: Indiana University Press.

Doane, Mary Anne (1991) *Femmes Fatales: Feminism, Film Theory, Psychoanalysis*. New York: Routledge.

Donnelly, Barry (1990) 'Catcher in the Rye: Robert B. Parker's P.I.', *The Armchair Detective*, 23 (Winter): 12–25.

Douglas, Jack D. (1976) *Investigative Social Research*. Beverly Hills: Sage.

Duranti, Allesandro and Goodwin, Charles (eds) (1992) *Rethinking Context: Language as an Interactive Phenomenon*. Cambridge: Cambridge University Press.

Durgnat, Raymond (1974) *The Strange Case of Alfred Hitchcock, or the Plain Man's Hitchcock*. Cambridge, MIT Press.

Eaton, Walter Prichard (1909) 'The Movies', *American Magazine*, September, 498.

Ebert, Roger (1989a) 'Review of *Blow Out*', in *Roger Ebert's Movie Home Companion, 1990 Edition*. New York: Andreas and McMeel. pp. 79–80.

Ebert, Roger (1989b) 'Review of *The Conversation*', in *Roger Ebert's Movie Home Companion, 1990 Edition*. New York: Andreas and McMeel. pp. 154–5.

Ebert, Roger (1989c) 'Review of *Fatal Attraction*', in *Roger Ebert's Movie Home Companion, 1990 Edition*. New York: Andreas and McMeel. pp. 248–9.

Ebert, Roger (1989d) 'Review of *Black Widow*', in *Roger Ebert's Movie Home Companion, 1990 Edition*. New York: Andreas and McMeel. pp. 77–8.

Ebert, Roger (1989e) 'Review of *Broadcast News*', in *Roger Ebert's Movie Home Companion, 1990 Edition*. New York: Andreas and McMeel. pp. 97–8.

Ebert, Roger (1992) 'Interview with Oliver Stone', in Oliver Stone and Zachery Sklar, *JFK: The Book of the Film*. The documented screenplay, based on 'On the Trail of the Assassins' by Jim Garrison; 'Crossfire: The Plot That Killed Kennedy' by Jim Marris; public sources; Oliver Stone's research notes; compiled by Jane Rusconi. New York: Applause Books. pp. 249–53.

Edelstein, David (1987) 'Review of *Black Widow*', *Village Voice*, February 16: 70.

Ediger, Jeffrey (1993) *A Phenomenology of the Listening Body*. Unpublished doctoral dissertation, Institute of Communications Research, University of Illinois at Urbana-Champaign.

Edmunds, Lowell (1985) *Oedipus: The Ancient Legend and Its Later Analogues*. Baltimore: Johns Hopkins University Press.

Ehrlich, Mathew C. (1991) 'The Romance of Hildy Johnson: The Journalist as Mythic Hero in American Cinema', in *Studies in Symbolic Interaction*, Vol. 12. Greenwich, CT: JAI Press. pp. 89–104.

Einstein, Daniel (1981) 'Review of *The Conversation*', in Frank N. Magill (ed.), *Magill's Survey of Cinema: English Language Films, Second Series, Vol. 2*. Englewood Cliffs, NJ: Salem Press. pp. 515–18.

Eisner, Elliot W. (1991) *The Enlightened Eye: Qualitative Inquiry and the Enhancement of Educational Practice*. New York: Macmillan.

Ekman, Paul (ed.) (1973) *Darwin and Facial Expression: A Century of Research in Review*. New York: Academic Press.

Eliade, Mircea (1958) *Patterns in Comparative Religion*. Translated by Rosemary Sheed. New York: New American Library.

Erens, Patricia (ed.) (1990a) *Issues in Feminist Film Criticism*. Bloomington: Indiana University Press.

Erens, Patricia (1990b) 'Introduction', in P. Erens (ed.), *Issues in Feminist Film Criticism*. Bloomington: Indiana University Press. pp. vx–xxvi.

Everson, William K. (1972) *The Detective in Film*. Secaucus, NJ: The Citadel Press.

Faludi, Susan (1993) *Backlash*. New York: Knopf.

Farber, Stephen (1974) 'A Nightmare World with No Secret: Review of *The Conversation*', *New York Times* May 12, Sec. II: 13.

Farberman, Harvey (1979) 'The Chicago School: Continuities in Urban Sociology', *Studies in Symbolic Interaction*, 2: 3–20.

Farberman, Harvey (1991) 'Symbolic Interactionism and Postmodernism: Close Encounter of a Dubious Kind', *Symbolic Interaction*. 14: 471–88.

Farberman, Harvey and Perinbanayagam, R.S. (1985) 'Introduction', in Harvey Farberman and R.S. Perinbanayagam (eds), *Studies in Symbolic Interaction: Supplement 1: Foundations of Interpretive Sociology: Original Essays in Symbolic Interaction*. Greenwich, CT: JAI Press. pp. 3–12.

Featherstone, Mike (1990) *Consumer Culture and Postmodernism*. London: Sage.

Finch, Janet (1993) 'It's Great to have Someone to Talk to: Ethics and Politics of Interviewing Women', in Martin Hammersley (ed.), *Social Research: Philosophy, Politics and Practice*. London: Sage. pp. 166–80.

Fine, Gary Allan (1990) 'Symbolic Interactionism in the Post-Blumerian Age', in George Ritzer (ed.), *Frontiers of Social Theory: The New Syntheses*. New York: Columbia University Press. pp. 117–57.

Fine, Gary Alan and Sandstrom, Kent L. (1988) *Knowing Children: Participant Observation with Minors*. Newbury Park, CA: Sage.

Flam, Jack (1991) 'Invader: Review of *A Life of Picasso, Vol. I: 1881–1906* by John Richardson with the collaboration of Marilyn McCully', *New York Review of Books*, 38 (6) (March 28): 3–4, 6–7.

Fonow, Mary Margaret and Cook, Judith A. (1991) 'Back to the Future: A Look at the Second Wave of Feminist Epistemology and Methodology', in Mary Margaret Fonow and Judith A. Cook (eds), *Beyond Methodology: Feminist Scholarship as Lived Research*. Bloomington: Indiana University Press. pp. 1–15.

Forman, Henry James (1933) *Our Movie Made Children*. New York: Macmillan.

Foster, Hal (1988) 'Preface', in Hall Foster (ed.), *Vision and Visuality*. Seattle: Bay Press. pp. ix–xiv.

Foucault, Michel (1970) *The Order of Things*. New York: Vintage.

Foucault, Michel (1975) *The Birth of the Clinic*. New York: Vintage.

Foucault, Michel (1977) *Discipline and Punishment*. New York: Pantheon.

Foucault, Michel (1980) *Power/Knowledge*. New York: Pantheon.

Franklin, Sarah, Lury, Celia and Stacey, Jackie (1991) 'Feminism and Cultural Studies: Pasts, Presents and Futures', *Media, Culture & Society*, 13: 171–92.

Freccero, John (1971) '*Blow-Up*: From the World to the Image', in Roy Huss (ed.), *Focus on Blow-Up*. Englewood Cliffs: Prentice-Hall. pp. 116–28.

Freud, Sigmund (1915/1959) 'A Case of Paranoia Running Counter to the Psychoanalytic Theory of the Disease', in James Strachey (ed.), *Sigmund Freud, Collected Papers*. Vol. 2. New York: Basic Books. pp. 150–61.

Frisby, David (1992) 'Between the Spheres: Siegfried Kracauer and the Detective Novel', *Theory, Culture & Society*, 9: 1–22.

Frow, John and Morris, Meaghan (1993) 'Introduction', in John Frow and Meaghan Morris (eds), *Australian Cultural Studies: A Reader*. Urbana: University of Illinois Press. pp. vii–xxxii.

Gabbard, Krin and Gabbard, Glen O. (1987) *Psychiatry and the Cinema*. Chicago: University of Chicago Press.

Gamman, Lorraine (1989) 'Watching the Detectives: The Enigma of the Female Gaze', in Lorraine Gamman and M. Marshment (eds), *The Female Gaze: Women as Viewers of Popular Culture*. London: The Women's Press. pp. 8–26.

Gamman, Lorraine, and Marshment, M. (eds) (1989) *The Female Gaze: Women as Viewers of Popular Culture*. London: The Women's Press.

Gaonkar, Dilip Parameshwar (with McCarthy, Robert J. Jr) (1994) 'Panopticism and Publicity: Bentham's Quest for Transparency', *Public Culture*, 6: 547–75.

Gardner, Helen (1959) *Art Through the Ages* (4th edn). New York: Harcourt.

Garrison, Jim (1988) *On the Trail of the Assassins*. New York: Sheridan Square Press.

Geertz, Clifford (1988) *Words and Lives*. Stanford, CA: Stanford University Press.

Gelmis, Joseph (1982) 'Review of *Chan Is Missing*', *Newsday*, April 23 (Part II): 11.

Ginzburg, Carlo (1986) *Clues, Myths, and the Historical Method*. Baltimore: Johns Hopkins.

Glaser, Barney G. and Strauss, Anselm L. (1964) 'Awareness Contexts and Social Interaction', *American Sociological Review*, 29: 669–79.

Gledhill, Christine (1978) 'Klute 1: Contemporary Film Noir and Feminist Criticism', in E. Ann Kaplan (ed.), *Women in Film Noir*. London: British Film Institute. pp. 6–21.

Gluck, Sherna Berger and Patai, Daphne (eds) (1991) *Women's Words: The Feminist Practice of Oral History*. New York: Routledge.

Goffman, Erving (1959) *The Presentation of Self in Everyday Life*. New York: Doubleday.

Goffman, Erving (1963) *Behavior in Public Places*. New York: Free Press.

Gomery, J. David (1979) 'Hollywood, the National Recovery Administration, and the Question of Monopoly Power', *Journal of the University Film Association*, 31 (Spring): 38–52.

Goode, Greg (1982a) 'The Oriental in Mystery Fiction, Part I', *The Armchair Detective*, 15: 196–202.

Goode, Greg (1982b) 'The Oriental in Mystery Fiction, Part II', *The Armchair Detective*, 15: 306–13.

Goode, Greg (1983a) 'The Oriental in Mystery Fiction, Part III', *The Armchair Detective*, 16: 62–74.

Goode, Greg (1983b) 'The Oriental in Mystery Fiction, Part IV', *The Armchair Detective*, 16: 257–61.

Goode, Greg (1983c) 'The Oriental in Mystery Fiction, Corrections', *The Armchair Detective*, 16: 96, 218, 322.

Goodman, Walter (1994) 'Television, Meet Life, Life, Meet TV', *New York Times*, June 19 (Section 4): 1.

Gottschalk, Louis, Kluckhohn, Clyde and Angell, Robert (1945) *The Use of Personal Documents in History, Anthropology, and Sociology*. New York: Social Science Research Council.

Graham, Allison (1991) 'Journey to the Center of the Fifties: The Cult of Banality', in J.P. Telotte (ed.), *The Cult Experience: Beyond All Reason*. Austin: University of Texas Press. pp. 107–21.

Gramsci, Antonio (1934–5/1975) 'On the Detective Novel and Detective Novels', in *Quaderni del Carcere*. Turin: Einaudi. pp. 2128–30.

Grossberg, Lawrence (1988a) *It's a Sin: Essays on Postmodernism, Politics & Culture*. Sidney: Power Publications.

Grossberg, Lawrence (1988b) 'Wandering Audiences, Nomadic Critics', *Cultural Studies*, 2: 377–91.

Grossberg, Lawrence (1989) 'On the Road with Three Ethnographers', *Journal of Communication Inquiry*, 13: 23–6.

Grossberg, Lawrence (1992) *We Gotta Get Out of This Place: Popular Conservatism and Postmodern Culture*. London: Routledge.

Guba, Egon C. and Lincoln, Yvonna S. (1989) *Fourth Generation Evaluation*. Newbury Park, CA: Sage.

Gunning, Tom (1988) 'What I Saw From the Rear Window of the Hostel Des Folies-Dramatiques, or The Story Point of View Films Told', in Andre Gaudreault (ed.), *Ce que je vois de mon cine . . . La representation du regard dans le cinema des premiers temps*. Paris: Merudiens Klincksieck.

Gusfield, Joseph (1963) *Symbolic Crusade: Status Politics and the American Temperance Movement*. Urbana, IL: University of Illinois Press.

Habermas, Jürgen (1992) *The Structural Transformation of the Public Sphere: An Inquiry into a Category of Bourgeois Society*. Cambridge: MIT Press.

Hall, Stuart (1981) 'The Whites of their Eyes: Racist Ideologies and the Media', in George Bridges and Rosalind Brunt (eds), *Silver Linings*. London: Laurence and Wishart. pp. 36–7.

Hall, Stuart (1988) *The Hard Road to Renewal*. London: Verso.

Halliwell, Leslie (1990) *Halliwell's Filmgoers' and Video Viewers' Companion*, (9th edn). New York: Harper.

Hanke, Ken (1989) *Charlie Chan at the Movies: History, Filmography, and Criticism*. Jefferson, NC: McFarland & Company.

Hansen, Miriam (1986) 'Pleasure, Ambivalence, Identification: Valentino and Female Spectatorship', *Cinema Journal*, 25 (Summer): 6–32.

Harper, Douglas (1994) 'On the Authority of the Image: Visual Methods at the Crossroads', in Norman K. Denzin and Yvonna S. Lincoln (eds), *Handbook of Qualitative Research*. Thousand Oaks, CA: Sage. pp. 403–12.

Harpers World (1907) August 24: 1246.

Hawthorne, Nathaniel (1850/1984) *The Scarlet Letter*. San Diego: Harcourt, Brace and Jovanovich.

Haycroft, Howard (1972) *Murder for Pleasure: The Life and Times of the Detective Story*. New York: Biblo and Tannen.

Hayes, Will H. (1928) 'The Motion Picture Producer's and Distributor's Association', *Outlook*, April 11: 576.

Heung, Marina (1987) 'Review of *Black Widow*', *Film Quarterly*, Fall: 54.

Higashi, Sumiko (1991) 'Ethnicity, Class and Gender in Film: De Mille's *The Cheat*', in Lester D. Friedman (ed.), *Unspeakable Images: Ethnicity and the American Cinema*. Urbana: University of Illinois Press. pp. 112–39.

Hirsch, Foster (1981) *The Dark Side of the Screen: Film Noir*. New York: A.S. Barnes & Company.

Hoberman, J. (1986) 'Review of *Blue Velvet*', *Village Voice*, September 23: 58.

Hoberman, J. (1987) 'Review of *Fatal Attraction*', *Village Voice*, September 29: 68.

Hogan, David J. (1988) 'Review of *Black Widow*', in Frank N. Magill (ed.), *Magill's Cinema Annual, 1988: A Survey of Films of 1987*. Englewood Cliffs, NJ: Salem Press. pp. 75–8.

Hornsby-Smith, Michael (1993) 'Gaining Access', in Nigel Gilbert (ed.), *Researching Social Life*. London: Sage. pp. 52–67.

Horton, Andrew S, (ed.) (1991a) *Comedy/Cinema/Theory*. Berkeley: University of California Press.

Horton, Andrew S. (1991b) 'Introduction', in Andrew S. Horton (ed.), *Comedy/Cinema/Theory*. Berkeley: University of California Press. pp. 1–24.

Horton, Arnold (1982) 'Review of *Chan is Missing*', *Films in Review*, December: 623.

House, Ernest R. (1990) 'An Ethics of Qualitative Field Studies', in Egon G. Guba (ed.), *The Paradigm Dialog*. Newbury Park: Sage. pp. 158–64.

Hsiung-Ping, Chiao (1991) 'The Distinct Taiwanese and Hong Kong Cinemas', in Chris Berry (ed.), *Perspectives On Chinese Cinema*. London: British Film Institute. pp. 155–65.

Hughes, Everett C. (1963) 'Good People and Dirty Work', in H.S. Becker (ed.), *The Other Side*. New York: Free Press. pp. 23–36.

Hunt, Jennifer and Manning, Peter K. (1991) 'The Social Context of Police Lying', *Symbolic Interaction*, 14: 51–70.

Huss, Roy (ed.) (1971a) *Focus on Blow-Up*. Englewood Cliffs: Prentice-Hall.

Huss, Roy (ed.) (1971b) 'Antonioni in the English Style: A Day on the Set', in Roy Huss (ed.), *Focus on Blow Up*. Englewood Cliffs: Prentice-Hall. pp. 7–12.

Irigaray, Luce (1985) *Speculum of the Other Woman*. Translated by Gillian G. Gill. Ithaca: Cornell University Press.

Irving, John (1978) *The World According to Garp*. New York: E.P. Dutton.

Izod, John (1988) *Hollywood and the Box Office, 1895–1986*. New York: Columbia University Press.

Jaehne, Karen (1987) 'Review of *Blue Velvet*', *Cineaste*, 15 (3): 38.

James, Caryn (1991) 'Now Starring, Killers for the Chiller 90's', *New York Times*, March 10 (Section 2): 1, 20–2.

Jameson, Fredric (1983) 'Postmodernism and Consumer Society', in Hal Foster (ed.), *The Anti-Aesthetic: Essays on Postmodern Culture*. Port Townsend, WA: Bay Press. pp. 115–25.

Jameson, Fredric (1987) 'Reading Without Interpretation: Postmodernism and the Video-Text', in Derek Attridge, et al. (eds), *The Linguistics of Writing: Arguments Between Language and Literature*. Manchester: Manchester University Press. pp. 198–223.

Jameson, Fredric (1990) *Signature of the Visible*. New York: Routledge.

Jameson, Fredric (1991) *POSTMODERNISM, or, The Cultural Logic of Late Capitalism*. Durham: Duke University Press.

Jameson, Fredric (1992) *The Geopolitical Aesthetic: Cinema and Space in the World System*. Indiana: Indiana University Press.

Jansen, Sue Curry (1988) *Censorship: The Knot that Binds Power and Knowledge*. New York: Oxford University Press.

Jay, Martin (1988) 'Scopic Regimes of Modernity', in Hal Foster (ed.), *Vision and Visuality*. Seattle: Bay Press. pp. 3–23.

Jay, Martin (1993a) *Downcast Eyes: The Denigration of Vision in Twentieth-Century French Thought*. Berkeley: University of California Press.

Jay, Martin (1993b) *Force Fields: Between Intellectual History and Cultural Critique*. New York: Routledge.

Johnson, Richard (1986–7) 'What is Cultural Studies Anyway?', *Social Text*, Winter: 38–80.

Johnston, Claire (1975/1988) 'Dorothy Arzner: Critical Strategies', in Constance Penley (ed.), *Feminism and Film Theory*. New York: Routledge. pp. 36–45. (Originally published in 1975.)

Kaplan, E. Ann (1978) 'Introduction', in E. Ann Kaplan (ed.), *Women in Film Noir*. London: British Film Institute. pp. 1–5.

Kaplan, E. Ann (ed.) (1988) 'Introduction', in E. Ann Kaplan (ed.), *Postmodernism and its Discontents*. New York: Verso. pp. 1–11.

Kapsis, Robert E. (1992) *Hitchcock: The Making of a Reputation*. Chicago: University of Chicago Press.

Katovich, Michael A. and Haller, Margot (1993) 'The Violent Female in Film: From *Femme Fatale* to *Retro Fatale* and Beyond'. Paper presented to the 1993 Annual Meeting of the American Sociological Association, Miami Florida, August 13.

Kawin, Bruce F. (1978) *Mindscreen: Bergman, Goddard and First-Person Film*. Princeton: Princeton University Press.

Kayser-Jones, Jeanie and Koenig, Barbara A. (1994) 'Ethical Issues', in Jaber F. Gubrium and Andrea Sankar (eds), *Qualitative Methods in Aging Research*. Thousand Oaks, CA: Sage. pp. 15–32.

Keane, Marian E. (1988) 'A Closer Look at Scopophilia: Mulvey, Hitchcock, and Vertigo', in Marshall Deutelbaum and Leland Poague (eds), *A Hitchcock Reader*. Ames: Iowa State University Press. pp. 231–48.

Kilborne, Peter T. (1994) 'In A Growing Number of Stories, Hidden Microphones Are Listening', *New York Times*, May 28 (Section A): 6.

Klinger, Barbara (1984/1986) '"Cinema/Ideology/Criticism" Revisited: The Progressive Genre', in Barry K. Grant (ed.), *Film Genre Reader*. Austin: University of Texas Press. pp. 74–90. (Originally published in *Screen*, 25 [January–February 1984]: 30–44.)

Koch, Stephen (1973) *Stargazer*. New York: Praeger.

Kolker, Robert Phillip (1980) *A Cinema of Loneliness: Penn, Kubrick, Coppola, Scorsese, Altman*. New York: Oxford University Press.

Kolker, Robert Phillip (1988) *A Cinema of Loneliness: Penn, Kubrick, Spielberg, Altman*. (2nd edn). New York: Oxford University Press.

Konigsberg, Ira (1988) 'Review of *Fatal Attraction*', in Frank N. Magill (ed.), *Magill's Cinema Annual, 1988: A Survey of Films of 1987*. Englewood Cliffs, NJ: Salem Press. pp. 118–21.

Kracauer, Siegfried (1971) *Schriften I*. Frankfurt: Suhrkamp.

Krafsur, Richard (ed.) (1976) *The American Film Institute Film Catalog of Motion Pictures. Vols. 1 and 2. Feature Films 1961–1970*. New York: R.R. Bowker Company.

Kristeva, Julia (1977) *About Chinese Women*. New York: Urizen.

Krug, Gary (1992) 'Technologies of the Real, and Realist Ethnographies of Video Texts', *Studies in Symbolic Interaction*, 13: 59–75.

Krutnik, Frank (1991) *In A Lonely Street: Film, Genre, Masculinity*. New York: Routledge.

La Belle, Jenjoy (1988) *Herself Beheld: The Literature of the Looking Glass*. Ithaca: Cornell University Press.

Lacan, Jacques (1973/1978) *The Four Fundamental Concepts of Psycho-Analysis*. New York: Norton & Company.

Lacan, Jacques (1988) *The Seminar, Book I: Freud's Papers on Technique*. Cambridge: Cambridge University Press.

Lather, Patti (1993) 'Fertile Obsession: Validity After Poststructuralism', *The Sociological Quarterly*, 34: 4: 673–94.

Lathrop, George Parsons (1891) 'Edison's Invention', *Harper's Weekly*, July 13: 447.

Lau, Jenny Kwok Wah (1991) 'A Cultural Interpretation of the Popular Cinema of China and Hong Kong', in Chris Berry (ed.), *Perspectives On Chinese Cinema*. London: British Film Institute. pp. 166–74.

Lears, Jackson (1994) 'Review of David Nasaw, *Going Out: The Rise and Fall of Public Amusements*', *New York Times Review of Books*, January 9: 29.

Lee, Keehyeung (1991) 'Orientalism in Japanese Colonial Discourse'. Unpublished manuscript, Department of Sociology, University of Illinois at Urbana-Champaign.

Lee, Leo Ou-Fan (1991) 'The Traditions of Modern Chinese Cinema: Some Preliminary Explorations and Hypotheses', in Chris Berry (ed.), *Perspectives On Chinese Cinema*. London: British Film Institute. pp. 6–20.

Lee, Raymond (1993) *Doing Research on Sensitive Topics*. London: Sage.

Leff, Leonard J. and Simmons, Jerold L. (1990) *The Dame in the Kimono: Hollywood, Censorship, and the Production Code from the 1920s to the 1960s*. New York: Grove Weidenfeld.

Leitch, Thomas M. (1991) *Find The Director and Other Hitchcock Games*. Athens: University of Georgia Press.

Lengermann, Patricia M. and Niebrugge-Brantley, Jill (1990) 'Feminist Sociological Theory: The Near-Future Prospects', in George Ritzer (ed.), *Frontiers of Social Theory: The New Syntheses.* New York: Columbia University Press. pp. 316–46.

Levin, Martin (1977) *Hollywood and the Great Fan Magazines.* New York: Arbor House.

Lewallen, Avis (1989) 'Lace: Pornography for Women?', in Lorraine Gamman and Margaret Marshment (eds), *The Female Gaze.* Seattle: The Real Comet Press.

Lincoln, Yvonna S. and Denzin, Norman K. (1994) 'The Fifth Moment', in Norman K. Denzin and Yvonna S. Lincoln (eds), *The Handbook of Qualitative Research.* Newbury Park: Sage. pp. 575–86.

Lindesmith, Alfred and Strauss, Anselm (1949) *Social Psychology.* New York: Holt.

Lindsay, Vachel (1915) *The Art of the Moving Picture.* New York: Macmillan.

Lonergan, Bernard (1963/1977) 'Consciousness and the Trinity', a talk given in the spring of 1963 at the North American College in Rome and reprinted in Walter J. Ong, S.J. *Interfaces of the Word.* Ithaca: Cornell University Press. pp. 121–2.

Lurie, Susan (1981–2) 'The Construction of the Castrated Woman in Psychoanalysis and Cinema', *Discourse*, 4 (Winter): 52–74.

Lyman, Stanford (1990a) *Civilization: Contents, Discontents, Malcontents and Other Essays in Social Theory.* Fayetteville: University of Arkansas Press.

Lyman, Stanford (1990b) 'Anhedonia: Gender and the Decline of Emotions in American Film, 1930–1988', *Sociological Inquiry*, 60: 1–19.

Lyman, Stanford (1990c) 'Race, Sex, and Servitude: Images of Blacks in American Cinema', *International Journal of Politics, Culture and Society*, 4: 49–77.

Lyons, Arthur and Truzzi, Marcello (1990) *The Blue Sense: Psychic Detectives and Crime.* New York: Warner Books.

Lyotard, Jean-François (1984) *The Postmodern Condition: A Report on Knowledge.* Minneapolis: University of Minnesota Press.

Macdonald, Ross (1973) *On Crime Writing.* Santa Barbara: Capra Press.

McGrady, Mike (1987) 'Review of *Black Widow*', *Newsday*, February 6, Part III: 3.

McHale, Brian (1992) *Constructing Postmodernism.* New York: Routledge.

McLean, Adrienne L. (1993) 'It's Only that I do what I Love and Love what I Do: *Film Noir* and the Musical Woman', *Cinema Journal*, 33: 3–16.

Magill, Frank N. (ed.) (1986) *Magill's Cinema Annual Cumulative Indexes: 1982–1986.* Englewood Cliffs, NJ: Salem Press.

Mankiewicz, Frank (1992) 'About the Debate', in Oliver Stone and Zachery Sklar *JFK: The Book of the Film.* The documented screenplay, based on 'On The Trail of the Assassins' by Jim Garrison; 'Crossfire: The Plot that Killed Kennedy' by Jim Marris; public sources; Oliver Stone's research notes; compiled by Jane Rusconi. New York: Applause Books. pp. 187–9.

Mannheim, Herman (ed.) (1960) *Pioneers in Criminology.* Chicago: Quadrangle.

Manning, Peter K. (1977) *Police Work.* Cambridge, MA: MIT Press.

Marchetti, Gina (1991) 'Ethnicity, the Cinema, and Cultural Studies', in Lester D. Friedman (ed.), *Unspeakable Images: Ethnicity and the American Cinema.* Urbana: University of Illinois Press. pp. 277–309.

Marrs, Jim (1989) *Crossfire: The Plot that Killed Kennedy.* New York: Carroll and Graf.

Martin, J.B. (1985) *Ben Hecht: Hollywood Screenwriter.* Ann Arbor, MI: UMI Research Press.

Marx, Gary T. (1986) 'The Iron Fist and the Velvet Glove: Totalitarian Potentials Within Democratic Structures', in James E. Short, Jr (ed.), *The Social Fabric: Dimensions and Issues.* Beverly Hills: Sage. pp. 135–62.

Marx, Gary T. (1988) *Undercover: Police Surveillance in America.* Berkeley: University of California Press.

Marx, Gary T. (1992) 'Under-the-Covers Undercover Investigations: Some Reflections on the State's Use of Sex and Deception in Law Enforcement', *Criminal Justice Ethics*, Winter/Spring: 13–24.

Mast, Gerald (1976) *A Short History of the Movies.* Indianapolis: Bobbs-Merrill.

234 THE CINEMATIC SOCIETY

Mayne, Judith (1988) *Private Novels, Public Films.* Athens, GA: University of Georgia Press.

Mayne, Judith (1990) *The Woman at the Keyhole: Feminism and Women's Cinema.* Bloomington: Indiana University Press.

Mead, George Herbert (1925/1926/1964) 'The Nature of Aesthetic Experience', in A. Reck (ed.), *George Herbert Mead: Selected Writings.* Indianapolis: Bobbs-Merrill. pp. 294–305.

Merleau-Ponty, Maurice (1962) *Phenomenology of Perception.* London: Routledge.

Merleau-Ponty, Maurice (1964a) *The Primacy of Perception.* Evanston: Northwestern University Press.

Merleau-Ponty, Maurice (1964b) *Sense and Non-Sense.* Evanston: Northwestern University Press.

Merleau-Ponty, Maurice (1968) *The Visible and the Invisible.* Evanston: Northwestern University Press.

Metz, Christian (1982) *The Imaginary Signifier: Psychoanalysis and the Cinema.* Bloomington: Indiana University Press.

Meyrowitz, Joshua (1985) *No Sense of Place.* New York: Oxford University Press.

Mills, C. Wright (1956) *The Power Elite.* New York: Oxford.

Mills, C. Wright (1963) *Power, Politics and People: The Collected Essays of C. Wright Mills* (ed. with an introduction by Irving Louis Horowitz). New York: Ballantine.

Mitchell, Richard J. Jr (1993) *Secrecy and Fieldwork.* Newbury Park: Sage.

Modleski, Tania (1988) *The Women who Knew Too Much: Hitchcock and Feminist Theory.* New York: Methuen.

Modleski, Tania (1990) 'Hitchcock, Feminism and the Patriarchal Unconscious', in P. Erens (ed.), *Issues in Feminist Film Criticism.* Bloomington: Indiana University Press. pp. 58–74.

Moore, Suzanne (1989) 'Review of *sex, lies and videotape*', *New Statesman* and *New Society.* September 15: 44.

Morris, Meaghan (1988) 'At Henry Parkes Motel', *Cultural Studies*, 2: 1–47.

Mulvey, Laura (1975/1989) 'Visual Pleasure and Narrative Cinema', in L. Mulvey, *Visual and Other Pleasures.* Bloomington: Indiana University Press. pp. 14–26. (Originally published in *Screen*, 1975.)

Mulvey, Laura (1989) 'Afterthoughts on "Visual Pleasure and Narrative Cinema" inspired by King Vidor's *Duel in the Sun* (1946)', in L. Mulvey, *Visual and Other Pleasures.* Bloomington: Indiana University Press. pp. 29–38.

Munden, Kenneth (ed.) (1971) *The American Film Institute Catalog of Motion Pictures Produced in the United States. Vols. 1 and 2. Feature Films 1921–1930.* New York: R.R. Bowker Company.

Munsterberg, Hugo (1916) *The Photoplay: A Psychological Study.* New York: D. Appleton and Company.

Musser, Charles (1991) 'Ethnicity, Role-Playing and American Film Comedy: From Chinese Laundry Scene to Whoopee (1884–1930)', in Lester D. Friedman (ed.), *Unspeakable Images: Ethnicity and the American Cinema.* Urbana: University of Illinois Press. pp. 39–81.

Nasaw, David (1994) *The Rise and Fall of Public Amusement.* New York: Basic Books.

Neale, Stephen (1990) 'Questions of Genre', *Screen*, 31: 45–66.

Nichols, Bill (1981) *Ideology and the Image: Social Representation in the Cinema and Other Media.* Bloomington: Indiana University Press.

Ong, Walter J. (1977) *Interfaces of the Word.* Ithaca: Cornell.

The Oxford English Dictionary, (1989, 2nd edn). Prepared by J.A. Simpson and E.S.C. Weiner. Oxford: Clarendon Press.

Pace, Eric (1991) 'Edward H. Land is Dead at 81: Inventor of Polaroid Camera', *New York Times*, March 2: 13.

Parish, James R. and Pitts, Michael R. (1974) *The Great Spy Pictures.* Metuchen, NJ: Scarecrow Press.

Parish, James R. and Pitts, Michael R. (1986) *The Great Spy Pictures II.* Metuchen, NJ: Scarecrow Press.

Park, Robert E. (1926/1967) 'The Urban Community as a Spatial Pattern and a Moral Order', in Ralph Turner (ed.), *Robert E. Park on Social Control and Collective Behavior*. Chicago: University of Chicago Press. pp. 56–68.

Penley, Constance (1989) 'A Certain Refusal of Difference: Feminism and Film Theory', in C. Penley, *The Future of Illusion: Film, Feminism and Psychoanalysis*. Minneapolis: University of Minnesota Press. pp. 41–56.

Penzler, Otto (1977) *The Private Lives of Private Eyes, Spies, Crimefighters, and Other Good Guys*. New York: Grosset and Dunlap.

Permutter, Ruth (1985) '*Rear Window*: A Construction Story', *Journal of Film and Video*, 37, Spring: 53–65.

Persons, Stow (1958) *American Minds: A History of Ideas*. New York: Henry Holt.

Petley, Julian (1988) 'Review of *Fatal Attraction*', *Monthly Film Bulletin*, January: 14.

Pitts, Michael R. (1979) *Famous Movie Detectives*. Metuchen, NJ: Scarecrow Press.

Pitts, Michael R. (1990) *Famous Movie Detectives. Vol. II*. Metuchen, NJ: Scarecrow Press.

Place, J.A. and Peterson, L.S. (1974/1976) 'Some Visual Motifs of Film Noir', in Bill Nichols (ed.), *Movies and Methods: An Anthology*. Berkeley: University of California Press. pp. 324–38. (Originally published in *Film Comment*, 10 (1) (Jan-Feb. 1974).)

Punch, Maurice (1986) *The Politics and Ethics of Fieldwork*. Newbury Park: Sage.

Punch, Maurice (1994) 'Politics and Ethics in Qualitative Research', in Norman K. Denzin and Yvonna S. Lincoln (eds), *Handbook of Qualitative Research*. Thousand Oaks, CA: Sage. pp. 83–98.

Radway, Janice (1989) 'Ethnography Among Elites: Comparing Discourses of Power', *Journal of Communication Inquiry*, 13: 3–11.

Ray, Robert B. (1985) *A Certain Tendency of the Hollywood Cinema, 1930–1980*. Princeton: Princeton University Press.

Raschke, Debrah (1988) 'Review of *Fatal Attraction*', *Cineaste*. 16: 44.

Richardson, Laurel (1994) 'Writing as a Method of Inquiry', in Norman K. Denzin and Yvonna S. Lincoln (eds), *The Handbook of Qualitative Research*. Newbury Park: Sage. pp. 516–29.

Rickey, Carrie (1982) 'Review of *Chan Is Missing*', *Village Voice*. April 27: 52.

Rifkin, New (1982) *Antonioni's Visual Language*. Ann Arbor, MI: UMI Research Press.

Robbe-Grillet, Alain (1958) *The Voyeur*. New York: Grove.

Robbe-Grillet, Alain (1991) *Ghosts in the Mirror*. Translated by Jo Levy. New York: Grove Weidenfeld.

Roberts, Jerry (1989) 'Newspaper Videos: Copley Los Angeles Newspapers' Film Critic Lists the 25 Best Pictures Available in Video Stories and Much, Much More', *Editor and Publisher*, April 22: 80–81, 112–13. (I would like to thank James W. Carey and Matt Ehrlich for bringing this source to my attention.)

Rohmer, Eric and Chabrol, Claude (1979/1988) *Hitchcock: The First Forty-Four Films*. New York: Continuum.

Room, Robin (1985) 'Alcoholism and Alcoholics Anonymous in U.S. Films, 1945–1962: The Party Ends for the Wet Generation'. Paper presented at an International Group for Comparative Alcohol Studies Conference on Cultural Studies on Drinking and Drinking Problems, September 24–28.

Rorty, Richard (1989) *Contingency, Irony, Solidarity*. New York: Cambridge University Press.

Rorty, Richard (1991) *Objectivity, Relativism, and Truth*. New York: Cambridge University Press.

Rorty, Richard (1994) 'Towards a Liberal Utopia', *Times Literary Supplement*, No. 4760, June 24: 14.

Rosaldo, Renato (1986) 'From the Door of his Tent: The Fieldworker and the Inquisitor', in James Clifford and George E. Marcus (eds), *Writing Culture*. Berkeley: University of California Press. pp. 77–97.

Rose, Dan (1990) *Living the Ethnographic Life*. Newbury Park, CA: Sage.

Rose, Jacqueline (1976–77/1988) 'Paranoia and the Film System' in C. Penley (ed.), *The Future of Illusion: Film, Feminism and Psychoanalysis*. Minneapolis: University of Minnesota Press. pp. 141–58.

Ross, Andrew (1989) *No Respect: Intellectuals & Popular Culture*. New York: Routledge.

Ross, E.A. (1928) *In World Drift*. New York: Macmillian.

Rothman, William (1982) *Hitchcock: The Murderous Gaze*. Cambridge: Harvard University Press.

Rubenstein, Leonard (1979) *The Great Spy Films*. Secaucus, NJ: Citadel Press.

Ryan, Michael and Kellner, Douglas (1988) *Camera Politica*. Bloomington: Indiana University Press.

Said, Edward (1979) *Orientalism*. New York: Vintage Books.

Said, Edward (1989) 'Representing the Colonized: Anthropology's Interlocutors', *Critical Inquiry*, 15: 205–25.

Samuels, Charles Thomas (1971) 'The Blow-Up: Sorting Things Out', in Roy Huss, (ed.), *Focus on Blow-Up*. Englewood Cliffs: Prentice-Hall. pp. 13–28. (Originally published in *American Scholar*, Winter, 1967–68: 120–31.)

Sanders, William B. (ed.) (1976) *The Sociologist as Detective* (2nd edn). New York: Praeger.

Sartre, Jean-Paul (1943/1956) *Being and Nothingness*. New York: Philosophical Library.

Sawyer, Charles (1987) 'Review of *Black Widow*', *Films in Review*, April: 227.

Sayre, Nora (1974) 'Review of *The Conversation*', *New York Times*, April 8: 44.

Scarce, Rik (1994) '(No) Trial (But) Tribulations: When Courts and Ethnography Conflict', *Journal of Contemporary Ethnography*, 23: 123–249.

Schatz, Thomas (1981) *Hollywood Genres: Formulas, Filmmaking and the Studio System*. New York: Random House.

Schopen, Bernard (1989) *The Big Silence*. New York: The Mysterious Press.

Schrader, Paul (1972/1986) 'Notes on Film Noir', in Barry Keith Grant (ed.), *Film Genre Reader*. Austin: University of Texas Press. pp. 169–82. (Originally published in *Film Comment*, 1972, 8: 813.)

Schroeder, William Ralph (1984) *Sartre and his Predecessors: The Self and the Other*. New York: Routledge.

Scott, James F. (1971) '*Blow-Up*: Antonioni and the Mod World', in Roy Huss (ed.), *Focus on Blow-Up*. Englewood Cliffs: Prentice-Hall. pp. 89–97.

Shalin, Dmitri N. (1992) 'Critical Theory and the Pragmatist Challenge', *American Journal of Sociology*, 98: 237–79.

Sharff, Stefan (1991) *Alfred Hitchcock's High Vernacular: Theory and Practice*. New York: Columbia University Press.

Shohat, Elia (1991) 'Ethnicity-in-Relations: Toward a Multicultural Reading of American Cinema', in Lester D. Friedman (ed.), *Unspeakable Images: Ethnicity and the American Cinema*. Urbana: University of Illinois Press. pp. 215–50.

Silver, Alan and Ward, Elizabeth (1979) *Film Noir: An Encyclopedia Reference to the American Style*. Woodstock, NY: The Overlook Press.

Silverman, Kaja (1988) *The Acoustic Mirror: The Female Voice in Psychoanalysis*. Bloomington: Indiana University Press.

Silverman, Kaja (1992) *Male Subjectivity at the Margins*. New York: Routledge.

Silverstone, Roger (1988) 'Television Myth and Culture', in J.W. Carey (ed.), *Media, Myths, and Narratives: Television and the Press*. Newbury Park: Sage. pp. 20–47.

Simmel, Georg (1924) 'On Visual Interaction', in R.E. Park and E.W. Burgess (eds), *Introduction to the Science of Sociology*. Chicago: University of Chicago Press. pp. 256–65. (Originally published 1908.)

Simone, Sam P. (1982) 'Alfred Hitchcock, Advocate of Freedom: A Study of *Foreign Correspondent, Saboteur, Lifeboat*, and *Notorious*'. Unpublished doctoral dissertation, Department of Theater and Cinematic Arts, Brigham Young University.

Sklar, Robert (1975) *Movie-Made America*. New York: Random House.

Slide, Anthony (1983) 'Review of *Dead Men Don't Wear Plaid*', in Frank N. Magill (ed.), *Magill's Cinema Annual, 1983: A Review of 1982 Films*. Englewood Cliffs, NJ: Salem Press.

Slover, George (1971) 'Isolation and Make-Believe in Blow-Up', in Roy Huss (ed.), *Focus on Blow-Up*. Englewood Cliffs, NJ: Prentice-Hall. pp. 107–15.

Smith, Louis M. (1990) 'Ethics, Field Studies and the Paradigm Crisis', in Egon G. Guba (ed.), *The Paradigm Dialog*. Newbury Park: Sage.

Smythe, Dallas W. (1981) *Dependency Road: Communications, Capitalism, Consciousness and Canada*. Norwood, NJ: Ablex.

Sobchack, Vivian (1991) 'Postmodern Modes of Ethnicity', in Lester D. Friedman (ed.), *Unspeakable Images: Ethnicity and the American Cinema*. Urbana, IL: University of Illinois Press. pp. 329–52.

Sontag, Susan (1977) *On Photography*. New York: Farrar, Straus, and Giroux.

Spender, Stephen (1984) 'Introduction', in Malcolm Lowry, *Under the Volcano*. New York: New American Library. pp. vii–xxii. (Originally published 1947.)

Spoto, Donald (1976) *The Art of Alfred Hitchcock*. New York: Hopkinson and Blake.

Spoto, Donald (1983) *The Dark Side of Genius: The Life of Alfred Hitchcock*. New York: Ballantine.

Springer, Claudia (1991) 'Comprehension and Crisis: Reporter Films and the Third World', in Lester D. Friedman (ed.), *Unspeakable Images: Ethnicity and the American Cinema*. Urbana: University of Illinois Press. pp. 167–89.

Stacey, Jackie (1994) *Star Gazing: Hollywood Cinema and Female Spectatorship*. New York: Routledge.

Stam, Robert (1989) *Subversive Pleasures: Bakhtin, Cultural Criticism and Film*. Baltimore: Johns Hopkins University Press.

Stam, Robert (1991) 'Bakhtin, Polyphony and Ethnic/Racial Representation', in Lester D. Friedman (ed.), *Unspeakable Images: Ethnicity and the American Cinema*. Urbana: University of Illinois Press. pp. 251–76.

Stam, Robert and Pearson, Roberta (1983) 'Hitchcock's Rear Window: Reflexivity and the Critique of Voyeurism', *Enclitic*, 7 (1) Spring: 136–45.

Staples, William (1994) 'Small Acts of Cunning: Disciplinary Practices in Contemporary Life', *Sociological Quarterly*, 35 (4): 645–64.

Sterritt, David (1982) 'Review of *Chan Is Missing*', *Christian Science Monitor*, July 1: 18.

Stoller, Paul and Olkes, Cheryl (1987) *In Sorcery's Shadow*. Chicago: University of Chicago Press.

Stone, Oliver and Sklar, Zachery (1992) *JFK: The Book of the Film*. The documented screenplay, based on 'On the Trail of the Assassins' by Jim Garrison; 'Crossfire: The Plot That Killed Kennedy' by Jim Marris; public sources; Oliver Stone's research notes; compiled by Jane Rusconi. New York: Applause Books.

Strauss, Anselm (1993) *Continual Permutations of Action*. New York: Aldine de Gruyter.

Studlar, Gaylyn (1983) 'Review of *Chan Is Missing*', in Frank N. Magill (ed.), *Magill's Cinema Annual: A Survey of 1982 Films*. Englewood Cliffs, NJ: Salem Press. pp. 113–15.

Studlar, Gaylyn (1985) 'Masochism and the Perverse Pleasures of the Cinema', in Bill Nichols (ed.), *Movies and Methods: Volume II*. Berkeley: University of California Press. pp. 602–21.

Sweet, Louise (1987) 'Review of *Black Widow*', *Monthly Film Bulletin*, July: 201.

Symons, Julian (1985) *Bloody Murder: From the Detective Story to the Crime Novel: A History*. New York: Viking.

Taubin, Amy (1987) 'Review of *Fatal Attraction*', *Village Voice*, October 6: 67.

Taussig, Michael (1990) 'Violence and Resistance in the Americas: The Legacy of Conquest', *Journal of Historical Sociology*, 3: 209–24.

Taussig, Michael (1993) *Mimesis and Alterity*. New York: Routledge.

Telotte, J.P. (1989) *Voices in the Dark: The Narrative Patterns of Film Noir*. Urbana: University of Illinois Press.

Telotte, J.P. (ed.) (1991) *The Cult Film Experience: Beyond All Reason*. Austin: University of Texas Press.

Thomas, Kevin (1982) 'Review of *Chan Is Missing*', *Los Angeles Times*, August 13 (Calendar section): 7.

Thomas, William and Thomas, Dorothy Swaine (1928) *The Child in America*. New York: Alfred A. Knopf, Inc.

Thompson, Jon (1993) *Fiction, Crime and the Empire*. Urbana: University of Illinois Press.

Todorov, Tzvetan (1977) 'The Typology of Detective Fiction' in T. Todorov (ed.), *The Poetics of Prose*. Ithaca: Cornell University Press. pp. 42–52.

Toobin, Jeffrey (1994) 'Cash for Trash', *New Yorker*, July 11: 34–41.

Truffaut, François (1984) *Hitchcock: The Definitive Study of Alfred Hitchcock* (rev. edn with the collaboration of Helen G. Scott). New York: Simon and Schuster.

Truzzi, Marcello (1976) 'Sherlock Holmes: Applied Social Psychology', in William B. Sanders (ed.), *The Sociologist as Detective* (2nd edn). New York: Praeger. pp. 50–86.

Tseëlon, Efrat and Kaiser, Susan B. (1992) 'A Dialogue with Feminist Film Theory: Multiple Readings of the Gaze', *Studies in Symbolic Interaction*, 13: 119–37.

Tuska, Jon (1978) *The Detective in Hollywood*. Westport, CT: Greenwood Press.

Tuska, Jon (1984) *Dark Cinema: American Film Noir in Cultural Perspective*. Westport, CT: Greenwood Press.

Tyler, Stephen A. (1986) 'Post-Modern Ethnography: From Document of the Occult to Occult Document', in James Clifford and George E. Marcus (eds), *Writing Culture*. Berkeley: University of California Press. pp. 122–40.

Ulmer, Gregory (1989) *Teletheory: Grammatology in the Age of Video*. New York: Routledge.

Urry, John (1990) *The Tourist Gaze*. London: Sage.

Van Maanen, John (1978) 'On Watching the Watchers', in P.K. Manning and J. Van Maanen (eds), *Policing*. Santa Monica, CA: Goodyear. pp. 309–49.

Van Maanen, John (1988) *Tales of the Field: On Writing Ethnography*. Chicago: University of Chicago Press.

Variety (1990) 'All-Time Film Rental Champs, by Decade', May 2: 114–36.

Verdon, Timothy and Henderson, John (eds) (1990) *Christianity and the Renaissance: Image and Religious Imagination in the Quattrocento*. Syracuse: Syracuse University Press.

Vidich, Arthur J. and Lyman, Stanford M. (1985) *American Sociology: Worldly Rejections of Religion and their Directions*. New Haven: Yale University Press.

Vidich, Arthur and Lyman, Stanford M. (1988) *Social Order and the Public Philosophy*. Fayetteville: University of Arkansas Press.

Vidich, Arthur and Lyman, Stanford M. (1994) 'Qualitative Methods: Their History in Sociology and Anthropology', in Norman K. Denzin and Yvonna S. Lincoln (eds), *The Handbook of Qualitative Research*. Newbury Park, CA: Sage. pp. 23–59.

Vidich, Arthur J., Bensman, Joseph and Stein, Maurice R. (eds) (1964) *Reflections on Community Studies*. New York: Wiley.

Voltaire (Arouet, François-Marie) (1748/1966) 'Zadig', in D.M. Frame (ed.), *Voltaire's 'Candide,' 'Zadig,' and Selected Short Stories*. Bloomington: Indiana University Press. pp. 110–21.

Warren Report (1964) *Report of the President's Commission on the Assassination of President John F. Kennedy*. Washington, DC: US Government Printing Office.

Weber, Max (1904/1958) *The Protestant Ethic and the Spirit of Capitalism*. New York: Scribner's.

Weis, Elisabeth (1982) *The Silent Scream. Alfred Hitchcock's Sound Track*. London: Associated University Press.

West, Cornel (1989) *The American Invasion of Philosophy*. Madison: University of Wisconsin Press.

Westin, Alan F. (1967) *Privacy and Freedom*. New York: Atheneum Publishers.

Wiley, Norbert (1994) *The Semiotic Self*. London: Polity Press.

Williamson, Judith (1987) 'Review of *Black Widow*', *New Statesman*, July 24: 17.

Williamson, Judith (1988) 'Review of *Fatal Attraction*', *New Statesman*, January 15: 28.

Wilmington, Michael (1987) 'Review of *Fatal Attraction*', *Los Angeles Times*, September 18 (Calendar Section): 1.

Wilson, Colin (1985) *The Psychic Detectives: The Story of Psychometry and Paranormal Crime Detection*. San Francisco: Mercury House.

Winsten, Archer (1982) 'Review of *Chan is Missing*', *New York Post*, June 4: 44.

Wolcott, Harry F. (1994) *Transforming Qualitative Data*. Thousand Oaks, CA: Sage.

Wong, Eugene Franklin (1978) *On Visual Media Racism: Asians in American Motion Pictures*. New York: Arno Press.

Wood, Robin (1965) *Hitchcock's Films*. London: Zwemmer.

Wood, Robin (1977/1986) 'Ideology, Genre, Auteur', in Barry K. Grant (ed.), *Film Genre Reader*. Austin: University of Texas Press. pp. 59–73. (Originally published in *Film Comment*, 13 (1) [January-February 1977]: 46–51.)

Wood, Robin (1982) 'Fear of Spying', *American Film* (November): 28–35.

Wood, Robin (1989) *Hitchcock's Films Revisited*. New York: Columbia University Press.

Yarbrough, Jeff (1992) 'Heart of Stone', in Stone, Oliver and Sklar, Zachery, *JFK: The Book of the Film*. The documented screenplay, based on 'On The Trail of the Assassins' by Jim Garrison; 'Crossfire: The Plot that Killed Kennedy' by Jim Marris; public sources; Oliver Stone's research notes; compiled by Jane Rusconi. New York: Applause Books. pp. 508–16.

Zaretsky, Eli (1976) *Capitalism, the Family and Personal Life*. New York: Harper & Row.

Zelizer, Barbie (1992) *Covering the Body: The Kennedy Assassination, the Media, and the Shaping of Collective Memory*. Chicago: University of Chicago Press.

Zizek, Slavoj (1992) 'Alfred Hitchcock, or, The Form and its Historical Materialism', in Zizek Slavoj (ed.), *Everything You Always Wanted to Know About Lacan (But Were Afraid to Ask Hitchcock)*. London: Verso. pp. 1–14.

INDEX

absolutist stance, 204
aesthetics: of looking, 46; postmodern, 8–9
Allen, Woody, 109
Altheide, David L., 208–9
Antonioni, Michelangelo, 129, 135–6, 163
autoethnography, 199

Bakhtin, Mikhail M., 140, 141; and carnival of theatre, 14; and mimesis as fraud, 197; and polyphony, 90. *See also* Stam, Robert
Barris, Alex, 53
Barthes, Roland, 197
Baudrillard, Jean: and hyperreality, 200; and media and simulacra, 198, 199, 200
Behind That Curtain, 89
Benjamin, Walter, 25
The Big Sleep, 52
The Big Store, 66–7
Biga, Tracy, 76, 79
Black Widow, 2, 5, 73, 149–56; and female gaze, 139–40; and feminine self-image, 157–8; as film noir, 136; gazing structures of, 150; and narcissistic gaze, 157–8; and polyphony, 150; and sexism, 141; and violence, 157; water symbolism in, 155
Blow Out, 10, 181
Blow-Up, 6, 51, 114–15, 128–36; and the camera, 128–30; and colour, 129–30, 135; lesson of, 137; morality in, 136–7; and photography, 128–9; Peeping Tom in, 114; and reality, 128–9, 135; and self, 129
Blue Velvet, 4, 73, 76–82, 85 n. 1; and comedy, 64, 65; and gendered gaze, 58, 76–8, 80–2; and modernism, 76; multiple gazes in, 76, 78–9, 81–2; and violence, 55
Blumer, Herbert, 11, 20, 28, 32, 38 n. 4
Bozovic, Miran, 61 n. 7
Breen, Joseph, 20
Broadcast News, 4, 64, 65, 67, 68–73; and feminine gaze, 68, 70–1

camera's gaze, 114; and crime, 25; and ethnography, 190, 196–7; and family, 25, 40 n. 22; ideological heritage, 31; lens of, 26; and morality, 137; as *Rear Window*, 121; and science, 24–5, 31; and truth, 6, 118, 130; and visual code, 25–6
capitalism: crime and camera, 25; cultural logics of, 6; and individuals, 6; local, 9; and monopoly, multinational-consumerism, 9; and private space, 5, 6; stages of, 9, 22; and phases of voyeuristic film, 9
Cartesian eye, 195
censorship, 208; early, 18–19, 20; opposition to, 19; and the Production Code, 20
Chan is Missing, 89, 103–9; and Asian self, 103; and assimilation, 104; as collage, 103–4, 107–8; and identity, 104–5; as multi-voiced, 107–8; and stereotypes, 107
Charlie Chan, 23, 88–100, 111–12 n. 9, n. 10, 142, 143; blundering character of, 66; and *Chan is Missing*, 103, 109; as ethnic hero, 59; and Mr Moto, 101, 102; pragmatic method of, 97–9, 110; and racism, 59, 99–100; and *Zelig*, 109
Charlie Chan at the Opera, 88, 89, 94–100; and anti-feminism, 95; geometric structure in, 96–7
Chinatown, 48, 51, 57
cinema: history of, 2, 10 n. 7, 16–19, 39 n. 11; and individual, 29; postmodern, 1; primitive-realist, 8, 9; sociological impact of, 13–14; and sociology, 13, 212–13; and surveillance society, 13–14, 15
cinematic: apparatus, 193, 200; culture, 24, 28, 32–3, 50, 200; gazing, 29–30, 31, 33; imagination, 33–4, 36; self and Herbert Blumer, 28, 29, 32–3, 38 n. 4, realism, 21–2; voyeurism, 163, 191
Citizen Kane, 35, 41 n. 35
colour, 4, 129–30, 135
comedy: and audience, 4, 66; ethnic, 92, 94; and female voyeur, 72, 73, 74–5; and neutralization of danger, 64; and reflexivity, 66; and voyeurism, 64–6

ABOUT THE AUTHOR

Norman K. Denzin is Professor of Sociology, Communications and Humanities at the University of Illinois, Urbana-Champaign. He is the author of numerous books, including *Sociological Methods, The Research Act, Interpretive Interactionism, Images of Postmodern Society, The Recovering Alcoholic* and *The Alcoholic Self,* which won the Cooley Award from the Society for the Study of Symbolic Interaction in 1988. He is the editor of *Studies in Symbolic Interaction: A Research Journal* and *The Sociological Quarterly.* He is also co-editor of the Sage publication, *Handbook of Qualitative Research* and co-editor of *Qualitative Inquiry.*